Small Cities and Towns in Global Era

Small Cities and Towns in Global Era

Emerging Changes and Perspectives

Edited by

R.N. Sharma
R.S. Sandhu

RAWAT PUBLICATIONS

Jaipur • New Delhi • Bangalore • Hyderabad • Guwahati

ISBN 978-81-316-0575-2

Published by
Prem Rawat for **Rawat Publications**
Satyam Apts, Sector 3, Jawahar Nagar, Jaipur 302 004 (India)
Phone: 0141 265 1748/7006 Fax: 0141 265 1748
E-mail: info@rawatbooks.com
Website: www.rawatbooks.com

New Delhi Office
4858/24, Ansari Road, Daryaganj, New Delhi 110 002
Phone: 011 2326 3290

Also at *Bangalore, Hyderabad* and *Guwahati*

Typeset by Rawat Computers, Jaipur
Printed at Chaman Enterprises, New Delhi

Contents

Part Two
Case Studies

Preface

There has been a rich tradition in Western literature on understanding the 'city' for its various forms, processes and institutions. Historical-evolutionary, Ecological, Weberian and Marxist perspectives, and a few others, have provided rich insights into understanding the urban as different from the rural communities, and also comparative forms of cities and towns emerging in various societies. If Lewis Mumford considered city as the 'symbol of possible', Henry Lefebvre saw it 'attacking the countryside, corroding and dissolving it'. If city has been a key factor in evolution of civilisation, new morality, autonomy and new production systems, it is also considered to be responsible for dismantling communities, decaying social environment and distorting personality.

In Indian context, for decades, scholars (more so sociologists and anthropologists) found no useful purpose in studying city as separate from village. For them, an Indian city was more an extension of rural reality where caste, kinship and religion played an equally relevant role. This proved to be an over-simplified view, and a few studies were carried out across the disciplines which focused on emerging key cities through Indian history and their morphology; and also a few industrial cities (or towns) with emerging new inequalities and socio-cultural life situations. However, the focus of such studies was mainly on a few economically vibrant or capital cities. Thousands of small cities and towns (more so the bazaar towns) hardly attracted researchers to understand their 'urbanity' and their age-old contribution to vast agrarian communities in the country. The tradition initiated by Prof. Radha Kamal Mukherjee (through his study of Gorakhpur town in Uttar Pradesh) or Richard G. Fox (through his study of Tezibazaar town – some 50 kms away from

Banaras city) was hardly carried forward by urban sociologists in the country. In fact, several reviews of research studies in urban areas (more so in the sociological field) carried out by the Indian Council of Social Sciences Research (ICSSR) at different points of time invariably pointed to a serious bias in research favouring the large (Indian) cities. Whatever research on urban growth (or the lack of it), it has emerged mainly due to the contribution of researchers from human geography and demography.

The recent decades of neo-liberalisation of world economies through the 'global regime' have brought 'city' under special focus. The 'post-modern' city has emerged as one of the key catalytic agents of the new world order. 'A few mega cities are intensely concentrated pockets of activity through which policies, finance and production flow' (M. Castells). The result is that the 'global city' has drawn attention of several eminent researchers across the world, and a rich discourse on political economy of such cities has emerged. Even in developing economies like India, China or Korea, a few mega cities have become focus of research for understanding their role in developing market-driven economies in their own countries, and in the process, emerging forms of networking in terms of finance, exchange of technology and skills and market linkages.

Thus, a few Indian cities are now going through major transformation in terms of mega housing, infrastructure and commercial projects. In the process, the 'right to city' (David Harvey) is being re-written or encroached upon by a privileged section of citizens who, through their active partnership in globalising economies, are dominating the scene in terms of their high lifestyles, economic opportunities and new privileges. In contrast, the poor are being driven out from strategic locations of city spaces to peripheries and confronting new inequalities and challenges.

In such a globalising regime, what is happening to small cities and towns in India, which for centuries remained functional in their regions of influence? Are they being dismantled and being written off the map, or are they being co-opted into the neo-liberal economy? If so, what are their gains or losses? These are the issues related to small cities and towns in India which need to be understood by researchers and policy makers. Unfortunately, the past bias of scanty research on these towns appears to be reinforced in the present situation also where only aggregate data related to a few aspects of their economies or demographic profiles is made available. The need is strongly felt for conducting extensive research, more so interdisciplinary, for understanding the changes or stagnation in these urban settlements. It is in this context that it was considered relevant to organise an all-India seminar on 'Small Cities and Towns in Global Era: Emerging Changes and Perspectives', at the Tata Institute of Social Sciences, Mumbai, on 29–30 August, 2011. Several leading researchers from different disciplines participated in the seminar.

The themes under focus were: emerging changes or stagnation in small cities and towns; their economies, labour market and linkages with the regions under their influence; changes in socio-cultural values; issues in gender and ethnic exclusion; spatial dynamics and issues; institutions of governance and role of civil society; regional politics and identities; and finally, emerging perspectives on small cities and towns in the global era.

The present volume is thus an outcome of assembling a few leading papers from the two-day deliberations during the seminar. One paper (published by one of the editors elsewhere) is also included. In all, the volume includes eight papers which raise broader issues and relate them to relevant perspectives. Equally significant are an equal number of case studies of a state (Punjab) and individual towns presented in a separate section. The editors are grateful to all the contributors who took out time from their busy schedules for writing their papers. If this volume attracts the attention of urban researchers in India to focus their research on this neglected area (status of small cities and towns in rapidly changing India), our effort would prove meaningful.

The national seminar and this volume were made possible due to generous grants sanctioned by Dr S. Parasuraman, Director, Tata Institute of Social Sciences (TISS). We are very grateful for his kind support not only for making the funds available but also his continued encouragement for publishing this volume. Prof. S. Siva Raju, Prof. Swapna Banerjee-Guha, Dr A. Shaban and Dr Anita Rath of the TISS, helped in various ways during the seminar and encouraged us to bring out this volume. Our thanks to them. Very special thanks to Ms Priyanka Bhosale who put in so much effort during the preparations of the seminar and then editing this manuscript.

Finally, we extend thanks to Rawat Publications for bringing out this volume nicely.

R.N. Sharma
R.S. Sandhu

Introduction

R.N. SHARMA

The rapid changes emerging at global level, under the market-driven neo-liberal economy, are unparalleled and unprecedented. These changes cut across the countries, their existing production systems, work environments and living styles of people. Under these processes, the human settlements, rural or urban, are also undergoing a sea change. Information technology, mobility of people with specialised skills and growing needs of more and more resources – natural or otherwise – are effecting conventionally organised human habitations. On one hand, new rights and lifestyles are emerging for people with privileged partnerships in the global processes, on the other, there are millions who are involuntarily being displaced from their traditional habitats or sources of livelihood, for meeting new demands of ever-expanding production systems and markets.

This mega transformation has thus had a massive impact on the conventionally existing cities or towns. A few large cities, all across the world, are competing to become 'world class' through their mega transformation. As stated by M. Castells (1998), 'these mega cities are intensely concentrated pockets of activity through which policies, finance and production flow'. In the process, traditional systems of regional production and distribution of goods or services are being reorganised or disintegrated under the present global era. In fact, the mega cities are transforming into huge agglomeration economies (or city-regions), which suck and consume resources of their regions and even far beyond. The 'right to the city' is being re-shaped or infringed upon (Harvey, 2008).

These processes and their impact are relevant and applicable to Indian society which has also adopted the neo-liberal paradigm of growth, more so since the 1990s. A few relevant questions arise here: Under this mega trans-formation, what is the fate of thousands of small cities and towns, which for decades have been serving the regions under their influence? What kind of changes are emerging in these 'bazaar' or 'administrative towns' under the global regime? Have there been efforts on the part of researchers to capture these changes, or the recent research on urban areas remains indifferent to small cities and towns, as has been the case in past?

Neglected Research on Small Cities and Towns

The neglect of small cities and towns by government for any major policy thrust by revitalising their economies and using their immense potential for a balanced regional growth, is also very much evident when one looks at the research conducted by academics on urbanisation and urban devel-opment in the country. Such a bias has repeatedly been brought to notice by a few leading researchers in the field. Kundu and Bhatia (1995) rightly observe: 'Indifference on the part of research community on issues relating to urban structure, thus, helps in institutionalising existing inequality and accentuating the bias against small and medium towns in the developing world.' Similar disappointment is also expressed by a few other researchers who have done a comprehensive review of research on towns and cities, since independence (see, for instance, review of research on urbanisation and urban development in India by Ashish Bose in 1973, Victor S. D'Souza in 1985, Meera Kosambi in 1994, Richard G. in 1991, Sujata Patel and Kushal Deb in 2006, and research in urban sociology by S. Bhowmik in 2009. Expressing such concerns, Kosambi (op. cit.: 30) observes: 'Most studies of urban society concentrate on large cities.' Patel and Deb (op. cit.: 21), in their evaluation of urban studies, also recall the main thrust of urban research mainly focusing on the large cities. Similarly, Sujata Patel (ibid.: 21) observes: 'Though this introduction suggests that there is tremendous diversity of and about urban experience, I have been able to include examples mainly from metro-politan cities. Unfortunately, there is very little published work on small and medium towns in India.' This is totally in contrast with the emerging research on a few large Indian cities which are competing to become 'world class'. For a summary view of such research, see Nair (2005), Banerjee-Guha (2009: 95–107) and Sharma (2010: 69–91).

It is not to say that studies on small cities and towns are singularly missing, but these are more evaluative studies of government programmes like the IDSMT. A few non-evaluative studies can be recalled here: 'The Role of Small Cities in Regional Development' by O.P. Mathur (1984); 'Growth Dynamics of SMTs: A Case Study of Bihar, M.P. and Haryana' by Shalini Gupta (1995); and a study of 'Industrial Growth in Gobindgarh Town' by Kundu and Bhatia (op. cit.). Senior bureaucrats like M.N. Buch and P.S.A. Sundaram have also been supporting the cause of policy thrust in favour of small cities and towns. The need is of serious research related to socio-cultural and economic life of such settlements and their contribution to the regions, under their influence. In this context, one can recall the rich tradition of research with socio-cultural focus on small cities or towns, in earlier decades. Radhakamal Mukherjee and Baljit Singh (1965) conducted a socio-cultural study of Gorakhpur city (then with a population of about 1,80,000). Likewise, Richard G. Fox (1991) studied business traditions in a small town Tezibazar – 50 kms away from Banaras city. Such studies are now hardly conducted by sociologists or scholars from other professions though some studies are conducted of fringe villages under direct influence of large cities or agglomerations [see, for instance, Fox, 1991; Yadav, 1987 and Gill, 1991].

Deliberations on Small Cities and Towns (of India) in Global Era

It is in the above context that a strong need was felt to deliberate the fate of thousands of small cities and towns of India, under the present global regime. Accordingly, a national seminar on the theme 'Small Cities and Towns in Global Era: Emerging Changes and Perspectives' was organised at the Tata Institute of Social Sciences (TISS), Mumbai, during 29–30 August 2011. The thrust of the two-day deliberations was to discuss relevant themes related to emerging changes in small cities and towns across India and in the process to develop some perspectives for such changes (or even stagnation) since the opening up of Indian economy to global market forces. Accordingly, the sub-themes under focus were: impact of change on their economies, labour markets and forward-backward linkages of the regions under their influence; changes in socio-cultural values and issues in gender and ethnic exclusions; emerging uses of space and role of real estate; status of infrastructure and interventions if any for upgrading it; institutions of governance and their status; role of civil society and political identities; and finally, emerging perspectives on small cities and towns in India in present global era.

As expected, the trend of scanty research on such urban settlements also influenced the quality of papers, more so the case studies across the regions. In contrast, the theoretical debate on possible influences and trends proved to be quite rich, with opening up areas of research in future. The need was evidently felt repeatedly on the part of Indian urban researchers to take up the challenge by creating useful research in the area.

The Present Volume

In all, about 20 presentations were made by participants of the seminar and they fairly represented various regions of the country. The papers in the present volume are a welcome outcome due to their contribution by leading urban researchers from various areas of specialisations. All the

4 ❖ R.N. Sharma

papers, except one, included in this volume were presented in the seminar. The paper '"Citiness" and "Urbanity": The Privilege of Mega Cities' was also recently published in the journal, *Bangladesh Sociological Studies* (Volume 3, Number 2). As the paper has direct relevance to the theme of the present volume, it adds to the scanty research on small cities and towns in the country.

The volume is divided into two parts: (1) theoretical perspectives, and (2) case studies. The first part begins with the paper by Swapna Banerjee-Guha, which sets the tone of discourse on 'Small Cities and Towns in Contemporary Urban Theory, Policy and Praxis'. It provides an excellent political-economy perspective on the dominant role played by a few mega cities which, according to the author, are emerging as 'champions of urbanity', particularly due to 'their contribution in raising the economic efficiency of shining India, while serious academic engagement and related discourses on smaller cities and towns have been relegated to a near redundancy'. For Banerjee-Guha, 'the state policy in India has gone on to promote modernisation with an open thrust towards building huge infrastructure for locating development in or near leading urban centres'. The author makes a survey of the 'planning approach' of Government of India which in recent years gets tilted towards 'control and direction of use of prime lands in such city regions'. Banerjee-Guha concludes her paper by highlighting the need of a corrective urban policy (by Government of India and various states) by making a case for a 'multi-layered planning'. In her own words, 'One competing argument favouring multi-layered planning is that the suggestions put forth by the locals having greater knowledge of the regional resource and ecological characteristics may get recognition.'

The paper 'Emerging Perspectives on Small Cities and Towns' by Annapurna Shaw is again a high-quality paper, presenting a critique of urban policy and planning of Indian government since independence. Shaw also highlights the fact that though the neglect by Central or state governments of small cities and towns is all-pervasive, in present paradigm of market-driven development with global linkages, 'the private sector views such settlements with opportunity of their serving as intermediate centres and points of a global supply chain'. This emerging fact is very much visible in states like Gujarat and Tamil Nadu, where the aggressive policy of industrialisation by these states is co-opting such cities and towns which are strategically located. In the process, they are getting new job opportunities and even attracting manufacturing units. For Shaw though the 73rd and 74th Constitutional Amendments, aimed at devolution of (political and financial) power to these settlements and their rural counterparts, were initiated by the government in the early 1990s, their outcome, so far, has been more than satisfactory. The same can be stated about the JNNURM, which more favours the large cities with sound financial resources. The author advocates an 'inclusive policy' where development also goes to the backward regions and their urban settlements. Shaw also highlights the fact that private sector is making deep inroads into small urban pockets and rural areas for turning them into new markets for consumer goods and services.

The paper '"Citiness" and "Urbanity": The Privilege of Mega Cities' by R.N. Sharma, also one of the editors of the present volume, further pushes the agenda of attracting the attention of policy makers, development experts and academicians towards the growing dominance of a few large Indian cities for creating a favourable environment for their emerging as the 'privileged' city-regions for neo-liberal economic development. In the process, thousands of small cities or towns are being co-opted into the process of being 'written off the map' both by the policy makers and urban researchers in the field. In simple terms, 'citiness' refers to small community-oriented towns gradually taking shape as cities, with the expansion of their socio-economic and cultural institutions – the process that started in Europe during the Middle Ages. The term 'urbanity' within the fold of reason is interpreted by Marxist and Weberian scholars as a product of 'modern' and 'post-modern' city, mainly in terms of expanding base of capitalism, spatial forms and various institutions emerging from the relationship of class and property. According to the author, a few large Indian cities, with their global linkages, are more and more being accepted as representing 'centrality' of citiness and urbanity. Indian researchers also show a distinct bias in their favour by ignoring the cause and relevance of small cities and towns, and the key role played by them in their regions of influence. The paper concludes that in terms of quality of life, opportunities for growth and basic dignity of life, small cities and towns appear to have no future in India.

The volume also has two important and leading papers which explore forms of 'city (and town) culture and values' being shaped and re-shaped under the neo-liberal market-oriented urban India. Rowena Robinson, in her paper 'Culture of Small-Town India', using available literature, including electronic media and newspaper reports, tries to develop a perspective on India's small-town culture. She proposes that the consumer culture of mass cities is swaying the sleeping towns in far-reaching areas, resulting in raising aspirations, along with marked divergences between the preferences and aspirations of small town dwellers and those who live in metropolises like Mumbai, Delhi or Bangalore. In what ways these value changes (and objective reality in terms of flowing consumer goods towards the town) are altering dynamics of social life in small towns, is the main research question probed in the paper. In the tradition of anthropological writings about urban transition in Western communities, Robinson explores the process of Indian metropolitan cities by liberating the youths of small towns from rigid and orthodox values. How are the forward and backward linkages emerging, needs to be researched. The author particularly probes the IT sector and its influence on the towns – both in terms of creating new opportunities and growing mobility among the knowledge workers towards the metropolises. For her, things appear to be going well for the small towns due to their increasing consumer power. She also draws attention on the downsides as well. These are in terms of poor infrastructure, poor governance, poor resources and growing violence and crime. Finally, Robinson contextualises the cultural capital in changing towns and even the countryside. For her, ethnic and community networks are disintegrating or taking new forms, though with different implications in terms of caste, gender or class. The paper thus puts forth many propositions in the context of changing towns which can form useful areas of research in future.

The next paper 'The Academic Bias against Towns: A Cultural Audit' by Rajesh Gill also raises the basic question: Does the urban way of life (referring to the metropolitan culture) percolate to the smaller and lesser urban settlements too? This has been examined in terms of infrastructure, governance, population attributes, technological development and the culture. Gill highlights the growing socio-cultural and economic differences between the mega cities and the rest of urban India. In the earlier part of her paper, she recalls great urban theorists who raised the comparative issues about primary relationships and values represented through the folk cultures and the secondary relationships represented through the emerging 'city' on Western horizon. In Indian context, Gill refers to 'unequal advantages' due to exclusionary urban development, asking for the 'right to the city'. In changing urban India, she recalls varying perceptions of people about their needs, aspirations and value preferences. This has been examined more in the context of Chandigarh, which itself manifests duality of views across the classes. Like the previous paper by Robinson, Gill also raises several propositions about changing urban India which require new insights and scope for future research.

Biraj Swain, in her paper 'Small Towns, their Limited Resourcing Options and Equity Deficits' presents a revealing and much desired investigation into the resource generation and financial options available to small cities and towns of India, and for that sake of several other nations now competing for attracting global finance for developing infrastructure in their urban settlements. For her, such urban centres would have taken shape as reasonably 'first-port-of-call' for first generation migrants, but for the lack of resources and ever-shrinking opportunities. According to her, the available estimates from UNICEF and WHO suggest that India would need to invest approximately ₹ 96 billion between 2001 and 2015 to the MDG target for urban water, and ₹ 208 billion for urban sanitation. However, there is a large concern over the lack of basic infrastructure in urban India, especially the smaller urban areas being incapable to mobilise needed resources. Swain presents an interesting case of a small city, Ratlam in western Madhya Pradesh, which opted out of mobilising a loan from the Asian Development Bank (ADB) due to the fear of not being able to repay the debt. She then makes a case for such small cities to come out of the trap of 'resource-deficit spiral'. The author extends the argument to more serious deficits in funding schemes meant for improving job opportunities and quality of life of the urban poor. Finally, she makes valuable suggestions towards improving resource bases of hundreds of small cities in the country.

Abdul Shaban and Sanjukta Sattar's paper 'Industrial Dispersal and Clustering in India during Post-Reform Period and the Role of Small and Medium Towns' is a well-documented and well-critiqued paper on the ever-live issue of deflating over-concentrated economic activity (and therefore, population) from the mega cities, towards undeveloped regions in the country. The aggregated data on industrial clustering vis-à-vis its dispersal at the national level is segregated at the state and then district level, both in terms of emerging organised/informal industrial/service based clusters of growth and, therefore, the variations in the working population. The authors have derived several useful and revealing conclusions from the trends emerging, more so after the liberalisation of Indian economy in 1991. For Shaban and Sattar, the number of workers in the organised sector of Indian economy has contracted in the post-liberalisation phase, but the informal sector has experienced a robust growth across the districts of several states. For them, there are two distinct dynamics underway with regard to the dispersal of industrial and commercial sectors in the country. First, at the absolute level, the concentration of workers has been growing in Class I cities, especially in the million-plus cities. Secondly, when the distribution of workers per thousand of population in different size-class of cities is measured, it shows some evidence of dispersal of industrial and commercial activities during the post-reform period. However, for the authors, the dispersal is largely confined to and around major industrial regions/clusters in the country. It is also revealed that the role of small and medium towns with regard to absorption and (geographic) expansion of market and provision of cheap factor of production is becoming very important in north-western, western and southern regions of the country.

The paper 'Financing and Access to Basic Amenities in Small and Medium Towns of India under Globalised Regime' by Debolina Kundu presents a detailed database across the regions within the country, and the emerging perspective(s) on the role of central and state governments towards financing much-needed infrastructure base in small cities and towns. For achieving it, the author presents a trend of growth of small cities and town, highlights emerging spatial patterns in access to basic amenities in these settlements, and then makes a noteworthy attempt to analyse the financing patterns of urban development across the size-class of towns for the select states as well as at the national level, more so in the context of 13th Central Finance Commission data as well as the allocations under the JNNURM-based programmes and their outcomes. The author also highlights the fact that the JNNURM has provided substantial assistance to cities and towns for infrastructure development and housing the poor, and has been effective in renewing the country's focus on the urban sector. However, the analysis exhibits a move towards polarised development and in-built big-city bias, especially in the developed states. For the author, for revitalising small cities and towns with growth potential efforts should be made for making special provisions for unconditional general grants addressed towards their infrastructure and housing needs till the time they develop the capacities to receive project fundings. This will make the growth process inclusive, where the urban poor (and small cities and towns) would be partners in the developmental process, and ensure equitable and sustainable urban growth.

Part Two consists of case studies focusing on specific towns, with the exception of the paper by R.S. Sandhu and Jasmeet Sandhu extending its scope to small cities and towns across the Punjab state. It would be relevant to state here that the contributors of the present volume do not necessarily confine their definition of town versus city to the rigid census definitions. Class I cities have been defined as urban settlements with their population of one lakh or above. Given the trend that large cities are expanding rapidly in their population size, and over 50 cities now crossing their population above one million and much more, in no way these are comparable with the cities with their population, say, below half a million. The term 'urban agglomeration' used by the census is equally problematic from the socio-cultural research viewpoint. It is due to the fact that 'development authorities' of several large cities keep on adding fringe areas to their jurisdiction, though such extended areas may be in contrast different in terms of status of infrastructure and socio-cultural traits of their residents. The contributors of case studies of cities/towns in the present volume, therefore, focus more on the main city, within its municipal boundaries.

The paper 'Urban Development and Small Towns in Punjab', authored jointly by R.S. Sandhu and Jasmeet Sandhu, presents a detailed critique of the neglected status of small cities and towns across, the otherwise, prosperous Punjab state. This neglect is equally visible in biased research favouring the large cities. In their own words, 'We are more knowledgeable about stars and planets but lesser known about our cities and towns'. For the researchers, 'although there has been tremendous advancement in database management system, yet a lot of information particularly at the local level remains unrecorded, unorganised and inaccessible; and officials concerned consider it as confidential and a personal property'. Within such constraints, the authors make an admirable approach in dissecting, through whatever available data, the small cities and towns across Punjab and bring out revealing trends in their growth or decline. Within the regions of state, there have emerged marked disparities in the levels of urbanisation. The researchers observe that, like other Indian states, the major cities and developed regions are turning economically more vibrant and attracting more migrants from within or outside the state. For them, a majority of small cities and towns are developing without systematic planning. The disparities in levels of infrastructure are revealing, though the health facilities have favoured the small towns and rural areas, if not in quality, at least in coverage of the remote areas. The researchers conclude the paper with the observation that the small towns in Punjab are ignored by planning and development processes, and the poor live in slum-like conditions as marginalised by their municipal authorities.

Another joint paper 'The Changing Face of Urban India: Allahabad City in Context' by K.N. Bhatt and Lalit Joshi presents an excellent critique of the changing (or rather decaying) city of Allahabad, which in the past was considered a jewel of Uttar Pradesh, due to its rich history. The city which was at the forefront of the nationalist movement against the British colonisers and a prime educational centre of the eastern region, according to the authors, is in a state of decay due to the neglect by corrupt and indifferent planners, the land sharks converting open spaces into a concrete jungle, the decaying infrastructure, and totally chaotic development of its fringe areas. Such a state of affairs is perceived by the authors within the Marxist perspective where the 'use' value of land in the city is fast changing into the 'exchange' value, and thus, turning into the 'force of production'. The authors present a detailed landscape of the city as developed by the colonisers, and then extended by the natives into a 'prime bazaar city' due to its religious significance. In its present status, the old city languishes in neglect. Seven decades of planning and governance has not brought any relief from congestion, high density of population, traffic jams, encroachments and illegal constructions. For the authors, the deteriorating physical environment of the city, due to depleting open spaces, is a serious matter but of nobody's concern. The civil society groups are no match for the powerful vested interests.

The paper 'The City of Terror: Deprivation, Segregation and Communal Conflicts in Malegaon' by Abdul Shaban presents a stark case of a bubbling city with 'low technology' based powerloom industry, but its labour force living in abject poverty, poor working conditions and uncertainties of life due to the town turning into a riot-prone area. Thus, a large majority of Muslim migrant population lives in the city in grinding poverty and penury. According to the author, the financing of production of cloth and its trade, from spinning to dying, is under the control of a handful of Hindu (Marwari) merchants who further segregate the population of city into their secured residential places vis-à-vis the rest of the areas (with Muslim-dominant population) living in 'spaces of fear' and deprivation. According to Shaban, the migrant youths who join the powerloom work, get aged with deadly diseases like tuberculosis or malnutrition. The author also peeps into the causes of communal disharmony and violence. For him, 'though the city has been an important base for powerloom industry for over a century, the lack of development in the town shows continued apathy and lack of vision of planners and policy makers to harness economic potentials (for a better cause) of such industrial towns'.

The next three papers focus on cities in tribal and hilly areas. The two are Shillong and Tura in the state of Meghalaya, and the third one, Port Blair (in Andaman Islands and also its administrative headquarters). Port Blair and Shillong also happen to be tourist destinations.

The paper 'Ethnic Conflicts in a Small City: The Case of Shillong' by Nikhlesh Kumar mainly focuses on inter-ethnic relationships more based on tensions and conflicts in a small multi-ethnic, multi-religious city (Shillong) in the north-eastern region of India. Initially, the paper draws from historical writings more related to the role of British colonisers in establishing this city in 1867. There, the first conflict took place between the Khasi tribal chiefs (the original community in the area) and the Britishers. With the shifting of Chief Commissioner's office (of the province of Assam), the immigration of various communities from outside regions led to setting the ground for inter-ethnic conflict in the city. There also came Christian missionaries and a centre of Ramakrishna Mission. This helped 'modernising' local Khasis on one hand, and making them 'identity-conscious', on the other. This drew lines of conflict for supremacy by the native tribal community (the Khasis) and the outside settlers. Their conflict for 'identity' extended to the national level, with a need on the part of Central government to intervene in the affairs of Meghalaya state. The author provides a detailed account of a steady and sustained effort by the Khasis to maintain hold on the city and, therefore, the region. He probes the role of various Acts introduced by the Indian government in protecting tribal properties and their customary practices. In the process, according to the author, a tertiary identity, that of the 'Scheduled Tribe', has emerged in the area.

The paper by Umesh Kumar and D.N. Pandey on 'Morphological and Demographic Changes in Port Blair Town and their Impact' provides a detailed account of Port Blair town which is, though a highly sensitive region, both ecologically and due to inhabiting some of the most ancient tribals known in human society, growing rapidly as a tourist destination. Thus, the present paper endeavours to study the growth of Port Blair town against the backdrop of resource scarcity (more so drinking water), in addition to its impact on the primitive tribal groups. The authors present rich data on changing morphology of the city-region, tracing its history from the British (colonial) period till today. How the fringe areas of Port Blair are re-shaping due to their exploitation for commercial (tourism and transport) purposes, is well argued. The paper also shows the far reaching consequences due to the growing migrant population within the island. Thus, the fringe areas are going through functional and physical transformation which is adversely affecting the ecology of the region. The tourist activity is now extended to the far areas for which a transport route is encarved through the inhabitation of Jarwa tribals. According to the authors, this is bound to destroy this most primitive community whose number is around 250 (in 2002). The Onges tribe is also on the verge of disappearance, so are the Great Andamanese and the Sentinelese. The Indian government appears to be insensitive to these delicate issues, while eco-tourism is taking its toll.

The status that is enjoyed today by Shillong, the capital city of Meghalaya, was in fact enjoyed in history by another town known as Tura. It is one of the oldest towns in Meghalaya, and had been the headquarters of the entire Garo Hills Division since 1866. Interestingly, after the formation of the state of Meghalaya, it grew rapidly during 1971–81, with an abnormally high growth rate of 127 per cent during the period. However, its topography has not supported its further growth, due to its isolated location and unsupportive urban/economic activities. The result is that it now shows steadily falling growth rate, just opposite to Shillong city, which has attracted more population along with trade, commerce and tourism. Sumit Mukherjee and Amlan Biswas, in their paper, provide a vivid description about the causes of historic growth of Tura town and then its steady decline.

V. Anil Kumar's paper 'Urban Governance and Planning in Karnataka' presents an overview of the status of quality and infrastructure in small cities and towns across the Karnataka state. For him, the status of urban governance and planning vis-à-vis district and taluk towns is in a deplorable state. The author presents a critique of the provision of District Planning Committee (DPC) under the 74th Constitutional Amendment, according to which the DPCs are to perform the role of integrating the town/city planning with the district-level planning, including both the urban and rural areas. However, for him, nowhere is it visible. The planning of small cities and towns is lost in red tape with little coordination among the involved government departments. By citing the case of Dharwad city, Anil Kumar highlights the fact that in spite of rich heritage of this historic town linking the Bangalore-Pune highway, it starves for basic facilities like water and sewage system. For the author, the situation is in no way better for several other small cities and towns of Karnataka which languish due to scarcity of resources and poor basic infrastructure.

Finally, the paper on 'Munger: A Bazaar Town in Decline' by Sheema Fatima reveals the sad and steady decline of Munger town in Bihar state, which was historically a significant district town along the river Ganga, and particularly became relevant to the British colonisers due to its strategic topography. Today, it has declined to a stagnant sleepy town, and according to the author, it could be attributed to utter failure on the part of the state government to utilise these small cities and towns with ample potential for their own growth and better economic opportunities in the region. According to her, the story of Munger town also reminds of the fact that most colonial centres remained a source of administrative and economic benefits for the Britishers, without creating any strong urban dynamics for balanced regional growth through their forward and backward linkages.

Concluding Remarks

In Indian society, for decades, researchers (more so sociologists and anthropologists) found no useful purpose in studying 'city' as a separate category of social reality. For them, urban India existed more an extension of rural reality where caste, kinship and religion have played an equally relevant role. Those a few studies, which emerged in urban context, mainly focused on large cities that grew more under the colonial legacy. Thousands of small cities and towns, particularly the bazaar towns, hardly attracted researchers in the field to understand their 'urbanity' as well as their age-old contribution to vast agrarian communities in the country. The policy thrust of Indian government also favoured large cities for development and capital formation. The need has evidently been felt repeatedly on the part of urban researchers to take up the task of useful research in the area.

In last two decades or so, the process of globalization has stirred up societies in various ways. The new market systems have emerged under new global regime, many of which cut across the countries. Under their influence, on one hand, new rights and lifestyles are emerging for the privileged participants in the global process, on the other, there are millions others who remain deprived of gains of such development.

Instead, many of them are involuntarily being displaced from their habitats and very sources of livelihoods, for meeting new demands of ever-expanding production systems and market linkages. This mega-transformation has created significant impact on conventionally existing cities and towns. A few cities across the countries are coming up the hubs of flow of capital and new technologies under the ever-expanding information technologies and labour markets. In this process, traditional centres of regional production and distribution of goods and services are getting reorganized or disintegrated.

In the above context, there is a strong need of understanding the impact of such changes on Indian urban settlements, especially the small cities and towns which, as stated above, have remained neglected in urban research. With this relevant objective, the present volume is an outcome of national a seminar held at the Tata Institute of Social Sciences (TISS), Mumbai theme of the seminar was 'Small Cities and Towns in Global Era: Emerging Changes and Perspectives'. The selected papers in the present volume, which is divided into two sections, mainly fall under two categories: those focusing on the global agenda and its possible impact on urban settlements, and those which detail out the emerging changes and their impact on socio-cultural and economic life situations of citizens of specific cities (and towns) under their focus. In other words, the first section is more based on theoretical underpinnings and emerging perspectives on changing small cities and towns of India, while the second section contains case studies on such settlements.

This is a modest effort towards needed research in this very neglected area of research. It is expected that the volume will inspire the future researchers to make systematic efforts in grasping the rapid changes under the present global era and their impact on thousands of small cities and towns of India.

References

Banerjee-Guha, S. (2009) 'Neo Liberalising the "Urban": New Geographies of Power and Injustice in Indian Cities', *Economic and Political Weekly.* Vol. XLIV, No. 22, May 30.

Bhowmik, Sharit (2009) 'Urban Sociology'. In Yogesh Atal (ed.). *Sociology and Social Anthropology in India.* New Delhi: ICSSR.

Bose, Ashish (1973) *Studies on India's Urbanisation, 1901–1971.* New Delhi: Tata McGraw-Hill.

Castells, Manuel (1998) *The Information Age: Economy, Society and Culture. Vol. III: End of Millennium.* Malden/Oxford: Blackwell.

D'Souza, Victor S. (1985) 'Urban Studies'. In *Survey of Research in Sociology and Social Anthropology, 1969–79.* Vol. I. New Delhi: Satvahan, sponsored by ICSSR.

Fox, Richard G. (1991) 'Colonial Town in Prismatic Society'. In M.S.A. Rao (ed.). *A Reader in Urban Sociology*. New Delhi: Orient Longman.

Gill, Rajesh (1991) *Social Changes in Urban Periphery*. New Delhi: Allied Publishers.

Gupta, Shalini (1995) *Growth Dynamics of Small and Medium Towns in India: A Case Study of Bihar, M.P. and Haryana*. www.unesco.org/most/dsp57-en.htm (retrieved on 03.08.2009).

Harvey, David (2008) 'The Right to the City'. *New Left Review*. Vol. 53, September–October.

Kosambi, Meera (1994) *Urbanisation and Urban Development in India: Research in Sociology and Anthropology: Third Survey*. New Delhi: ICSSR.

Kundu, Amitabh and Sutinder Bhatia (1995) 'Industrial Growth in Small and Medium Towns and their Vertical Integration: The Case of Gobindgarh, Punjab, India'. UNESCO/MOST Discussion Paper No. 57, http://www.unesco.org/ most/disp57en.htm (retrieved on 08.03.2009).

Mathur, O.P. (1984) *The Role of Small Cities in Regional Development*. Nagoya: UNCRD.

Mukherjee, Radhakamal and Baljit Singh (1965) *A District Town in Transition: Social and Economic Survey of Gorakhpur*. Bombay: Asia Publishing House.

Nair, Janaki (2005) *The Promise of the Metropolis: Bangalore's Twentieth Century*. New Delhi: Oxford University Press.

Sharma, R.N. (2010) 'Mega Transformation of Mumbai: Deepening Enclave Urbanism'. *Sociological Bulletin*. Vol. 59, No. 1.

Yadav, C.S. (ed.) (1987) *Studies on Rural-Urban Fringe*. New Delhi: Concept Publishing.

Part One
Theoretical Perspectives

1

Small Cities and Towns in Contemporary Urban Theory, Policy and Praxis

SWAPNA BANERJEE-GUHA

Since 1970s, the discourse that has gone to dominate international urban research has consistently underscored the significance of global cities in international economic and urban systems overpowering attempts to understand the 'urban' in diversity in size and region-specific characteristics. Accordingly, a large number of works have come out with meticulous analyses of such cities, particularly their contribution in raising the economic efficiency of countries and regions while serious academic engagement and related discourses on smaller cities and towns have been relegated to a near redundancy. The above unidirectional approach towards 'urban' with the spotlight on global cities is integrally connected with an increasing neo-liberalisation of the global order, backtracking of welfare state, and renewed convergence of investment with a massive importance of the corporate sector in planned development initiatives. In the process, concepts of decentralisation and balanced urban development along with imperatives of growth of smaller cities and towns in association with their local/regional resource-base have considerably fallen off the said mainstream global research agenda. Their merit in the aforesaid research agenda mainly lies in their ability to serve the global urban hierarchy, remaining at its tail-end as secondary investment nodes. No proper data or official statistics on these settlements exist in the offices of international research or planning institutes. Policy and planning perspectives for them largely follow the same globalisation-oriented development models that help them join the race of attaining 'globalness'. The ground realities at a wider scale reflect a corresponding notion of 'new urbanism' characterised by acute urban competitiveness and place-marketing. Obviously the large global cities are only identified as 'champions of urbanity' by the said entrepreneurialist perspective for reproduction of the above unidirectional approach to 'urban' in developing countries too. Projected as the quintessential form of a unified vision of urban planning, these cities actually act as vital links between the contemporary urban imaginations of global capital, largely contributing towards the construction of hegemony of globalisation. The perspective partly rests on the inequalities of the existing urban systems, but more on the construction of newer areas of decline and growth, targeting, at times, the smaller cities and towns. India, too, has been no exception to this. Similar trends in urban discourse and planning, often state-supported, with a clear stress on mega cities have been found to dominate the planning and praxis of urban development in the country, especially since 1990s, with a perilous shift in urban planning, making it anti-poor, elitist and indifferent to redistribution of resources. Smaller cities and towns in the process have lost their significance in regional planning agendas that earlier centred largely on decentralisation and balanced development. The 21st century urban planning has become more brazen in reinforcing the importance of mega cities in achieving success in globalisation (Banerjee-Guha, 2011).

A parallel trend of urban research and theorisation, however, has always existed, challenging the above. Theorists of this trend, at micro level, have focused on the contradictions of neo-liberalised global cities, their increasingly uneven pattern of wealth distribution and last but not the least, acceleration of their isolated and elitist nature of growth, particularly in contemporary times that in several ways has proved detrimental to the goal of a socially just urban development; at macro level, they have stressed on the imperatives of a well-knit urban system and the significance of smaller cities and towns that stand for a more distributed pattern of development based on social justice. In India, too, researchers belonging to this alternative school have been considerably vocal, focusing on the need for exploring the potential of smaller 'ordinary cities' – based on their regional-local resource base, for the purpose of reducing regional disparity. According to this viewpoint, symbiosis between these settlements and the existing resource potential in their 'upland' (Dickinson, 1964) happens to be the key to balanced regional development. The above line of argument has posed a formidable challenge to the fragmentary, global-city oriented discourse of contemporary times.

Researchers of the above genre, hailing from different parts of the world (Knox, 1995; Friedman, 1995; King, 1990; Kundu, 1986, 2011; Shaw, 1996; Banerjee-Guha, 2002a; Robinson, 2002, 2011), have pointed out that both from academic and planning perspectives it is improper not to take into account the relevance of smaller cities in the urban systems as only they can exposit the diversities of 'urban' that have the potential of forging a close link with the surrounding region. They argue that world

city research focusing only on global cities and that too on their significance in international economy and the global urban hierarchy essentially
suffers from a structural rigidity that does not allow an understanding of
the diversity of 'urban' – in size, economy and socio-cultural nuances.
Friedman (1986) noted that it was only the economic momentum that
became the determining factor for all explanations in the above approach:
'the economic variable is likely to be decisive for all attempts at explanation' (Friedman, 1995: 317). He even asked whether the world city
research incorporated only a specific class of cities having some specific
characteristics that make them different from majority of the urban
agglomerations of the world. Friedman (1995) stated that the tendency to
categorise cities into a hierarchy and the resultant undue thrust on few
cities went to leave out many more cities that lacked 'globalness' despite
having varied characteristics and experiences on social and cultural fronts.
King (1990), too, while exploring the nuances of colonial urbanism,
cautioned about the myopic nature of the world city research and its
lopsided perspective (Taylor, 2000). On the same lines, Knox (1995)
argued that even the so-called focus on global cities was also one-sided as
it only highlighted the overpowering economic significance of such cities
and not their multiscalar inequality that resulted from the entrepre-
neurial/competitive agenda of the global city framework (Kundu, 1996;
Banerjee-Guha, 2009). However, researches in the Global North focusing
on the contradictions of capitalist urbanisation and the unequal nature of
global cities were few (Harvey, 1973; 1985; Castells, 1989; Pickvance,
1986; Sassen, 1991) and till early 1990s, large cities of the Global South,
because of their 'economic irrelevance' (sic), remained almost excluded
from the lens of the traditional world city research.

The above mentioned urban research with focus on contradictions
of global cities and globalisation nevertheless gained momentum with
time. Way back in 1970s, in his 'Social Justice and the City', Harvey
(1973) had advocated for justice in city planning. In 1980s, at a macro
scale, he (1985) analysed the urbanisation process of capital as the
primary force behind emerging inequality in inter and intra-urban
systems. Some years later, Sassen (1994) noted that the few major cities
that could succeed to become global cities and nodes of a disproportion-
ately large corporate power also happened to be the convergence points of
a huge mass of the poor and the underprivileged, occupied by a large
number of underclass immigrant population that went to create 'spaces
of difference' (Berner and Korff, 1995) inside such cities. The issues that
significantly appeared in the realm of urban research from this time
onwards were intra-urban inequality (Smith, 1996), segmentation,
ghettoisation and gentrification, all that intensified with the tightening
of the neo-liberal regime. Implications of neo-liberalism on city life, governance, economy, culture and, finally urban planning that reflected a

wider restructuring of the economy surfaced as associated issues. The earlier world city hypothesis could not capture these realities that had started showing up in western cities way back in the 1970s and in non-western cities from the 1990s (Cohen, 1981; Abu-Lughod, 1995). In the following years, post-Fordist neo-liberal urban restructuring and the associated issues assumed a critical place in urban studies (Harvey, 1991; Machimura, 1992) that got linked up with the wider body of research on contradictions of globalisation at diverse scales (Banerjee-Guha, 2002b), proving in the long run that not all urban research required to follow a rigid spatial systems analysis, rather they belonged to a larger body of interdisciplinary explanatory framework that offered valuable critique on the functioning of capital at global and local scales along with the associated role of state and non-state institutions.

Having affinity with the above viewpoint emerged a huge bunch of researches in the Global South, including India, on urban systems and regional development focusing on the significance of small cities and towns for balanced growth. Studies on patterns of urban growth, rural-urban migration, regional and urban disparity, urban poverty, crisis of urban policy and many related issues went to form the body of this research that was further enriched by organic knowledge drawn from diverse spaces. Imperatives of developing lower order cities and towns, utilising their growth potentials – notwithstanding their placement in the global economic/urban hierarchy – for achieving balanced regional development, happened to be a significant underlying approach of a number of these studies (Kundu, 1989; Kundu and Gupta, 1996; Banerjee-Guha, 1993, 2002a; Shaw, 1996, 1999). Their interdisciplinary character acted as a catalyst to promote their explanatory resilience.

Post-1970 Realities at Macro and Urban Levels

Post-1970 focus on globalisation and global cities in world city research has got a lot to do with the prevailing politico-economic trend at the global level. A careful look at the world scenario reveals that since 1970s, a new urban order was found to rule the world coinciding with the crisis of the Fordist-Keynesian regime and breakdown of the Bretton Woods system. It was a time when the world capitalist system became increasingly neo-liberalised, impacting countries and regions across the world, especially those of the Global South and encroaching into their developmental path (Banerjee-Guha, 2009). Political geographies of urban governance simultaneously transformed from a welfarist orientation to get superseded by a 'new urban' political outlook that mainly focused on the issues of urban and regional economic competitiveness, famously analysed as a shift to urban manageliarism embedded in the concept of market-rule and entrepreneurism. As a natural process, it got entwined with debates on globalisation and its implications in national and local economies on the one hand, and change in the macro-economic situation and policies, on the other. The salient characteristics were: dismantling of institutional constraints upon marketisation, universal backtracking of the welfare state, increased commodification, shrinking of the organised sector jobs, etc. Simultaneously, despite deregulation and privatisation of state-owned and state-provided services, a new kind of vociferous state intervention with larger entrepreneurial capacity was brought in, to roll forward new forms of governance that ostensibly suited a market-driven globalised economy (Brenner and Theodore, 2002). Despite variations between regions and countries, the pattern attained a universal status. At urban level, it was characterised by increasing constraints in municipal planning, exercise of power of elected civic bodies, privatisation of basic services, withdrawal of the state from urban development, escalating support to private-public partnerships especially in infrastructure projects and increasing gentrification of urban space to accommodate the increasing demand of elite consumption (Banerjee-Guha, 2006). The process became an obvious phenomenon in the developing world since late 1980s and by 1990s, countries like Mexico, Brazil and India became the major nodes of its consolidation. Meanwhile, the tempo of urbanisation in these countries had started experiencing a sharp increase that reached a hyper rate during the 1980s. From 1950–1990, urban population of developing countries increased fourfold with the majority living in large cities (Burgess et al., 1997). During 1980s, a number of countries started adopting supply side economic policies seeking to derive efficiency in service delivery by privatisation that led to a consensus regarding national development and urban development. In the process, increasing efficiency and productivity through investment (with an assurance of best return) emerged as a key factor that paved the way for private sector in urban development, that led to the latter's entanglement with investors' choice of concentrating resources in certain centre. This paved way for creating private cities and intensified social and spatial inequalities among existing urban settlements. It is important to mention here that in the late 1980s, aid donors and global economic institutions, through a series of initiatives, officially recognised the significance of an urban focus in development policies. The thrust, as usual, was on large cities that would act as diffusion centres of the neo-liberal ideology they wanted to promote. State-capital alliances started becoming a common practice and accordingly, global investment of international financial institutions (IFIs) got converged in large urban centres backed by an ideology of return-based sector-oriented investment. The chronology of a series of recommendations will make the picture clearer: in 1988, the urban focus was approved in the OECD recommendations; in the same year, it was again approved by the Global Strategy 2000; in 1991, UNDP's Urban

Development Policy Paper approved it; in the same year, approval came from World Bank's Urban Sector Policy Paper; finally in 1993, the Bank's Housing Sector Policy Paper accepted the urban focus recommendation. The process was further underpinned by rapid technological progress and increasing integration of trade, production, investment, finance and labour circuits, all mediated by the growing role of transnational corporations, international banks and financial institutions (IFIs). The opening up of national economies and reduced power of the state made independent management of economic affairs increasingly difficult. Important instruments of macro-economic management too could not be determined unilaterally while conventional macro-economic interventions became more difficult to sustain (Griffin and Khan, 1992). At this point there emerged a standardised urban policy in several developing countries at the behest of international financial institutions that went at par with state fiscal austerity, market liberalisation and public sector privatisation, the three pillars of the 'Washington Consensus' (Goldman, 2005) with an orientation towards a more export-based economy and greater efficiency.

The above shift had also a link with the changing attitude towards urban development by major economic institutions. Before 1980s, urban economies were seen as an outcome of national and international economic decisions. Harris (1992) argued that although national development strategies highlighted the employment-generating character of urban economies, the field of urban development was largely neglected and the economic potential of large urban economies was never seen with a proper perspective. With a more open world economy, the role of large cities was found much more instrumental in nationalising the concentrated development pattern that gradually led to implementation of urban development initiatives as advocated by international institutions. Here lies the significance of the standardised policy of urban development for all mega cities for attaining globalhood that almost became a 'fait accompli' for medium and small cities, irrespective of their resource potential and economic base. So far as the issue of regional development is concerned, the contemporary state institutions considerably got disengaged from practical urban development to emerge as a more vociferous institution for facilitating corporate-led development and, in the process, gentrifying selective metropolitan centres/regions for enabling them to attract global investment.

The Indian Scenario

In India, in current times, the focus of planning on large cities and a heightened effort of injecting globalness to smaller cities thus needs to be seen as a fallout of the above process that has close association with globalisation of the economy. The state policy in India has gone on to promote modernisation with an open thrust towards building huge infrastructure for locating development in or near leading urban centres. Private cities with upscale infrastructure are coming up in the outskirts of second or third-tier cities making enclave development a significant strategy even in urban planning. Hence, large areas inside the cities or in their peripheries with diverse land-use pattern are being acquired and handed over to corporate groups for making differently planned cities following the infrastructural norms of 'global cities', causing severe loss of livelihood to millions of farmers or other existing users of those lands. All these, regardless of the methods used, have increased urban-rural or urban-urban disparity in regional systems underlying which lays the methodology of economic productivity of selective investment. As we are focusing on the smaller cities in this article, let us briefly look at the post-independence urban policy in India with special reference to such cities.

In the absence of any explicit urban development policy of respective state governments, the national urban policy in the country always reoriented itself to the prevailing body politic in response to which fiscal measures and projects were decided. A careful observation of the policy documents will bring out the conflicts between different regional forces, on the one hand, and between the concepts of capital accumulation and distributive justice, on the other. Also, the main corpus of the policy has always addressed the large cities. The smaller cities and towns and non-metropolitan urban areas, for all practical purposes, have grown without any properly laid-down policy either at Centre or at state and local levels. Few state governments came out with properly laid-out policy and in many cases the job was entrusted to special planning bodies that were not in a position to adopt an all-round perspective for urban and regional development at a macro scale. Over and above, it was the Central government's national urban policy brought out as a part of the Five-Year Plan documents that was largely followed by the state governments (Banerjee-Guha, 2002a).

The crux of the national urban policy at the initial plan periods was modernisation with a focus on large-scale projects for achieving fast development. A sizeable part of the modern sector was already concentrated in the large urban centres that reiterated their position as the pivot of industry, trade and commerce. Dynamism of the spatial economy of the country was made to be represented only by these centres. It was reflected in the urban sector's 27 per cent share in the country's gross domestic product in 1950–51; by 1980, it became 47 per cent and by 2000, 60 per cent. The main stakeholders were the large cities. During 1980s, excessive concentration was, however, identified as a major problem of urban growth. One must note that from 1970 onwards the concept of new towns had already started being discussed by professional planners and architects as alternate urban strategies.

During the first two plan periods, ministerial arrangements were made; institutions were set up for management of urban administration for which bodies of skilled professionals were created. Both plans expressed concern over haphazard urban growth in the country in response to which enactment of town and country planning legislation was taken up for drawing master plans for urban areas with land regulation rules. During the Third Plan, the process got materialised through necessary financial and legislative measures and for the first time, an urban planning and land policy was formulated having a broad perspective of balanced urban development taking into consideration the role of smaller cities, towns and rural areas. Actually, the Third Plan had been the most vocal about dispersal, decentralisation and significance of municipal administration covering areas of physical planning, housing and other services in all urban areas. Subsequently, central assistance was also provided to the states to prepare master plans and chalk out suitable urban and regional development policies. Although different types of cities were earmarked as targets, yet it were the largest cities that were primarily taken up for implementation. Plenty of criticisms, however, came up that the legislations were nothing but elaboration of the old British laws that had a tendency of overriding the indigenous forms of urban spatial organisation. Many years after, in 1983, the Task Force appointed by the Planning Commission also mentioned that the concepts of deconcentration, dispersal of economic activities, planning of garden cities and suburbs, highlighted in the initial years of planning, leaned heavily on colonial legacies (Planning Commission of India, 1983). By this time, however, involvement of the government in sale and development of urban land and granting lease-hold and not ownership to users came up as major strategies along with a national shelter policy, under which sites and services projects for the economically weaker sections were included as a prime project. The Fourth Plan made arrangement to provide funds for housing and urban development to metropolitan authorities and state housing boards through the Housing and Urban Development Corporation (HUDCO), although most of the funds again went to the large cities. Several gigantic urban projects were initiated, such as, development of new state capitals in Punjab, Odisha and Gujarat and creation of large planning regions around metropolitan cities. For the first time, the idea was mooted to make the development efforts of towns and cities self-financed and the state becoming a facilitator than a provider of urban services (Banerjee-Guha, 2002b). In the Fifth Plan, thus, concern was expressed about generating maximum possible revenues through public participation in land development. However, the contradiction between supporting the largest metropolitan cities on the one hand, and advocating urban dispersal on the other, became clearer by then. Bardhan (1991) commented that the first contradiction was the result of the pressure from the urban middle and upper class located in large cities and the second was an indicator of appeasing the regional forces. Fifth Plan document, therefore, had the promise of financial assistance to metropolitan development for projects of national importance in the largest cities with simultaneous objectives to develop smaller towns and new urban centres (Banerjee-Guha, 2002a). Accordingly, in the Sixth Plan, financial assistance was allotted for the programme of Integrated Development of Small and Medium Towns (IDSMT) launched by the Central government to regenerate smaller urban centres. Seventh (1985–90) and Eighth (1990–95) Plans continued with the above contradictions but in a different manner. On the one hand, there was still an emphasis on the need for strengthening smaller and medium urban centres, while on the other, as suggested by the National Commission of Urbanisation in 1985, all urban local bodies, including the smaller ones, were planned to be given more power (sic), made more independent (as a result of withdrawal of state financial support) and manage their development projects by involving the private sector. The suggestions were approved formally in the 74th Constitutional Amendment in 1992. Innumerable smaller urban local bodies by this Act were made independent (sic) but financially weaker with reduced budgetary allocation and shrunken economic base. Their additional responsibility of raising funds from the capital market became a critical issue as it led to a compromise on pro-poor projects (Banerjee-Guha, 2009). Gradually, discourses in favour of private sector entry in the provision of urban services, cost subsidies, user charges and most importantly, efficiency of service provision (Banerjee-Guha, 2009) gained ground. The trend of concentration in large cities had already set in; in 1991, 300 urban agglomerations with a population of 1,00,000 and above went to account for more than 65 per cent of the total urban population of the country. With the opening up of the economy in 1991 to achieve a faster pace of capital accumulation, the above trend actually went to represent the official policy, making the contradiction between larger and smaller cities almost redundant in the official lexicon. Centralisation became the prime 'mantra' that got exemplified in the 'mega city (having population of 4–8 million) programme' of the Central government with an objective to develop infrastructure in large cities, while the earlier policies of strengthening smaller urban centres receded backstage (Chakraborty, 1996). Private sector investment in mega cities became an official priority and no anti-monopoly measures were taken (Bagchi, 1987) to curb the consequent inter-urban disparity or the strain on infrastructure of large cities that the above process led to. The focus on large cities that were identified as GEMs (generating economic momentum) fitted the bill of a larger neo-liberal world order in which economic changes had huge organisational and spatial implications for cities, characterised by a rescaling of their functions, activities and relations (Smith, 2002). Voices of criticism were many, expressing concern over the reduced role of state in urban development, allowance to market forces to go unchecked and using population size alone for selecting cities for development programmes. Arguments were also raised in favour of spatial redistribution of resources and benefits among different regions and urban centres of diverse size classes (Kundu, 1993; Banerjee-Guha, 2002a). But the process continued unabated.

In the pre-reform days, although the metropolitan regions in India were by far the most developed regions in terms of infrastructure, (e.g., power, roads, housing, telecommunications, health, education, etc.), there were other regions too that received state support. Post-1991, with the state largely moving away from location decisions accepting corporate/foreign investment as a major factor to boost economic growth, a renewed vigour was seen in revitalising the metropolitan cities and only a few selective regions. Chakravorty (2000) identifies some major changes in the locational pattern of investment from pre-reform to post-reform days that have relevance to our above argument. In the post-reform days, with the state becoming a weaker player and the source of capital turning to be primarily private, comprising 87 per cent of the total investment, he finds it is only the mega cities, districts close to them and a few coastal areas that received the maximum investment compared to the smaller urban centres and other interior areas of the country. A careful look at the pattern will indicate that post-reform urban planning, based more on private sector initiative, was no longer only city-centric, rather it extended to the peri-urban and beyond, bringing back primacy in the urban system in a more expansive manner, from the core urban district to the wider periphery that the core started appropriating (Banerjee-Guha, 2009; Kundu, 2011) gradually, in a phased manner.

Both the Tenth and Eleventh Plans have identified very low degree of urbanisation in the country in recent time with a decline of population in big cities. The Eleventh Plan has simultaneously predicted that with rapid economic growth in future, the pace of urbanisation would certainly push up, but it needs to occur in a more distributed manner. Many (Banerjee-Guha, 2010; Kundu, 2011) have associated the decline in population growth in mega cities with an indirect monitoring of immigration of the underclass, both urban and rural, into these cities. I have stated elsewhere (Banerjee-Guha, 2009) that in the past few years, there has been a drastic elitist shift in the discourse of urban planning and praxis in the country with the voice of the rich in large cities becoming particularly formidable, that has led to gradual appropriation of larger proportion of urban space and infrastructure for elitist consumption. The above trend of 'bourgeois urbanism' essentially reflects the process of neo-liberalisation of urban policy at macro level, rescaling of the 'urban' imagery and, as mentioned, redundancy of smaller cities and towns in the urban planning agenda. One needs to remember that in 2007, the High Power Expert Committee (HPEC) stated that India's financial services would not be able to derive significant IFS (International Financial Services) revenues, unless cities like Mumbai came up as IFCs (International Financial Centres), following the framework of GFCs (Global Financial Centres). The Committee's stated vision (HPEC, 2007) brought the logic of the government's focus on large cities out in the open.

HPEC, in its 2011 report on India's Urban Infrastructure and Services (HPEC, 2011), notes that towns with population less than 1,00,000, experienced a declining annual growth rate during 1991–2001: from 3.2 per cent, it came down to 2.3 per cent; that they lack a strong economic base and suffer from weak managerial and governance systems. Even though the Report expresses concern over the above trend and recommends intervention through public policy, it simultaneously reiterates that it is the 'market force that will by and large shape the future of Indian cities', for which significance of large metropolitan cities as investment hubs cannot be ignored. All its major intervention methods (Kundu, 2011) in the form of enhancing private-public partnership, generating larger tax revenues, mobilising funds through bonds and other innovative financial instruments go well with only the functioning system of larger cities and not smaller cities or towns. In the same manner, the Eleventh Plan document, while expressing concern over lopsided urban growth and suggesting a spatially balanced urban development, in policy prescription advocates for a growth (at a rate of 9–10%) oriented development path while putting emphasis on massive investment on infrastructure in wealthy and prosperous cities. Who does not know the mandate of the JNNURM (Jawaharlal Nehru National Urban Renewal Mission), the largest ever post-independent national urban policy initiated in 2005 focusing on large cities (Mahadevia, 2006), upscaling their infrastructure through private investment, changing their governance system, making them beautiful and slum-free, thereby legitimising a process of exclusionary urbanisation? Way back in 1970s, Samir Amin made observations on changes in the social formations of peripheral countries with the entry of foreign corporate sector in development and planning. He noted how a larger section of the society living in towns and villages would remain out of the orbit of the capitalist sector, how the poor in big cities would struggle for survival while a small section of elites enjoy the growing convergence of wealth, and finally how development *per se* would reflect an uneven pattern with almost a total exclusion of the poor from modern capitalist planning. One wonders how well Amin's analysis fits the contemporary urban development trend in India.

Alternative Theorisation and Associated Perspectives

Since mid-1990s, a large number of researchers started focusing on the diversity of metropolitan life from interdisciplinary perspectives. Discourses emerged in various disciplines of social science, including cultural studies, that sought to explore urban landscape as key spaces of representation and symbolisation (Westwood and Williams, 1996), identity politics (Keith and Pile, 1993) and collective memory (Boyer, 1994). In short, the multi-dimensional nature of the social and cultural life of cities (Appadurai, 1990) along with the potential of the local and regional resource base of the surrounding areas got emphasised. As Shields (1995) argued:

> We need to construct multi-dimensional analyses which, rather than imposing monological coherence and closure, allow parallel and conflicting representations to coexist in analysis. (Shields, 1995: 245)

Highlighting the 'extraordinary' diverse nature of city life and its economies, Amin (1994) and Thrift (1996) argued that reciprocity with regional economies and resource base and a supportive communication network can make wonder for small towns and cities to survive a volatile globalised system (Banerjee-Guha, 2002a). Subsequently came the argument in favour of 'ordinary' and 'creative' cities, a concept with which the smaller urban centres could identify themselves all the world over, amidst the growing uncertainty that was emerging in the globalised world about their identity and existence. Notwithstanding the significance of researches on large cities as economic nodes, the above argument earned credibility, not just as a survival metaphor for towns and smaller cities, but more as an alternative perspective to nurture them as nodes of regional and subsequently, of national economic importance.

> The important point is that the complex interweaving of place-based and wider relational webs and the ways in which they bring together the multiple space-times of the city, has tended to be ignored. (Amin and Graham, 1997: 418)

Smaller cities, conceived in the above manner, can even offer a framework of revival in the face of the danger of getting pushed out from the globalised framework of 'either compete or perish', by shaping up as representative centres of their respective regions, having a symbiotic relation with the local resource base and all other associative elements, an idea floated long back by Dickinson (1964) while conceiving cities and their regions in a reciprocal relational framework.

> The city is a human phenomenon ... its complex relations with its surroundings are as much cultural and administrative in nature as they are economic. The relations between the city and its surroundings can be ... determined through historical evaluation. (Dickinson, 1964: 8)

Building on the diverse critiques of modernist planning and global urban gaze, the above viewpoint has an underlying base of reflective forms of consumption and cultural production that has all the potentials of developing intricate linkages carved out with inputs from physical planning, but incorporating the region in the context. The approach is more normative, tied with active policy and planning debates (Amin and Graham, 1997). Montogomery (1995), on a similar line, developed his argument based on the diverse characteristics of these urban centres with mixed-use urban landscapes and a fully animated time-space interaction, enlivened with a rich array of economic, social and cultural activities that again could be an answer to their problems of decay, alienation and endangered economic base. The creative cities debate shifted the focus from large to smaller centres (Griffiths, 1995) and also deflected the stress of understanding cities only through a globalised framework for the purpose of reviving their growth possibilities. The strands of this new urban utopia shifted from the paradigmatic time-space sample of global cities (that bypasses the debate of their contradictory characteristics of first worlding and third worlding) as spaces of power and centrality to capture the changing relationship in inter-urban and rural-urban frameworks through organic interaction that may extend over large regions. The complex interlinkage between place-based relational webs in a regional construct became a central concern of these strands that needs to be taken up seriously by future urban researchers. The ensuing development dilemma of small and medium towns can be juxtaposed in this concept by which the 'urban' can be conceived as both a concentrated complex and a part of diverse regional relational webs, as well. The 'urban' thus becomes an embedded and heterogeneous range of time-space processes (Harvey, 1996) that cannot be examined independently, dissociated from the diverse spatio-temporalities of the region at large. Largely ignored by global city researchers, the above theorisation recognises the social complexity of urban economy and offers a more subtle perspective on urban multiplicity – as Harvey states, 'Multiple processes generate multiple real' (Harvey, 1996: 259), stressing the interconnections with the located milieu that may even find a place for the 'ordinary cities' in the complex time-space circuits of the globalised world. Zukin (1995) suggests that cities grown in this manner will have more propensities to accommodate and encourage a broader pool of economic possibilities in an urban area and make use of alternative forms of growth. According to Zukin, such cities will tend to be more just and less indifferent to the poorer inmigrants and will have a natural tendency to bring together the economically marginalised and unearth their hidden capacity, otherwise suppressed by exploitation. In short, the wealth of diversities and differences embedded in their organic locatedness will act as a source of their economic creativity. Refuting criticisms that the above idea underestimates the economic cost of regenerating smaller cities and, therefore, is wrong in economics, Amin and Graham (1997) stated that a sense of place and belonging generated through the above mechanism would tap the hidden potential of these cities and mitigate the economic risk of the process.

Ensuing Praxis

I will now discuss a few efforts made in a few places. There may be many more. To start with, let us look at the Third National Development Plan of Japan initiated in late 1970s that came out with an official objective to prevent expansion of overgrown cities and encourage growth of regional urban centres. With a very small usable land area, the country has always faced problems related to excessive concentration. The huge urban mass of the overgrown Tokyo-Osaka-Nagaya region, stretching over a continuous area of 600 kilometres (Murayama, 2000), is an outcome of this. The acute metropolitanisation has conversely affected the development of many interior areas of the country, leading to decline of economic activities in smaller towns, causing huge outmigration (Tsutsumi, 1996). It was the Third National Development Plan (1979–1987) document that for the first time put stress on development of local cities to serve as economic, social and cultural centres of their respective areas. The associated policy, known as Teiyu-Kan (Integrated Local Settlement Policy), was developed on the basis of local and regional resource potential of smaller urban centres that are located in the interior parts of the country. Despite a worldwide neo-liberal stress on large cities from 1980s onwards and overgrowth of cities like Tokyo or Osaka, the policy continued in subsequent plans too with official support. Amidst the contradiction between concentration and dispersal, the Japanese government strove to achieve a balanced urban development and establish a multi-nodal spatial economy (Ministry of Land, Government of Japan, 1998), working in close collaboration with voluntary and non-profit organisations. The overall urban development pattern of Japan, however, still reflects a strong trend of metropolitanisation.

In 2009, a new urban action (URBACT) network called 'Creative Clusters' launched a project known as 'Obidos Charter and Pact for Creativity' from Obidos in Portugal to connect small and medium cities in Europe with a broader network to make use of the creativity of their citizens for viable and sustainable urban development (URBACT, 2009). The project aimed at involving creative people in a new model of urban development with an understanding that settlement size should not be the main criterion for its success. On the other hand, accessibility was considered a major pre-requisite to help such creative clusters to diversify their economy in a way that would use primarily the local/regional resource base and in synchronisation, build economy-based cultural events to make the efforts economically viable, similar to what Amin and

Graham had suggested in 1997. Subsequently, Clayton and Moris (2010) came out with the idea that medium cities actually possess a competing quality of life offerings that could offer opportunities for firms and individuals to take advantage of benefits of co-location without associated high costs, that usually pose as incriminating factors in case of big cities. They identified a number of factors that are important for reviving medium cities. These are: (i) economic relationships with other cities, (ii) close functional interaction with the surrounding region with a purpose to regenerate the latter, (iii) investing in workforce skill, (iv) developing strategy in response to changes in the economy, and (v) specialised activities for utilising the enriched potential of the settlement and its region to the maximum.

All the above efforts, including Teiyu-Kan of Japan, considerably echo the alternative viewpoints that have been making rounds in the academic/intellectual circle in India in recent decades aiming at a more balanced and equitable urban development. Considering the status of urban development in different regions, one can see that there exists tremendous possibility of applying these ideas according to the need and potential of respective regions. For example, the entire northeastern region, large parts of southern, western and northern West Bengal, Northern Himalayas including Himachal Pradesh, Jammu and Kashmir, large tracts of Uttar Pradesh, Rajasthan, Haryana, Bihar, Jharkhand and Gujarat that are rich in resources of diverse nature can be brought under suitable development programmes having the alternative viewpoint. Specific industries and economic activities, using local resource base, can be located in small cities and towns in several areas that will highlight traditional industries or landscape-based industries/activities. Such endeavours can be pursued under local city and region development programmes based on a multi-centred concept of development that India can capture well due to an already well laid-out urban spatial structure. There is an urgent need to decentralise economic activities to smaller urban centres by not just relocating pollutant industries/activities of mega cities, but by developing more of those activities that find support from local/regional resource base for their growth and development. States having strong panchayati raj system ought to be selected first for implementing such decentralised measures.

It is not very difficult to pinpoint the malady of centralised planning. Similarly, it is difficult to ignore the greater potentiality of decentralised, multilayered planning as a superior institutional framework (Marjit, 1999), especially in a huge country like India. One competing argument favouring multi-layered planning is that the suggestions put forth by the locals having greater knowledge of the regional resource and ecological characteristics may get recognition. Moreover, a decentralised planning mechanism with region-specific perspectives having modestly designed small-scale long-term plans (as the methodology) has a greater possibility of creating harmonious partnerships among regional government institutions, local civic bodies and non-governmental organisations that may be able to prioritise questions of social justice and ecological modernisation (Harvey, 1996) in urban development and decide to keep out the big corporate sector from planning and development of smaller urban centres.

> Alternative anti-capitalist possibilities are to some degree already present, even though they are the subject of acute contestation and struggle ... The issue is not one, therefore, of gazing into some misty crystal ball or imposing some classic form of Utopian scheme in which a dead spatiality is made to rule over history and process. The problem is to ... advance a more socially just and politically emancipatory mix of spatio-temporal processes rather than acquiesce to those imposed by finance-capital ... Integration of the urbanisation question into the environmental-ecological question (of the region) is a sine qua non for the twenty-first century. (Harvey, 1996: 420, 429)

If properly implemented, this will go a long way to establish the concept of integrative urban planning in praxis and pave way towards creating a viable development alternative for innumerable small cities and towns in India and many other countries as well, not merely for their own survival, but more for achieving a balanced regional development in which the role of the 'urban' will be differently worked out to finally challenge the rigid one-dimensional perspective of the contemporary neo-liberal urban framework.

References

Abu-Lughod, J. (1995) 'Comparing Chicago, New York and Los Angeles: Testing Some World City Hypothesis'. In P. Knox and P. Taylor (eds). *World City in a World System.* New York: Cambridge University Press.

Amin, A. (1994) *Post-Fordism: A Reader.* Oxford: Blackwell.

Amin, A. and S. Graham (1997) 'The Ordinary City'. *Transactions of the Institute of British Geographers.* Vol. 22, pp. 411–29.

Amin, Samir (1977) *Imperialism and Unequal Development.* New York: Monthly Review Press.

Appadurai, A. (1990) 'Disjuncture and Difference in the Global Cultural Economy'. *Public Culture.* Vol. 2 (2), pp. 1–24.

Bagchi, A. (1987) 'Towards a Political Economy of Planning in India'. *Contribution to Political Economy.* No. 3, pp. 15–38.

Banerjee-Guha, S. (2000a) Metropolitan Dominance and Regional Disparity in India: Observations from Relevant Planning Measures of Japan, VRF Series Monograph. No. 358, Japan: Institute of Developing Economies.

———. (2002) 'Shifting Cities: Urban Restructuring in Mumbai'. *Economic and Political Weekly*. Vol. 37(2), pp. 121–28.

———. (2006) 'Post-Modernism, Post-Fordism and Flexibilised Metropolis: Dialectical Images of Mumbai'. In S. Raju et al. (eds). *Colonial and Post-Colonial Geographies of India*. New Delhi: Sage, pp. 205–22.

———. (2009) 'Neoliberalising the Urban: New Geographies of Power and Injustice in Indian Cities'. *Economic and Political Weekly*. Vol. 44(22), pp. 95–107.

———. (2011) 'Choto Shohorer Ki Hobey? (What Will Happen to Small Cities?)'. *Anushtup*. Special Issue on West Bengal, pp. 14–19.

Bardhan, Pranab (1991) 'The Macro-economic Performance of India in a Comparative Political Economy Perspective'. In D. Banerjee (ed.). *Essays in Economic Analysis and Policy*. New Delhi: Oxford University Press, pp. 87–108.

Berner, E. and R.K. Korff (1995) 'Globalisation and Local Resistance: The Creation of Localities in Manila and Bangkok'. *International Journal of Urban and Regional Research*. Vol. 19(2), pp. 209–22.

Boyer, C. (1994) *The City of Collective Memory*. Cambridge, USA: MIT Press.

Brenner, N. and N. Theodore (2002) 'Cities and the Geography of Actually Existing Neoliberalism'. *Antipode*. Vol. 34(3), pp. 349–79.

Burgess, R. et al. (1997) *The Challenges of Sustainable Cities: Neoliberalism and Urban Strategies in Developing Countries*. London: Zed Books.

Castells, M. (1989) *The Informational City: Information Technology, Economic Restructuring and the Urban-Regional Process*. Oxford: Blackwell.

Chakraborty, S.C. (1996) 'Too Little, in the Wrong Place? Mega City Programme, Efficiency and Equity in Indian Urbanisation'. *Economic and Political Weekly*. Special Number, pp. 2568–72.

Chakravorty, S. (2000) 'How Does Structural Reform Affect Regional Development? Resolving Contradictory Theory with Evidence from India'. *Economic Geography*. Vol. 76(4), pp. 358–94.

Clayton, N. and K. Morris (2010) *Recession, Recovery and Medium-Sized Cities*. Norwich: Exeter City Council.

Cohen, R.B. (1981) 'The New International Division of Labour, Multinational Corporation and Urban Hierarchy'. In M. Dear and A.J. Scott (eds). *Urbanisation and Urban Planning in Capitalist Society*. London: Methuen Press.

Dickinson, R.E. (1964) *City and Region*. London: Routledge and Kegan Paul.

Friedman, J. (1986) 'The World City Hypothesis'. *Development and Change*. Vol. 17(1), pp. 69–84.

Friedman, J. (1995) 'Where We Stand: A Decade of World City Research'. In P.L. Knox and P.J. Taylor (eds). *World Cities in a World System*. Cambridge: Cambridge University Press, pp. 21–47.

Goldman, M. (2005) *Imperial Nature: The World Bank and Struggle for Social Justice in the Age of Globalisation*. New Haven: Yale University Press.

Griffin, K. and A. Khan (1992) *Globalisation and Developing Countries*. Geneva: UNRISD.

Griffiths, R. (1995) 'Cultural Strategies and New Modes of Urban Intervention'. *Cities*. Vol. 12(4), pp. 253–65.

Harris, N. (ed.) (1992) *Cities in the 1990s: The Challenge for Developing Countries*. London: UCL Press.

Harvey, D. (1973) *Social Justice and the City*. Baltimore: Johns Hopkins University Press.

———. (1985) *The Urbanisation of Capital*. Oxford: Basil Blackwell.

———. (1991) *The Condition of Post Modernity*. Oxford: Blackwell.

———. (1996) *Justice, Nature and the Geography of Differences*. Oxford: Blackwell.

High Power Expert Committee (HPEC) (2007) *Making Mumbai an International Financial Centre*. New Delhi: Sage Publications for Ministry of Finance, Government of India.

———. (2011) *Report on Indian Urban Infrastructure and Services*. New Delhi: National Institute of Urban Affairs.

Keith, M. and S. Pile (1993) *Place and the Politics of Identity*. London: Routledge.

King, A.D. (1990) *Global Cities: Post-Imperialism and Internationalisation of Capital*. London: Methuen.

Knox, P. (1995) 'World Cities in a World System'. In P. Knox and P.J. Taylor (eds). *World Cities in a World System*. London: Routledge.

Kundu, A. (1986) 'Migration, Urbanisation and Inter-regional Inequality'. *Economic and Political Weekly*. Vol. 21(46), pp. 2005–08.

———. (1989) 'National Commission on Urbanisation: Issues and Non-Issues'. *Economic and Political Weekly*. Vol. 24(2), pp. 1185–88.

———. (1993) *In the Name of the Urban Poor: Access to Basic Amenities*. New Delhi: Sage Publications.

———. (2011) 'Politics and Economics of Urban Growth'. *Economic and Political Weekly*. Vol. 46(20), pp. 10–12.

Kundu, A. and S. Gupta (1996) 'Migration, Urbanisation and Regional Inequality'. *Economic and Political Weekly*. Vol. 31(47), pp. 3391–98.

Machimura, T. (1992) 'Urban Restructuring Process in Tokyo in 1980s'. *International Journal of Urban and Regional Research*. Vol. 16(1), pp. 114–28.

Mahadevia, D. (2006) 'JNURM and the Poor in Globalising Mega Cities'. *Economic and Political Weekly*. Vol. 41(31), pp. 2299–3403.

Marjit, S. (1999) 'Decentralised Financing, Governance and Public-Private Co-operation'. *Economic and Political Weekly*. Vol. 34(21), pp. 1197–201.

Ministry of Land, Government of Japan (1998) The Fifth Comprehensive National Development Plan Document. Tokyo.

Montogomery, J. (1995) 'Urban Vitality and the Culture of Cities'. *Planning Practices and Research*. Vol. 10(2), pp. 101–9.

Murayama, Y. (2000) *Japanese Urban System*. Amsterdam: Kluwer Academic Publishers.

Pickvance, C. (1986) 'Comparative Urban Analysis and Assumptions About Causality'. *International Journal of Urban and Regional Research*. Vol. 10(2), pp. 162–84.

Planning Commission of India (1983) *Task Force on Housing and Urban Development*. New Delhi: Government of India.

Robinson, J. (2002) 'Global and World Cities: A View from off the Map'. *International Journal of Urban and Regional Research*. Vol. 26(3), pp. 531–54.

———. (2011) 'Cities in a World of Cities: The Comparative Gesture'. *International Journal of Urban and Regional Research*. Vol. 35(1), pp. 1–23.

Sassen, S. (1991) *The Global City*. Princeton: Princeton University Press.

———. (1994) *Cities in a World Economy*. New Delhi: Pine Forge Press.

Shaw, A. (1996) 'Urban Policy in Post-Independent India: An Appraisal'. *Economic and Political Weekly*. Vol. 31(4), pp. 224–28.

———. (1999) 'Emerging Patterns of Urban Growth in India'. *Economic and Political Weekly*. Vol. 34(14), pp. 969–78.

Shields, R. (1995) 'A Guide to Urban Representations and What to do About It?'. In A. King (ed.). *Representing the City: Ethnicity, Capital and Culture in the 21st Century Metropolis*. London: Macmillan, pp. 227–52.

Smith, N. (1996) *The New Urban Frontier: Gentrification and the Revanchist City*. New York: Routledge.

Taylor, P. (2000) 'World Cities and Territorial States Under Condition of Contemporary Globalisation'. *Political Geography*. Vol. 19(1), pp. 5–32.

Thrift, N. (1996) 'New Urban Eras and Old Technological Fears: Reconfiguring the Goodwill of Electronic Things'. *Urban Studies*. Vol. 38(8), pp. 1463–93.

Tsutsumi, K. (1986) 'Depopulated Regions in Japan: A Model on Social Change in Peripheral Regions'. In K. Kobayashi and Y. Kita (eds). *Exploring Sustainability*. Japan: Regional Planning Research Group, pp. 251–59.

URBACT (2009) *Small and Medium Sized Cities Enter the Stage of the Creative Economy*. Report of URBACT. Obidos. Portugal.

Westwood, S. and J. Williams (1996) *Imagining Cities: Scripts, Signs and Memories*. London: Routledge.

Zukin, S. (1995) *The Culture of Cities*. Oxford: Blackwell.

2

Emerging Perspectives on Small Cities and Towns

This paper examines the policy towards small towns and cities in the pre-reform or nationalist period comparing and contrasting it with what has happened post-1991. Policy making has to be understood as an outcome of domestic concerns and politics as well as broad developments at the global level. The 1970s and 1980s were marked by the official view that small cities and towns could play an important developmental role. The National Commission on Urbanisation (1988) recommended upgradation of a list of fast-growing towns as potential generators of economic momentum for their surrounding regions. But there was a lack of effective follow-up to the recommendations. In the post-liberalisation period, official interest in these settlements has reduced even further, triggering a prevailing viewpoint of these being disadvantaged areas because of government neglect. This is in contrast to private sector views of small cities and towns serving as intermediate and end-points of a global supply chain. They are important as links to a global supply chain of goods and lately, even services. Thus, for the private sector, there is increasing interest in smaller urban settlements as markets for goods and also as pools of cheaper labour for service industries.

For balanced and sustainable urban growth able to absorb a near doubling of the urban population by 2030, it is necessary, however, to have a broader view of these small towns and see them as generators of both economic and social momentum for the surrounding regions. With a significant agricultural base, less pollution, and more green spaces, many such towns are still pleasanter places to live as compared to large cities. But even these advantages are fast disappearing without planned development and upgradation of basic infrastructure. The present paper is organised as follows: In the next section the role of small cities and towns during the nationalist period, 1951–1991, is discussed, which is followed by policy developments in the post-liberalisation period. The next section looks at these developments from the point of view of inclusiveness and the emerging pattern of urbanisation in the country, followed by two contrasting perspectives towards small urban settlements, and finally, some suggestions are made on how to bring these left-out urban areas to the forefront of policy.

At the start, it is necessary to make a distinction between 'small cities' and 'small towns' for not only do they differ in terms of population size, but also in terms of growth dynamics and growth potential. By small cities, this paper refers to settlements less than 500,000 and up to 100,000 in size. Small towns would refer to all urban places below 100,000. The prospects for growth and development are strong for small cities with marketing firms and private corporations regarding them as the new drivers of the urban economy. On the other hand, the situation and future of smaller urban places is less certain.

It is well known that with population accretion occurring at the top of the urban system, existing large cities have grown larger and larger while smaller urban places of less than 1,00,000 have kept losing population. Urban settlements of less than 1,00,000 (one lakh) accounted for 55.37 per cent of the total urban population in 1951. This has fallen to 31.38 per cent in 2001. The declining trend has been particularly striking at the bottom-end of the system where towns with a population of 20,000 and less, which had accounted for 29.69 per cent of total urban population in 1951, contained only 9.36 per cent of the total urban population in 2001. Smaller cities, on the other hand, have done better in the last 60 years. In 1951, cities with a population of 100,000 to one million accounted for 25.57 per cent of the total urban population. In 2001, their share had increased to 30.78 per cent (Bhagat and Mohanty, 2009). Data is not separately available for the size class 100,000 to 500,000 but most of the cities in this range have been able to graduate upwards in size over the last 50 years.

The provisional results of the 2011 Census indicate a big increase in the number of towns in the country, from 5,161 in 2001 to 7,935 in 2011. With a net addition of 2,774 towns, this is an increase of 53.7 per cent during the last decade. Of these, 2,552 are new towns or Census towns. These non-statutory towns now account for 49 per cent of all urban places in the country, up from 36 per cent in 2001. This upsurge in new towns is a positive development, indicating a 'bottom-up' dynamic that has been weak or missing from the urbanisation process of prior decades. But whether this increase in new towns is largely the result of the reclassi-fication of villages to towns or whether it is more an outcome of the merger of adjoining villages to a pre-existing larger urban centre is not known as yet.

What is known is that over the last two decades, small cities and towns are beginning to show changes in their economic and social aspects. Aggregate data on these aspects is now available through the NSS. Using NSS unit level data, several economists have provided us with a rare glimpse into some aspects of differences in this regard between large, medium and small towns in India for the period during the 1990s. Himanshu (2006) and Kundu and Sarangi (2005) used the following size class classification: large cities/towns for settlements with a population of one million and above, medium cities/towns for settlements with a population of 50,000 and one million, and small towns with a population less than 50,000. Table 1 shows the head count ratio of poverty by size class of towns.

Table 1

Head count ratio of poverty by size class of urban areas

	HCR 87–88	HCR 93–94	HCR 99–00	Change 87–88 to 93–94	Change 93–94 to 99–00
Rural areas	35.5	31.2	28.7	–4.3	–2.6
Small towns	43.6	38.5	35.3	–5.1	–3.2
Medium towns	55.6	26.8	24.0	–6.7	–2.8
Large towns	22.6	17.4	16.5	–5.3	–0.8
Urban areas	35.0	28.5	25.4	–6.6	–3.1

Source: NSS various rounds, cited from Himanshu (2006).

To be noted is the higher levels of poverty in small towns compared to the medium and large towns. In fact, poverty in small towns is slightly higher than even rural areas. Secondly, poverty decline has been stronger for small and medium towns as compared to the large cities. Kundu and Sarangi's (2005) analysis of NSS data for the period 1993–2000 has also indicated the above trends.

Small and medium towns have experienced higher growth in consumption expenditure as shown in Table 2 although their level of both income and expenditure is considerably lower than that of large cities.

Table 2

Real monthly per capita consumption expenditure (1993–94 prices)

	1987–1988	1993–19994	1999–2000	Compound annual growth in (%) 87–88 to 93–94	Compound annual growth in (%) 93–94 to 99–00
Rural areas	287.4	286.6	298.9	–0.05	0.70
Small towns	365.0	383.5	423.3	0.83	1.66
Medium towns	424.1	452.9	505.0	1.10	1.83
Large towns	570	610.9	649.1	1.16	1.02
Urban areas	430.3	464.8	518.4	1.29	1.84

Source: NSS various rounds, cited from Himanshu (2006).

The compound annual growth rate in monthly per capita consumption expenditure is higher in small and medium towns in the latest period shown. It is these trends of both declining poverty and increasing purchasing power that have promoted the view that the smaller urban places are the emerging engines of growth. Smaller urban places also are less unequal as compared to large cities and this is shown in Table 3.

Table 3

Gini-coefficients of monthly per capita consumption expenditure

	1987–88	1993–94	1999–2000	Change 87–88 to 93–94	Change 93–94 to 99–00
Rural areas	27.3	25.8	26.3	–1.5	0.5
Small towns	30.0	29.3	32.2	–0.7	2.9
Medium towns	31.3	30.1	33.0	–1.2	2.9
Large towns	34.9	32.7	36.0	–2.2	3.3
Urban areas	32.7	31.9	34.6	–0.8	2.7

Source: NSS various rounds, cited from Himanshu (2006).

While all urban areas have experienced growing inequality, small and medium towns had lower levels of inequality and lower growth rates of inequality in the 1990s. This trend has raised the hope that smaller urban settlements can help in poverty reduction, in fact some view them as being critical for effective poverty reduction.

The above data would imply that smaller urban settlements should have an increasing role to play in a national-level strategy of urbanisation and economic development. Unfortunately, it is just the opposite, and has been so since the onset of economic liberalisation in 1991. As has been observed, in the last two decades, 'unfortunately, medium and small

towns have got least attention from planners and policy makers'
(Himanshu, 2006). This was not always the case. The next section
provides an overview of policies towards smaller urban settlements in the
early plan years.

Small Cities and Towns in the Nationalist Period, 1951–1991

During the nationalist period, the urbanisation process in India was
guided, implicitly or explicitly, by two major policy elements. The first
and more dominating one was a top-down approach which gave highest
priority to urban-based industrial development. From the Second Plan
period (1956–60) till the mid-1980s, industrial development through an
import substitution strategy led to huge investments in heavy industries
such as iron and steel, engineering, chemicals, machinery and machine
tools. The spatial focus of this strategy was the already developed areas
and the dominant discourse on urbanisation and urban policy following
from this way of conceptualising development was the large cities, particularly metropolitan cities. But, as it further worsened the existing pattern
of polarised development, inherited from 200 years of colonial rule,
starting from the late 1960, attempts were made to reverse the polaris-
ation through industrial decentralisation. The focus of the latter policy
was the smaller towns and cities. Thus, the nationalist period was
marked simultaneously by both a top-down approach as well as a
bottom-up more decentralised approach towards urban settlements
(Banerjee and Schenk, 1984).

Industrial concentration was very high at the start of this period
with 75 per cent of the nation's industries located in three major cities –
Bombay, Calcutta and Madras. Inter-state differences in per capita
income were also high, with Bihar having an average income that was 40
per cent below the national average while West Bengal was around 40 per
cent above the national average. From the Second Plan (1956–1961)
onwards, the emphasis on heavy industries began to receive priority in
Plan allocation, and during the period 1956 to 1966, industries gravitated
to metropolitan regions and large cities. Thus, industrial development
remained confined to already industrially developed areas. The Second
Plan also saw the limitations of large-scale and highly capital-intensive
industrial development in absorbing surplus labour and a small allocation
of 4 per cent of the Plan outlay was made to cottage and small industries,
which were seen as good sources to obtain supplies of consumer goods.

As the infrastructure and facilities for promoting the growth of
cottage and small industries was weak or non-existent, the government
hoped to enable the growth of a small-scale industrial sector through the
establishment of industrial estates, in small towns and cities. These

industrial estates would fulfil several objectives: namely, industrial decentralisation, encouraging industrial growth in backward regions and developing and strengthening the base of small towns and rural areas (Mathur, 1979). However, this aspect of India's development policy 'never became a centerpiece of economic development policies, unlike in China' (Banerjee and Schenk, 1984: 200) and investment allocations to cottage and small industries declined to 1.6 per cent in the Fourth Plan. This was partly due to their limited success.

By 1974, industrial estates had been established in 130 out of 800 towns of population ranging from 20,000 to 100,000. But only a small percentage of the output of these estates were consumer goods. Reviews of the estates in 1967 indicate that more than half the output (53%) consisted of engineering goods, 11.6 per cent of electrical engineering goods, 14.6 per cent of chemical goods and only around 20 per cent accounted for consumer goods. The early industrial estates established in small towns were not related to the local market or the rural sector. They were able to provide employment to only 83,000 persons by 1969. Over time, they became unsustainable and languished (Mishra et al., 1974). By the mid-1970s, the limitations of the early industrial estate policy had become apparent and there was a policy reversal that favoured the location of industrial estates near larger cities (Mathur, 1979).

The 1970s was also the period when there was a general concern among a large number of developing nations about the unbalanced nature of urban settlement systems in their countries. A United Nations Report of 1977 indicates that many less developed countries were strongly inclined to adopt appropriate policies and measures to achieve deceleration of their largest cities and to favour the growth and development of small and intermediate size cities. Both for reasons of efficiency and equity and the failure of trickle-down mechanisms from the largest urban centres to smaller places, small and intermediate cities were viewed as more desirable.

These global developments in policy influenced India's approach towards small and medium towns. They are reflected in the Fifth Plan (1974–1979), which recommended the 'promotion of development of smaller towns and new urban centres' along with three other major recommendations. The plan launched a Central government scheme called Integrated Urban Development Programme (IUDP) the guidelines of which were issued in December 1974. Unfortunately, this scheme 'did not have any strong non-metropolitan bias that was so much needed' (Ganguly, 1986: 9). The guidelines suggested inclusion of all metropolitan and million-plus cities, all towns with a population of three lakhs and above, all capital towns of the states irrespective of their size and other medium and small cities and areas of national importance. But, being so open ended, 'the IUDP scheme in effect had little to offer to the small and medium towns' (Ganguly, 1986: 10). By 1978–79, it covered 31 cities and towns in 11 states. But of these 17, or more than a half, were big cities. Quite clearly, the IUDP was inadequate to address the problems and issues of small and medium towns. At the end of 1978–79, the IUDP in its original form was discontinued.

In the meantime, at the international level, by the late 1970s, there was a shift towards clear and specific planning actions for small and medium towns, and the example of urban decentralisation policies in countries such as South Korea, Japan and China was to influence urban policy making in India (Shaw, 1995). On the basis of the strong recommendation of a Task Force which had submitted its report to the government in 1977, the Central government initiated a new scheme at the start of the Sixth Plan (1979–1984) solely for small and medium towns. This was the IDSMT (Integrated Development of Small and Medium Towns), launched in 1979–80. Its aim was the slowing down of growth rate of metropolitan cities and increasing the growth rate of smaller urban settlements. Programme components eligible for Central assistance on a matching basis included land acquisition and development for basic housing schemes including sites and services, traffic and transportation associated with shelter and employment, development of mandis/markets, provision of industrial estates, provision of other services and processing facilities and low-cost sanitation. Components for which funds were to be found from state plans included slum improvement/upgradation, urban renewal and small-scale employment generation activities; low-cost schemes for water supply, sewerage, drainage and sanitation; preventive medical facilities/health care; parks and playgrounds, and assistance in making modification in city master plans to permit mixed land use.

The vision behind the programme was that through the provision of civic and social infrastructure as well as economic components like markets, commercial centres and industrial estates, the selected towns would become effective growth and service centres for their rural hinterlands and absorb some of the migration to large cities. All towns with a population up to 100,000, as in 1971, were to be covered by the scheme. In the selection of towns, preference would be given to district headquarters towns, sub-divisional towns, mandi towns and other important growth centres. In the 6th Plan period, 235 towns with a population below one lakh were selected and they covered a population of 104.47 lakhs as of 1971, which increased to 146.36 lakhs in 1981 (Wishwkarma, 1986). The percentage share of the IDSMT towns' population to the total urban population was 9.57 per cent in 1971 and 10.23 per cent in 1984.

By the mid-1980s, several positive aspects of the scheme were noted. The upgradation of services and infrastructure of the towns had led to 'many secondary developments through backward and forward 'linkages', generation of more employment at the grassroots level, and development of their skills' (Wishwakarma, 1986: 44). But implementation hurdles were also noted. There were legal, administrative, technical and financial constraints. Moreover, development of the towns did not seem to have any impact on their hinterlands. Given that it was still too premature to expect such impacts and as the only project directed towards smaller urban settlements, the scheme was continued in the 7th Plan period during which 145 more towns were added and in Annual Plan of 1990–91, 77 more were added. The IDSMT remained an important programme through the 7th, 8th and 9th Plan periods but was finally discontinued in the middle of the 10th Plan in 2005, by which time, it had covered 1,854 towns and the population ceiling limit for town selection had been raised to 500,000.

In the 1980s, another important development in the area of urban policy was the setting up of the National Commission on Urbanisation by Rajiv Gandhi in 1985. The Commission submitted its seven-volume report in 1988 and made several observations on the role of smaller towns and cities in balancing growth and taking demographic pressure off the 'overloaded' larger cities and at the same time, stimulating the agricultural sector. It recommended a focus on intermediate size urban places, particularly those with the capacity to generate economic growth. Selecting 329 such towns on the basis of their demographic and economic potential as well as location and resources, these GEM (Generators of Economic Momentum) towns were suggested for up-gradation as they could play a critical role in spreading growth in their hinterlands (NCU, 1988, Vol. 2, Part 1: 55).

Small Cities and Towns, Post-1991

The post-reform period thus inherited two major policy directions with regard to small cities and towns. The first was the IDSMT, which was then in its 12th year of implementation. The second was the corpus of ideas and recommendations left by the National Commission of Urbanisation of 1988. The 1990s' thinking on urban issues was also influenced by what was happening globally with the shift from the state-directed development strategies of the past 40 years to market-driven and laissez faire strategies where the government takes a backseat. Such change in ideas involved a switch away from reliance on state to non-state actors and a focus on non-governmental organisations and civil society.

A major fallout of the shift in thinking was the re-emphasis on the large or metropolitan city as the focus of policy attention. This was seen throughout Asia, particularly as attempts at controlling the growth of large cities had failed and urban primacy continued unabated in many of the smaller countries despite government intervention to channel growth away from the largest cities (Rondenneli, 1991). In India, the Mega Cities Programme was launched and the problems of large cities highlighted. Large cities fitted the role of engines of growth and concentration of resources in them was justified as they were growing rapidly and contained a large percentage of the urban population, including the urban poor. Large cities were also most amenable to management by new public management tools and techniques that stressed the incorporation of the values and efficiencies of the private sector in publicly managed organisa-tions, such as those delivering basic urban services. Thus, while the focus of major reforms during 1991–2001 was on financial and industrial dereg-ulation, changes in thinking about the urban were already in place via the advocacy of new public management tools and techniques for the better management of cities.

Alongside the re-emphasis on the large city, the first decade after economic liberalisation policies initiated in 1990–91, was also important for the focus on decentralisation which occurred with the passage of the 73rd and 74th Constitution Amendment Acts in 1992 to give greater stability and power to rural and urban local bodies. These Acts sought to make the third tier of government more effective in self-administration but without adequate finances and financial control, this has been partial, so far, and only possible in the largest and better-off municipal corpora-tions. The municipal councils of small towns have not been much benefitted. In the 1990s, the government's role in the land market also began to show a gradual change with its declaration of wanting to act as an 'enabler and facilitator' rather than as a land developer (Shaw, 1996). To further this end, in 1999, the Central government scrapped the Urban Land (Ceiling and Regulation) Act of 1974 as a Central Act. The Act was seen as preventing transactions of large plots of land and as giving the government too much discretionary control over the land market in the large cities. As of now, most of the major states in the country have repealed the Act in their own legislative assemblies.

In these ways, the decade of the 1990s laid the ground work for the introduction of more thorough reforms which were launched thereafter. It was in the second decade after economic reforms were initiated, that a direct attempt was made to reform the urban sector through the launching of a specific programme. In 2001, a decade after economic reforms had started in India, the Central government launched its 'urban sector reforms' aimed at increasing the efficiency of urban local bodies. This took the form of an Urban Reform Incentive Fund in 2003 where state governments were offered incentives to undertake reforms. In December 2005, this idea was incorporated in the Central government's massive urban programme, called the Jawaharlal Nehru Urban Renewal Mission (JNNURM) by which ₹ 50,000 crores (₹ 5,00,000 million) was to be pumped into the urban system for the next seven years, 2005–6 to 2011–12, for all kinds of infrastructure creation and improvement of urban governance.

The programme, a flagship of the UPA (United Progressive Alliance), the present ruling coalition, was started in December 2005 and is of particular importance to metropolitan regions. JNNURM has two sub-components: urban infrastructure and governance, and basic services for the urban poor. The two sub-missions cover the 35 million plus-cities, all state capitals and a few other cities of national importance making a total of 65 cities for which the Centre is planning to spend ₹ 39,150 crores (₹ 3,91,500 million) by 2012 to upgrade slums and create new infrastructure.

Towns and cities that are not among the selected 65 are covered by two other schemes within the JNNURM programme: Urban Infrastructure Development Scheme for Small and Medium Towns (UIDSSMT) and Integrated Housing and Slum Development Programme (IHSDP). The financial allocation for them was ₹ 10, 850 crores (₹ 1,08, 500 million). Thus, after 2005, the IDSMT was discontinued and replaced by these two programmes, both under the umbrella of JNNURM.

With just 21.7 per cent of JNNURM funding and bifurcation into two smaller programmes, policy focus on smaller urban places is greatly reduced. The guidelines of both these programmes do not make a size distinction when it comes to eligibility for the schemes. They are applicable to 'all cities/towns as per 2001 Census excepting cities/towns covered under JNNURM'. While this gives greater flexibility to the states in town selection, chances are that the largest towns and cities, not covered by JNNURM, are likely to get selected. There is some economic justification for this, as reviews of IDSMT have shown that very small towns cannot emerge as growth centres even with upgradation and the optimal town size for this purpose being between 1 lakh and 3 lakhs.

However, a major drawback to the present programmes remains and it has to do with its narrow and limited focus. From the broad focus of the IDSMT, which covered civic and social infrastructure as well as economic components for strengthening the economic base, the UIDSSMT has a much narrower focus on civic schemes alone. It provides Central assistance for components such as urban renewal, water supply, sanitation, solid waste management, drainage, sewerage, storm water removal, roads, parking lots, heritage areas and the preservation of water bodies. In the Special Category States, there is an added component which is the prevention of soil erosion/landslides. The result is that many more towns can be covered via single agenda schemes under the given resources but the impact of these schemes on the towns' role as growth centres is likely to be negligible. The completion of the scheme would result in the achievement of a minimal level of basic municipal services. The IDSMT's more comprehensive programme of investment, which included marketing facilities, transport and preventive health facilities, has been scaled down. By the end of 31 March 2008, three years after programme launching, 649 projects in 524 towns had been started. Most are single-agenda projects to increase water supply. As of June 2010, this had increased to 763 projects in 640 towns at an approved cost of ₹ 12,920 crores (Sivaramakrishnan, 2011). The projects are for improving water supply, sewerage, roads and drainage.

As in the case of the other components of JNNURM, 'the pattern of better-off states taking the bulk of the funds is repeated in UIDSSMT' (Sivaramakrishnan, 2011: 28). Maharashtra with ₹ 2,700 crores and Andhra Pradesh with ₹ 2,460 crores lead in terms of approved costs though Tamil Nadu leads in terms of number of projects sanctioned. Table 4 shows the distribution among leading states by number of projects, number of towns covered and approved costs as of September 2010.

Table 4

State-wise distribution of number of projects under UIDSSMT as of September 2010

State	*Number of projects	*Number of towns covered	*Approved costs	**% Urban population 2011
Tamil Nadu	123	115	882.7	48.45
Maharashtra	94	86	2,699.9	45.23
Andhra Pradesh	84	69	2,460.0	33.49
Uttar Pradesh	64	46	1,169.6	22.28
Gujarat	52	52	438.1	42.58
Madhya Pradesh	47	33	762.6	27.63
Jammu & Kashmir	45	13	398.7	27.21
Karnataka	38	30	682.5	38.57
Rajasthan	37	35	609.9	24.89
Assam	30	28	207.8	14.08
West Bengal	26	25	385.7	31.89
Others	98			

*Source: www.jnnurm.nic.in as cited in Sivaramakrishnan (2011).
**Census of India 2011: Provisional Population Totals, Paper 2, Vol. 1 of 2011, www.censusindia.gov

What is to be noted is the presence of large states, both urbanised and less urbanised, in getting schemes approved under UIDSSMT. Small states, however, have not fared well and it has been pointed out that 'smaller states like Himachal Pradesh, Jharkhand, Chhattisgarh, Sikkim or Tripura have very few projects sanctioned, five or less in each case, despite the fact that the small and medium towns in these states badly needed help' (Sivaramakrishnan, 2011: 30). Also to be noted is the fact that apart from Jammu and Kashmir, looking at the number of projects and the number of towns covered, in most states, it works out to one new project per town with just a few towns getting more than one project. These features of the UIDSSMT have developmental implications which are discussed in the next section.

Small Towns and Cities and the Issue of Inclusive Development

From the above review of policy developments with regard to small towns and cities in the post-liberalisation period, it is clear that the Central government's latest approach has been scheme-oriented rather than an outcome of a well-thought-out policy. In this regard, it has actually taken a backward step by removing the holistic focus of the older programme, the IDSMT which aimed at upgradation of both the economic as well as the civic infrastructure of selected towns. By replacing it with the narrow scheme-focus of the UIDSSMT, more towns are being covered in a shorter time period but once a particular basic amenity such as water supply is improved, its long-term effects on the town's economic growth or on its role as a service centre for the surrounding region are uncertain. Its impact is likely to be very different in the better-off states as compared to the poorer and/or less urbanised states.

For small towns and cities located in the economically dynamic and more urban states, such improvements could be highly beneficial, increasing their attractiveness as alternate locations for new industries and services. In such states, 'high growth rates have led to a spiral of commercial and service sector activity' (11th Five-Year Plan, Vol. 1: 139), which in turn will enable them to attract migrants and workers from the surrounding regions. For small towns and cities located in economically stagnant regions, improving only the water supply or just the sewerage alone will not be as beneficial. The quality of life of local residents will improve but the location of the town in a backward state will mean that the impact of this in terms of the attraction of new industries or services will be limited. As noted in the 11th Five-Year Plan document (2007: 139): 'the backward areas continue to lack even basic amenities such as education, health, housing, rural roads, drinking water and electricity. Livelihood options are also limited as agriculture does not give adequate returns and industry is virtually absent, leading to limited trade and services.' Improving a single dimension of civic infrastructure will not go far enough towards improving such towns.

Table 5 shows the diverging nature of urban growth in this country where there a number of states that are more economically advanced and having higher than average levels of urbanisation. These states are also becoming urban faster. In contrast, there are a few other states that are economically stagnant and with lower levels of urbanisation. These states are showing a slower pace of urban change as shown below:

Table 5

Diverging pattern of urbanisation, 2011

More urban states			Less urban states		
State	% urban	% change 01–11	State	% urban	% change 01–11
Punjab	37.49	3.57	Rajasthan	24.89	1.5
Haryana	34.79	5.87	U.P.	22.28	1.5
W. Bengal	31.89	3.92	Bihar	11.30	0.84
Gujarat	42.58	5.22	Assam	14.08	1.18
Maharashtra	45.23	2.8	Jharkhand	24.05	1.81
Andhra P.	33.49	6.19	Odisha	16.68	1.69
Karnataka	38.57	4.58	Chhattisgarh	23.24	3.15
Goa	62.17	12.41	Madhya P.	27.63	1.17
Kerala	47.72	21.76	Himachal P.	10.04	0.24
Tamil Nadu	44.04	4.41	India	31.16	3.35

Source: Census of India, 2011. Provisional Totals, Paper 2, Volume 1.

A second problem with UIDSSMT is inherent in the way Central allocations are made in JNNURM in that larger states are favoured. Since the basis of allocation is the urban population of the city or of the state concerned and its proportion to total population, small states are disadvantaged. They quickly reach their ceiling allocations with but a few projects. This becomes a major drawback in the case of the UIDSSMT, which is supposed to focus on medium and small towns. Such towns are the only types of towns in the more remote and hilly states along the Himalayas and the North-east. As can be seen from Table 6, urban growth has been very high in several of the smaller states. In fact, the decadal urban growth rates of most of the small states have exceeded the national average in the period 2001–2011. As a result, their change in level of urbanisation from 2001 to 2011 has also been higher than average.

Table 6

Urban growth in India's small states, 2001–2011

States	% urban population	Change in % urban from 2001 to 2011
Uttarakhand	30.55	4.88
Sikkim	24.97	13.9
Arunachal Pradesh	22.67	1.92
Nagaland	28.97	11.74
Manipur	30.21	5.1
Mizoram	51.51	1.88
Tripura	26.18	9.12
Meghalaya	20.08	1.22
India	31.16	3.35

Source: Census of India, 2011, Provisional Population.

With a rapidly growing urban population, these states need more support to upgrade their towns and small cities than what has been forthcoming under UIDSSMT. Apart from Goa, which is a high per capita income state, all these states have few alternate avenues for revenue generation and their ability to deal with such increases is likely to be much more limited as compared to the larger and older urban centres in the country. In fact, 'the mechanical application of the state plan ceiling on the one hand and proportionate urban population formula on the other have resulted in significantly reduced allocations for these towns' (Sivaramakrishnan, 2011: 35) located in smaller states.

Other than Goa, all the smaller states, shown in Table 6, fall into the category of 'lagging region' as defined by lower than the national average of SDP per capita and lower than the average of growth in SDP per capita (Ghani, 2009). These characteristics are also prevalent in much of the eastern and northern regions of the country covering large states such as Bihar, Odisha, Jharkhand, Uttar Pradesh, Madhya Pradesh, Chhattisgarh and Rajasthan. These large states are also those that have lower levels of urbanisation and have experienced lower rates of urban growth during 2001–2011. Yet they have many towns, some of which have the potential to emerge as important urban centres for a larger region. Such settlements could play a catalytic role in the development of the lagging areas.

In the past, policy had targeted backward areas as sites of new industry but this did not produce the expected results. Focusing on selected urban centres in the backward areas of both large and small states could be a way out as it would lead to the creation of non-agricultural employment and services. We see this idea also contained in the NCU's suggestion of encouraging the development of 329 GEM (Generators of Growth Momentum) towns in the country. The GEMs were made up of both National Priority Cities (NPCs) and State Priority Cities (SPCs) and no town below 20,000 was considered. Interestingly, the on-going JNNURM's choice of 65 cities closely reflects the criteria suggested by the NCU in its listing of National Priority Cities. In the choice of State Priority Cities, however, there are some stark differences between the NCU and the JNNURM counterpart, which is the UIDSSMT.

The NCU had stressed the need to focus on certain criteria for the selection of State Priority Cities: (1) rapidly growing towns, that is, those growing above the average or national rate of urban growth in the preceding census period; (2) headquarters of all districts where the urban population was more than 30 per cent of the total population of the district; and (3) the headquarters of all districts with a rural population of more than 90 per cent. As high population growth could be a proxy for economic growth, population growth momentum (PGM) was taken to be a signal for economic growth momentum (EGM). Regarding the second criterion, more urbanised districts were likely to have better urban infra-structure, and so, extending and building on this made economic sense. Criterion (3)'s rationale was the need to discourage migration from rural areas to the big cities and to develop regional growth centres. In fact, the NCU stressed that 'one of the objectives of positive urbanisation policy should be to open up the rural hinterland and generate economic activity within the regional nexus so that the need for long-distance migration is minimized' (NCU, 1988, Vol. 2, Part 1: 73).

This latter focus is completely missing in the guidelines to the states regarding the selection of towns for UIDSSMT. Thus, in the choice of towns, as made by various states, the largest or most economically viable towns, not covered under JNNURM's UIG, have generally been selected. Such towns or small cities would clearly fulfill the first two criteria mentioned above. It is regarding the third or the selection of towns in rural districts that there have been very few instances. Yet this is an aspect that could promote inclusive development of both backward regions and backward states. Merely focusing on the largest towns in the more urbanised districts will not broaden the base of urban growth and the huge economic benefits that are coming from it, post-liberalisation.

Two Contrasting Perspectives

The large city focus of post-liberalisation urban policy, the withdrawal of a separate programme geared towards smaller urban settlements and smaller proportionate funding have led to a prevailing viewpoint that smaller urban settlements are officially neglected and disadvantaged areas. In fact, some academics have even referred to them as representing 'subaltern urbanisation' as contrasted with the elite or exclusionary urbanisation being witnessed in metropolitan cities (Kundu and Sarangi, 2005). These sobering perspectives of the nature and pattern of contemporary urbanisation in India, however, present a sharp contrast to the upbeat forecasts, in the popular media, of the smaller urban settlements both as markets and as suppliers of cheap human capital. Viewing them as intermediate and end-points of a global supply chain, small cities and towns have become very important to the private corporate sector seeking new outlets for goods and services, cheaper location sites, and lower wage bills (Rastogi, 2010). Stories in the popular media and the identification of leading sports personalities with small towns have strengthened the perception of an emerging 'shining India' from the dusty by-lanes of provincial towns.

In the last two decades, there has undoubtedly been some market deepening with FMDGs (fast moving durable goods) such as TVs, refrigerators and fans, and cars and two-wheeler ownership as well as mobile telephony extending deep into heartland India.[1] It indicates rising affordability among middle class households as well as more extravagant lifestyles of the elites and richer households.[2] The latter is seen in the case of Aurangabad town in Maharashtra, which prides itself as having the highest ownership per capita of BMWs in India. But such market inclusion of smaller settlements has happened without the solving of their basic infrastructure problems, without the availability of good quality higher education and medical facilities and in most cases, without proper roads and easy connectivity to surrounding areas. Thus, their capacity to emerge as growth centres serving the surrounding hinterland, both through the provision of higher order goods and services as well as a market for rural goods, is limited, and outward and long-distance migration from rural areas to large cities continues unabated.

Conclusion

This paper attempted a review of urban policy towards smaller towns and cities in the country since the First Five Year Plan was adopted in 1951 to the present. While the need to spread development to all parts of the country was acknowledged early, an actual policy to enable this dates back to the 1960s. Globally, the attention on small towns and intermediate-sized cities became stronger during the 1970s when several developing nations began to focus on their growth and development through concerted government policy. Likewise, in India, a major programme towards this was initiated by the Central government in 1979 as the IDSMT. Its aim was to improve both civic as well as economic infrastructure of the towns selected in order to make them effective growth and service centres for the surrounding hinterland, but it was not easy to implement and took a long time to complete. Post-liberalisation, the IDSMT was terminated in 2005–06 and revised as the UIDSSMT, a component of the larger programme, JNNURM.

This programme, a truncated version of the IDSMT, aims to upgrade civic infrastructure in any town or city not covered by the

JNNURM's major component the UIG. Its limited focus and ad hoc nature makes it a less important programme, both in terms of financial allocation and its impact on the country's emerging urban problems. One such problem is that of growing inequality in the urban areas of the country. In the last 20 years, the rate of urban growth has quickened in the more developed and urbanised states as compared to the less urbanised and poorer states. Moreover, within larger states, both more developed and less developed, there are sharp economic differences as well. At the same time, some of the smallest states are also urbanising very fast. The divergence in the pattern of urbanisation has become starker since 2001. Government policy must attempt to address this. A blanket policy for all the states will only heighten disparities and not serve the purpose of inclusiveness. A three-pronged approach is needed.

In the case of policy for small cities and towns, a three-pronged approach would entail the following: in the economically dynamic and more urban states, the existing UIDSSMT can be continued to be implemented as is; in the economically stagnant and less urban states, the scope of UIDSSMT could be increased to include economic infrastructure and social facilities to be upgraded in selected small towns and cities; in the smaller and fast urbanising states, allocations under UIDSSMT should be increased so that more towns and more projects can be covered.

The UIDSSMT, in these ways, can be modified to increase the inclusiveness of urban growth in the country by focusing on fast-growing towns and cities of intermediate size located in smaller states and in the backward regions. The first volume of the 11th Five-Year Plan (2007–2012) is titled 'Inclusive Growth' where there is a separate chapter on 'regional imbalances'. The Backward Regions Grant Fund as envisaged in the 11th Plan to provide special assistance to such areas does not have an urban focus. Adding the criterion of selecting dynamic urban places in rural districts for projects under UDISSMT could be another step in the right direction.

Notes

1. 'An increasingly affluent middle class is harder to ignore.' 10 July 2008. http://knowledge.wharton.upenn.edu/india/article.
2. 'Small town India, the new destination for designers.' 18 May 2011. http://www.fashionunited.in/news/fashion.

References

Banerjee, T. and S. Schenk (1984) 'Lower Order Cities and National Urbanisation Policies: China and India'. *Environment and Planning.* A16: 487–512.

Bhagat, R. and S. Mohanty (2009) 'Emerging Pattern of Urbanisation and the Contribution of Migration in Urban Growth in India'. *Asian Population Studies*. 5 (1): 5–20.

Census of India (2011) *Provisional Population Totals, Paper 2, Volume 1 of 2011: Rural-urban Distribution, India*. Series 1. Downloaded from: http//www.censusindia.gov.in

Ganguly, Rabin (1986) 'Role of Secondary Cities and the Strategy for their Integrated Development'. *Nagarlok*. 18 (4): 5–22.

Ghani, Ejaz. (ed.) (2010) *The Poor Half Billion in South Asia: What is Holding Back Lagging Regions?* New Delhi: Oxford University Press.

Government of India (2007) *Eleventh Five Year Plan 2007–2012. Vol. 1: Inclusive Growth*. New Delhi: Planning Commission.

Himanshu, H. (2006) *Urban Poverty in India by Size-class of Towns: Levels, Trends and Characteristics*. Delhi: Centre de Sciences Humaines. Downloaded from: http://www.csh-delhi.com/team/downloads/publiperso/urban_IGIDR_paper.pdf

Kundu, Amitabh and Niranjan Sarangi (2005) 'Issue of Urban Exclusion'. *Economic and Political Weekly*. 40 (33): 3642–46.

Mathur, O.P. (1979) 'The Problem of Regional Disparities: An Analysis of Indian Policies and Programmes'. In F.C. Lo and K. Saleh (eds). *Growth Pole Strategy and Regional Development Policy*. Oxford: Pergamon Press.

Mishra, R.P., K.V. Sundaram and V.L.S. Prakasa Rao (1974) *Regional Development Planning in India*. New Delhi: Vikas.

National Commission on Urbanisation (NCU) (1988) *Report of the National Commission on Urbanisation*. Vol. 2, Part 1. New Delhi: Government of India.

Rastogi, Aseem (2010) Rural and Small Towns: The Next Big Opportunity for Indian Retail? September 24. Downloaded from: http://trak.in/tags/business/ 2010/09/24/rural-india-retail-opportunity/

Rondeinelli, D.A. (1991) 'Asian Urban Development Policies in the 1990s: From Growth Control to Urban Diffusion'. *World Development*. 19: 791–803.

Shaw, A. (1996) 'Urban Policy in Post-independent India: An Appraisal'. *Economic and Political Weekly*. 31(4): 224–28.

Shaw, Annapurna (1995) 'Satellite Town Development in Asia: The Case of New Bombay, India'. *Urban Geography*. 16 (3): 254–71.

Sivaramakrishnan, K.C. (2011) *Re-visioning Indian Cities: The Urban Renewal Mission*. New Delhi: Sage Publications.

Wishwakarma, R.K. (1986) 'From IDSMT to UBS: Issues in Policy Formulation and Implementation'. *Nagarlok*. 18 (4): 42–49.

3

'Citiness' and 'Urbanity'
The Privilege of Mega Cities*

R.N. SHARMA

The experience about urbanisation and industrial growth in India, in the earlier decades since independence, brings out the fact of over-concentration of urban (and industrial) economy in a few leading urban agglomerations which have emerged as the extensions of their mega cities (see, e.g., Sharma and Shaban, 2006; Shaban, 2006; Sita and Bhagat, 2007; Kundu, 2009). In the process, the small cities and towns, with their number exceeding 4,000 in the country (Census of India, 2001), though for decades serving their hinterlands and regions under influence, are 'now' virtually getting written off or becoming 'off the map' (Robinson, 2002) both for the policy makers and the urban researchers in the country. The present paper, while delineating this process, advocates the need of pro-active planning for improving the quality of life and economic opportunities for the inhabitants of these cities and towns. The paper argues that the perspective about 'citiness' and 'urbanity' (Rondinelli, 1983; Ruby, 1999; Clencey, 2004; Bell and Jayne, 2009: 683–99), which remained the privilege of mega cities in the developed societies, is now becoming relevant in Indian context (as also in so-called developing countries) where a few leading cities in command and control of capitalist formations are being conceived as representing such 'urbanity' and 'citiness'.

Citiness and Urbanity: The Twin Concepts

Before proceeding further with the above objective of the present paper, it would be relevant to present a workable definition of the twin concepts, citiness and urbanity. In simple terms, 'citiness' refers to small community-oriented towns gradually taking shape as cities, with the expansion

---

*Originally, the present paper was published in *Bangladesh Sociological Studies* (Vol. 3, No. 2). The paper is reproduced here with due permission of its Editor.

of various socio-economic and cultural institutions, including relevant basic services and amenities. During the Middle Ages, the European towns took such forms in terms of spatial expansion, architectural grandeur and growing bases for trade and commerce. As stated by Body-Gendrot and Beauregard (in Beauregard and Body-Gendrot, eds., 1999: 7): 'These cities of the Middle Ages are still the backbones of the current urban fabric in Europe ... the most 'working class' neighbourhoods in Paris today were already working class a century ago.'

The term 'urbanity' has been interpreted in several ways by researchers with the changing forms of cities and their roles in transforming the Middle Ages cities into industrial centres, with the advent of 'reasoning' under European Enlightenment and subsequently industrial revolution. Urbanity then carried varied notions to urban researchers and philosophers during the 'modern' and 'post-modern' (the global) periods. A brief account of it is presented here.

To initiate with the classic writings on city, Max Weber (quoted in Eisenstadt and Shachar, eds., 1987: 58) 'emphasised the complexity, rich variety, and numerous constellations; all historically rooted, of the political, economic and social relations existing in cities. His analysis of different civilizations highlighted the specific historical constellations of forces shaping the political and social structure of society as a whole and its cities in particular'. Another great writer on the city, Henry Lefebvre (1996: 127), referring to the evolving city during the Enlightenment Period, observed: 'In the past, reason had its place of birth, its feat, its home in the city. In the face of rurality, and of peasant life gripped by nature and the sacrilized earth full of obscure powers, urbanity asserted itself as reasonable.' This 'urbanity' within the fold of reason was subsequently interpreted by Marxist and Weberian scholars as a product of 'modern' and 'post-modern' city, mainly in terms of expanding base of capitalism, spatial forms and various institutions emerging from relations of class and property. The newly emerging city as an arena of contesting interest groups, originating from class, race, ethnicity and recently environmental activism, is seen creating new forms of urbanity. Thus, R. Ruby (in Beauregard and Body-Gendrot, op. cit.: 241–48) considers the urbanity '... as the shape and social linkage of morals, daily life in the city, and social contact within the city's boundaries ... . Urbanity does not express itself only through its spatial and material aspects ... we consider the city as a place of sociability, as a system of relations between different spaces, as a simple network of uncontrolled fluxes, as an imposed way of life, and/or as a moment of liberation of human kind ...' Thus, for Ruby, citizenship is not only a right but also a collective action. For Jayaram (2010: 53), the citizens would like a more exclusive definition of the citizenship, restricting it by a rigidly defined 'nativity'.

'Urbanity' is also perceived through social justice, which requires that '... existing groups have equal access to material well-being, symbolic recognition, and decision-making power, and that future generations inherit an environment that has not seriously deteriorated. To put this in another way, social justice is based on material equality, social diversity, democracy, and environmental sustainability' (Fainstein in Beauregard and Body-Gendrot, op. cit.: 251).

Though the modern age brought rapid urbanisation in Western societies, with small urban communities transforming into cities and urban agglomerations, it has also increased spatial and economic inequality, ethnic segregation, social movements and contested role of state as an agent of reform (Fainstein, ibid.). For neo-Marxists (like Lefebvre and Harvey), the growing 'citiness' has also confronted large-scale transformation of city, mainly under the influence of the ever-expanding capital and new technologies. This is more evident in the global era where a few cities in the prosperous North are emerging as the centres of transnational finance and headquarters of multi-national corporations which command and control expansion of capital and production systems across the nations (Sassen, 2000; Harvey, 2008). In the process, core and periphery in the hierarchy of cities (and towns) are emerging not only within the North but also in 'developing societies'. So, small cities and towns are being left out to their dismal conditions – more so in developing societies. The foregoing discussion elaborates these new forms which are fragmenting people and their life situations not only within the cities but across various societies.

Facets of Urbanity in Global Era

Elaborating on the role of mega cities in Western societies in influencing the mindset of policy makers and urban researchers in the field, Bell and Jayne (2009: 684–85) observe:

> The failure of urbanists specifically to consider small cities is related to the way in which 'the city' is viewed. Small cities have been considered irrelevant – they are supposed not to be cities that tell a story about urbanity, but rather speak of a failure to be urban. Hence, they are of little interest to serious theorists and theories. Explaining the form, function and meaning of the city at different times – variously described as modern or post-modern, industrial or post-industrial, fordist or post-fordist – has been the key aim of urban writing for over a hundred years ... When the most high-profile of urbanists talk about new and transformed urbanity, they have invariably done this via what they consider to be the most high-profile cities.

Pushing forward their argument in favour of small cities and towns, by recognising their valuable role in sustaining livelihoods of their inhabitants and those under their regions of influence, Bell and Jayne (ibid.: 685) state: 'It is clear that such models of city-ness are delineated with reference to a limited number of measures relating to population size and the presence of particular types of economic activity that they are often used to generalize about, or measure the success or failure of, all cities.' The economic activity cited in the mega cities refers to 'centrality of governance, trade, financial services, insurance, scientific knowledge, mass media, consumption, culture, entertainment, and so on' (ibid.: 688).

Bell and Jayne are not the lone advocates of focusing on small cities and towns for their valuable contribution to the regions and countryside under their influence. There are other researchers in Western context who point out the prevailing bias among researchers in the field and policy makers favouring the large (mega) cities of the first world. Some of these researchers (see, for instance, Harris, 1978; T. LeGates, 1996) highlight the need of recognising such a trend emerging in the 'mass cities' of developing societies which over-concentrates economic activity (urban and industrial) – for right or wrong – and tends to replicate so-called citiness and urbanity of the first world. Rondinelli (1983: 381–82) also reminds about the prevailing view, more so among the economists, that 'in developing countries where capital is scarce, the highest rates of return from investment are achieved in the larger cities and the vast size to which some primate cities were growing in the developing world was not economically inefficient'. For Rondinelli (ibid.: 382), 'the arguments do not hold for a wide range of processing, commercial, service, and small-scale manufacturing activities. They can be efficiently located in secondary cities and small market towns'.

Then, there are other factors which bring out the darker side of these mega cities due to over-concentration of economic activities and therefore, population-sizes. Rondinelli states (ibid.: 382):

> The growth of primate cites and metropolitan areas has created serious economic and social problems, and most developing countries lack the resources to cope with them. The largest cities in Latin America are experiencing severe problems in housing, transportation, pollution, employment and service supply. High levels of unemployment among squatters and recent immigrants to metropolitan areas continue a poverty-stricken existence. (Moreover), in calculating the returns from investment in primate cities, macro-economists often overlooked or undervalued the social costs of massive urban agglomeration.

Robinson (2002: 535) aptly summarises the above situation in the following words: 'In both the broader and the more narrow economic approach to identifying world cities, a view of the world off cities emerges where millions of people and hundreds of cities are dropped off the map of much research in urban cities, to service one particular and very restricted view of significance or (ir)relevance of certain sections of the global economy.' Here, one can recall the often quoted view of Sassen (2000) about 'global cities' which are turning out as key agents of global economy. Her key point is that the spatially dispersed global economy requires locally-based and integrated organisation, and this, she suggests, takes place in the global cities (quoted in Robinson, op. cit.: 535).

The Indian Scenario

What relevance does the foregoing discussion in Western context, where the 'urbanity' and 'citiness' are seen through the mirror of globalisation and global cities, have for Indian cities (and towns)? The present paper makes a modest effort to seek an answer to it. In Indian situation, historically, a few cities which served colonial interests of trade and administration emerged as the growth engines or primate cities for their regions, leaving behind hundreds of medium cities and towns, which, though neglected, served as 'bazaar' towns for their regions and countryside. This process kept on reinforcing the concentration of business and industrial growth in a dozen million-plus cities. The rapid urbanisation in the last 20 years or so in the country coincides with the liberalisation of its economy in 1991, under the market-driven global agenda. In 2001, 35 million-plus cities in the country sheltered a staggering 107.88 million people, with an average of three million persons in each of these cities (Sharma and Shaban, 2006: 21). This phenomenal growth of 'mass cities' has resulted in over-concentration of economic activity on one hand, and vast inequalities within their populations, reflected through growing slum populations, on the other. According to an estimate, during 2003–04, the top eight million-plus cities of India accounted for 36.1 per cent of the total bank deposits in the country, 51.4 per cent of the formal bank credit and 33.3 per cent of the total equity (the FDI) (ibid.: 28). Such is the background of less than a dozen mega cities in command and control of capital and its direction of use, against the total number of 4,368 cities and towns in India (Census of India, 2001). Within Maharashtra state, such regional inequalities are revealing. Over one-third of the total urban population of Maharashtra is concentrated in the Mumbai region alone. Almost a half of the 'net share in domestic product' of the state comes from only the two agglomeration economies – Mumbai and Thane and Pune-Pimpri-Chinchwad (Sharma and Shaban, op. cit.: 27).

The statistical (census) data for the growth of various categories of towns in India, with its spread over a century, again, brings out the fact that over the decades the Class I cities (with population over 1,00,000) have been gaining rapidly in their population sizes, as compared to the small towns whose populations remain stagnant or even decline (Table 1). In fact, presently, the 35 million-plus cities account for 37.81 per cent of the total urban population in the country (Census of India, 2001).

Table 1

Number of towns and percentage of urban population by size-class

Census years	No. of towns by size-class						Percentage of urban population by size-class					
	I	II	III	IV	V	VI	I	II	III	IV	V	VI
1901	24	43	130	391	744	479	26.0	11.2	15.6	20.8	20.1	6.1
1911	23	40	135	364	707	485	27.4	10.5	16.4	19.7	19.3	6.5
1921	29	45	145	370	734	571	29.7	10.3	15.9	18.2	18.6	7.0
1931	35	56	183	434	800	509	31.2	11.6	16.8	18.0	17.1	5.2
1941	49	74	242	498	920	407	38.2	11.4	16.3	15.7	15.0	3.1
1951	76	91	327	608	1124	569	44.6	9.9	15.7	13.6	12.9	3.1
1961	102	129	437	719	711	172	51.4	11.2	16.9	12.7	6.8	0.7
1971	148	173	558	827	623	147	57.2	10.9	16.0	10.9	4.4	0.4
1981	218	270	743	1059	758	253	60.3	11.6	14.3	9.5	3.5	0.5
1991	300	345	947	1167	740	197	65.2	10.9	13.1	7.7	2.6	0.3
2001	393	401	1151	1344	888	191	68.6	9.67	12.2	6.8	2.3	0.2

Class I: Greater than 1,00,000 population
Class II: 50,000–1,00,000 population
Class III: 20,000–50,000 population
Class IV: 10,000–20,000 population
Class V: 5,000–10,000 population
Class VI: Less than 5,000 population

This over-concentration of urban (and industrial) economy in a few mega cities and their satellite towns (urban agglomerations) is getting reinforced under the global era. According to Sita and Bhagat (in Shaw, 2007: 59), 'the overwhelming functional dominance of these cities is out-of-all proportion to their numbers'. They further observe (ibid.: 63–68):

The fast growing metro of Faridabad has emerged adjacent to Delhi along with Meerut. Surat and Pune (near Mumbai) are also growing fast... Two clusters of metropolitan dominance are clearly emerging, centered around the cores of Mumbai and Delhi ... The growth in Delhi urban area is primarily due to the Census towns that have shown extremely high growth rates in 1991–2001. Ghaziabad, Loni, Noida, Faridabad, Gurgaon and Bahadurgarh also experienced higher growth than the Delhi UA.

The growth rate in Chennai UA is primarily due to numerous satellite towns, namely Abattur, Avadi, Tiruvottiyur, etc.

The satellite towns of Mumbai UA, that is, Thane, Kalyan-Dombivli, Ulhasnagar, Mira-Bhayandar and Navi Mumbai (all now municipal corporations) have growth rates (1991–2001) varying as 20.03, 47.42, 196.29 and 128.76 per cent; while the Greater Mumbai UA showed a growth rate of 29.94 per cent. Bangalore UA's constituted towns' growth is amazing, with the Dasarahalli, Bhatarayanapura, Mahadevaoura, and Yelahanka showing a growth rate (1991–2001) of 567.97, 902.17, 440.66 and 85.49 per cent, respectively.

Likewise, the constituent towns of Hyderabad UA show a growth rate for the above period, varying between 55 per cent and over 100 per cent.

In the 'Shining India' (under the market-driven economic growth), a strong advocacy is emerging among the planners and other growth-agents for market efficiency and cost-effectiveness by pushing the agenda of growth through 'viable' urban agglomeration economies. As aptly observed by Kundu and Bhatia (1995):

> There is an advocacy for market efficiency and re-structuring of the existing institutional system for urban economic development ... . Implicitly this supports the process of emergence of a few global cities linked with the national and international markets, often at the cost of small and medium towns. Also, it amounts to outright dismissal of the strength of local level institutions in the smaller towns .... Indeed many of these towns have played a healthy role in the development of their regional economy. Unfortunately, the growth potentials of these towns are being ignored or underplayed in the present perspective of global-isation ... . A strong lobby is emerging, particularly in large cities; pleading for vigorous implementation of management solutions ... . This pro-liberalisation perspective would enable the larger cities to corner much of the advantage from the system.

As stated above by Kundu and Bhatia, there is a governmental view – more prevailing among the present policy makers (of the 'Shining India') and a few economists – that considers urban agglomerations as inevitable, given their favourable cost-effect and external economies. For instance, Mohan (2006: 63), a leading contributor to urban planning in the country, observed: 'Agglomeration economies are very important for reducing the costs of new firms as they enter the manufacturing world. There are also many economies of scale in the provision of urban infra-structure ... . Hence, agglomeration of economic activities and people, that is urbanisation, should be seen as positive for overall development. Hence, it should be supported by policy actions ...' For him, 'the problems of different sized towns have to be dealt with according to their respective needs. Large cities have to be regarded as national cities. While each of them is a regional centre, each performs national functions as well. They should be seen as performing a useful as well as productive role for the region and the country as a whole' (ibid.: 72).

A similar view is expressed by Arup Mitra (in Shaw, 2007: 165): 'Concentration (of economic activities) not only strengthens forward and backward linkages but also reduces the cost of operation by developing complementary services. The effective price of infrastructure services like power, water supply, roads, etc., gets reduced if there is concentration of users of these services. In all, interdependence of industries in terms of input-output linkages, ancillarisation and availability of infrastructure contribute to the growth of agglomeration economies.'

A somewhat more favourable approach for a decentralised industrial/urban growth was long back advocated by economists Lefeber and Datta-Chaudhuri (1971: 168–69). By recalling John Lewis' foreseen dangers of excessive population concentration and industrial agglomeration in the four largest cities of India on the not unreasonable assumption that 'the incremental social over-heads' requirements of the large urban concentrations will prove to be relatively greater than those of smaller complexes', Lefeber and Datta-Chaudhuri considered it 'not very impossible to place large industries in towns with population of one to two lakhs, as has already been demonstrated by Government of India by setting up several heavy industries in isolated and less developed regions ...' They also admitted that the 'efforts to promote private investment in non-industrial areas were not successful in spite of considerable subsidies and capital expenditure to provide the basic infrastructure' (ibid.: 170–71).

Indian Mega-Cities Replicating 'Citiness' and 'Urbanity' of Global North?

Given the logic and direction of urban/industrial growth in a few 'mass cities' of India, under the agenda of market-driven economy linked to transnational business and trade, the issue emerges: what should be the relevance of concepts of 'citiness' and 'urbanity' in Indian context? And a corollary of the above: what status then over 4,000 small cities and towns must carry in terms of their right to 'urbanity' and therefore a decent quality of life? The following sections of this paper highlight the above issues.

Given the hegemony of a few mega cities of the Global North on command and control of finance and trade, and therefore, their centrality in representing the citiness and urbanity, there has emerged a favourable perspective among the theorists from developed societies about their playing the role of 'world class' cities. The issue then emerges about the status of 'mass cities' from several 'developing' societies in terms of their representing such urbanity and citiness – if not at the global level – in the context of their own societies. Here, the observations of Robinson (op. cit.: 534–35) are relevant:

> In World Systems Theory more generally, countries across the world are seen to occupy a place within the hierarchy of the world economy, and possibly make their way up through the categories (core, periphery, semi-periphery) embedded in the world economy approach ... The country categorisations of core, periphery and semi-periphery in world-systems theory have therefore been transferred to the analysis of

cities, and overlain, albeit with a slightly different geography, on an extant but outdated vocabulary of categorisations (such as first/third world) within the field of urban studies … . This 'league table' approach has shaped the ways in which cities around the world have been represented – or not represented at all – within the world cities literature.

The 'non-assigning' status of 'world cities' to the 'mass cities' of Third World, perhaps, is due to their lack of proper infrastructure, over-crowding with a large proportion of population living in slums in dehumanising conditions, lack of 'civility', poor institutional set-up for promoting (private) business, and limited role of finance and trade across the nations. It is imperative to understand the status and image of mega cities in the Global South (more so in Indian context) vis-à-vis the vast number of small cities and towns existing for decades in these societies. Ironically, the step-motherly treatment by researchers or policy makers to small cities and towns in Western societies appears to be (more than) replicated in Indian society. Several researchers (e.g., Bose, 1973; D'Souza, 1985; Kosambi, 1994; Kundu and Bhatia, 1995; Rao et al., 1991; Patel and Deb, 2006; Bhowmik, 2009) have highlighted such a bias of urban researchers more focusing on large cities. Kundu and Bhatia (1995: 5), in this regard, observe: 'Indifference on the part of research community on issues relating to urban structure, thus helps in institutionalising existing inequality and accentuating the bias against small and medium towns in the developing world.'

Even researchers beyond India, like Preston, 1979; Simmons, 1979; Rondinelli, 1980 et al. (in Kosambi, 1994: 82–83), have advocated a more balanced and dispersed growth, given variety and backwardness of different regions in the country:

> Most Asian countries suffer from gross imbalances in spatial devel-
> opment, aggravated by overall population growth and rural-urban
> migration. The set of solutions suggested for rectifying the situation is to
> disperse urbanisation so that large cities on the one hand and rural
> communities on the other, are linked through village service centres
> market and small cities, and intermediate cities and regional centres, and
> to check rural to urban migration through multi-faced rural development.

The above valuable suggestions for a balanced urban and regional growth might be realistic, say, two decades back. Today, no such direction of growth is visible. Instead, a few mega cities as discussed earlier, supported by present growth paradigm and promoted by their respective states, are competing to become 'world class' for attracting foreign investment, mainly under capitalist formations. The centrality of mega cities in the Global North is being operationalised, in Indian context, in the form of their turning into the 'core' for influencing the regions under their influence, and in turn, functioning as the 'peripheries' to the Global North centres of business and finance. This is taking shape through urban renewal by investing billions of rupees in creating high-grade infrastructure, luxury housing, shopping malls, sky-scrappers, corporate offices, tourist centres, and so on. This is happening mainly through debt financing (Harvey, 2008). Metro rails, widened roads with fly-overs (for rapid transit systems), tapping water supply sources from even 100 kms away, and pushing the poor inhabitants away from central parts of these cities is visible all around (for details, see Sharma, 2010: 69–91). Speculation and profiteering in the real estate has emerged as the most visible outcome of such a mega-transformation which leaves no scope for a majority of average citizens to own even an ordinary house in extended suburbs of these cities. International standards (as claimed) in health, education and related services are emerging – again beyond the reach of even middle class inhabitants. Thus, mega-transformation of these 'mass' cities is resulting in creating wealth for the privileged (with an un-holy nexus between the builder mafia and corrupt bureaucrats and politicians), while a large section of ordinary citizens is being pushed into further deprivation and hardships.

This is the form of 'urbanity' and 'citiness' taking shape in a few rapidly growing cities, under the present 'Shining India' project. These cities are emerging as the hubs for business, more so the information technology, and high cadre (and costly) educational, health and related institutions. They are creating consumer culture for the privileged, while the millions of slum-dwellers in these cities struggle for their day-to-day survival. For the latter, the right to city for a decent living is as elusive as it is for the inhabitants of small cities and towns.

The future agenda of urban planners appears to further compound the concentration of population and economic activity in these growth engines. It is projected (and accordingly the planning process initiated) that in the next 10 to 15 years, the population of Greater Mumbai UA and the Delhi UA would reach around 25 million each. In Mumbai, in order to give boost to the real estate even beyond Navi Mumbai, another floating road (across the sea) of around 22 kms at the current prices of ₹ 9,000 crores is proposed which would connect the Nava Shiva (in Navi Mumbai) to Shewri (in Mumbai city) (Sharma, ibid.: 81). The Metro project in Mumbai, linking Varsova-Ghatkopar-Mankhurd, has already begun, with an estimated cost of ₹ 19,000 crores, though the transport experts in the city, like Sudhir Badani, estimate the final cost of the project to be four times higher than the estimated one by the Maharashtra government.

The scenario of future growth of Delhi UA is mind-boggling. The Delhi-planners (the DDA) have conceived five 'mega cities' within the national capital of India, for housing another 73 lakh people. According to media reports (*The Hindustan Times,* Mumbai Edition, January 8, 2008),

'These mega cities have been planned to accommodate 60 per cent of the 230 lakh population by 2021. The DDA Board has cleared the draft zonal plans, which provides for these mega cities.' The future growth of other economic hubs like Kolkata, Chennai, Bangalore, Hyderabad, Ahmedabad and Pune would not lag behind.

There are no research studies available to ascertain the implications of such over-growing urban agglomerations on the regions under their influence. The extent of resources (natural or otherwise) being appropriated from distant regions for sustaining the fast-growing consumer cultures of these mega cities, is not researched. For instance, Delhi UA now gets water from the Tehri dam, over 150 km away from the city. Mumbai UA is appropriating water from far areas at the cost of diversion of such water meant for irrigation and drinking in rural areas of the region. Moreover, this all is happening in a country where over a half of the population, mainly in rural areas, is still struggling for 'food security'. And lastly, what is the relevance of such a growth to over 4,000 cities and towns spread all across the country? The following and the last section of this paper looks at the fate of these cities and towns.

Relevance of 'Urbanity' and 'Citiness' to Small Cities and Towns

According to the Census of India (2001), among the counted 4,368 cities and towns in the country, the Class I cities with population of one lakh and above are only 393. In contrast, 401 towns are with a population range of 50,000 to 99,000; 1,151 with the population between 20,000 and 50,000; 1,344 towns within the range of 10,000 to 20,000 and 1,079 towns with the population 10,000 or below (Srivastava, 2009). There are no detailed analytical studies across categories of these cities and towns for understanding their economies, quality of life, spatial forms and institutional administration dealing with basic services and public utilities. A possible explanation for such a dearth of research in the area emerges from the observations of Rao, Bhat and Kadekar (1991: 1–2): 'There is a view prevalent in some circles of sociologists that the distinction between rural and urban sociology is not meaningful in the Indian context because about 80 per cent of the people live in villages ... and there is no dichotomy in India between the village and the traditional city as both are elements of the same civilization.' However, this view has undergone a sea-change in the last 20 years or so, not because a large population has become urban (till this date not more than 30 per cent Indian population is urban), but due to rapid transformation of a few mega cities in the present global era, which is influencing traditional India in a significant way. This change is emerging through rapid growth of consumer markets, growing neo-rich upper-middle class with fair consumer power, significant growth of knowledge workers in the IT sector, impact of new media (through television, electronic gadgets) raising aspirations of people all around and, above all, emerging forward and backward linkages of market-driven economic growth in these leading cities and their regions under influence (for 'political-economy of this transformation', see, for instance Banerjee-Guha, 2009). It is, therefore, not surprising that the traditional rural India which, for centuries, remained an egalitarian culture within Hindu civilisation, is now being written off as no more a dominant cultural entity. So much so, that a leading sociologist, Gupta (2005: 751–58), finds today's Indian villages more as a 'rural debris'. In his own words, 'The village in India, once considered with life 'unchanging' and 'idyllic' has in recent decades seen profound changes ... The town is not coming to the country, as much as the country is reaching out to the town, leaving behind a host of untidy rural debris ... The village is shrinking as a sociological reality, though it still exists as space.' What Gupta states about today's Indian villages is also fairly applicable to hundreds of those small cities and towns which are being written off by 'Shining India'.

A few leading researchers like A. Kundu, O.P. Mathur and K. Sivaramakrishnan have been writing on the need of research and policy interventions for these small cities and towns. The National Commission on Urbanisation set up by the Government of India in 1986 also tried to highlight the neglect and stagnation of these urban settlements which are spread all across the regions. A few studies of small settlements on the peripheries of large cities were conducted by researchers in the field, but these settlements have now become a part of their respective urban agglomerations.

Given such a poverty of research in the area, a more often quoted assessment by Kundu, Bagchi and Kundu (1999: 1893–1906) of basic services in these urban settlements is reproduced here for depicting their poor quality of life:

> According to the 1991 Census data, the percentage of households having all the three amenities (toilets, electricity and drinking water) in Class III, IV and V towns (with population between 5,000 and 50,000) is about 30 per cent, while that for Class I cities (more than 1,00,000 population), it is twice as large ... . More specifically, the state governments and para-statal institutions did not exhibit sensitivity in favour of small and medium towns.

A few other interventions, without any significant outcomes, can be recalled here. Since the Fifth Plan, the Government of India has been implementing a scheme, known as Integrated Development of Small and Medium Towns (IDSMT), but nothing significant has been achieved for making them viable to attract private investment (see Sharma and Shaban, op. cit.: 2006). The National Commission on Urbanisation (1986) identified 538 small cities and towns as 'generators of economic momentum' (GEM), but the recommendation of the Commission for developing them got lost in bureaucratic red tape. A recent evaluation about the 'Poverty Levels of Living and Employment Structure in the Small and Medium Size Towns' in states of Punjab, Gujarat and Andhra Pradesh (see, CSO Project of Institute for Human Development: 1–13) brings out more the darker status of these towns than their bright future. The study, which covered the period 1987–88 to 1990–00, observed (ibid.: 10):

> The analysis shows that in all regards, that is with respect to various dimensions of development, there is significant disparity across different size class of urban centres. In fact, level of development in urban centres is very much a function of the size of the urban centre. This is true for all the states in India, where the small and medium towns are at a greater disadvantage as compared to the large cities and particularly with regards to the metropolitan cities. And the gap between the metropolitan cities and the small towns is quite large with regards to all aspects of development.

Interestingly, the present 11th Five-Year Plan has suggested the need of a long-term National Urban Policy (Para 11.7), in order to prevent the haphazard growth of urban areas by strengthening the IDSMTs. The scheme appears to be subsumed in another scheme meant for the large cities (Bhowmik, 2010: 76). Government of India now appears to be committed for the mega-transformation of large cities. Though it is also true that given their poor quality of infrastructure and resource base, these cities needed large funds since decades for creating better living conditions and economic momentum. Government's new urban renewal scheme, called the Jawaharlal Nehru National Urban Renewal Mission (JNNURM) for funding infrastructure and related projects in over 60 large cities (the million-plus or nearing million-cities), at a huge cost of ₹ 150,000 crores (around $33 billion) in a period of 10 years is a case in point (see, the website of JNNURM). Maybe, it is assumed that once they create the momentum of growth, their impact would help the small cities and towns to grow in their regions.

Small Cities and Towns: 'Children of Lesser God'

One of the leading experts on urbanisation in India, Ashish Bose, often quotes his favourite phrase: 'God made the city in heaven, while the devil made the town.' In terms of quality of life, opportunities for growth and basic dignity of life, small cities and towns appear to have no future in India. Other than routine government jobs in institutional sets-up, like local self-governments, region-based administrative services, low-profile educational and health institutions, and routine trade and services, there are no attractive growth potentials for skilled or non-skilled manpower. As discussed earlier, even the basic amenities like water, transport and electricity are in a very poor condition or somehow being managed by para-statal bodies. Though the modern media like television, mobile phones and (basic) computer education have reached a majority of these settlements, the same have more raised aspirations (and therefore, the feelings of deprivation and uncertainty) among their youths who do not have adequate outlets for achieving a better life status. Thus, a few who excel in their educational and skill achievements, rush to large cities for better avenues.

The basic issue, therefore, is almost the absence of institutional infrastructures for retaining skilled manpower through attracting economic opportunities. Most pathetic instances are the irregular electric and water supply to these small cities and towns, which not only make the life of their inhabitants difficult and frustrating but also create low momentum for reverse migration from large cities to these settlements. One can see with own eyes, groups of youths from all across the classes more disorganised (and even criminalised) than living a purposeful and dignified life.

These small cities and towns of today's India are really 'children of lesser god', with hardly any rights and privileges for offering a dignified and meaningful life to their inhabitants. Their 'citiness' and 'urbanity' are a 'non-issue' before 'shining India', where the privileged and the neo-rich classes (minus the squalors) in a few mega cities are competing for a 'world class' city life. The 'right to city' (Harvey, 2008) is a highly divided reality in urban India.

References

Banerjee-Guha, S. (2009) 'Neo Liberalising the "Urban": New Geographies of Power and Injustice in Indian Cities'. *Economic and Political Weekly.* Vol. XLIV, No. 22, May 30.

Beauregard, R.A. and Sophie Body-Gendrot (eds) (1999) *The Urban Moment: Cosmopolitan Essays on the Late 20th Century City.* California: Sage Publications.

Bell, David and Mark Jayne (2009) 'Small Cities: Towards a Research Agenda'. *International Journal of Urban and Regional Research.* Vol. 33, No. 3, September.

Bhowmik, Sharit (2009) 'Urban Sociology'. In Yogesh Atal (ed.), *Sociology and Social Anthropology in India.* New Delhi: ICSSR.

———. (2010) 'Urban Poverty and the Eleventh Five Year Plan (EFYP)'. How Inclusive is the Eleventh Five Year Plan? People's Mid-term Appraisal. Delhi: Centre for Budget & Governance Accountability.

Bose, Ashish (1973) *Studies on India's Urbanisation, 1901–1971.* New Delhi: Tata-McGraw Hill.

Census of India (2001) *Primary Census Abstracts, 1991* and *2001*. New Delhi: Government of India.

Clencey, G. (2004) 'Local Memory and Worldly Narrative: The Remote City in America and Japan'. *Urban Studies*. Vol. 41, No. 12.

D'Souza, Victor S. (1985) 'Urban Studies'. In *Survey of Research in Sociology and Social Anthropology, 1969–79*. Vol. I, New Delhi: Satvahan, sponsored by ICSSR.

Eisenstadt, S.N. and A. Shachar (eds) (1987) *Society, Culture and Urbanisation*. California: Sage Publications.

Fainstein, Susan S. (1999) 'Can We Make the Cities We Want'. In R.A. Beauregard and Sophie Body-Gendrot (eds.), *The Urban Moment*. California: Sage Publications.

Gupta, Dipankar (2005) 'Whither Indian Village: Culture and Agriculture in "Rural" India'. *Economic and Political Weekly*. Vol. VXL, No. 8, February 9.

Harris, Barbara (1978) 'An Unfashionable View of Growth Centres'. In R.P. Misra et al. (eds), *Regional Planning and National Development*. New Delhi: Vikas Publishing House.

Harvey, David (2008) 'The Right to the City'. *New Left Review*. Vol. 53, September–October.

Institute for Human Development (undated) Poverty Levels of Living and Employment Structure in the Small and Medium Sized Towns. CSO Project, IHD, New Delhi. http://www.mospi.nic.in/research_studes_poverty_levels. htm (retrieved on 8.4.09).

Jayaram, N. (2010) 'Revisiting the City: The Relevance of Urban Sociology Today'. *Economic and Political Weekly*. Vol. XLV, No. 35, 28 August.

JNNURM (2005) Jawharlal Nehru National Urban Renewal Mission. Government of India. Website: www.jnnurm.ac.in

Kosambi, Meera (1994) *Urbanisation and Urban Development in India: Research in Sociology and Anthropology: Third Survey*. New Delhi: ICSSR.

Kundu, Amitabh and Sutinder Bhatia (1995) 'Industrial Growth in Small and Medium Towns and Their Vertical Integration: The Case of Gobindgarh, Punjab, India'. UNESCO/MOST Discussion Paper No. 57, http://www.unesco.org /most/disp57en.htm (retrieved on 08.03.2009).

Kundu, Amitabh, S. Bagchi and D. Kundu (1999) 'Regional Distribution of Infrastructure and Basic Amenities in Urban India: Issues Concerning Empowerment of Local Bodies'. *Economic and Political Weekly*. July 10: 1893–1906.

Lefeber, Louis and Mrinal Datta-Chaudhuri (1971) *Regional Development Experiences and Prospects in South and South-East Asia*. Paris: Mouton.

Lefebvre, Henry (1996) *Writings on Cities*. Translated and Edited by E. Kofman and E. Lebas. Oxford: Blackwell.

LeGates, Richard T. (1996) *The City Reader*. London: Routledge.

Mathur, O.P. (1984) *The Role of Small Cities in Regional Development*. Nagoya: UNCRD.

Mitra, Arup (2007) 'Industry-Urban Nexus: The Role of Urban Agglomeration Economies'. In A. Shaw (ed.), *Indian Cities in Transition*. New Delhi: Orient Longman.

Mohan, Rakesh (2006) 'Urbanisation in India: Patterns and Emerging Policy Issues'. In Sujata Patel and Kushal Deb (ed.), *Urban Studies*. New Delhi: Oxford University Press.

National Commission on Urbanisation (1987) *Interim Report*. New Delhi: Government of India.

Patel, Sujata and Kushal Deb (ed.) (2006) *Urban Studies*. New Delhi: Oxford University Press.

Rao, M.S.A., Chandrashekar Bhat and L.N. Kadekar (eds) (1991) *A Reader in Urban Sociology*. New Delhi: Orient Longman.

Robinson, Jennifer (2002) 'Global and World Cities: A View from Off the Map'. *International Journal of Urban and Regional Research*. Vol. 26, No. 3, September.

Rondinelli, Dennis A. (1983) 'Towns and Small Cities in Developing Countries'. *The Geographical Review*. Vol. 73, October.

Ruby, Christian (1999) 'Promised Scenes of Urbanity'. In Robert E. Beauregard and Sophie Body-Gendrot (eds), *The Urban Moment*. California: Sage Publications.

Sassen, Saskia (2000) *Cities in a World Economy* (2nd Ed.). Thousand Oaks: Pine Forge Press.

Shaban, A. (2006) 'Regional Structures, Growth and Convergence of Income in Maharashtra'. *Economic and Political Weekly*. Vol. XLI, No. 18, May 6.

Sharma, R.N. (2010) 'Mega Transformation of Mumbai: Deepening Enclave Urbanism'. *Sociological Bulletin*. Vol. 59, No. 1, January–April.

Sharma, R.N. and A. Shaban (2006) 'Metropolisation of Indian Economy: Lessons in Urban Development'. *The ICFAI Journal of Governance and Public Policy*. Vol. 1, No. 2, September.

Sita, K. and R.B. Bhagat (2007) 'Population Change and Economic Restructuring in Indian Metropolitan Cities: A Study of Mumbai'. In A. Shaw (ed.), *Indian Cities in Transition*. New Delhi: Orient Longman.

Sivaramakrishnan, K.C., Amitabh Kundu and B.N. Singh (2005) *Oxford Handbook of Urbanisation in India*. New Delhi: Oxford University Press.

Srivastava, Rahul (2009) Middle India: Towns vs. Cities. The Research Forum Goa. http://infochangeindia.org/200502066107/Urban-India/Backgrounder/MiddleIndia-Towns (retrieved on 08.03.2009).

4

Culture of Small-Town India

ROWENA ROBINSON

It is the economists rather than the sociologists or anthropologists who have turned our attention forcefully in recent times towards small-town India. Though sociologists and anthropologists have studied towns such as Agra, Lucknow, Banaras and Shimla and cities such as Delhi or Mumbai, they have principally worked within the dichotomous framework of the rural *versus* the urban. Thus, they have rarely tried to understand the differences between the cultural worldviews of the metropolis and the small town. For them, it is the differences (and the similarities) between the culture of the village and the culture of the city/town that is of interest.

In this paper, I have employed the available literature, including electronic media and newspaper reports, to try and develop a perspective on India's small-town culture. The reports of marketing firms and recent economic surveys have begun to give us indications of marked divergences between the preferences and aspirations of small-town dwellers and those who live in the metropolises of Delhi, Mumbai or Bangalore. It is in Aurangabad rather than in Mumbai that the costly cars like Mercedes Benz and the BMW brands are hiking up their sales; it is in Rohtak rather than in Delhi that the craze for expensive branded shoes is growing phenomenally.

What can we read from these signs of shifting consumption patterns? Is consumption enough to tell of significant cultural change? Is it just that there is now more money in small-town India? What about other indications of the altering dynamics of social life in the small town? What kinds of structural changes can we perceive happening there? Apart from consumption, we will have to turn our attention to altering income and class patterns, new genres of employment and opportunities for mobility, the shifting caste, family and gender dynamics and the changing expectations of small-town inhabitants with regard to governance.

The literature on India's middle classes is now growing. The paradoxical location of the middle classes – facing backwards and forwards; centred in the political discourses of a 'Shining India' but showing sharp strains of exclusion within; enabled by democracy and yet unwilling to extend that democratic opportunity to the working poor, the unemployed or the marginalised – has been pointed out. We have come to understand the 'gentrification' of urban spaces – cleaning and sanitising these for the lives and leisure activities of the middle classes and closing off access to them by the working class or the poor. It has been argued, on the other hand, that friendship and social networks formed through educational and occupational links have begun to occupy greater importance in the lives of the middle classes, replacing the tighter bonds of a shared caste location.

Not too many, however, draw attention to the fact that it is the small-town middle class population that is showing the greatest increase. To what extent can we extrapolate from findings that refer largely to the middle classes in the metropolises to define or comprehend the provincial or the small-town middle classes? There are questions for us to address here: do these remain regional middle classes as opposed to the global middle classes of, say, Mumbai or Delhi? On the other hand, do they form a link between the villages and the big cities? Do they play the role of intermediary transformers or connectors – extending the lifestyles of the city into the rural areas? Or are they set to create a society different from both the city and the village?

The Economics of Small Towns

Small towns are seeing new businesses emerge and a rapid globalisation of their economies. Telecommunications have spread and satellite and cable television are easily available. The mobile market is expanding rapidly and communication is aided by the spread of courier services, malls, cinema multiplexes and video libraries. There is an explosion of real estate and of finance companies. Some of these may run with black money when they are not registered, or take the form of chit funds. There is an emphasis on the acquisition of marketable skills and this is evidenced by the spread of English-learning classes, tuition centres and English-medium private schools. The auto sales industry has seen rapid growth in small towns.

Market professionals designate Indian cities as Tier I, II and III cities or sometimes as metros, key urban towns (KUT) and rest of urban India (ROUI). Their studies, popularised through the media, have riveted readers through their catchy titles such as 'The Dhoni effect: The rise of small-town India' (an Ernst and Young study of 2008) and 'The Bunty Syndrome', a study by advertising agency Euro RSCG that came out in 2007. These titles capture the cultural location of small towns, as well as their sudden entry into the marketing limelight. Babli and Bunty are popular names in small-India for girls and boys, respectively; there was even a popular 2005 Bollywood film of the same name. Its characters originated from small-town India. Dhoni is, of course, India's cricket hero, originating from Ranchi. The title signifies the coming of age of the Indian small town, just as Dhoni comes of age as India's suave, sure and immensely successful cricket captain.

The KUT category includes towns such as Pune, Chandigarh, Jaipur, Ahmedabad, Lucknow, Ludhiana, Cochin, Vijaywada, Vizag and Nagpur. The ROUI towns include Aurangabad, Allahabad, Gwalior, Bhubaneshwar, Moradabad, Rohtak, Faizabad, Hasan, Shimla and Shillong. It is recognised that these towns constitute huge and developing markets, not just for essentials but also for luxury goods and entertainment products. These towns are now better connected physically, there is greater media incursion and increased awareness and the levels of prosperity are growing. There are 51 districts in the country which have at least one town with a population greater than 5,00,000. If one puts them all together, there is a bigger market here than the four largest metros combined. Tier II towns such as Nagpur, Surat, Coimbatore or Jaipur are seeing an increase in the ratio of spending to earning.

The top metros fulfil only 30 per cent of the total consumption market; the key urban towns, the rest of urban India and rural India together constitute 70 per cent. The growth potential of the latter market is the greater. For instance, in the telecom sector, subscriber growth in the four metros is 58 per cent, but it is even higher in the rest of India at 93 per cent. Towns such as Chandigarh, Pune or Indore have three-quarters the affluence levels of Mumbai. Greater connectivity has increased the reach of small-town India. With real estate being substantially less expensive, marketers find it cost-effective to set up organised retail in smaller towns.

Small towns look attractive in terms of purchasing power, product consumption and time spent on the media. Media reach has increased significantly, giving easier access to credit and greater disposable incomes. Perceptions of small towns are different from those of the big city people. Surveys show that in the metros, Dhoni is seen as an 'icon' or a 'star', but in small-town India, he is associated with his status as 'captain' and as 'rich'. The middle classes are not shy to spend any longer and have greater income to indulge. Entertainment is increasingly becoming an important item of expenditure. Though there is much greater sensitivity to branding, it is not the case that the major brands are imported. Again, market surveys have shown that eight of the top ten brands in the country are of Indian origin.

The core group is young and is in Tier II or III towns. This alters the ways in which we need to think of them even from an economic perspective. It does not always hold that attitudes or preferences 'trickle-down' from the metropolis to the small town. Market surveys show that the consumer in the small town has high confidence in his abilities and is proud of being Indian. There is a constant need for adventure, yet the family – usually nucleated but not cut off from the extended family or wider circle of kin – remains the cornerstone of social life. Youngsters cite their parents as their role models.

There is a two-wheeler advertisement that catches the confidence of the small-town young man, who declares that the same road that leads from the small town to the big city also leads from the big city to the small town. New advertisements such as the ones by HDFC or Mastercard focus on 'giving' back to one's family or parents, while other advertisements highlight the Indian origin of the brand they are offering. Indeed, a new series of watches by Titan – the Titan Raga Crystal collection – sold not just in the metropolises, but right down to the small cities and towns.

Things seem to be going well for the small towns. The percentage growth in the number of malls is twice that of the metros. People in small towns want premium products and established brands. They spend much more on LCD televisions and on other lifestyle and wellness products. They are willing to spend much more on leisure products and options. IT is now going to the small cities. There are lower labour costs and real estate costs are also lower. There are reduced staff attrition rates. Several multi-specialty hospitals are opening or planning to open big centres in the smaller towns, where land is much cheaper and expansion possible. Better infrastructure, greater accessibility and the huge demand-supply gap in health care are creating these opportunities.

The online marketing company, eBay, has a two million strong community from 240 towns in India; some of these towns sell ethnic specialty or regional products to a global community: clothes, jewellery, Alphonso mangoes. In the lifestyle category, a piece of jewellery sells every six minutes, while a mobile handset sells every seven minutes. The social networking site Bigadda has 50 per cent of its users from non-metros and 60 per cent of its page views. Gameplexes are opening up in the small towns. People want something that others don't have, and aren't afraid to spend on it. Lifestyle spending on shoes, clothes, deodorants, perfumes, jewellery, luxury cars and the like is high. Internet use has increased in these towns from 5 per cent in 2000 to 36 per cent in 2009. Aurangabad is famous for purchasing 151 Mercedes Benz in a day. Its silica-free water is attracting beer manufacturers and its residents are enjoying new entertainment pursuits, including bowling and roller-coaster rides.

There are several factors pushing growth in small towns. The development of SEZs and the availability of real estate (both for purchase or rent) at competitive prices is a strong impetus. This has improved physical connectivity; the reach of the Internet and information technologies has also brought small towns closer to the rest of the world. Some of the Tier III cities are close to big metropolises such as Delhi, Mumbai or Bangalore. Towns such as Hyderabad, Ahmedabad, Surat and Baroda have seen phenomenal expansion and a big push on infrastructure, including roads, air connectivity and the like. The prices of land have soared and created new wealth. The BPO industry has provided new work opportunities, as have the new malls, multiplexes, gameplexes, and so on. Women are now working outside the home and have incomes to spend. Lifestyles can improve and choices broaden.

There are downsides as well. There are smaller labour pools in small towns; highly professional talent is not easily available. Where would the new hospitals find doctors or nurses? There are serious infrastructural limitations – uninterrupted electricity, clean water, sewage and sanitation services and the like. Many roads are still narrow; civic facilities are poor. Governance is also often poor; areas of small towns are still impoverished, ill-connected and badly serviced. There are increasing divides between the groups that have managed to ride the globalisation wave and those with fewer skills and much less resources who find themselves not much better or sometimes worse off.

Culture and Consumption: Money and Forms of Capital

It is Simmel (2004) who set out most elaborately the implications of an extended money economy for the culture of the city and its inhabitants. While Weber looked at money through the lens of increasing rationalisation, Marx focused on alienation and fetishism but principally in the economic sphere. It was Simmel who extended the analysis of money towards a cultural and symbolic exploration. He saw money as bringing into being a 'calculative' spirit; but also as demanding greater awareness and intellect on the part of the citizen of the industrialising capitalist city. Urban life overstimulates and causes individuals to become blasé or emotionally exhausted, so that they might seek more and more thrills and engage in riskier behaviour.

Money, the individual and modernity are intimately linked. Money becomes pure symbol, separated from its substance value. It frees the person, allowing movement of property and things, and does not involve the full person but only the product of labour exchanged on the market. Thus, the use of money overcomes physical and social distances. However, money becomes the measure of all things, including persons. Legal rights become monetary claims; emotional considerations are replaced by calculability and subjective values become objectified through money. The value of an object is determined not by its use but by the desire that people have to obtain it. The rich can reshape the purpose of money bringing out its malleability. They can spend, save or invest it; the poor have to spend on specific needs.

Veblen's (2005; *original* 1899) theory of conspicuous consumption is familiar to us – specifically his view that the leisure class, in particular, spends or wastes money on socially visible goods (as opposed to privately consumed goods) in order to display its higher status. He also points out that women of the leisure class are withdrawn from the labour force; the conspicuous leisure of a woman is proof of her husband's or father's status. Her lack of occupation as well as her jewellery and clothing act, in their very passivity, as strong indicators of the wealth required to support them. They also speak of the ease with which such wealth must have been acquired.

Bourdieu (1984) offers us a theory of distinction or taste, as well as a model of the overlapping but theoretically distinct forms of capital. For him, forms of capital can intersect and can even be converted, one into another. Economic capital is the command over economic resources; social capital consists of the resources based on group membership, relationships and networks of influence and support; cultural capital includes the forms of knowledge, education and other cultural advantages that a person has which gives him/her a higher position in society; and, symbolic capital consists of the resources that an individual might have on the basis of social prestige or recognition.

Bourdieu would distinguish between 'consumption' as in ownership, expenditure, ingestion or use from 'consumption' as deciphering or decoding the cultural meaning, thereby presupposing the mastery – practical or explicit – of a code. 'Taste', for Bourdieu, is traced to education and social origin; in fact, social origin must be responsible for what cannot be taught – the extra-curricular or avant-garde culture. Tastes can be socially accounted for – not just the taste for the flavours of food but even far more refined or elaborate tastes for particular forms of culture, modes of leisure and entertainment or works of art.

People of taste most likely have cultural capital in all its forms – embodied, objectified and institutionalised. Embodied capital includes those properties of the self which are consciously or passively acquired, such as linguistic skills or capital. Physical objects such as books, works of art, or scientific instruments are forms of objectified cultural capital. Both institutionalised capital and physical goods or objectified capital are likely to be more easily acquired with economic resources. Institution-alised capital includes academic credentials or qualifications, the marks of recognition of scholastic establishments.

Theorists of late capitalism bring out the hyper-reality of contem-porary life. The free-floating signifier rarely touches down on a particular signified, but shifts endlessly, distancing us emotionally and 'really' from 'experience' and even meaningfulness. Wars are watched on television and filmed by 'embedded' journalists to get the best shot for prime-time viewing. There are 'good guys' and 'bad guys' and little to distinguish the real war as it is watched from a film. One recalls Simmel's prescient suggestion that urbanites are blasé because they see too much at too rapid a pace. They cannot feel anything anymore. They get burned out. In such a world, there can never be any fulfilment or, indeed, meaning but only the ceaseless pursuit of 'desire'. Desire is infinite in a world where everything can be bought: from clothes to a new lifestyle to a new self and new identity. The boredom is kept at bay by the pursuit of adventure and risk; the more dangerous the activity, the more pleasurable it is. However, once a quest is mastered, the search is on for a new one, because repetition would bring ennui.

The Other Side of Small Towns

Till this point, we have discussed the 'newness' of small towns: the new forms of communication, new patterns of growth and new opportunities for work and occupational expansion. What is the other side of this new process of the spread of capitalism in the small town? Basile and Harriss-White (1999), tracing the social history of accumulation in small-town Arni in south India, argue that a corporatist socio-economic structure is emerging in the town, which produces an institutional framework for the self-governance of the economy and an ideological framework to minimise conflict between capital and labour, the individual and the society.

What this means, in effect, is that economy and society overlap in the corporatist regime, through organisational structuring. Caste provides the ideological backdrop for this corporatist project. Caste enables the overlap between economy and society and diffuses conflict. Accumulation of the local capitalist class is marked by petty crime (adulteration, cheating at all levels, including in pricing) and fraud (especially when it comes to taxation). The hegemony of the local capitalist class is that of forward dominant castes, though OBCs are making some inroads and patriarchy; labour remains largely from lower castes (Most Backward Classes and Scheduled Castes), as well as disorganised and deliberately casualised.

Evidence from Tamil Nadu's Tiruppur (Cawthorne, 1995) also suggests that clustering of the unregulated knitwear industry benefits the merchants and capitalists, while providing labour with only limited and small gains in wages. Labour, presumably largely lower-castes and consisting of men, women and children, continues to be paid low and to work in poor conditions. On the other hand, capital is concentrated, organised and thus enabled to increase its profits, principally through pressure on the labour rather than through technological advances for displacing or enhancing labour. Though the author does not elaborate on the caste divisions, it would not be wide off the mark to assume that Tiruppur is unlikely to show a very different order of stratification from Arni, also from the same state, Tamil Nadu.

Derné's research (1994) in Banaras is not projected as the findings from a small town (as opposed to metropolis or village), but can be presented here. He shows the continuing importance of joint family living among the merchants – upper middle class and upper caste. They closely monitor the behaviour of their female relatives, would not like them to work outside the home and, in fact, would not permit them to leave the home either unless with permission and accompanied. Men are free in their own behaviour and travel unrestrictedly whether for business or for recreation. However, they seek to restrict their wives' movements outside the home in the name of their honour and the honour of the whole family.

Even working women manage to get by only if they behave docilely at home and in front of their husbands. They need to establish as close a relationship as possible with their men, and may succeed in influencing them to set up a separate home from the parents. It is, however, through men that they act and they can do this only if they 'satisfy' their husbands and appear on the surface obedient and submissive. Men may want their wives to wear modern clothes such as jeans and T-shirts but women should dress to please their husbands and in accordance with their wishes. While the conjugal tie is becoming more important, it is not allowed to openly disturb the joint family norm and it, by no means, signifies the equality of the man and the woman in their relationship.

In terms of caste and familial relations, there are certainly changes in small towns, but substantial continuities in ideology persist. In particular, gender relations show the introduction of new expectations as well as the emphasis on traditional responsibilities for women and the stability of the household. Further, it becomes clear that those who have a little – some resources, some access to education – can benefit far more in the changing economy than those with very little or nothing at all. In other words, small town elites are enabled in consolidation of their advantages, and some opportunities open for others in terms of increasing labour/work options, and through government-sanctioned reservations in education and employment.

Culture of Small Town

It is hard to assert that small towns have not changed at all culturally. Even statistical evidence manifests certain structural alterations, and these must signal or be the effects of particular cultural shifts. Yet, it is possible for there to be great change, even while certain rigidities – of caste or of patriarchy – remain or, in fact, reassert themselves. What does this reassertion tell us sociologically? Let us attempt below to examine this and other related questions – which were raised at the start of this paper.

A new era of hedonistic consumption is sweeping the small-town India. Conspicuous consumption is central to that culture, wherein it is lifestyle or publically consumed goods that are the focus of spending –

houses, cars, 'good looks' (explained further below), membership of private clubs and gyms as well as celebrations such as weddings. It is not surprising that there has been a 20 to 25 per cent increase in wedding spending. Entertainment is another growing expenditure for small-town urbanites. The acquisition of wealth is accompanied by attempts to remove or keep women out of the workforce or enforce greater restrictions on their movement – these turn into signifiers of not just economic but also social and familial status and prestige.

Signs of change are visible particularly in the 'shopping mall' culture that has seized small-town India. Shopping malls are becoming a significant social space which youngsters, in particular, use to meet and exchange information, socialise with colleagues or celebrate important occasions. The space may or may not become a substitute for the domain of the domestic space. Sometimes, it is used to meet with friends or colleagues away from the family, but this is not always the case. Youngsters, who go for evening tuitions, can use it to meet their friends or significant others. It is a safe, comfortable space with eating/entertainment options, and offers privacy from the family. However, families also come together to the mall – more often to eat or watch a film, but perhaps even to shop.

The malls have increased phenomenally the degree to which youngsters have become aware and conscious of national and international brands of clothing and consumer items. It is the 'in thing' to window shop, update oneself on the latest brands or plan one's next purchase. The malls are a place of prestige, as well as security. People like to get themselves photographed at the mall, in front of their favourite brand showroom or icon. The McDonald's golden arch is particularly popular. Perhaps these images speak of aspirations for an international lifestyle: one that is increasingly 'in front' of us, so to speak, through film, television and the Internet, but also maybe just beyond our actual reach.

The malls have generated alternative modes of employment for young people (in sales, security and customer assistance). The management, when recruiting, often looks for 'good looks' as well as the ability to speak English. The mushrooming of English-speaking coaching classes in small-town India which promise fluency in 60 or 90 days is partly linked to this phenomenon.[1] Interestingly, the share of the wallet, as marketers put in, for personal grooming is as high as 9 per cent across urban India. Small-town India accounts for a considerable portion of this expenditure. It has been shown by market surveys that small-town women pay large amounts for age correction, body sculpting and removing skin imperfections.

What is more telling, perhaps, is that men too are spending much more in this category. In the last few years, the male 'skin-whitening category', which was non-existent just a decade ago, has grown phenomenally (150% growth) and now constitutes a 100 million dollar industry. Much of this growth has been fuelled by small-town (or what marketers sometimes refer to as 'middle') India. Apart from the desire for the perfect face and body to increase one's marriage prospects (particularly but not only for women), perhaps some of these new opportunities for employment with their attendant criteria for successful selection – 'handsomeness' or 'good looks' – feed this phenomenon.

The efforts to convert wealth (consumption as ownership) into symbolic capital (consumption as mastery of the code), however, may well be fraught with greater difficulties. In the small town, the concentration of capital in a few hands reinforces the position of local elites. If this concentration takes a corporatist form, then social and economic capital go hand in hand and can be turned more readily into symbolic and cultural forms. On the other hand, these elites may remain regional or provincial elites unless, at least inter-generationally, they manage to connect with the educational and cultural goods valued in the more globally-linked metropolises.

In crucial ways, the elites of small towns and villages are linked. Landed village elites have extended their influence into the town, investing in new economic activities. This is Bagchi's 'haveli capitalism' (see Bagchi 1999; also Parthasarathy, 2011). Local political power and capital rests in their hands. This creates the basis for primitive accumulation: primitive because each entrepreneur has to chart his own course in capital accumulation and this is based, importantly, on non-capitalist forms of exploitation and primitive also because corruption and fraud are crucial in the accumulation process (Basile and Harriss-White, 1999). It also creates a social formation with particular types of labour processes and relations that rely on the greater exploitation of human labour and its intentional informalisation and casualisation.

Ideologically, too, the village elites and those of the township are linked, particularly when it comes to norms of caste or gender behaviour (see Derné, 1994). For the Dalit or the tribal in the village, it has been suggested (Gidwani and Sivaramakrishnan, 2003), circular migration to the township may become a means to move away from degrading forms of labour performed for caste patrons. Often migration is undertaken to disengage from relations of subjugation, even if it economically offers few extra rewards. Dalits and tribals can accumulate small surpluses to remit home, enhancing livelihood, but also diffusing, wittingly or otherwise, political sensibilities and, thus, providing impetus for regional political movements among the downtrodden.

The sharp increase in violence, including domestic violence, is in part signal of the destabilising effects of rapid and somewhat unruly capitalist expansion. Gangs of young men who come into the big cities in fancy cars and display both risky behaviour ('for the thrill') on the roads as well as often unconcealed antagonism or outright violence towards metropolitan women – particularly young, educated, fashionable and/or unaccompanied – are the subjects of many newspaper reports. At the same time, in small-town India, divorce rates are increasing, not just among the affluent but also among the middle class and the lower middle class.

What are the small towns watching on television? Newer serials, whose popularity is assessed by their TRPs, are using village and small-town settings in different parts of the country, and not just Gujarat as preferred earlier. Some of these serials, such as *Bidaai* set in Agra, were not even advertised on hoardings in Mumbai. Clearly, their audience resides elsewhere. Small towns are avid watchers of the soap operas. Serials such as *Pavitra Rishtaa* (set in Maharashtra) or *Pratigya* (Allahabad), *Balika Vadhu* (Rajasthan), *Veerawali* (Punjab), *Santaan* (Kanpur), *Na Aana Is Des Laado* (Haryana) or *Raja Ki Aayegi Baraat* (Himachal Pradesh) make people across the country aware of different regional cultures, languages, cuisine and dress.

On the other hand, the soaps are continuously obsessed with conventional problems involving marriage, the difficulty of marrying off a daughter with 'dark' complexion, the generation gap, the absorption of an educated daughter-in-law into the husband's family, the concerns of family honour and reputation, and the like. In marketers' terms, they cater to small town and big city viewers who have 'reverse aspirations', who desire, in other words, the return of tradition and the comforts that convention and continuity bring. They diffuse regional and religious customs and rituals across the country (if in stereotypical and contrived ways) and, sometimes, even engender their revival. Most of these rituals and *pujas* are the preoccupation of women of the household and sanctify and valorise traditional wifely behaviours.

Conclusion

The influence of rapidly-changing global economics is entirely visible in India's small towns and that is what draws our attention to them in the first place. One might recall Derné's (2008) sectioning of the middle class, based on research in a small North Indian town, into the global or transnational elite and the ordinary non-elite. The choices available to these groups are different, their options differ, their lifestyles are not similar but they are exposed to the processes of economic globalisation and of cultural change that are spreading, especially through the media. Moreover, both groups consider themselves middle class and even, to an extent, modern.

The second group has less access to the fruits of globalisation, especially economic globalisation, and may not have the kind of transnational connections that the first group does. Nevertheless, it is Derné's argument that even those with less access to globalisation can be influenced by it. This is a class that is locally-oriented (ibid.: 44) but affected nonetheless by the effects of globalisation on its families, cultural orientations and understandings of class, gender and even nationalism. Perhaps small-town middle classes belong largely to the latter group, but there will be some among them that are part of the transnational elite.

Resistance to changes can be great, especially when it comes to issues of gender and the family. The new economics of the body or what Foucault would refer to as the 'care of the self' demonstrates an increasing awareness of and valorisation of sexuality and good looks for both men and women. However, for women, the attractiveness is to be channeled towards their husband or potential husband's needs and desires. Men want their women to dress in modern clothes but only for their pleasure. Of course, the effects of globalisation can hardly be contained so securely. Once transitions start occurring and women are in the employment market, have some spending power of their own and receive greater education, a greater degree of change is likely.

The opposition to the rapid change (as well as the effects of change) can be seen in the increase in violence of all sorts – rape, domestic violence, road rage, random street violence, often but not only against women – in small towns (and, indeed, across India). It can be seen in the increasing divorce rates, or other forms of class discontent and urban unease. In small towns, the opposition can be quelled due to the patriarchal and caste-based character of the elite. The capitalist class has the overlapping economic, social and symbolic capital needed to suppress or contain resistance or conflict. It may even rely on brute force or on influence in local government. The direct political influence of small-town elites is far greater. Further, there are material and ideological connections between rural and small-town urban elites; the metropolitan middle classes may face a wider range of influences as well as changing structures that force them to adjust or alter their expectations to a greater extent. It is far more difficult to contain class opposition, or enforce norms that will maintain traditionalism in gender and family. The state – with its own aim of creating a globally competitive India – will have to be relied on more, if metropolitan middle class aspirations are to be achieved.

In a sense, the small-town middle classes may actually turn into sites of opposition to the metropolises. With their wider political influence – their numbers are much greater and their clout in provincial affairs often extends even down to the village level – they may work to siphon off state and federal resources for urban development that till now the big metropolises have perceived as their exclusive right. Rather than mimicking the big cities, they may actually seek to create a new amalgam of traditional expectations and modern accomplishments. The reassertion of traditional norms in the midst of so much change speaks of this effort, and in its course, villages and small towns are perhaps not far apart.

We have talked about how small towns are engaging in new leisure activities and about what they are watching on the small screen. In both areas, we have seen the reassertion of familial and traditional gender norms. Indeed, many of the soaps on television show a great deal of violence, particularly but not only in the domestic sphere, and against women. The makers of serials such as *Balika Vadhu* may claim that they do not support the practice of child marriage, or other serial producers may likewise claim that they do not condone violence. However, *Balika Vadhu* showed the continuing *success* of the child marriage which was its central focus. This and other contemporary serials depict in agonising detail the ill-treatment to women or their disciplining (including through physical force) into the appropriate behaviour for wives, daughters and daughters-in-law. The ratings of these serials indicate considerable popular approval of such depictions. Further, the emphasis on rituals, and the spread of rituals through their elaborate representation in such serials, is clearly an important part of the way in which norms about *streeachar* and proper womanly behaviour are diffused and reasserted. Even rituals that may have been fading away in significance are revived through such serials.

In the end, the long-term effects of change in small towns are difficult to foresee. What one can say with greater surety is that the conflicts are likely to be perceived for some time to come; and at least in the short and perhaps even the middle-term, these will increase. Culturally, as we have already noted, the small towns may seek to keep at bay the effects of globalisation on norms of gender, family and caste. Patriarchy and the caste/class nexus may labour to keep women and the so-called lower castes away from the benefits of globalisation and economic and social change. Through its serials and some of its other productions, television and the media may in fact work against the process of secularisation, but by bringing global ideas and diverse channels of opinion to the small towns and villages, they open up the world and the effects are unlikely to be expected.

Newer opportunities cannot be completely contained even by elite action. As women and those at the bottom of the social hierarchy gain greater access to education, employment and income, the trends of change will be contrary and perhaps even unanticipated. Already, increasing divorce rates among young couples show both the acceptance of divorce among wider social circles as well as the greater options – economic and social – for women. The law and the courts have certainly aided to this process. Indeed, as some of the evidence may indicate, we should not underestimate the wider political influences and sensibilities that may enter the small towns, through the metropolis directly or more diffusely through the global media. On the one hand, the city and the media may spread greater consumerist influences, and groups and individuals may hope to translate newly-acquired economic resources into more highly valued social, cultural or symbolic goods. On the other hand, these influences may provide the momentum for more radical local and regional political action by the exploited.

Note

1. I am indebted to Mr Sumit Srivastava, Lecturer at the Centre for Globalisation and Development Studies, University of Allahabad, for the insights of this and the preceding two paragraphs, communicated to me via e-mail.

References

Bagchi, Amiya Kumar (ed.) (1999) *Economy and Organisation: Indian Institutions under the Neo-Liberal Regime*. New Delhi: Sage Publications.

Basile, Elisabetta and Barbara Harriss-White (1999) Corporate Capitalism: Civil Society and the Politics of Accumulation in Small Town India. QEH Working Paper Series – QEHWPS38. Paper for the Gordon White Memorial Conference. Institute of Development Studies, Sussex, 30 April–1 May.

Bourdieu, Pierre (1984) *Distinction: A Social Critique of the Judgment of Taste*. London: Routledge.

Cawthorne, Pamela M. (1995) 'Of Networks and Markets: The Rise and Rise of a South Indian Town, The Example of Tiruppur's Cotton Knitwear Industry'. *World Development*. 23(1): 43–56.

Derné, Steve (1994) 'Hindu Men Talk About Controlling Women: Cultural Ideas as a Tool of the Powerful'. *Sociological Perspectives*. 37(2): 203–27.

———. (2008) *Globalization on the Ground: Media and the Transformation of Culture, Class and Gender in India*. New Delhi: Sage Publications.

Gidwani, Vinay and K. Sivaramakrishnan (2003) 'Circular Migration and the Spaces of Cultural Assertion'. *Annals of the Association of American Geographers*. 93(1): 186–213.

Parthasarathy, D. (2011) 'Planning and the Fate of Democracy: State, Capital and Governance in Post-independence India'. In Vincent Pollard (ed.), *State Capitalism, Contentious Politics and Large-scale Social Change*. Leiden: Brill.

Simmel, Georg (2004) *The Philosophy of Money*. New York and London: Routledge.

Veblen, Thorstein (2005) (1899) *The Theory of the Leisure Class: An Economic Study of Institutions*. Delhi: Aakar Books.

5

The Academic Bias against Towns

A Cultural Audit

RAJESH GILL

A quick scan of public policy on urban India since independence clearly indicates a heavy tilt towards large cities, primarily the metropolitan and mega cities, in terms of planning of infrastructural and industrial inputs. Long ago, during the 1980s, the National Commission on Urbanisation (NCU) in its report had stressed upon the fact that in view of the persistent flow of rural migrants towards urban centres and the burgeoning populations of already bulky cities, greater attention must be paid to develop the infrastructure and employment opportunities in small and medium towns, in order to correct the skewed spatial urban growth. But, the largest of cities have continued to attract the rural as well as urban migrants, their unlivable conditions and congestion notwith-standing. Further, it is these metropolitan cities which have always fascinated anthropologists, sociologists and urban ecologists, who developed rich theoretical frameworks to describe and explain the city culture and its social consequences. Mumford, Simmel, Weber, Wirth and other eminent theorists perceived these large heterogeneous urban centres as spaces that contrasted with the traditional community-based rural settlements. Later, following Marxian interpretation, Castells conceptualised cities as spaces for collective consumption and crystallisation of class structures, along which the city population took shape. Cities have been understood as consuming centres, their productive aspect having been believed to have been outlived. Like all social theories, urban theory too has been heavily subjective and biased towards large cities, offering almost negligible explanation about the cultural life of smaller towns which hardly had any resemblance with the huge metros. Even the electronic media, particularly 'Bollywood' in India, has always depicted urban culture peculiarly of metros like Mumbai and Delhi as the culture, and has seldom focused upon the less urban centres. It is argued in the present paper that this trend reveals an academic bias especially in the conceptualisation of urban culture towards the large cities. There is an urgent need to develop alternative conceptual frameworks to capture the culture peculiar to towns which are not as large, heterogeneous and differentiated as cities, hardly behaving like 'melting pots'. The paper interrogates the existing cultural explanations of city life in view of the changed reality in the wake of global connectivity through information technology, making space a redundant category. The question then is: does the urban way of life percolate to the smaller and lesser urban settlements too? It is high time social scientists interested in urban studies go beyond large cities and choose to understand the cultural ethos of towns, their internal variations notwithstanding, in comparison to that of cities, especially in the context of India, which displays a huge gap between its cities and towns in terms of infrastructure, governance, population attributes, technological development and culture.

'City' for every one, including a layman, a rural migrant, an academician, a policy maker – primarily means a big city, usually a million-plus or a mega city, with a huge population, sufficiently good municipal income, skyscrapers, glamorous malls, institutions of higher education, expanded markets, seats of power and a rich infrastructure. When, for instance, a student in a remote village of India, after completing education, plans to try his luck for a job in a city, he thinks only of Mumbai, Delhi, Bangalore, Kolkata, Chennai and not, say, Rohtak or Hoshangabad or Agra. The academic fixation on the largest cities is similarly evident from the preoccupation of even our policy makers with these cities. In one of his writings, Kundu and Bhatia (www.unesco. org/most/dsp57) argue:

> … much of the current policy debate and media discussion on the problems of slums and deficiency of amenities is restricted to a few large cities. The fact that greater attention is paid to these cities in the policies and programmes for poverty alleviation and provision of amenities can possibly be explained in terms of strong vested interests in favour of larger cities. These cities have greater visibility and consequently get selected for slum improvement and poverty alleviation programmes by international and national agencies. Further, it becomes easier to cover a larger number of poor households in absolute terms because of the size factor, if larger cities are selected under the programmes.

India, like most of the developing countries of the world, has been experiencing highest growth rates in Class I cities, while the towns, medium and small, have usually either been growing extremely slow or have been sending migrants to the largest cities. Even, the National Commission on Urbanisation in its report of 1988 underlined this fact and stressed upon the need to render small and medium towns more attractive to prospective migrants. However, the fact remains that the largest cities have the best of infrastructure in place and that goes a long way in attracting migrants from all over the country as well as the world towards these settlements, despite the overcrowded and unmanageable ambience.

Large Cities: Centres of 'Growth' and 'Identitites'

In the era of liberalisation, both private and public investments have further been concentrated in the large metros, leaving the small towns in even a greater state of neglect. Given the fact that life opportunities are positively associated with the size of the city, it is but natural for such cities to experience a burgeoning growth in population. The substantially better financial status of the municipal bodies of metros is another important factor leading to a top-heavy urban structure in India.

Having been established by numerous studies that the wages go on rising as one moves higher in urban hierarchy and further with the coming in of ICT revolution, there is a growing craze among youth, in search for well-paid jobs, heading for the metro cities, if not across borders. It is the largest of the cities that continue to fancy everyone, i.e., the rich and the poor, men and women, educated and illiterate, rural and urban, and so on. Further, since these cities also happen to be the seats of power, in political, cultural and financial sense, these tend to grab the large chunk of state and Central funds for infrastructural development. Consequently, these cities land up with the best of roads, schools, colleges, universities, courts, markets, malls, cinemas, industries, banks, hotels, etc., making them still more preferred. It is ironical that despite their enormous contribution to the environmental havoc created by heavy traffic, industrial pollution, heaps of garbage, etc., the large metros happen to be the torchbearers for the international agenda of green cities.

The same obsession with the large metro city is discerned as one looks at the relevant literature, especially in urban sociology. Urban anthropologists and sociologists, fascinated with the revolutionary impact of industrial city that followed Industrial Revolution, developed theories underlining urban social disorganisation, mainly focusing upon the large industrial cities. The smaller cities, popularly known as towns, were primarily conceptualised as traditional, conventional, producing only orthogenetic change, due to their relatively homogeneous character and dominance of indigenous culture. Secularisation in terms of the complete irrelevance of ethnic identities – religious, regional, linguistic, racial and caste – was conceived to be a characteristic mainly of the large metropolitan cities, undergoing secondary urbanisation, while the smaller towns reinforced the local culture and identities.

Urban studies have throughout been preoccupied with the large cities, most often the metropolitan and the mega cities, hardly ever talking about the smaller towns, which have usually been called large villages, given their greater resemblance to the rural settlements. Especially the social theory focusing upon the cultural transformation brought in by urbanisation has mainly preoccupied itself with the largest cities. Due to the rise of industrial city initially in the Western Europe and then in US, the modern city was modeled upon European or American cities, with the assumption that cities in the rest of the world would undergo the same urban experience. Over a period of time, however, it has been realised that urbanisation never occurs in a vacuum and that the cultural context in which it takes off remains a very significant catalyst in the process, often resulting in extremely different outcomes. Hence, Tokyo has to be different from Los Angeles and Singapore has to be different from Dhaka and Colombo has to be different from Beijing. However, what has persisted is the continuous focus upon the largest of the cities, especially in terms of theorising of the social and cultural impact of urbanisation.

Literature indicates that in the developing countries, largest cities have remained the engines of urbanisation. Initially, this phenomenon was captured in terms of 'urban primacy' where one largest city dominated the economy, polity and culture in a region, more often in the developing regions, unlike the urban hierarchy characterising the Western societies. Over the years, as India experienced rapid urbanisation after independence, every state of the country was dominated by one largest city, usually the state capital, which enjoyed not only the political, but even economic, industrial and cultural dominance over the region. Demographically speaking, the largest cities in the country have throughout experienced the highest growth rates, mainly due to the edge enjoyed by these over other relatively smaller urban centres, in terms of better infrastructure and job opportunities. Despite the persistent emphasis by urban planners upon the expansion of small and medium towns, rural migrants have continued to throng the largest cities, rendering the phenomenon of step-migration, so characteristic of initial phases of urbanisation redundant.

Futility of the Ideal Typical Conception of 'City'

The preoccupation of scholars specialising in urban sociology on large cities is evident right from the beginning. Even Ferdinand Tonnies, in his masterwork *Gemeinschaft and Gesellschaft (1987 [1940])*, talked about the (large) city characterised by disunity, rampant individualism and selfishness in contrast to the village, characterised by social cohesion and communitarianism. According to Tonnies, within the *Gesellschaft* character of the modern city, there existed a rational and calculating attitude among inhabitants, primarily concerned with their own self-interest, to *look out for Number One*. Tonnies' ideas of the modern city get very well reflected through the poem of Robert Crowley (1961):

> And this is a city, in name but in deed
> It is a pack of people that seek after meed (profit)
> For officers and all, do seek their own gain
> But for the wealth of the Commons, no one taketh pain
> And hell without order, I may it well call
> Where every man is for himself and no man for all.

Tonnies was among the first few scholars to initiate sociology of the city. Following him, his contemporary, Emile Durkheim (1964) too wrote about the 19th century city. His concepts of 'mechanical' and 'organic' solidarity go parallel with Tonnies' concepts of *Gemeinschaft* and *Gesellschaft*, respectively. Although conscious of the problems cities were likely to create for the individual, i.e., impersonality, alienation, disagreement and conflict, for him the city still was superior in terms of its 'organic solidarity'. He wrote:

> The yoke that we submit to in modern society is much less heavy than when society completely controls us as it does in rural society, and it leaves much more place open for the free play of our initiative ....

While Tonnies apprehended the destructive tendencies of the city, Durkheim looked at the city as a source of social cohesion emerging out of increased division of labour and great human development, necessitated by an acute degree of interdependence that followed social differentiation and division of labour.

City life received serious academic attention later by Georg Simmel (1964), who focused upon the mental characteristics of the city. In his remarkable work *The Metropolis and Mental Life* (1964), Simmel describes the impact city life has on the mental temperament of the individual. He argued that due to the multiple stimuli offered by the city, there is an 'intensification of nervous stimuli' with which the urban dweller learns to cope. Just like Tonnies, Simmel too treats city life as more rational and calculative. Simmel wrote:

> If all the clocks and watches in Berlin would suddenly go wrong in different ways, even if only by one hour, all economic life and communication of the city would by disrupted for a long time.

The most interesting argument put forth by Simmel was in relation to the tremendous significance of money in city life. He wrote:

Money is concerned only with what is common to all; it asks for the exchange value, it reduces all quality and individuality to the question: how much?

Due to the very large population and density, Simmel argued that urban dwellers developed an indifferent and apathetic attitude, conceptualised by him as *blasé* attitude, full of detachment. He felt that people in a city responded with their 'head' as against their rural counterparts who acted with their 'heart'. Although Simmel like Durkheim believed in the liberating power of the city for its dwellers, still he wrote:

> ... under certain circumstances, one nowhere feels as lonely and lost as in the metropolitan crowd.

His writings ultimately bring him closer to Tonnies.

Another significant scholar in the field, Max Weber (1958), in his famous essay *The City* conceptualised the city on the basis of his comparative analysis of cities in different cultural and social contexts. But, for him, only the fortified, economically and politically self-sufficient cities of medieval period could be called cities. Weber's conception of the city was far more insightful and comparative than the simplistic one provided by the earlier scholars. For him, not all cities would produce the mental illness cited by Simmel or a detachment depicted by Tonnies.

These conceptualisations of urban life were obviously depicting large cities and definitely not the small towns, which were mostly treated as resembling the rural communities. This is evident in the writings of Robert Ezra Park (1967):

> In a small community it is the normal man, the man without eccentricity or genius who seems most likely to succeed. The small community often tolerates eccentricity. The city rewards it. Neither the criminal, the defective, nor the genius has the same opportunity to develop his innate disposition in a small town that he invariably finds in a great city.

The most significant and culturally relevant conceptualisation of city was offered by Louis Wirth (1938) in his famous essay: *Urbanism As a Way of Life*. Wirth defined the city as a process of 'social segmentalisation' as a result of the interest-specific human relationships as they existed in the city. Like all his predecessors, Wirth too apprehended social disorder and disorganisation as a consequence of large size and density of the cities. Impersonalisation has been identified as the most prominent characteristic of urban life by most of the classical writers on the city.

By and large, then, one finds various explanations on urban life primarily based upon ideal typical conceptions of the city. While Tonnies puts the urban society in contrast to the rural, by calling the former *Gesellschaft* and the latter *Gemeinschaft,* Durkheim conceptualised rural and urban societies in terms of *Mechanical* and *Organic* solidarity. In fact, the social disorganisation approach that developed in context of the industrial city, particularly in Chicago School, is based entirely on the large industrial city, characterised by anonymity, social segmentalisation and individualisation necessitated by the demographic and spatial structuring of the large metropolitan city. But, the question is: does this ideal typical conception of 'city' explain the small and medium cities and towns, which have a relatively low anonymity, individualisation and segmentalisation?

Let us take an example of the conceptualisation of the cultural change generated by a city in terms of 'heterogenetic' change proposed by Redfield and Singer (1954). According to them, the population of the orthogenetic city is relatively homogeneous and such a city contributes to maintaining and reintegrating the Great Tradition. Further, in their opinion, all orthogenetic cities are pre-industrial while heterogenetic cities are primarily industrial and post-industrial. Conception of the industrial city as a 'melting pot' further depicted life in the large city, especially the American, giving way to an 'urban' man (woman), while his/her native ethnic identities got irrelevant. Empirical and historical evidence, however, refutes such simplistic conceptualisations of city, especially since cities have been known to reinforce the process of ethnicisation and fundamentalism (Gill, 2000).

City Seen as an Urban Divide

There is enormous literature pointing out the futility of using 'city' as an insulated category while in fact it is a highly differentiated space, contextual in character, offering different things to different people residing in it. For instance, the recent report on 'State of the World's Cities 2010/2011, Bridging the Urban Divide' by UN-HABITAT (2008) forcefully underlines the phenomenon of 'urban divide', more visible in relatively less-developed countries of the world. It says that the spatial divide in cities of developing countries does not just reflect income inequalities among households; it is also a byproduct of inefficient and poor urban planning. It further states that the access to 'urban advantage' is greatly determined by the socio-cultural factors apart from the formal land and labour markets. The 'urban advantage' refers to:

> The abundance and variety of goods, services, amenities and opportunities which cities make available compared with rural areas. Social connections or 'human capital' are also part of that. The urban advantage is a function of the density and scale of public, business, education, health, cultural and other institutions a city manages to concentrate.

The urban divide between the rich and the poor, between those who enjoy the 'shopping malls' and those who are penniless, thus gradually has led to social exclusion, by pushing the poor and marginalised to the periphery not just in terms of spatial city but even in terms of access to life opportunities offered by the city. Such an unequal access to the 'urban advantage' especially in developing countries has led to the challenging of the exclusionary urban development, asking for 'right to the city'. In some places, it has been used as a theoretical and political framework focusing on enforcement, empowerment, participation, self-fulfillment, self-determination and various forms of human rights protection at the city level.

'Inclusive City': What about the Small Towns?

State of the World's Cities 2010/2011 Report by UN-HABITAT (2008) brings out the need to develop 'inclusive city' by which it implies:

Cities share a few basic features that can take different forms in various conditions: they provide the opportunities and supportive mechanisms that enable all residents to develop their full potential and gain their fair shares of the 'urban advantage'. In an inclusive city, residents perceive themselves as important contributors to decision-making, ranging from political issues to the more mundane routines of daily life ... . The concepts of human relations, citizenship and civic rights are all inseparable from urban inclusiveness. (2008: XIX)

According to this report, an inclusive city thus could be built by using the following strategies:
* Assessing the past and measuring progress;
* More effective, stronger institutions;
* Building new linkages and alliances among the various tiers of government;
* Demonstrating a sustained vision to promote inclusiveness; and
* Ensuring the redistribution of opportunities.

Further, urban experience so far indicates that fiscal health of an urban settlement greatly contributes to the infrastructural development as well as reduction in the urban/opportunity divide. Numerous studies have shown that the largest metropolitan cities have much better basic services both for the rich as well as the poor as compared to the small and medium towns, due to which migrants throng these cities. The municipal corporations of these cities are much more comfortable financially, better connected politically with the funding agencies and attractive for the multinational companies, giving them a clear-cut edge over the small and medium towns, with local municipal bodies reeling under fund starvation and administrative neglect. Despite the 74th Constitutional Amendment Act, providing for a decentralised and people-friendly local administration, the smaller towns continue to be ill-administered with completely feudal and centralised power structures. The urban divide in these towns is further likely to aggravate with the privatisation of housing and urban management. The phenomenon of 'gated communities', so characteristic of large cities, has invaded smaller towns in a big way. A direct outcome of such gated communities especially in smaller towns, already eroding the democratic essence of urban space, has been reflected through greater social exclusion, enhancing the urban divide between those with an easy access to urban advantage and those without it.

Size Alone Cannot Define a City or Town

Cities have always been distinguished from each other in terms of size, varying with the census definitions among different countries. Taking the example of India, it has always been the largest cities that have fancied the immigrants for the infrastructure, job opportunities and glamour offered by them. However, while size is a very important variable for the purposes of town planning, fiscal planning and land use planning, it may be irrelevant for the human interpretation of it. Human beings may be using their own typology of cities, with absolutely no connection with the ones developed for technical and academic purposes. For instance, significant distinction is made by residents between small towns and large metropolitan cities, with the frequent use of phrases like 'small town mentality', 'urban jungle', 'life in a metro' and the like. Moreover, it is the 'global city' that dominates the urban scene in contemporary times. Mumbai, the most cosmopolitan and globally-connected city, and Bangalore, the IT hub, happen to be the ultimate choice for young aspirants, looking for greener pastures within India. The sole criterion for assessing a city today is the amount of money and life opportunities it can offer, irrespective of whether it breeds social disorganisation or not. Here, once again, smaller towns are at a disadvantage because they just cannot compete with the global cities in terms of life opportunities.

That cities cannot be squeezed neatly into quantitative categories is evident from the following statement of John Rennie Short in his work *Urban Theory*:

> Statistical definitions lend precision but lack subtlety ... the term 'urban' is plastic and elastic; we will use it to refer to cities in general but especially the large sort of cities that are commonly recognizable as more than simply large villages. The term applies across a band of different city sizes, but the emphasis is on places that are both quantitatively and qualitatively different from large rural villages. (2006: 2)

No doubt then that except for the benefit of using straight-jacket definitions of city for purposes of measurement and quantification, it evades a simple definition due to its complexity. The fact is endorsed in the following statement:

> Conventionally, villages have populations counted in hundreds, towns in thousands, cities in hundreds of thousands and metropolitan cities in millions ... a dense agricultural area can have a population equivalent to that of a small city. (Angotti, 1993: 6)

Miles (2007) feels that the idea of a city is so variable that size says little of what makes city life attractive. A received image of the European city is a knot of streets in which people live closely, a romanticised notion which ignores social distinctions and the hierarchies of streets. While cities may be defined for technical purposes in the census, these are likely to have different meanings for the common people, especially in terms of their social and cultural implications.

People's Perceptions about Cities and Towns

Quite interestingly, a layperson's perception of a city in terms of large or small may have no connection with the size or other formal census categorisations. For instance, Chandigarh, which is now a metropolitan city as per Census 2011 and is the most modern and planned Indian city, was treated as a small town till recently not because of its size but primarily because it did not have the social and cultural flavour of a large city. For the youth, it was and still is a dead city while for the professionally qualified, it is no match for cities like Bangalore, Hyderabad, Delhi and Mumbai. At the same time, however, Chandigarh remains an attractive destination for the rural youth of Punjab and Haryana, primarily from humble backgrounds, due to the glamour and (fast) life that, for them, exists in the city.

It is very strange that despite the metros being conceptualised as 'crowd' both by academics as well as common people, these continue to be the most-sought-after destinations by people from all types of background. The poorest of the poor and the richest of the rich, everybody strives to land in a metro, of course for different reasons. Yet, it is very interesting to engage in the ethnographic accounts of people in their reading of these towns and cities. Some of these are given below.

'I Love to be a Part of this Crowd!'

For a group of women, married to men living and working in Mumbai, hailing from Punjabi families, mainly in and around Delhi, Mumbai is the place they love to be in. They hate the thought of going back permanently to Delhi and getting settled there due to its small town culture. Since most of their kinsmen stay in and around Delhi, especially those of their husbands, they feel imprisoned once they land there, completely robbed of their liberty and freedom. While in Mumbai, they feel absolutely free. They could wear anything they liked, eat anything they preferred, remain out of home any time of the day or night, without any fear of being quizzed. They loved this freedom of a metro, which was absolutely absent in the small town culture of Delhi.

'A Heaven Called Chandigarh!'

For scores of young agile boys who have been born and brought up in remote villages of Punjab; who have been sweating out in the scorching sun while working in the fields, fascinated by the glittering urban world on television and cinema, Chandigarh is the destination. For them, living in Chandigarh means enjoying freedom from the shackles of village life, the toil and sweat; it also implies eating noodles, pizzas and burgers and wearing western attire and enjoying dating. For them, Chandigarh is an ideal city.

'I Can Write my Own Biography Here!'

It is only the largest of the cities where a migrant having been burdened through generations by the caste, income and occupational stigmatised identities can escape into a state of individual freedom. For thousands of men and women coming from remote villages and small towns of Uttar Pradesh, Bihar, Chhattisgarh or even Punjab and Haryana, having grown up under the clutches of caste ethnocentrism and poverty, a metro offers a space where it is possible for them to create a new identity. The universities and colleges of Indian metros are today brimming with thousands of such young boys and girls struggling hard to get out of their traditional social handicaps and write their own biographies, academically called 'choice biographies' (Beck, 1992).

What Happens in Towns?

Just as all cities are not identical, all towns too are very different in spirit. On comparison with the cities, especially the metropolitan, towns seem to be less evil and less wounded. Many of the characteristics of a city, narrated by scholars like Simmel, Durkheim, Mumford, Banfield and others, emanating out of a huge size of population and heterogeneity, i.e., anonymity, segmentalisation, individualisation, alienation, etc., may not be found in towns to the same extent as in metros. But the question is: does that make these towns more attractive to migrants? Certainly not! The same anonymity of large cities that creates insecurity among senior citizens gives a sense of freedom to youngsters from the clutches of caste, gender and class identity. The secondarisation of relationships which Wirth considered an outcome of the urban way of life tends to reduce the burden of social obligations for a migrant, who finds it possible here to live the way he likes to. In fact, many of the vices, integral to a metro, are totally missing in smaller towns, but does that make them more attractive to migrants? It is a fact that unlike the initial phenomenon of step migration, whereby a rural migrant used to first migrate to a nearby urban settlement within the same region, today he/she prefers to move directly to a metro, simply because it offers tremendous life opportunities to everyone irrespective of age, educational qualifications, skills, and so on.

Before drawing conclusions, it needs to be remembered that the towns, small and medium, vary substantially between themselves in terms of their functional type, location, social and demographic composition, political and commercial potential and so on. Thus, a town which happens to be a birthplace of the Chief Minister of a state shall be very different from another town without any such privileged identity. Similarly, a town which is a pilgrimage centre shall be very different from a trade town, given different levels of heterogeneity and commercial character.

It is a known fact that in smaller towns most of the institutions governing formal land and labour markets, basic services and infrastructure, are weak or dysfunctional, constantly under the influence of vested interests of those few in power – economic, political and social. While public institutions in these towns are totally lacking, private vested interests fill the void, acting as a substitute for the public provisions meant for collective good. Urban planning is often rendered merely as an instrument of exclusion, thanks to the manipulation by those in power, ironically in the name of master planning. In almost all the towns of Punjab, for instance, gated communities have taken over, having ensured enclaves of wealth, totally marginalising the poor spatially, socially and politically.

The UN-HABITAT Study (2008) had indicated that public transport was one of the most effective ways of reducing inequalities in cities. In 10 Asian cities surveyed, however, it was found that political role of non-governmental organisations advocating stronger political commitment along with freedom of expression and other human rights made enormous contribution to improvement in social inclusiveness. With the provision of health, education and other social welfare functions having been granted constitutional status in India, effective efforts by civil society groups could do a great job towards reducing urban divide. But most of the NGOs and civil society groups in India are stationed in metropolitan and mega cities, leaving smaller towns at the mercy of the local administration. Public transport system in these cities is completely lacking, again leading to a heavy dependence of residents upon private transport, with an unequal access and affordability.

Quite interestingly, while large metros grant anonymity to their residents, people in North Indian towns, given a smaller population, find an intense temptation to exude consumerism with a view to earn a special status within the town. This paper hypothesises that while most of the classical urban sociologists and anthropologists have associated city life with vices, social disorganisation and indifference, the same would not apply to towns where the well-off people are likely to exhibit a greater degree of conspicuous consumption in order to earn a privileged position, with lesser degree of anonymity and impersonalisation. Struggles to grab political power in these towns are more likely to be governed by parochial identities of religion, caste and *gotra,* although the trend would be different in different kinds of towns.

Conclusion

To conclude, while demographers and economists have largely considered the relatively low development of the small and medium towns in terms of their infrastructure and fiscal status for their lower growth rate in comparison to large cities, it is argued here that cities continue to be the preferred destinations for migrants also because of the relatively secular and anonymous ambience offered by them. More systematic studies of an ethnographic nature are required to understand the bias against smaller towns among not only the academics and planners, but also among the migrants and original residents of these towns. In fact, there is a need to theorise upon the social and cultural ethos in these towns, which are likely to be extremely distinct from the one conceptualised for large cities. As one scans through the popular conceptions of cities being a breeding ground for broken families, increasing divorces, gender violence, child abuse and social disparities, one is led to assume as if smaller urban settlements would be just the opposite, a haven to live in. But empirical evidence does not substantiate this assumption and the fact remains that it is the same cities, full of crime, insecurity, apathy and social disorganisation, which continue to pull migrants towards them, either for the better opportunities offered there, or the relatively secular ambience where one can breathe more easily than in the village or small town; or the more liberal cultural milieu that pulls one out of the clutches of communitarian identities. Thus, despite these cities being projected as a case of 'urban divide' or 'dual cities' for the huge disparities existing within them in terms of access to urban opportunities, these continue to be a haven for those struggling to get rid of their age-old social disabilities, and for that small towns are no substitute.

References

Angotti, T. (1993) *Metropolis 2000: Planning, Poverty and Politics*. London: Routledge.

Beck, U. (1992) *Risk Society: Towards a New Modernity*. London: Sage.

———. (1998) *World Risk Society*. Cambridge: Polity.

Castells, Manuel (1972) *The Urban Question*. London: Edward Arnold. (Reprintedj in 1977).

Crowley, Robert (1961) Quoted in Lewis Mumford. *The City in History*. New York: Harcourt, Brace and World, p. 343.

Durkheim, E. (1893) *The Division of Labor in Society*. New York: Free Press. (Reprinted in 1964).

Eames, Edwin and Judith Granich Goode (1977) *Anthropology of the City: An Introduction to Urban Anthropology*. Englewood Cliffs, NJ: Prentice Hall.

Gill, Rajesh (2000) 'Cities and Ethnic Identities: A Case of De-ethnicization or Re-ethnicization?' *Sociological Bulletin*. Vol. 49, No. 2, September.

———. (2003) 'Planning Urban Settlements for People: A Social Agenda'. *Urban India*. Vol. XXIII, No. I, January–June.

Kundu, Amitabh and Sutinder Bhatia (1995) 'Industrial Growth in Small and Medium Towns and their Vertical Integration: The Case of Gobindgarh, Punjab, India'. UNESCO/MOST Discussion Paper No. 57. http://www.unesco.org/most/dsp57

Miles, Malcolm (2007) *Cities and Cultures*. New York: Routledge.

Miles, Steven and Malcolm Miles (2004) *Consuming Cities*. New York: Palgrave Macmillan.

Park, Robert E. (1916) 'The City: Suggestions for the Investigation of Human Behaviour in the Urban Environment'. In Robert E. Park and E.W. Burgess (eds), *The City*. Chicago: University of Chicago Press, pp. 1–46. (Reprinted in 1967).

Redfield, Robert and Milton Singer (1954) 'The Cultural Role of Cities'. *Economic Development and Cultural Change*. Vol. 3, pp. 53–73.

Schneider, Jane and Ida Susser (eds) (2003) *Wounded Cities, Destruction and Reconstruction in a Globalized World*. Oxford: Berg.

Sharma, Kalpana, Slumdogs and Small Towns of India, http://southasia.oneworld.net/opinioncomment

Short, John Rennie (2006) *Urban Theory: A Critical Assessment*. New York: Palgrave Macmillan.

Simmel, Georg (1905) 'The Metropolis and Mental Life'. In K. Wolff (ed.), *The Sociology of Georg Simmel*. New York: Free Press, pp. 409–24. (Reprinted in 1964).

Spates, James L. and John J. Macionis (1982) *The Sociology of Cities*. New York: St. Martin's Press.

Tonnies, Ferdinand (1887) *Fundamental Concepts of Sociology (Gemeinschaft and Gesellschaft)*. Translated by Charles P. Loomis. New York: American Book Company. (Reprinted in 1940).

UN-HABITAT (2008) *State of the World's Cities 2010/2011, Bridging the Urban Divide*. London: Sterling.

Weber, Max (1905) *The City*. Translated and edited by Don Martindale and G. Neuwirth. Glencoe: The Free Press, pp. 63–89. (Reprinted in 1958).

Wirth, Louis (1938) 'Urbanism As a Way of Life'. *American Journal of Sociology*. Vol. 4, pp. 1–24.

6

Small Towns, their Limited Resourcing Options and Equity Deficits

BIRAJ SWAIN[1]

South Asia in general and India in particular are fast urbanising. By the census of 2001, the urban population of India had grown to 27.1 per cent. While conventional economics would like to celebrate this trend as growth of aspirations and opportunities, a simple enquiry would reveal reasons far less celebratory. Failing rural livelihoods, agrarian crisis and dispossession of the marginalised from traditional common property resources make a heady cocktail for this rural outflow. While there have been a slew of announcements of programmes and schemes by the federal government and Planning Commission, taking cognisance of the urban reconfiguration, their adequacy is still a far cry. Information asymmetry, capacity constraints combined with serious lack of revenue and non-revenue resources make these towns (with less than a million population) languish in squalor and crumbling infrastructure.

This paper investigates the resource generation, financial options available for these small towns and cities which could have made these a reasonable first-port-of-call for first-generation migrants, but for the lack of resources and ever-shrinking opportunities. It examines closely the case of Ratlam in Madhya Pradesh, its reasons for opting out of an Asian Development Bank (ADB) loan in 2005. It examines a select set of cities and towns which have opted for concessional loans from the multi-lateral development banks and the debt burden such instruments generate. It concludes with a call for equity in practice (planning and resourcing) so that these places could be made appropriate for a tenable future. The paper concludes with comments on the (in)capacities of such sites which make them obvious zones of discrimination and the need for investment in capacities for the true realisation of the 74th amendment.

The provisional result of Census 2011 is the apparent increase in urbanisation. At one level, this may not seem to be all that significant, with the proportion of urban residents going from 27.81 per cent of the total population in 2001 to 31.16 per cent in 2011, or an increase of only 3.35 percentage points over a decade. This is not really a very major shift. A rate of urbanisation of less than one-third of the population is significantly lesser than the rate in many other developing countries, even those at similar levels of per capita income.

Nevertheless, it has created some excitement because for the first time since independence, the decadal increase in the size of the urban population (by 90.99 million people over 2001–11) is greater than that of the rural population (by 90.47 million).[2] It is not only in the smaller states that urbanisation appears to be proceeding apace. In some larger states such as Tamil Nadu, the proportion of urban population to total population is already approaching nearly a half, while Maharashtra and Gujarat are not too far behind. As per UN-HABITAT statistics, the urban population of India will be approximately 32.5 per cent of the total population in 2015, compared to 27.7 per cent in 2000.[3]

The 2001 Census of India put the number of urban households having access to basic sanitation within household premises at 61 per cent, but there are reasons to approach the statistics with caution. There are no systematic methods and regular systems for monitoring and generating data for the status of urban water and sanitation from the state level upwards to the central government agencies. Even if 61 per cent of India's urban population had adequate excreta disposal facilities in 2000, inadequate sewage systems and wastewater treatment facilities along with a high quantum of solid waste generation are causing an impending health catastrophe. Looking at the basic infrastructure facilities draws a fairly bleak picture. Examining the status of housing, public transport and power supplies draws an even bleaker picture!

The mid-term review of the Ninth Plan in 2000 by the Planning Commission found that the service levels of water supply in most of the cities and towns were far below the desired norm, and in smaller towns, even below the rural norms. It also found that urban sanitation was very poor: 'At the start of the Ninth Five-Year Plan (1997), although 49 per cent of the population had provision for sanitary excreta disposal facilities, only 28 per cent had sewerage systems. Where sewers were present, they generally did not have adequate treatment facilities. In the case of solid waste disposal, only about 60 per cent of the generated waste was collected and disposed of and of this, only 50 per cent was disposed of safely. Separate arrangements for safe disposal of industrial, hospital and other toxic and hazardous wastes were found to be generally nonexistent.'[4] For urban water, official reports tend to give greater weightage to physical and financial progress rather than to the quality, reliability and sustainability of services, which leads to problems in identifying coverage based on a strict definition of the term.

Assessing the financial status of water and sanitation in urban India is hampered by the weak information base in the sector. Few urban water supply and sanitation bodies report against a set of monitoring indicators, let alone publicly forecast and monitor against those indicators. Consequently, relatively little information is available to scrutinise the performance of urban water supply and sanitation organisations. Estimating financial gaps for the urban sector water and sanitation is normally done by extrapolating per capita investment requirements based on the experience of a few cities under the coordination of the Planning Commission. For a large country like India, average estimates of per capita investment requirements based on just a few cities may not provide an accurate national picture.

UNICEF/WHO (United Nations Children's Fund/World Health Organisation) have given a rough prediction that India would need to invest approximately ₹ 96 billion between 2002–15 to reach the MDG target for urban water and ₹ 208 billion to meet the target for urban sanitation. The financial figure requirements get further complicated with widely variant numbers being estimated by different groups. The World Bank-supported Expert Committee Group on Infrastructure Privatisation (ECGIP) arrived at ₹ 301 billion per annum year-on-year for each year of the Ninth Five Year Plan to achieve the desirable coverage. The Ministry of Urban Development has projected investment needs of ₹ 282 billion for urban water and ₹ 232 billion for urban sanitation for the Tenth Five-Year Plan (2002–07). If the Ministry of Urban Development's investment needs are matched by actual spending, there would appear to be enough resources in the sector to achieve the Millennium Development Goals targets for urban water sanitation coverage by 2015. However, there is a large concern over the lack of basic infrastructure in urban India, especially in smaller urban areas outside the major cities, many of which have poor water infrastructure and no sewerage system at all.

It is important to note that even if there is a large financial outlay for urban areas and all of this outlay is matched by actual spending, it does not guarantee that those with the worst WATSAN provision will enjoy substantially improved coverage by 2015. Inequity in public spending in towns and cities – and the resultant difference in coverage levels between poor and wealthy areas – will remain a major issue. A break-up of resource outlays for maintenance and new physical infrastructure in different socio-economic parts of urban areas are required for an informed public debate about the equity of public spending. It is also important to look at equity between urban and rural areas, as there is a temptation for large towns and state capitals to corner large spending outlays and public subsidies and transport surface water and/or mine ground water from afar to satisfy their needs, which can be at the expense of the water needs of rural areas and smaller towns.

The Number of Towns and Cities Increased to 7,935, as per 2011 Census Provisional Data

The increase in urban population is the outcome of three separate factors: the natural increase in population within urban areas, the migration of people from rural to urban areas, and the reclassification of settlements from rural to urban. All three factors have been at work over the past decade. The last factor is likely to have played a major role simply because there has been a significant, even remarkable, increase in the number of urban conurbations in the latest census. The number of urban settlements has increased from 5,161 in 2001 to 7,935 in 2011, an increase of 54 per cent, which dwarfs the 32 per cent growth in the urban population.

The 2011 Census classifies an area as urban if it fulfils any one of two conditions. First, any area that comes under a corporation, municipality or town panchayat is automatically classified as urban and is defined as a 'statutory town'. Secondly, a location is considered to be urban if it contains a population of 5,000 or above, has a density of at least 400 persons per square kilometre, and where 75 per cent of the male workforce is employed in non-agricultural occupations. It is then defined as a 'census town'.

One of the significant processes that has been at work in India over the past decade is the significant increase in the number of census towns – that is, places that are not recognised as urban areas in a statutory sense but fulfil the criteria laid down by the census. These account for more than 90 per cent of the increase in the total number of urban settlements. In a few states (such as Karnataka, Haryana and Jharkhand), the number of statutory towns has actually fallen, while the number of census towns has increased very sharply. Overall, the number of census towns has increased by more than 180 per cent, while there has been more than a threefold increase in their numbers in Bihar, Kerala, Punjab and Uttar Pradesh.[5]

Options for Infrastructure Financing in Small Towns, 7,935 of them and Still Counting

The metropolitan and other large cities are expected to make capital investments on their own, besides covering the operational costs for their infrastructure services. Most of the development projects under the new guidelines (JNNURM), undertaken through institutional finance rather than budgetary support, are required to be self-financing and also recover the capital costs. A strong case has been made for making the public agencies accountable and financially viable. The costs of borrowing have spiked, and as a consequence, they can no longer lend money at a rate below that prevailing in the market. This has come in the way of taking up socially desirable schemes that often turn out as financially un-renumerative. Projects for the provision of water and sanitation facilities, improvement of slum colonies, investments in public health posts, etc., which generally require a substantial component of subsidy, have, thus, received a low/no priority in this changed financing scenario.

Multiple options have been tried out, from HUDCO's subsidised, part-financed loans to ILFS's (Infrastructure Leasing and Financing Services) utility funding and grant-financing of improved urban services to bilateral aid (Government of UK's Department for International Development) for strengthening urban services to multi-lateral development bank funds for a host of urban reforms, i.e., ADB and World Bank. All these financing modus, claiming to be geared towards making urban local bodies and utilities more accountable, are combined with various urban reforms as a package such as:

1. Property tax rationalisation
2. Municipal accounting capacity building
3. Registration of all revenue and non-revenue generating land/property
4. Using land as a resource for fund raising
5. Cost recovery on services
6. Legislations/operating procedures for urban regulation
7. Service delivery for the poor in unconnected areas

This paper now examines the case of Ratlam (a small city in the state of Madhya Pradesh, India), which opted out of ADB's Urban Water Supply and Environment Improvement Project in 2005. This case is symptomatic of most of the small towns in India and even of South Asia.

Between a Rock and a Hard Place: Ratlam

ADB financing for water sanitation and sewerage projects comes in the form of loans. Ratlam and Ujjain[6] withdrew from the negotiated UWSEIP on the plea that the debt created by the loan would be difficult for the city to service. Other cities too were known to be facing the financial burden of the loan. The present analysis is limited in scope and has only drawn attention to some critical issues in this regard. Government of India is the borrower and the state governments, through their respective Urban Development Departments, the implementing parties. Although the cities covered by the respective projects have been placed under some obligation, yet there is minimal awareness at the city level about the loan obligations, nor does the accounting set-up provide for any kind of reporting regarding the debt burden on the city (Urban Local Body/Public Health Engineering Department) or the amount of repayment that has to be made by the city. In fact, even at the state-level, there is no information on the amount of repayments made to ADB as the loan is channelised through the central government as additional central assistance, and repayments by the state are made to the central government. The entire management of the loan rests with the ADB Division in the Department of Economic Affairs at Delhi. The accounting for loans received and repaid is done by the Aid, Accounts and Audit Division in the Department. The ADB Division not only takes care of repayments as per schedule but will also pre-pay a loan if it is to the country's advantage.[7]

Indebtedness at the state/city levels is managed by the Centre through centre-state-city fiscal arrangements. Any amount owed by a city to the state government can be adjusted from grants/revenues owed by the state to it (this remains a theoretical possibility only as a large chunk of salaries are paid from the grants). Similarly, any amount owed by the state government to the central government can be adjusted from grants/revenues due to it. In practice, liability for loan repayment is tossed up successively by the ULBs and state governments to the central government, which the latter cannot shrug off. State governments' debt has been accumulating in recent years due to their large and increasing GFD (gross fiscal deficit). Outstanding state debt in the country rose by 17.5 per cent at end-March 2004 over the previous year. In terms of GDP, the debt stock of states constituted 29.1 per cent as at end-March 2004, higher than the level of 27.8 per cent in the previous year. Analysis of Debt Outstanding to Gross State Domestic Product (GSDP) strengthens the view that debt levels were uncomfortably high with considerable deterioration in Debt/GSDP ratio:

Debt and GSDP ratio for 2002–03 and 2003–04

State	2002-3 Debt/GSDP	2003-4 Debt/GSDP
Rajasthan	42.8	54.0
Karnataka	24.9	29.0
Madhya Pradesh	38.0	53.1

Ratlam ULB's self-analysis: the financials of the corporation prepared by the consultants indicated that the ULB would be in a position to repay the loan. However, these projections assumed that there would be steep annual increases in the revenues generated from house tax, water charges and other sources of revenue to levels which may be considered to be politically and administratively impossible to achieve; the officials at the corporation were skeptical about being able to effect such steep increases and the real politic of the same. As it turned out, the city of Ratlam turned down the ADB loan for the following reasons:

1. It would be difficult for the Corporation to repay the loan (the city demanded an interest-free loan coupled with a three-fold increase in the compensation for octroi);
2. The interest rate of 12 per cent was too high and the ULB wanted it reduced to 8 per cent;
3. The allocation to consultancy at 7.3 per cent (2.2% Project Management Consultants and 5.1% Design and Construction Supervision Consultants) of total base costs of USD 234.2 million for the six cities in M.P. appeared to be excessive;
4. Transport Nagar project was not included in the overall project which could have generated revenue for Ratlam, it being on the Jaipur-Mumbai route with heavy passenger and freight traffic; and
5. Rising main was not included, considering the city has to draw water from a reservoir 63 metres below the city level and over 50-plus kilometres away, the mains constituted a crucial infrastructure for the city.

And, hence the city's ULB, irrespective of the party in power, refused the loan and the terms of the same consistently. The fact that they had defaulted on HUDCO finance was also a determinant of caution. However, this refusal doesn't mean Ratlam didn't need the financial assistance, neither does it mean that the city had been able to garner more attractive assistance in any better terms. But this refusal still calls for celebration because:

• It brought the acute problem of finance (in)access to small towns and the predatory financing conditions into sharp focus.
• It also meant, the town municipality, in spite of huge information asymmetry, could still do the number-crunching and opt out of an unattractive financing instrument which would have meant inter-generational loans/debt burden on the denizens of the city.

City and Site Specific or Pan-Indian?

It is neither a Ratlam or Madhya Pradesh specific problem, nor is the issue around debt financing by multi-lateral development banks. The malaise is much more widespread and deep-rooted, in fact pan-regional. Most ADB lending for water supply and sanitation projects is from the Ordinary Capital Resources (OCR) and the Asian Development Fund (ADF). In 2005, the total ADB lending for 32 loans comprising USD 4.4 billion was from Ordinary Capital Resources (76% of lending) and 40 loans comprising USD 1.4 billion from the Asian Development Fund (24% of lending) (Asian Development Bank, 2006). Loans from OCR are only made to comparatively 'more developed' countries, able to repay the debt. These loans are not concessional and interest rates are set by the market based on the LIBOR, plus a fixed spread (then at 0.6%), which is reset every six months. LIBOR is the London Inter Bank Offer Rate and is the interest rate offered by a specific group of London banks for US dollar deposits of a stated maturity. For example, the one-year LIBOR rate on 14 July 2006, was at 5.66 per cent (www.interestonlyloans.com). LIBOR-based loans have a floating interest rate until the borrower requests for fixing. The loans are payable over a 15 to 25-year period.[8]

ADB loans to India are from the OCR. ADF loans are made to the 24 'poorest' member countries with low debt repayment capacity at concessional rates (1 to 1.5% interest) with long grace periods (often eight years) and long repayment periods (they have a 32-year maturity period). ADB loans to Nepal are from the ADF.

Governments and other intermediaries on-lending these loans typically increase interest rates by 3 to 6.5 per cent. They also reduce repayment periods and grace periods. Table below illustrates how this works in water supply and sanitation projects in Bangladesh, India and Nepal:

Table 2

On-lending practices in water sanitation projects financed by ADB

Country	ADB project	Step 1	Step 2	Step 3
India	Urban Water Supply and Environment Improvement Project in Madhya Pradesh, case of Ratlam	ADB to Government of India (GoI) at LIBOR + 0.60% (OCR-25-year loan with 5-year grace period)	GoI to Special Purpose Vehicle Madhya Pradesh (SPVMP)	SPVMP to Town Municipality at 12%
Nepal	Small Towns Water Supply and Sanitation Sector Project	ADB to His Majesty Government of Nepal (HMGN) at 1.5% (ADF – 32-year loan, 8-year grace period)	HMGN to Town Development Fund (TDF) at 5% (20-year loan with 5-year grace period)	TDF to Water Users and Sanitation Committee at 8% (for 12 years with 3-year grace period)
Bangladesh	Second Water Supply and Sanitation Sector Project	ADB to GoB at 1.0% (ADF – 40-year loan, 10-year grace period)	GoB to Paurashava at 7.5% (20-year loan with 5-year grace period)	Paurashava to poor residents at 14% (market rate, through NGOs)

In fact, this problem is not just regional, i.e., South Asian but permeates the developed world as much:

So widespread is the (in)access to finance/resources that small towns in the United States are lobbying to access low-cost financing too.[9] Small towns and nonprofit groups warn they face higher borrowing costs because Congress failed to renew cheap incentives that encourage the purchase of their tax-exempt bonds. The 'bank qualified' incentives, as they are known, allowed small and rural municipal borrowers that sold $30 million or less in bonds to avoid going to Wall Street each time they needed to sell debt. Instead, local banks could buy the bonds and write off most of the costs they incurred to purchase and hold the debt. The incentives helped hundreds of social welfare projects throughout the country at below-market rates, i.e., from a drug-treatment centre in Billings, Montana, to a new nursing school building in La Crosse, Wisconsin.

Another small town in the US, city of Central Falls in the US state of Rhode Island, has filed for bankruptcy. It was a proud boomtown – textile mills and other manufactures dotted the landscape and anchored it in prosperity. Today, its website may still claim it to be a 'town with a bright future' but the reality is a different story; one where the money ran out and the city had to file for bankruptcy. What broke Central Falls was its generous pension system mixed up with a good amount of mismanagement. When the recession hit, the town just could not cope with its entitlements and the revenue couldn't even start to cover the cost. Sinking under 80-million dollars of debt, the mayor was stripped of his powers a year ago and the city was put in the hands of three different receivers sent from the state who tried all the tricks in the books. The local library and community centre were closed and all city services cut to the bone. Taxes were raised by almost 20 per cent but that only pushed people and business away. For months, the receivers tried to reach a deal with the 160 retired public safety workers. They were asked to accept cuts to their pensions of up to 50 per cent. Of course they said no and the agreement fell through. Declaring bankruptcy means the union deals will be cancelled and the city will be able to restructure its debt, but for the retirees, this means their pensions will be cut in half. Some fear that what happened in Central Falls might be a warning of more pain to come. Across the United States, cities, counties and states are going broke, struggling to recover from the recession and, in some cases, years of fiscal mismanagement. 'In Washington, the debt ceiling fights and discussions over possible cuts to Social Security and health benefits show how difficult it is to reinvent a system after too many years of living beyond its means, accompanied with predatory financing options'.[10]

Why Choose Such a Hard Option?

Considering the interest rates on such loans/instruments being so high on the end-users, it is important to understand the reasons why borrowers/institutions sign up for such modus:

- The water, sanitation, basic services' situation in towns is deplorable and there is a perception that large-scale financing is needed to address the problem, for example to bring water from a distant source. Municipalities are unable to raise enough revenue to cover the costs of the infrastructure and Central government grants are not available. Hence, small towns have no option but to take loans for expensive, infrastructure-heavy, cost-intensive projects often designed at state or Central levels. Often cheaper water and sanitation solutions could be designed, such as upgrading distribution systems and fixing leaks, which would remove the need for large financing.

- Although not as concessional as the loan made by ADB to Central government, on-lent loans are still cheaper than commercial loans available to local governments. Furthermore, many of the towns covered by these projects are not attractive investment destinations; hence alternative financing is not available. In some cases the end borrowers are unaware of the terms and conditions of the loans. In one municipality visited in Nepal, the officials were not even aware that the municipality was a guarantor for a loan taken by the local users' committee under an ADB-financed project. In India, repayments are made to ADB by the Central government and information regarding the amount of outstanding loans is not available with the end-borrower.

- Borrowers know that they will be bailed out by state or Central government if they are unable to repay loans and are therefore not very concerned about the terms and conditions.

Impact of Such Financial Bleeding

Tariff hikes to make projects financially viable: in order to be approved by the bank/financier Board of Directors, proposed projects must be financially viable, based on a calculation of the Financial Internal Rate of Return (FIRR). ADB projects are often designed centrally, by consultants, and not at the local level. This results in expensive projects due to over-designing of infrastructure, the cost of consultants and the interest rates on the loans. To make such projects appear financially viable, designs include huge increases in tariffs. These tariff increases are built into loan agreements as conditions. In the case of the town of Ratlam under the Urban Water Supply and Environmental Improvement Project in Madhya Pradesh, India, water tariffs were projected to increase by 8.4 times over a 16-year period. Often these increases in tariffs are included in loan documents without any agreement from the local government that is responsible for implementing the increases.

Contributions sought from water supply users are unaffordable for the poor: some projects are designed in such a way that part of the burden of loan repayment is passed on to the users through up-front cash and in-kind contributions. For the poorer residents in these towns, this contribution is unaffordable and means that they are unable to connect to the new water supplies, undermining the aim of delivering access to services for poorer communities. In some cases, residents were found to be mortgaging property and taking multiple loans in order to pay the up-front cash contribution. The time taken to raise these contributions also results in delays in project implementation. Since the loans have already been taken, these delays also eat into the time available for generating revenues for loan repayment.

Default in loan repayment, thus making the towns/cities even more unattractive and trapping them in a resource deficit spiral: end-borrowers are concerned about and in some cases struggling to repay loans. Under the Karnataka Urban Infrastructure Development Project, four towns which took loans under the project, in 1995, are falling behind on their repayments.

Table 3
Towns struggling to repay loans in Karnataka (crore rupees)

Town	Size of loan	Annual repayment	Repaid since 2001 (as of 2006)	% age repaid since 2001 (as of 2006)
Mysore	195.47	26.64	46.48	24%
Channapatna	17.09	2.68	0	0%
Ramnagara	44.88	6.48	0	0%
Tumkur	66.02	9.7	2.01	3%
Total	323.46	45.5	48.49	15%

If the scenario in one of the well-performing states, i.e., Karnataka is so bleak, one can only imagine the status of BIMAROU[11] states and for non-remunerative services like water, sanitation and public health, et al.

Way Forward: Putting the Last First, Equity Back in Focus

If these small towns are facing inter-generational development deficit, it is not without a reason. It is important to look beyond financial viability as the sole metric of success: the emergence of new poorer migrant populations laying claim to the city often through non-spectacular, incremental occupations of land, and the opening of small shops and industries. In many ways, these new forms vitalised urban life all over India and provided a material foundation to big cities. In recent years, these urban forms have been under attack from a coalition of neo-liberal reformers, right wing courts and elite civic groups.[12] Along with this, the land speculation and development of suburban enclaves by developers and finance companies are in full swing. We are entering an uncertain period of conflict in Indian cities. Spectacle has arrived; along with violence and the dream of 'making it' in the arena of global power. The terms of conflict are no longer between the past and the future, but among many endless presents. Some of the options could be:

- Setting, strengthening and engaging the city-level citizens' forums (which have proportionate representation of the poor and the people on the peripheries) and skills for informed debates;
- Transparency in contracts and loan agreements and throughout implementation of the project;
- A larger share of funds for the poor to be negotiated for (in all the three categories, i.e., authorised, unauthorised and resettled colonies) with the national and local governments;
- Greater local control/flexibility over use of loan/finance money advocated to ensure need-based intervention;
- Considering the information and power asymmetry, building capacities of the ULBs on a priority for informed dialogue between the state and the ULB and donors (if required); and finally
- Innovating an adequate instrument for financing capacity building: loans could be too expensive for a soft but essential task like training while grants could be too easy an instrument to win anyone's serious time and focus, hence the need to find/innovate the adequate modus.

In such a scenario, it becomes even more pertinent to make equitable resources available to the small towns and cities dotted across India and waiting to exhale.

Notes

1. The paper draws from the ADB Water Policy Implementation Review in 2005/6 for which the author was principal investigator for India and lead author for the international chapter on debt burden.
2. Ghosh, Jayati, Urban Challenge, *Frontline,* Volume 28, Issue 17, 13–26 August 2011.
3. WaterAid, Status of Drinking Water and Sanitation in India: Coverage, Financing and Emerging Concerns, 2005.
4. Ibid.
5. Ghosh, Jayati, *Urban Challenge*, Volume 28, Issue 17, 13–26 August 2011.
6. Ujjain, hosting the famous Kumbh Mela, used the religious event as the bargaining chip to negotiate a low/no-cost financing of the public health infrastructure (including water sanitation facilities' restoration and strengthening) for the city.
7. WaterAid, Water for All? Implementation of ADB's Water Policy in India: A Review, 2006.

8. Swain, Biraj and Wicken, James, The True Cost of Concessional Loans: On-lending Practices at the Asian Development Bank, WaterAid, 2007.
9. Ackerman, Andrew, Small towns lobby to restore access to low cost financing, *Wall Street Journal,* February 2011.
10. Al Jazeera, US small town files for bankruptcy, 2 August 2011.
11. Bihar, Madhya Pradesh, Assam, Rajasthan, Odisha, Uttar Pradesh.
12. Sunderam, Ravi, Technological Ruins, An essay from Nalini Rajan's edited volume Digitized Imagination, *The Hoot,* May 2011.

References

Ackerman, Andrew (2011) 'Small Towns Lobby to Restore Access to Low Cost Financing', *Wall Street Journal.* February.

Al Jazeera (2011) US Small Town Files for Bankruptcy. 2 August.

Dhar, Vijay and Nilanjana Sur (2009) Proceedings of the Workshop on, 'Alternative Sources of Financing Urban Development'. Ministry of Urban Development, in association with NIUA, New Delhi, 26 March.

Ghosh, Jayati (2011) 'Urban Challenge'. *Frontline.* Volume 28, Issue 17, 13–26 August.

Kundu, Amitabh (2000) 'Urban Development, Infrastructure Financing and Emerging System of Governance in India: A Perspective'. UNESCO.

McKinsey Global Institute (2011) *Urban World: Mapping the Economic Power of Cities.* June.

Ministry of Housing and Urban Poverty Alleviation, http://urbanindia. nic.in/as accessed on 5 August 2010.

Sunderam, Ravi (2009) 'Technological Ruins: A Short Essay'. In Nalini Rajan (ed.), *Digitized Imagination.* New Delhi: Routledge.

Swain, Biraj and James Wicken (2007) *The True Cost of Concessional Loans: On-lending Practices at the Asian Development Bank.* New Delhi: WaterAid.

WaterAid (2005) *Status of Drinking Water and Sanitation in India: Coverage, Financing and Emerging Concerns.* New Delhi: WaterAid India.

———. (2006) *Water for All? Implementation of ADB's Water Policy in India: A Review.* New Delhi: WaterAid India.

7

Industrial Dispersal and Clustering in India during Post-Reform Period and the Role of Small and Medium Towns

ABDUL SHABAN AND SANJUKTA SATTAR

The geography of industrial growth and development has historically been lopsided in India (Karan, 1964). The British Indian government encouraged development and localisation of industries (such as the textile industry) near the major port centres, and some basic industries (such as iron and steel industry in Chhotanagpur plateau area) were located near their sources of raw materials. In the post-independence period, attempts were made to disperse the basic and major industries for balanced regional development, and also small and medium-scale industries were encouraged in various ways to locate in remote and economically backward areas. Working Groups and Committees were set up by the Planning Commission to suggest measures for effective dispersal of the industries to small and medium towns, both to overcoming the regional inequality and to provide work opportunities to people in their own regions, and through this to overcome the issues arising out of migration of people to major cities. In this connection, the National Committee on Development of Backward Areas in its report on 'Industrial Dispersal' in 1980 suggested that planning for industrialisation and urbanisation has to go together (Planning Commission, 1980). Till 1991, the government efforts to disperse the industries to small and medium towns could not succeed to any significant scale due to inadequacy of infrastructure and human resources needed for industries in those towns and also due to the lack of local markets. The small and medium towns as such largely remain(ed) as functional hubs of administration ('tehsil' or district headquarters) or local *mandis* hardly offering any employment opportunities other than limited opportunities for rickshaw-pulling, head-loading, etc. After the liberalisation of economy in 1991, the government intervention with regard to directing industrial location to backward areas and small and medium towns took a backseat and market forces emerged as prominent factors to guide industrial location. In the above context, the present paper attempts: (a) to examine the changes in industrial policy in post-liberalisation phase vis-à-vis pre-liberalisation phase of Indian economy, (b) to find out the impact of these changes on location of industrial and commercial activities in India, and (c) to understand the role and position of small and medium towns with regard to dispersal of industrial and commercial activities and emerging industrial and service space economy of India. The organisation of the rest of paper is as follows. After briefly discussing the relationship between urbanisation and industrialisation in the following section, we highlight the major changes in industrial policy in India with respect to industrial location in pre- and post-economic reform periods. Besides, a brief overview of the pattern of industrial development in colonial period that necessitated the major policy initiatives in the post-independence period is also provided. To understand the role of urban systems in regional dispersal of industrial and commercial activities in the country, the next section maps the geographic locations of individual towns, which are then further correlated with geographic distribution of workers in subsequent sections. Then, using the data from Census of India (1991; 2001), the next section examines the growth of workers in major sectors and industries in different categories of towns, followed by the growth of enterprises[1] and workers in different states and districts of the country. This section also explores the existing geographical clustering of industries, and emerging industrial regions and belts. The last section concludes the paper.

Urbanisation and Industrialisation Linkage

Though not one-to-one, but a strong positive association exists between urbanisation and industrialisation. The location of an industry at a place often leads to concentration of population, and as such growth of a town. Many of the world cities and towns have evolved in this way. However, the industries can also be attracted by social overheads of a town, availability of labour, capital or existing market. In case of increasing economies of scale, this leads to further growth of the town and concentration of industries. The development and policy literature have very well acknowledged the potential existing in towns for initiating and accelerating economic growth. Francois Perroux mooted the idea of growth poles (Perroux, 1970; Monsted, 1974) which, in the context of space economy, would lead to 'urban-centred' growth (see Gore, 1984). Myrdal (1957) and Hirschman (1958) commended the role of urban centres in economic development; however, the dispute remains about the nature of impacts on the periphery – effectiveness of trickle-down/spread effect or polarisation/backwash. The new economic geography (Marshall, 1890; Krugman, 1991; Venables, 2005) and other literature, focusing on increasing economies of scale (Krugman, 1980; Gardiner, Martin and Tyler, 2011), free trade, and factor (land, labour) immobility, thick (labour) market effect (Helsley and Strange, 1990), and knowledge spillover (Henderson, 1988), productivity increase (Rosenthal and Strange, 2004) and strong inter-firm linkages, foretell the spatial clustering of economic activities. The diseconomies of scale can create spread effect but for market access and to get advantage of other associate benefits of agglomeration, the industries will remain within the periphery of the urban centres. Thus, the urbanisation at theoretical level is assumed to have strong linkage with industrialisation, and the spatial distribution of towns thus can strongly influence the spatial economy. Therefore, we also briefly examine the spatial system of towns and cities in the country, before examining the spatial patterns and dispersal of industrial and commercial activities.

Industrial Development in Colonial Period and Major Changes in Industrial Policy after Independence

The modern machine-based industrialisation in India started in mid-19th century with the location of cotton textile mills in major urban centres like Mumbai and Kolkata, and those slowly spread to Surat, Ahmedabad, and other centres. This was aided by the development of railway networks in the western region of India and specifically along the coasts during the 19th century. The modern industrialisation of India was started in different geographical settings and locations to that of earlier artisan-based industries, which flourished in India during medieval time. The new industries were located in port towns or in proximity to the raw material and transport routes (Planning Commission, 1980). The Kolkata region became the hub of jute textile industries, Mumbai emerged as a centre for cotton textile, while coal mining and iron smelting (due to location of raw materials) got concentrated along the West Bengal-Bihar (including present state of Jharkhand) border. Some semi-modern leather tanning industries were also located in and around Chennai. After World War I, the industrial pattern started changing and cotton textile industries started concentrating in Ahmedabad, the mining of other minerals grew in Central India and Assam, and thus the location of industries started shifting with its pattern changing. The period between the two World Wars saw emergence of some petroleum and engineering industries in Mumbai and Kolkata regions, while at the same time the traditional handicrafts and other industries suffered decline due to competition from modern industries, and decline in patronage due to decline of *zamindars* and *nawabs* (Planning Commission, 1980).

Table 1 shows the lopsided regional distribution of manufacturing workers in India from 1911 to 1971. The data show rise in the share of male worker in manufacturing sector in Maharashtra, Gujarat, Bengal and Tamil Nadu and the decline in the shares of many northern states (like Uttar Pradesh), most of which had flourishing artisan industry patronised by *zamindars* and *nawabs*. Also, together '... the cities of Bombay, Calcutta (including Howrah), Madras, Delhi, Ahmedabad and Bangalore accounted for 9.6 per cent of manufacturing employment in 1951 as against 4.7 per cent in 1921. The increase in concentration brings out one feature of the process of industrialisation, which is that growth generates further growth' (Planning Commission, 1980: para 2.4). It is also a fact that notwithstanding the industrial development in a few port-towns, India had limited modern industries prior to independence, and industrialisation prior to independence was in response to and shaped by colonial trade. Manufacturing was mainly located in Britain, and India was made a supplier of the needed raw materials and plantation agriculture like indigo (in Bihar) and tea (Assam, Kerala, and Karnataka). In other words, India largely became a supplier of raw materials to British industries and a market for their products, and this led to the squeezing of Indian economy and accumulation of capital in Britain (Dutt, 1940; Dutt, 1950). 'Had trading profits accumulated in domestic hands, there would

Table 1

State-wise distribution of male workers in household and non-household manufacturing (1911–1971) (percentages)

State	1911	1921	1931	1951	1961	1971
Andhra Pradesh	10. 6	9.4	9.8	9.0	9.3	8.7
Assam*	0.3	0.4	0.7	1.0	0.9	1.1
Bihar	5.7	5.6	5.4	3.3	6.7	5.4
Gujarat	5.0	5.3	5.2	5.8	5.6	6.4
Karnataka	4.2	4.4	4.1	4.7	5.2	5.6
Kerala	3.0	3.8	3.8	4.9	4.4	4.6
Madhya Pradesh	8.0	7.7	7.1	6.4	6.0	5.7
Maharashtra	9.7	9.6	10.2	12.9	12.9	14.3
Odisha	3.1	3.1	3.1	2.5	2.3	2.2
Punjab**	7.8	8.2	7.7	3.8	5.0	4.6
Rajasthan	6.1	5.6	5.7	4.0	2.9	3.3
Tamil Nadu	8.0	7.8	8.5	9.3	10.6	11.1
Uttar Pradesh	19.3	18.3	19.3	19.5	14.1	12.5
West Bengal	7.5	9.1	7.5	11.3	11.6	11.1
Delhi	0.3	0.5	0.6	1.0	1.4	1.9
Others	1.4	1.2	1.3	0.6	1.0	1.5

*Includes Mizoram, Meghalaya and Nagaland. **Includes Haryana.

Source: For 1911–1961, Census of India, 1961, Paper No. 1 of 1967. For 1971, Statistical Abstract India, 1977; as produced in Planning Commission 1980.

have been more domestic reinvestment and almost certainly more interest in domestic manufacturing' (Lewis, 1978: 22). Also, lack of agricultural modernisation had created a situation where it had become the only source for subsistence. The agricultural productivity was also not high to generate much demand for domestic industrial products (Lewis, 1978) over and above the supplies from Britain. The colonial preferences and biases in location of industries also greatly shaped the emergence of industrial regions of India after the post-independence period. The spatially concentrated development of banking (Rangarajan, 1982) and transport facilities (Raza and Aggarwal, 1986) further facilitated the spatial distortion in industrialisation in India and favoured Mumbai and Kolkata regions.

In independent India, the spatial and sectoral patterns of industrialisation have not only been produced by market forces but also been greatly shaped by government policies. The state and Central governments have used many policy instruments like subsidy, industrial licensing, infrastructure development and location of public industries in order to bring about the desirable changes offsetting the market advantages – for development of underdeveloped sectors and regions. Even after independence, there was continued decline of industries in northern Indian states and rise in the share of Maharashtra, Gujarat and southern states. Till 1971, the relative position of some of the states, like Bihar, remained unchanged (Table 1). Further, 'the share of the major industrial centres of Greater Bombay, Calcutta (including Howrah), Madras, Delhi, Ahmedabad and Bangalore in manufacturing employment rose from 9.6 per cent in 1951 to 12.9 per cent in 1971' (Planning Commission, 1980: para 2.16). Many steal and engineering industries were established in backward areas. Some secondary centres like Delhi, Kanpur, Bhopal, Bangalore, Nagpur, and Hyderabad also started emerging with industrial activity and thus setting in the process of industrial dispersal (Planning Commission, 1980). The National Committee on the Development of Backward Areas in 1980 pointed out: '... imbalances between the developed and backward states are not very substantial in household industries and small manufacturing establishments. However, the imbalances are very substantial for organised manufacturing' (Planning Commission, 1980: para 2.17). The government interventions towards dispersal of industries till 1970, were largely through location of public sector industries, but thereafter tools of concessional finance also started being used.

Industrial Policy and Spatial Dispersal of Industries

The policy instruments aimed towards dispersal of industries from major regions/towns and for developing economically backward areas have changed over the years in India. Three distinct phases in industrial policy of India can be indentified in the post-independence period. These are described as under:

The Phase of Deliberate Location of Public Sector Industries in Backward Areas

This policy instrument continued till 1970. In the initial phase of the period, the major aim was to reconstruct the Indian economy and speed up growth to overcome the relative backwardness which the country had suffered from the colonial rule. Therefore, the Industrial Policy Resolution 1948, the first industrial policy resolution of independent India, does not make any reference to development of backward areas or industrial dispersal. However, the Industrial Policy Resolution 1956 was a very elaborate one. This resolution made specific reference to the development of industries in backward areas and many heavy industries, and iron steel industries (like Bhilai Steel Plant in 1957, Durgapur Steel Plant in 1962) were set up in backward areas under the guidelines of this Industrial Policy Resolution. Third Five-Year Plan (1961–66) onwards, specific emphasis on dispersal of industries started being given (Planning Commission, 1980).

The Phase of Concessional Finance (1971 to 1991)

A number of financial instruments were used for industrial dispersal during this period. Some of the major instruments were the central investment subsidy scheme and the tax relief. Further, the government also attempted to develop infrastructure (transport, research and development facilities) in underdeveloped areas to attract the industries (Planning Commission, 1980). Many of these instruments even continue today: such as, infrastructure development schemes by Industrial Development Corporations at state levels, and concessional finance and tax rebates to industries in backward areas by central and state governments. The precursors of these types of instrument mainly were the Pande Working Group and Wanchoo Working Group set up by the National Development Council in 1969 to lay down criteria for identification of backward areas, and to deal with the incentives for starting industries in backward areas, respectively. Both the working groups submitted their reports in 1969. The Wanchoo Working Group, among others, recommended: (a) higher development rebates for industries in backward areas, (b) exemption from income and corporate tax for five years after development rebate, (c) exemption from import duties on machineries and components for industries set up in backward areas, (d) exemption from excise duties and sales tax on raw materials and finished products for five years, (e) transport subsidy up to 400 miles and beyond that transport cost for finished product be subsidised for backward areas in North-eastern states, and Andamans, and 50 per cent of the cost of transportation in case of backward areas in Jammu and Kashmir state (Planning Commission, 1980: para 4.7). This led to a major change in the way private sector was being attracted to the underdeveloped areas. Since 1971 onwards, the licensing policy was made more restrictive with respect to geographical location of industries. In 1971, the central government decided to restrict the licensing of some industries in certain radius of million-plus cities and cities with population above 5 lakh to 10 lakh (Planning Commission, 1980). The licensing policy was a negative instrument to stop location of industries in already developed/congested areas. However, it did not happen that the industries prohibited from major towns got located in less developed areas.

As the industrialisation in India was very polarised and clustered, the development of backward areas became an increasing concern of the government in 1970s and 1980s. The Census of India 1971 data reveals that about 21 per cent of workers in the non-household industries in the country were located in four metropolitan cities, Mumbai, Delhi, Kolkata, and Chennai (Table 2). Other five major cities, Ahmedabad, Bangalore, Kanpur, Pune and Hyderabad had about 7 per cent of the country's workers in this sector. The ratio of workers in non-household industries in the above metropolitan cities and the other five cities was much higher to other lower class towns and rural areas. To add to the financial incentives and accelerate the industrial dispersal, in 1988, the Government of India announced 'Growth Centre Scheme' for development of backward areas. Under this scheme, total 71 centres were proposed to be set up in the country. They were to be to be endowed with infrastructural facilities, regular and sufficient power and water supplies, telecommunication facilities, banking, and educational and research facilities (Planning Commission, 1980).

Table 2

Distribution of workers in non-household manufacturing, 1971

Towns	Share of employment in non-household manufacturing (%)	Number of workers in non-household manufacturing per 1,000 population
1. 4 metropolitan towns (Mumbai, Delhi, Kolkata and Chennai)	20.9	113
2. 5 major industrial towns (Ahmedabad, Bengaluru, Kanpur, Pune, Hyderabad)	6.6	93
3. All other towns above 50,000 population	27.5	64
4. All towns with population below 50,000	13.2	4
5. Rural areas	31.7	8
Total	100	20

Source: Census of India (1971), as presented in Planning Commission (1980).

The Phase of Neo-liberalisation and Increased Reliance on Market Forces

The neo-liberalisation of India since 1991 has led to many changes in the industrial policy. Whereas certain previous policy instruments for indus- trial dispersal have continued (like the transport subsidy to industries in backward areas), several others have been abandoned and new introduced. In sum, this phase has seen, (i) almost exit of the state from many types of industries through disinvestments, (ii) devolution of power to states for management of industrial policy, (iii) increased spatial competition among states through various policy incentives to attract the private (national and international) investments, (iv) significant structural changes in the economy from agricultural and industrial sectors to service and knowledge industry. To effect the neo-liberal changes, labour laws have been made flexible and deregulation of wages and pensions has been brought in.

The major highlight in this regard has been the Industrial Policy Statement, 1991, which advocated to, (a) abolish industrial licensing for most of the industries, (b) 51 per cent foreign direct investment (FDI) in some export-oriented industries, (c) referring sick public industries to Board for Industrial and Financial Reconstruction (BIFR), (d) shedding of excessive labour force in overstaffed public sector units, (e) privatisation of many public industries through disinvestment, and (f) closure or selling out of many sick industries (Ministry of Industry, n.d.). In fact, the main emphasis has now shifted to economic viability of industries rather than generation and promotion of development (in backward areas). Only at notional level, the rhetoric of balanced regional development has been emphasised. Although, in quite contradictory ways, the industrial policy also advocates: '... the spread of industrialisation to backward areas of the country to be actively promoted through appropriate incentives, institu- tions and infrastructural investments' (Ministry of Industry, n.d.). To further increase the competiveness of Indian export in international market and growth of economy, FDI up to 100 per cent has also been allowed under automatic route for most manufacturing activities in Special Economic Zones (SEZs) (Ministry of Commerce and Industry, 2003).

In sum, since 1991, the emphasis of the government has shifted from guaranteeing and providing employment to the people to create employ- ability, and this remains in consonance with reduction in size of the government through disinvestments and transferring many of its previous roles to the private sector. Though the central and state govern- ments continue to offer tax and subsidy incentives to the industries for their location in backward areas, (specifically, industrial development corporations in every state continue to develop industrial sites with infra- structure to pull private investments in backward areas) and encourage cluster development for economic efficiency (Government of India, 2006), the negative growth of formal sector workers continues, informalisation of economy is on rise and regional inequalities in income continue to sharpen (see Shaban, 2006).

Spatial System of Towns and Cities in India

As can be seen from Table 3 and Figure 1, the Indian urban system is top-heavy (higher concentration of population in a few million-plus cities), and is characterised by a regionally lopsided or clustered distribution of cities/towns. The concentration of population in major cities has further increased in post-liberalisation phase. For instance, the share of population of Class I towns in India increased from 56.7 per cent to 61.3 per cent in 2001. In contrast to this, the share of small and medium towns (towns with less than 100,000 of population) to the total towns in the country was 93 per cent in 1991 and 91.8 per cent in 2001. The major towns and cities in the country to a large extent are concentrated in Indo-Gangetic plains, western flank of Maharashtra and eastern and central Gujarat. Million-plus cities in rest of the regions show scattered

Table 3

Number of towns and population by size-class of towns in India, 1991 and 2001

Size class of towns (population)	No. of Towns		Town Share (%)		Population		Population Share (%)	
	1991	2001	1991	2001	1991	2001	1991	2001
VI (pop. <5,000)	289	232	6.34	5	1.0	0.80	50	3
V (5,000–9,999)	971	1,043	21.0	20.2	7.4	7.93	42	2.8
IV (10,000–19,999)	1,451	1,564	31.4	30.3	21.1	22.6	9.8	8.0
III (20,000–49,999)	1,161	1,396	25.2	27.0	35.3	42.3	16.3	15.0
II (50,000–99,999)	421	504	9.19	8	28.8	35.0	13.3	12.5
I (> 1,00,000)	322	422	7.08	2	122.3	172.4	56.7	61.3
Tier III (1,00,000–4,99,999)	272	353	5.96	8	50.5	68.0	23.4	24.2
Tier II (5,00,000–9,99,999)	32	42	0.70	8	22.1	31.1	10.2	11.0
Tier I (>10,00,000)	18	27	0.40	5	49.6	73.3	23.0	26.1
Total	4,615	5,161	100.0	100.0	215.7	281.1	100.0	100.0

Note: The classification of 1991 towns may differ from the reported towns in other publications. In this and other tables presented below, towns are identified with urban local bodies and only outgrowths are merged with their main towns. The number of towns reported in the Report on Indian Urban Infrastructure and Services, 2011, by the High Powered Expert Committee for Estimating the Investment Requirements for Urban Infrastructure Services, Ministry of Urban Development, Government of India, New Delhi, is 4,689. For the year 2001, the committee also reports 5,161 number of towns, but the population reported is 286.1 million. However, in the Town Directory, Census of India 2001 (data on CD), the total population of all the towns in 2001 is reported as 281.1 million.

Source: Census of India (1991; 2001).

distribution. Towns with a population of 10,000 to 19,999 are studded in Indo-Gangetic plains and in Tamil Nadu. The towns with population 20,000 to 49,999 are evenly distributed in a large part of the country. However, eastern Madhya Pradesh, Chhattisgarh, Odisha, western Jharkhand, central Andhra Pradesh, western Rajasthan and north-eastern states have lesser number of towns. This clustered spatial distribution and top-heavy nature of towns contribute to the polarised spatial economy (industrialisation) of India.

Industrial Concentration/Dispersal and Small and Medium Towns

The distribution of industrial and commercial sector workers in size-class of towns provides an insight into the dispersal/concentration of economic activities related to these sectors. The Primary Census Abstracts of Census of India (1991 and 2001) report the workers in household (HH) industries separately, but the workers in other secondary (mining and quarrying, non-household industries) and tertiary activities are clubbed together as 'other sectors'. Data presented in Tables 4 and 5 shows that together the secondary and tertiary sectors account for about 90 per cent of the total workers in Class I cities but the share gradually declines to below 75 per cent in most of the lower categories of towns. This shows that there exists a substantial share of workers in agriculture and allied sectors in the small and medium towns. Further, Table 4 shows that (a) although the share of HH industry workers at the all-India level has been around 3 and 5 per cent of the total urban workers in 1991 and 2005, respectively, the share has been substantial in lower class towns, (b) the share of HH industry workers has increased in all the urban centres and it has almost doubled in Class I towns during the period 1991–2001 (Table 4). The workers in HH industry per thousand of urban population have also substantially increased during the period. This indicates increased informalisation of urban employment/economy, and also that not much employment is being created in the organised sector (in the next section, we analyse the growth of informal/unorganised[2] sector enterprises vis-à-vis formal/organised sector in urban areas). The data related to 'other sectors' show that (a) where the share of workers in this group has marginally increased in most categories of towns during the period 1991–2001, it is largely stable in Tier I and II towns. The lower class of towns, on an average, have seen higher increase in the share of 'other workers' to their respective total workers. However, the Class I towns have higher number of other workers per thousand of population than other classes of towns, and this ratio rises with the size class of towns. There are indications of some dispersal of secondary and tertiary sector activities to the small and medium towns in the country as the changes in both the HH industry, and other sector workers per thousand of population have been higher in lower class towns. However, a large proportion of the increase may also be due to increased

Figure 1

Spatial distribution of towns in India by size-class, 2001

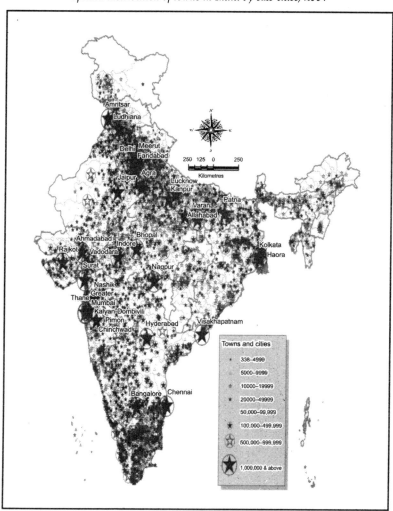

Source: Based on data from Census of India 2001.

informalisation and disguised unemployment in service sector of the economy of lower class towns.

Examining the shares of HH industry and 'other sector' workers in different classes of towns (without normalised by total population or number of workers in respective categories of towns), one finds that the share of Class I towns has substantially increased during 1991–2001. In

Table 4

The share (%) of household industry workers by size-class of towns, 1991 and 2001

Size class of towns (population)	Percentage to the total HH workers			Percentage to the total workers of the respective class of towns			HH industry workers/thousand of population of respective class of towns		
	1991	2001	Change	1991	2001	Change	1991	2001	Change
VI (pop. <5,000)	0.6	0.3	−0.3	3.5	5.0	1.5	11.4	17.6	6.2
V (5,000–9,999)	6.7	4.9	−1.9	6.1	8.2	2.1	18.1	29.1	11.0
IV (10,000–19,999)	13.5	11.3	−2.2	4.3	7.0	2.7	12.7	23.7	10.9
III (20,000–49,999)	22.5	18.8	−3.8	4.4	6.6	2.2	12.7	21.1	8.3
II (50,000–99,999)	14.3	13.9	−0.3	3.5	6.0	2.5	9.9	18.9	9.0
I (> 1,00,000)	42.5	50.9	8.4	2.3	4.4	2.1	6.9	14.0	7.1
Tier III (1,00,000–4,99,999)	22.2	21.9	−0.2	3.0	4.9	1.9	8.7	15.3	6.6
Tier II (5,00,000–9,99,999)	10.2	10.1	−0.1	3.2	4.9	1.7	9.2	15.4	6.3
Tier I (>10,00,000)	10.2	18.8	8.7	1.3	3.6	2.3	4.1	12.2	8.1
Total	100.00	100.00	—	3.1	5.2	2.1	9.2	16.9	7.6

Source: Census of India (1991; 2001).

Table 5

The share (%) of 'other workers' (non-household industries, mining & quarrying, and services) by size-class towns, 1991 2001

Size class of towns (population)	Percentage to the total workers in 'other sectors'			Percentage to the total workers of the respective class of towns			Workers in 'other sectors'/thousand of population of respective class of towns		
	1991	2001	Change	1991	2001	Change	1991	2001	Change
VI (pop. <5,000)	0.4	0.3	-0.1	71.8	77.2	5.4	222.1	270.8	48.7
V (5,000–9,999)	2.6	2.4	-0.2	63.9	67.0	3.1	183.7	237.4	53.7
IV (10,000–19,999)	7.6	6.8	-0.8	67.4	70.2	2.8	192.0	238.1	46.1
III (20,000–49,999)	13.7	13.3	-0.3	72.8	77.7	4.9	205.7	249.1	43.4
II (50,000–99,999)	12.6	11.9	-0.7	83.7	85.8	2.1	232.7	268.3	35.6
I (> 1,00,000)	63.2	65.3	2.2	93.6	93.4	-0.2	274.7	299.8	25.1
Tier III (1,00,000–4,99,999)	24.00	24.3	0.3	90.0	91.5	1.5	252.4	282.8	30.4
Tier II (5,00,000–9,99,999)	10.9	11.5	0.6	92.1	92.9	0.8	262.1	293.0	30.8
Tier I (>10,00,000)	28.3	29.5	1.2	97.6	95.2	-2.4	302.9	318.5	15.6
Total	100.0	100.0	0.0	85.3	87.3	2.0	246.4	281.4	35.1

Note: 'Other workers' comprise workers other than cultivators, agricultural labourers, and those engaged in household industry. Source: Census of India (1991; 2001).

Class I towns, the shares of HH industry workers and 'other workers' increased from 42.5 per cent to 50.9 per, and from 63.2 per cent to 65.3 per cent, respectively, during the period, while in rest of the classes of towns the shares have declined (see Tables 4 and 5; one must also keep in mind the number of Class I towns has also risen during the period from 322 to 422). This has also been due to a very high concentration of population in Class I towns: Class I towns formed only 8.3 per cent of the total towns in the country in 2001 but they constituted 61.3 per cent of the total urban population. This shows a very heavy concentration of industrial and service sector workers in major cities, and dispersal taking place only in terms of narrowing gaps between Class I towns and small and medium towns in ratio of workers per thousand of population in these sectors, not at the level of absolute concentration (which has risen in Class I towns in 2001 as compared to 1991).

Urban Economic Enterprises and their Geographic Clustering

There has been a significant increase in the number of establishments/enterprises in the country during 1990–2005. The total number of economic enterprises in the country increased from about 24.22 million in 1990 to 41.83 million in 2005, experiencing an annual compound growth rate (ACGR) of 3.98 per cent (Table 6). The growth rate of number of workers (employed in these enterprises) has relatively been lower than the growth rate in number of enterprises: the number of workers increased from about 77.14 million in 1990 to 100.90 million in 2005, with an ACGR of 1.94 per cent (Table 7).

Both the shares of enterprises and the workers have shifted in favour of rural areas in 2005 in comparison to 1990. At all-India level, the share of rural enterprises has increased from 59.9 per cent in 1990 to 61.1 per cent in 2005, while rural share of workers increased from 47.3 per cent in 1990 to 51.6 per cent in 2005. This is also significant due to the fact that some rural areas in 1990 have been classified as urban in 2001; in absence of that, the shares of the rural enterprises and workers would have been even higher. Rural areas experienced a decline in the share of enterprises related to mining and quarrying (from 85.1% to the total mining and quarrying enterprises in the country in 1990 to 71.4% in 2005), manufacturing (64.8% to 62.0%), and construction (55.9% to 53.4%). However, the rural share and number of workers in all these sectors have considerably increased in 2005 in comparison to 1990. Overall, the rural enterprises (ACGR 4.12% in rural areas and 3.77% in urban areas) and workers (2.57% and 1.32%) have grown higher than that of urban enterprises and workers. This shows that there has been a process of industrial dispersal from urban to rural areas during the period. The reasons for this may be from increasing factor cost in urban areas to regulation by the governments restricting and prohibiting the location of certain industries in urban centres.

Table 6

Growth of industrial enterprises by sector at all-India level, 1991 and 2005

Sectors	1990			2005			Annual compound growth rate (%) of enterprises 1990–2005		
	Rural-urban distribution of enterprise (%)		Total number of enterprises	Rural-urban distribution of enterprise (%)		Total number of enterprises			
	Rural	Urban		Rural	Urban		Rural	Urban	Total
Agriculture and allied activities	90.4	9.6	24,46,492	93.9	6.1	6,07,99,83	7.01	3.31	6.72
Mining and quarrying	85.1	14.9	48,746	71.4	28.6	84,805	2.75	8.96	4.03
Manufacturing	64.8	35.2	51,79,272	62.0	38.0	83,22,205	3.12	4.01	3.45
Electricity, gas and water supply	64.4	35.6	44,619	65.3	34.7	65,194	2.85	2.55	2.75
Construction	55.9	44.1	2,24,255	53.4	46.6	3,20,333	2.25	2.98	2.58
Wholesale trade, retail trade, restaurant and hotels	50.8	49.2	95,19,586	51.0	49.0	1,80,13,899	4.69	4.63	4.66
Transport, storage and communication	46.7	53.3	7,68,129	52.5	47.5	22,09,944	8.74	6.96	7.84
Financing, insurance, real estate and business services	33.2	66.8	4,35,421	40.8	59.2	13,07,204	9.77	7.24	8.17
Others	61.4	38.6	55,50,270	64.7	35.3	54,23,422	0.21	−0.80	−0.17
Total	59.9	40.1	2,42,16,790	61.1	38.9	4,18,26,989	4.12	3.77	3.98

Source: Computed using unit level data of Economic Census 1990 and 2005, obtained from Ministry of Statistics and Programme Implementation (MOSPI), New Delhi, on CD.

Table 7

Growth of total workers in industrial enterprises by sector at all-India level, 1990, 2005

Sectors	1990			2005			Annual compound growth rate (%) of workers 1990–2005		
	Rural-urban distribution of workers		Total number of workers	Rural-urban distribution of workers		Total number of workers			
	Rural	Urban		Rural	Urban		Rural	Urban	Total
Agriculture and allied activities	84.2	15.8	90,61,910	93.2	6.8	1,09,13,601	2.08	-4.62	1.34
Mining and quarrying	65.7	34.3	4,51,373	69.5	30.5	5,81,830	2.24	0.97	1.83
Manufacturing	47.6	52.4	2,29,56,105	53.1	46.9	25,481,715	1.53	-0.04	0.75
Electricity, gas and water supply	37.6	62.4	3,98,791	43.1	56.9	4,37,456	1.65	0.00	0.66
Construction	35.5	64.5	6,69,124	46.9	53.1	7,44,288	2.80	-0.63	0.76
Wholesale trade, retail trade, restaurant and hotels	40.8	59.2	1,76,88,210	43.5	56.5	3,29,41,362	5.02	4.19	4.54
Transport, storage and communication	27.2	72.8	27,27,748	41.5	58.5	43,92,734	6.64	1.85	3.46
Financing, insurance, real estate and business services	18.9	81.1	24,52,367	27.9	72.1	44,21,211	7.25	3.43	4.30
Others	42.6	57.4	2,07,33,776	47.7	52.3	2,09,89,924	0.90	-0.58	0.09
Total	47.3	52.7	7,71,39,404	51.6	48.4	10,09,04,121	2.57	1.32	1.94

Source: Computed using unit level data of Economic Census 1990 and 2005, obtained from Ministry of Statistics and Programme Implementation (MOSPI), New Delhi, on CD.

The growth of enterprises, specifically in the informal sector, during 1990–2005, has been higher than workers in both the rural and urban areas, indicating that enterprises are becoming less labour-intensive (Table 8). The size-class wise growth of urban enterprises shows some interesting trends. In the post-liberalisation phase, the growth of enterprises has become bi-polar. The growth rate has been higher of the enterprises employing either less than nine workers, i.e., informal sector enterprises, or of the enterprises employing between 101–500 workers. The ACGR of enterprises employing less than six workers and six to nine workers has been 3.98 per cent and 3.74 per cent, respectively, while the ACGR of workers in these size-class of industries has been 3.85 per cent and 3.92 per cent, respectively. The ACGRs of enterprises and workers employing 101–500 workers have been 3.12 per cent and 2.97 per cent, respectively, during the period 1990–2005. The number of enterprises and workers in size-class of enterprises employing 51–100 workers have experienced positive but low ACGRs. The other size-class of enterprises (in terms of their number and workers employed in) have experienced negative growth rates. This shows that both the consolidation of formal enterprises (employing more than nine workers) and in-formalisation of urban economy in general are underway in India. The subcontracting and breaking away of integrated formal industries on the line of process and manufacturing stage (vertical split/disintegration) is also spurring the growth of informal sector enterprises. The number of workers is also showing almost similar pattern of growth as enterprises (Table 9). At the aggregate level, the workers have only risen in enterprises employing 50 to 500 workers, or in the informal enterprises. In fact, whereas the decline in the workers of enterprises employing above 1,000 workers has been at –9.54 per cent per annum, the workers in the informal sector have increased at about 4 per cent per annum.

Dispersal of Industries: Evidence from State Level Data

We now attempt to examine the industrial dispersal of economic activities at the state and district levels. As the income data from different sectors of the economy is available for rural and urban areas, we rely on the share of workers employed in each of the region (rural and urban). If the share of workers of a sector in a state/district has increased in 2005 in urban areas in comparison to that of 1990, we call this concentration of industries related to that sector in urban centres and vice-versa. Notwithstanding the incorporation of rural areas into urban centres (through Census reclassification), the data at the state level shows that there has been a weak but steady trend across the states of industrial dispersal (Table 10). However, one must keep in mind that there has already been a very high concentration of economic activities in the large urban centres in the country and this dispersal is expected due to increasing congestion in these urban centres and also restrictive policies by the governments for

Table 8

Annual compound growth rate (%) of total urban enterprises by different size of workers, 1990, 2005

Sectors	Size-class of enterprises (employing number of workers)										Total
	<6	6–9	10–20	21–30	31–40	41–50	51–100	101–500	501–1,000	1,001 & above	
Agriculture and allied activities	3.42	1.52	-3.29	-1.41	0.83	-1.46	3.75	10.82	-6.34	-13.40	3.31
Mining and quarrying	9.75	8.57	2.53	-0.26	-0.48	-1.15	3.62	3.44	1.70	-2.41	8.96
Manufacturing	4.65	2.51	-6.14	-4.09	-2.20	-1.14	1.54	3.84	-1.84	-4.73	4.01
Electricity, gas and water supply	3.02	4.64	-0.52	0.14	0.02	-0.47	1.13	1.90	-2.56	-3.37	2.55
Construction	2.95	7.04	-4.12	-3.41	0.08	-0.98	1.42	6.76	0.00	0.00	2.98
Wholesale trade, retail trade, restaurant and hotels	4.68	4.81	-1.42	1.40	3.33	2.63	7.13	11.01	-0.27	-3.72	4.63
Transport, storage and communication	7.31	4.71	-2.55	-1.81	-1.24	-2.13	0.00	2.34	-1.58	-3.04	6.96
Financing, insurance, real estate and business services	8.08	7.36	-0.28	-1.10	-2.14	-1.99	-1.06	3.82	3.82	2.61	7.24
Others	-1.06	3.00	-2.06	-0.65	-0.46	-0.68	-0.21	0.56	-1.34	-3.02	-0.80
Total	3.98	3.74	-2.99	-1.40	-0.70	-0.73	0.82	3.12	-1.07	-3.45	3.77

Source: Computed using unit level data of Economic Census 1990 and 2005, obtained from Ministry of Statistics and Programme Implementation (MOSPI), New Delhi, on CD.

Table 9

Compound annual growth rate (%) of workers employed in urban enterprises with different size of workers, 1990, 2005

Sectors	Size-class of enterprises (employing number of workers)										Total
	<6	6–9	10–20	21–30	31–40	41–50	51–100	101–500	501–1,000	1,001 & above	
Agriculture and allied activities	3.07	1.61	-3.00	-1.36	0.89	-1.23	4.35	9.44	-7.37	-31.80	-4.62
Mining and quarrying	9.62	8.85	2.62	-0.32	-0.37	-1.05	3.68	3.95	2.09	-4.69	0.97
Manufacturing	3.85	2.61	-5.87	-3.89	-2.06	-0.98	1.96	3.68	-1.88	-10.15	-0.04
Electricity, gas and water supply	3.31	4.94	-0.25	0.14	0.06	-0.43	1.33	2.05	-2.39	-6.17	0.00
Construction	3.82	7.29	-3.96	-3.24	0.17	-0.93	1.80	6.20	1.98	-21.48	-0.63
Wholesale trade, retail trade, restaurant and hotels	4.80	4.97	-1.15	1.49	3.29	2.76	7.77	10.47	-0.62	-15.60	4.19
Transport, storage and communication	6.98	4.92	-2.48	-1.79	-1.26	-2.10	0.11	2.07	-1.55	-10.64	1.85
Financing, insurance, real estate and business services	7.92	7.59	-0.21	-1.11	-2.14	-1.92	-0.87	4.37	3.81	-2.58	3.43
Others	-0.92	3.31	-1.79	-0.62	-0.46	-0.68	-0.10	0.63	-1.48	-4.48	-0.58
Total	3.85	3.92	-2.75	-1.33	-0.68	-0.67	1.07	2.97	-1.14	-9.54	1.32

Source: Computed using unit level data of Economic Census 1990 and 2005, obtained from Ministry of Statistics and Programme Implementation (MOSPI), New Delhi, on CD.

industrial (particularly polluting industries) location. In 1991, the population living in urban centres in the country was 25.7 per cent, but the urban centres had 52.7 per cent of the total workers employed in economic establishments. In 2001, although the share of urban population had increased to 27.8 per cent, yet the share of workers in economic establishments in the urban centres to the total workers in all the economic establishments had declined to 48.4 per cent. At the all-India level, the decline in the share of workers in 2005 in comparison to 1990 has been –5.5 per cent in manufacturing, –5.7 per cent in the secondary sector (includes mining and quarrying, manufacturing, construction, electricity, gas and water supply), and –4.1 per cent in the tertiary sector or services. The major states which have experienced above 5 per cent decline in the share of workers in the manufacturing sector in the urban areas during the period are Punjab (–6.5%), Haryana (–11.6%), Uttar Pradesh (including Uttarakhand) (–12.5%), Bihar (including Jharkhand) (–7.3%), West Bengal (–5.6%), Maharashtra (–5.8%), Karnataka (–24.9%), Kerala (–5.3%). Thus, we see that highest dispersal has taken place in Karnataka, followed by Uttar Pradesh (including Uttarakhand), and Haryana. However, the share of urban centres may also decline due to industrial closure in urban centres and this is well proven by Table 10. The Table shows that workers in the manufacturing sector have experienced negative growth rate in major states like Karnataka, Uttar Pradesh, Bihar, Maharashtra, as well as at all-India level. This means that, among major states, meaningful dispersal of manufacturing sector from urban to rural centres has taken place only in Punjab, Haryana, West Bengal, and Kerala.

Manufacturing constitutes a major share of the secondary sector, which also includes mining and quarrying, construction, and gas and water supply. At all-India level, the urban share of secondary sector workers in 2005 was 46.9 per cent, the same as for the manufacturing sector. In Uttar Pradesh and Bihar, the share of secondary sector is higher than the manufacturing sector (which experienced decline during the period), showing that the rest of the activities in the secondary sector have been more than compensating the employment loss due to the decline of employment in manufacturing enterprises in these states. However, in Punjab and Maharashtra, the deficit remains and other sectors have not been able to compensate the losses of employment in manufacturing sector (Table 10). In case of Karnataka, besides manufacturing, the workers in other sub-sectors have also declined over the period, while the share of secondary sector has increased in Net State Domestic Product (NSDP) of the state from about ₹ 5,684 crore in 1990–91 to about ₹ 12,072 crore in 2004–05 at 1993–94 prices, indicating overall consolidation of secondary sector in the state during the period and replacement of labour by technology/machines, or simply, jobless growth in the sector.

There is relatively a higher concentration of service sector in urban centres than the secondary sector at the all-India level and states/UTs, except in Delhi, Mizoram and Gujarat (see Table 10). At all-India level, as against 46.9 per cent of the secondary sector workers to the total secondary sector workers, 56.3 per cent of the workers in tertiary sectors are located in urban centres. The dispersal of service sector employment to the rural areas has although taken place in majority of the states (except in Delhi, Sikkim, Arunachal Pradesh, Gujarat and Andhra Pradesh), the pace of dispersal has been slower (in terms of decline in the urban share). Further, except Bihar, in none of the states/UTs, the service sector workers have experienced negative growth rate (Table 11). In most of the states/UTs and at all-India level, the ACGR of number of workers in services has been much higher than the ACGR in secondary sector, and as such the service sector has been the main driver of the economy and employment in the post-liberalisation phase in India. The total number of workers in all the economic enterprises has experienced negative growth rates in Bihar, Karnataka, Kerala and Andaman and Nicobar Islands. This shows that the overall employment situation in enterprises in these states worsened during the period.

Shifting Geographies of Employment and Industrialisation

Below we briefly examine the changes and shifts that have taken place in India at the district level in terms of employment in economic establishments during 1990–2005. For this, we have plotted the relevant data on maps. Based on the clustering of workers, we can identify 13 major industrial and commercial clusters/regions/belts in the country (see Table 12 and Figure 2). The industrial regions like those around Delhi, Mumbai, Kolkata, Chennai, have persisted historically, while others have experienced significant growth and spread after independence. The Alwar-Jaipur-Ajmer industrial belt, and Hyderabad-Karimnagar-Karnool region, Jalpaiguri-Darjeeling-Cooch Behar belt and coastal Andhra Pradesh belt have taken their shape in a significant manner after 1990. The industrial corridors along Mumbai-Nashik-Nagpur-Bilaspur-Kharagpur railway line and National Highway 3 (Mumbai to Nashik) and 6 (Surat to Howrah) are taking shape. Further, as shown in Figure 1, there has been significant spread of industrial and commercial activities in and around the major industrial regions/belts. However, Madhya Pradesh, Chhattisgarh, Uttar Pradesh, Bihar, northern Odisha, western Jharkhand, Vidarbha and Marathwada regions of Maharashtra, southern Rajasthan, norther-eastern Karnataka, Uttarakhand, Himachal Pradesh, Jammu and Kashmir and north-eastern states largely remain untouched from industrial and commercial activities in the post-liberalisation phase.

As is evident from Figure 2, the trickle-down or dispersal of industrial and commercial activities has largely been in the periphery of the

Table 10

Share of urban workers to the total workers in respective sectors of enterprises

States	Urban					Total (rural+urban)				
	Agriculture and allied activities	Manufacturing	Secondary sector	Tertiary sector	Total urban	Agriculture and allied	Manufacturing	Secondary sector	Tertiary Sector	Total
Jammu & Kashmir	7.98	4.06	4.24	1.34	1.84	3.41	0.88	1.62	2.75	2.50
Himachal Pradesh	-0.08	1.59	1.76	2.59	2.28	8.49	2.29	2.52	3.03	3.06
Punjab	-3.46	-2.44	1.44	1.47	1.43	-1.52	-2.14	1.63	1.54	1.51
Chandigarh	1.75	1.21	1.23	2.79	2.26	10.12	2.80	2.76	3.71	3.67
Haryana	-3.06	4.15	4.03	4.05	4.00	-3.68	3.96	3.82	4.00	3.89
Delhi	5.25	2.46	2.27	3.43	3.13	7.16	3.07	2.81	3.57	3.64
Rajasthan	0.47	-3.56	-3.38	0.13	-0.99	6.29	-1.91	-1.79	1.32	0.50
Uttar Pradesh, including Uttarakhand	-2.53	-2.74	-2.54	-1.01	-1.35	-2.03	-1.26	-1.03	0.26	-0.14
Bihar, including Jharkhand	12.79	-1.57	-5.05	3.51	2.60	5.30	-2.20	-0.23	3.02	2.68
Sikkim	1.16	3.18	3.65	2.31	2.46	-6.01	-3.50	0.57	1.49	1.07
Arunachal Pradesh	4.02	1.05	0.60	1.57	1.55	2.95	-0.16	0.00	2.33	2.16
Nagaland	5.21	1.69	1.98	2.72	2.67	2.63	1.41	1.73	3.29	2.92
Manipur										
Mizoram	13.87	3.30	0.93	2.03	2.58	14.73	3.74	1.81	2.05	2.81

Cont'd...

...Cont'd

Tripura	6.25	1.45	1.51	2.71	2.57	1.31	0.76	1.05	3.61	2.92
Meghalaya	2.00	1.06	1.49	1.57	1.56	1.48	3.53	2.92	2.54	2.57
Assam	0.98	1.53	0.47	2.16	1.84	-5.54	2.24	1.48	2.88	1.97
West Bengal	-2.77	1.13	1.02	1.30	1.17	1.11	2.07	1.97	2.32	2.14
Odisha	3.19	0.65	1.04	0.87	0.95	6.32	2.09	2.29	2.20	2.51
Madhya Pradesh, including Chhattisgarh	2.38	2.05	1.64	2.60	2.35	1.76	1.76	1.60	3.37	2.69
Gujarat	5.52	2.55	2.60	4.55	3.84	4.38	1.20	1.24	3.98	3.26
Daman & Diu	-4.82	0.87	0.75	2.04	0.86	-2.88	14.93	14.10	4.60	8.24
D & N Haveli	18.83	18.32	17.96	11.11	14.54	0.60	14.21	13.93	7.57	11.56
Maharashtra	-0.28	-1.22	-1.13	1.67	0.85	4.95	-0.61	-0.57	2.26	1.68
Andhra Pradesh	5.67	2.42	2.91	5.67	5.00	6.97	1.14	1.48	4.91	4.20
Karnataka	-21.76	-6.25	-6.69	-1.41	-4.42	-5.62	-2.96	-3.31	-0.46	-2.24
Goa	-7.02	1.44	1.37	-0.05	0.09	-3.71	0.07	0.09	0.56	0.29
Lakshadweep	—	—	—	—	—	—	—	—	—	—
Kerala	7.30	0.76	0.69	2.15	2.03	-5.72	1.85	1.80	2.89	-0.34
Tamil Nadu	4.78	1.75	1.98	3.87	3.26	12.19	2.07	2.25	3.50	3.88
Puducherry	-0.33	-0.08	-0.17	3.79	2.75	3.33	2.92	2.74	3.84	3.51
A & N Islands	-1.50	-5.11	-4.12	2.80	1.47	-33.49	-6.60	-4.69	2.77	-10.31
All-India	-4.62	-0.04	-0.05	2.12	1.32	1.34	0.75	0.77	2.63	1.94

Source: Computed using unit level data of Economic Census 1990 and 2005, obtained from Ministry of Statistics and Programme Implementation (MOSPI), New Delhi, on CD.

Table 11

Annual compound growth rate (%) of workers in various sectors by state/UTs, 1990–2005

States	Urban					Total (rural+urban)				
	Agriculture and allied activities	Manufacturing	Secondary sector	Tertiary sector	Total	Agriculture and allied	Manufacturing	Secondary sector	Tertiary Sector	Total
Jammu & Kashmir	—	—	—	—	—	3.41	0.88	1.62	2.75	2.50
Himachal Pradesh	7.98	4.06	4.24	1.34	1.84	8.49	2.29	2.52	3.03	3.06
Punjab	-0.08	1.59	1.76	2.59	2.28	-1.52	-2.14	1.63	1.54	1.51
Chandigarh	-3.46	-2.44	1.44	1.47	1.43	10.12	2.80	2.76	3.71	3.67
Haryana	1.75	1.21	1.23	2.79	2.26	-3.68	3.96	3.82	4.00	3.89
Delhi	-3.06	4.15	4.03	4.05	4.00	7.16	3.07	2.81	3.57	3.64
Rajasthan	5.25	2.46	2.27	3.43	3.13	6.29	-1.91	-1.79	1.32	0.50
Uttar Pradesh, including Uttarakhand	0.47	-3.56	-3.38	0.13	-0.99	-2.03	-1.26	-1.03	0.26	-0.14
Bihar, including Jharkhand	-2.53	-2.74	-2.54	-1.01	-1.35	5.30	-2.20	-0.23	3.02	2.68
Sikkim	12.79	-1.57	-5.05	3.51	2.60	-6.01	-3.50	0.57	1.49	1.07
Arunachal Pradesh	1.16	3.18	3.65	2.31	2.46	2.95	-0.16	0.00	2.33	2.16
Nagaland	4.02	1.05	0.60	1.57	1.55	2.63	1.41	1.73	3.29	2.92
Manipur	5.21	1.69	1.98	2.72	2.67	14.73	3.74	1.81	2.05	2.81
Mizoram	13.87	3.30	0.93	2.03	2.58	1.31	0.76	1.05	3.61	2.92
Tripura	6.25	1.45	1.51	2.71	2.57					

Cont'd....

...Cont'd

Meghalaya	2.00	1.06	1.49	1.57	1.56	1.48	3.53	2.92	2.54	2.57
Assam	0.98	1.53	0.47	2.16	1.84	-5.54	2.24	1.48	2.88	1.97
West Bengal	-2.77	1.13	1.02	1.30	1.17	1.11	2.07	1.97	2.32	2.14
Odisha	3.19	0.65	1.04	0.87	0.95	6.32	2.09	2.29	2.20	2.51
Madhya Pradesh, including Chhattisgarh	2.38	2.05	1.64	2.60	2.35	1.76	1.76	1.60	3.37	2.69
Gujarat	5.52	2.55	2.60	4.55	3.84	4.38	1.20	1.24	3.98	3.26
Daman & Diu	-4.82	0.87	0.75	2.04	0.86	-2.88	14.93	14.10	4.60	8.24
D & N Haveli	18.83	18.32	17.96	11.11	14.54	0.60	14.21	13.93	7.57	11.56
Maharashtra	-0.28	-1.22	-1.13	1.67	0.85	4.95	-0.61	-0.57	2.26	1.68
Andhra Pradesh	5.67	2.42	2.91	5.67	5.00	6.97	1.14	1.48	4.91	4.20
Karnataka	-21.76	-6.25	-6.69	-1.41	-4.42	-5.62	-2.96	-3.31	-0.46	-2.24
Goa	-7.02	1.44	1.37	-0.05	0.09	-3.71	0.07	0.09	0.56	0.29
Lakshadweep	—	—	—	—	—	—	—	—	—	—
Kerala	7.30	0.76	0.69	2.15	2.03	-5.72	1.85	1.80	2.89	-0.34
Tamil Nadu	4.78	1.75	1.98	3.87	3.26	12.19	2.07	2.25	3.50	3.88
Puducherry	-0.33	-0.08	-0.17	3.79	2.75	3.33	2.92	2.74	3.84	3.51
A & N Islands	-1.50	-5.11	-4.12	2.80	1.47	-33.49	-6.60	-4.69	2.77	-10.31
All-India	-4.62	-0.04	-0.05	2.12	1.32	1.34	0.75	0.77	2.63	1.94

Source: Computed using unit level data of Economic Census 1990 and 2005, obtained from Ministry of Statistics and Programme Implementation (MOSPI), New Delhi, on CD.

major industrial regions. The pivots of these industrial regions remain the major urban centres. However, it does not apply in some states. The major towns of Uttar Pradesh, Bihar and Madhya Pradesh are examples in this regard. Patna, Varanasi, Allahabad, Lucknow, Kanpur, Indore, Bhopal, etc., have not created the expected levels of industrial and commercial activities in their regions. Thus, the level of urbanisation and major urban centres alone cannot be considered as sufficient conditions for development of industrial and commercial activities. It is also important to note that industrial and commercial activities in coastal Andhra Pradesh, Tamil Nadu and Kerala are largely led by the small and medium towns, or Tier 3 level cities.

The geographical distribution of workers in urban enterprises is also largely showing a similar pattern as the distribution of total workers (Figure 3). The figure also shows that workers in economic enterprises have grown significantly during the period in urban centres and have also experienced geographical spread, but this spread is mainly confined to the urban centres of surrounding districts of major urban centres. The manufacturing activities in urban centres are also concentrated only in a few regions, and form the core of the many industrial and commercial regions of the country mentioned above. There have been growths in the number of workers in manufacturing activities in majority of the clusters, but the geographical spread is again largely confined to the immediate vicinity (Figure 4).

There has been considerable informalisation of the workforce in urban areas across the country. The share of workers in informal sector enterprises in the country was 47.2 per cent in 1990, and has increased to 66.7 per cent in 2005, with an ACGR of about 4 per cent (Table 13). As against this rapid growth of the informal sector, the formal or organised sector has experienced negative growth rate (ACGR –2.0%). There are considerable number of workers in urban areas employed in enterprises related to agriculture and allied sectors, and this sector has experienced the highest decline (ACGR –16.3%). The decline is expected as urban centres evolve over the time: workers in agricultural and allied sectors, often in newly incorporated urban centres, move to secondary and tertiary sector activities both due to higher productivity in latter activities and also the land use changes. In the formal sector of the economy, only wholesale, retail, restaurant and hotels, financing, insurance, real estate and business services have experienced positive growth rates. Along with increased intensification of mining and quarrying activities by national and transnational companies in the post-liberalisation phase, many of the settlements based on mining activities have grown over the years and have been incorporated as urban centres and that is why the growth rate of mining workers has been higher during the period. Among the informal sector, it has been the service sector that has grown quite substantially in

Table 12

Major industrial regions/belts of India

	Region	Includes districts of	Core centre(s) based on size of employment
1.	Amritsar-Chandigarh belt	Amritsar, Jalandhar, Ludhiana, Chandigarh	Ludhiana
2.	Delhi-Agra-Moradabad region	Agra, Mathura, Faridabad, Gurgaon, Gautam Buddha Nagar, Delhi, Meerut, Muzaffar Nagar, Moradabad	Delhi
3.	Kolkata-Howrah-Kharagpur region	Kolkata, Howrah, Hoogli, Burdhaman, Medinipur East, Medinipur West, Bankura, South 24 Pargana, North 24 Pargana	Kolkata
4.	Dhanbad-Bankura region	Dhanbad, Bankura, Purulia, Ranchi	Dhanbad
5.	Pune-Mumbai-Ahmedabad belt	Mumbai, Pune, Raigarh, Thane, Nashik, Vapi, Surat, Anand, Ahmedabad	Mumbai, Surat, Ahmedabad
6.	Thiruvananthapuram-Thrissur-Kozhikode belt	Kolhapur-Belgaum-Dharwad	Kolhapur, Bharwad
7.	Bengaluru-Mysore- Chennai belt	Bengaluru, Mysore, North Arcot, South Arcot, Chennai, Chengai Anna	Chennai, Bengaluru, Mysore
8.	Madurai-Coimbatore-Salem-Tiruchirappalli region	Coimbatore, Madurai, Salem, Tiruchirappalli	Coimbatore, Madurai
9.	Thiruvananthapuram-Thrissur-Kozhikode belt	Thiruvananthapuram, Alappuzha, Ernakulam, Thrissur, Malappuram, Kozhikode	Thiruvananthapuram, Kozhikode

Cont'd...

...Cont'd

	Major regions emerging after 1990	
10. Jaipur-Alwar-Ajmer belt	Alwar, Jaipur and Ajmer	Jaipur
11. Hyderabad-Karimnagar-Karnool region	Hyderabad, Mehbubnagar, Medak, Karim Nagar, Warangal, Kurnool, and Nalgonda	Hyderabad
12. Coastal Andhra Pradesh belt	Visakhapatnam, East Godawari, West Godawari, Yanam, Krishna, and Gantur	Visakhapatnam
13. Jalpaiguri-Darjeeling-Cooch Behar belt	Jalpaiguri-Darjeeling-Cooch Behar	Jalpaiguri, Darjeeling

Source: Based on Figure 2.

Figure 2

Concentration of workers in economic establishments and industrial regions in India, 1990 and 2005

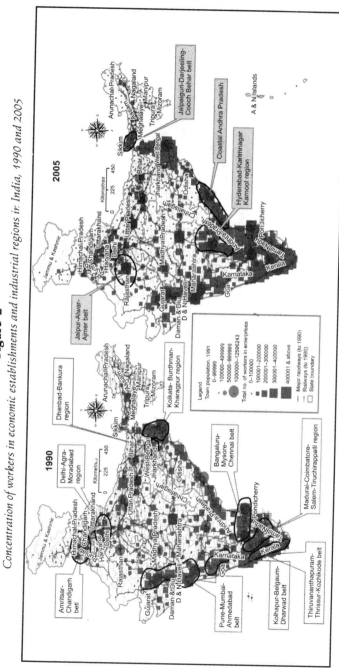

Source: Based on unit level data of Economic Census 1990 and 2005, obtained from Ministry of Statistics and Programme Implementation (MOSPI), New Delhi, on CD.

Figure 3

Distribution of total workers in urban enterprises by districts, 1990 and 2005

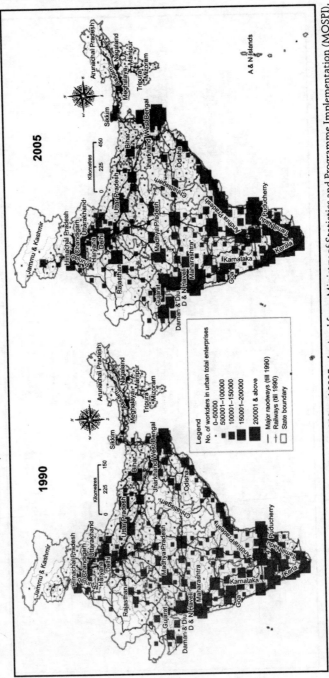

Source: Based on unit level data of Economic Census 1990 and 2005, obtained from Ministry of Statistics and Programme Implementation (MOSPI), New Delhi, on CD.

Figure 4

Distribution of number of workers in manufacturing enterprises in urban centres by districts, 1990 and 2005

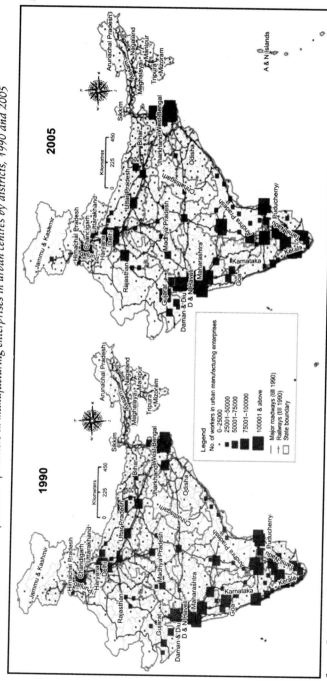

Source: Based on unit level data of Economic Census 1990 and 2005, obtained from Ministry of Statistics and Programme Implementation (MOSPI), New Delhi, on CD.

the post-liberalisation phase. While in the case of secondary sector, the expansion has substantially shifted from the formal to the informal sector. Another interesting characteristic of India's economy today is that the informal sector enterprises constituted 95.2 per cent of the total economic enterprises in the country in 1990, and this share had increased to 97.8 per cent in 2005.

The share of workers in urban informal sector enterprises to the total workers in all enterprises in urban areas is presented in Table 14. Although there is no neat geographic pattern of distribution of informal sector workers, the northern (also relatively underdeveloped) states of India like Bihar (83.1%), Uttar Pradesh (81.6%), Madhya Pradesh (76.1%), Assam (79.4%), and Odisha (68.5%) have a higher share of urban informal sector workers to their respective total workers in urban enterprises. These states also have a considerably higher share of their urban service sector workers as informal sector workers. In fact, in these states, the share of informal sector urban workers has been higher than the national average in all the sectors.

There has also been an interesting regional pattern in growth of workers in economic establishments during the period. Where the old industrial commercial clusters like Delhi-Agra-Moradabad region, Amritsar-Chandigarh belt, Pune-Mumbai-Ahmedabad belt, Bengaluru-Mysore-Chennai belt, coastal Andhra Pradesh belt, Madurai-Coimbatore-Salem-Tiruchirappalli region, and new industrial clusters like Hyderabad-Karimnagar-Karnool region have experienced higher growth rates of the total workers (rural+urban) during the period 1990–2005, the growth rate in the Kolkata-Howrah-Kharagpur region, Thiruvananthapuram-Thrissur-Kozhikode belt (except in southern part of this belt), and Thiruvananthapuram-Thrissur-Kozhikode belt has significantly been lower, indicating possible stagnation and decline of these industrial clusters (Figure 5). The Jaipur-Alwar-Ajmer belt and Jalpaiguri-Darjeeling-Cooch Behar belt have been growing at a moderate rate and also in these regions the growth is expanding to other neighbouring districts. A significant growth (though from the low base) of workers in enterprises has taken place in districts of Assam valley, and other north-eastern states. The districts of central Maharashtra, like Osmanabad, Bid and Jalna (in contiguous geographical area) are also showing a higher growth rate of workers. These high growth rate districts may grow as future industrial and commercial clusters. However, the growth in the north-eastern region, and Hyderabad-Karimnagar-Karnool region is mainly led by the urban centres (see Figure 5, right-hand-side map).

As emerges the trend, the formal sector in India has contracted and informal sector expanded in the post-liberalisation phase. Looking into specifically the urban centres, where a significant share of workers and

Table 13

Annual compound growth rate (%) and share (%) of urban informal sector enterprises and workers to the total enterprises and workers in urban areas, 1990–2005

Sectors	Enterprises				Workers			
	Share (%) of informal sector enterprises		ACGR (%) of enterprises 1990–2005		Share (%) of informal sector workers		ACGR (%) of workers 1990–2005	
	1990	2005	Informal sector	Formal sector	1990	2005	Informal sector	Formal sector
Agriculture and allied activities	98.7	99.4	3.4	-2.0	30.7	88.9	2.9	-16.3
Mining and quarrying	87.2	95.1	9.6	1.8	10.3	31.6	9.4	-1.0
Manufacturing	91.8	97.4	4.4	-4.3	38.3	62.7	3.5	-3.6
Electricity, gas and water supply	75.5	82.8	3.2	0.0	12.4	21.0	3.9	-0.7
Construction	96.1	98.3	3.1	-2.9	36.7	74.3	4.5	-6.8
Wholesale, retail, and restaurant and hotels	98.7	99.3	4.7	0.1	81.0	88.1	4.8	0.8
Transport	95.2	98.5	7.2	-1.7	34.2	65.3	6.7	-2.7
Financing, insurance, real estate, and business services	85.9	95.1	8.0	-0.5	30.6	55.0	7.8	0.3
Other sectors	91.7	92.2	-0.8	-1.3	34.8	38.3	0.1	-1.0
Total	95.2	97.8	4.0	-1.8	47.2	66.7	3.9	-2.0

Source: Computed using unit level data of Economic Census 1990 and 2005, obtained from Ministry of Statistics and Programme Implementation (MOSPI), New Delhi, on CD.

Table 14

Share (%) and changes in share of workers in urban informal enterprises to the total workers in urban areas, 1990 and 2005

	2005					Changes (share in 2005 less the share in 2005)				
	Agriculture and allied activities	Manufacturing	Secondary sector	Tertiary sector	Total urban informal sector workers	Agriculture and allied	Manufacturing	Secondary sector	Tertiary Sector	Total urban informal sector workers
Jammu & Kashmir	57.7	89.8	86.1	60.0	64.5	57.7	89.8	86.1	60.0	64.5
Himachal Pradesh	30.0	38.9	35.3	47.9	45.4	-60.5	-10.8	-10.7	5.7	2.5
Punjab	91.8	55.9	55.0	72.0	66.9	5.8	12.9	12.3	10.5	11.4
Chandigarh	94.0	54.2	50.3	39.1	41.4	13.6	19.2	14.2	12.0	12.1
Haryana	87.6	44.0	44.0	67.9	60.9	-4.3	9.8	9.7	3.4	6.6
Delhi	91.0	38.7	38.2	65.9	57.0	5.4	-7.5	-6.8	15.9	8.3
Rajasthan	92.7	72.7	70.3	70.4	70.7	3.5	20.6	20.4	7.4	11.2
Uttar Pradesh (UP)	96.2	76.7	76.1	83.4	81.6	—	—	—	—	—
Uttarakhand	75.6	69.1	66.9	67.1	67.2	—	—	—	—	—
UP including Uttarakhand	94.6	76.4	75.6	82.0	80.4	4.2	40.8	40.0	23.2	29.9
Bihar (BH)	98.6	89.7	88.7	81.9	83.1	—	—	—	—	—
Jharkhand (JH)	93.0	59.6	50.7	69.5	65.7	—	—	—	—	—
BH, including JH	95.5	76.5	70.3	77.3	76.3	10.1	40.3	36.5	20.7	24.1
Sikkim	24.2	70.6	65.8	42.4	43.7	-75.8	34.1	43.3	-2.2	2.8
Arunachal Pradesh	29.2	73.1	34.2	44.6	43.1	-66.6	17.7	2.2	10.1	8.1
Nagaland	96.1	85.6	85.8	42.0	44.3	3.0	52.1	54.5	11.0	12.9
Manipur	94.9	95.5	94.3	64.9	70.9	-3.8	11.8	12.2	7.3	7.8

Cont'd....

...Cont'd

Mizoram	99.8	89.6	86.8	55.7	63.4	27.4	15.6	26.9	7.7	13.5
Tripura	90.1	87.3	84.5	58.2	62.1	-2.0	27.0	26.5	12.8	14.4
Meghalaya	80.8	80.5	75.3	52.2	55.2	-8.0	16.6	20.3	8.3	9.5
Assam	95.2	86.8	86.7	77.7	79.4	20.8	41.8	50.3	28.4	32.4
West Bengal	84.6	62.5	61.1	66.9	65.3	1.3	21.5	20.5	15.7	16.9
Odisha	89.8	68.4	66.7	68.2	68.5	-1.3	20.5	19.8	21.0	20.6
Madhya Pradesh (MP)	96.6	83.5	80.6	74.2	76.1	—	—	—	—	—
Chhattisgarh (CHH)	94.8	62.0	58.8	70.6	68.1	—	—	—	—	—
MP, including CHH	96.1	79.4	76.3	73.5	74.5	3.7	20.0	22.2	18.3	19.1
Gujarat	93.1	49.3	49.6	76.0	67.5	28.6	12.2	12.1	16.6	16.8
Daman & Diu	100.0	86.0	84.5	64.4	70.0	14.4	33.4	33.7	3.2	4.8
D & N Haveli	59.8	15.4	15.9	62.7	34.4	-40.2	8.1	5.8	2.0	-6.2
Maharashtra	84.9	63.1	62.6	65.3	64.8	5.6	28.2	27.8	14.6	19.0
Andhra Pradesh	66.4	57.0	55.3	51.5	52.5	-22.5	9.3	6.8	-7.4	-4.0
Karnataka	81.2	66.0	65.5	64.9	65.2	78.7	49.4	50.0	28.9	42.1
Goa	84.4	74.5	69.8	60.3	62.3	9.9	19.5	19.6	18.1	18.1
Lakshadweep	81.1	44.6	39.0	41.0	45.0	81.1	44.6	39.0	41.0	45.0
Kerala	94.5	70.5	70.9	66.3	69.2	3.0	23.4	24.3	12.4	16.0
Tamil Nadu	95.5	70.1	69.9	71.7	71.6	4.7	16.9	16.7	13.2	14.5
Puducherry	88.9	39.6	41.6	50.4	49.4	-3.4	12.8	13.1	-1.0	3.4
A & N Islands	100.0	54.4	46.0	40.8	41.7	0.0	31.6	25.2	12.4	14.7
All-India	88.9	62.7	61.8	68.0	66.7	58.2	24.4	24.4	15.2	19.5

Source: Based on unit level data of Economic Census 1990 and 2005, obtained from Ministry of Statistics and Programme Implementation (MOSPI), New Delhi, on CD.

enterprises is located, we find that growth of the formal sector in urban areas has been very clustered in the NCR region, northern Punjab and southern Himachal Pradesh, Hyderabad-Karimnagar-Karnool region, Assam valley, capital regions of north-eastern states, and a few scattered centres in Maharashtra (Ahmadnagar, Jalna), Gujarat (Ahmedabad), and Tamil Nadu (Thanjavur and Kanyakumari) (Figure 6). In states like Uttar Pradesh, Bihar, and Madhya Pradesh, workers in the formal sector are either declining very fast or experiencing a very low growth rate. As against this, the workers in urban informal sector have experienced a significantly higher growth rate across the districts in the country (see Figure 6, right-hand-side map).

Conclusion

There is a considerable regional concentration of industrial and commercial activities in India. The old industrial hubs of India founded by the British have largely been foci of growth and expansion of industrial and commercial productions even in the post-independence period of the country. In the pre-liberalisation phase (before 1991), the government through various policy instruments, like licensing, investment subsidies, tax holidays, development of supporting infrastructures, etc., attempted to disperse the industrial and commercial activities to underdeveloped regions of the country but could hardly succeed much. After the liberalisation of the economy in 1991, most of the hard policy measures (like the licensing) with regard to industrial dispersal have been abandoned, and industrial location is largely left to the market forces. Class I cities still remain the hub of industrial and commercial activities and with a share of less than one-third of the population, they command about two-thirds of the workers in industrial and commercial sector activities in the country. The number of workers in organised sector of the economy has contracted in the post-liberalisation phase, but the informal sector has experienced a robust growth across the districts of the country. There are two distinct types of dynamics underway with regard to the dispersal of industrial and commercial sector in India. First, at the absolute level, the concentration of the workers is growing in Class I cities, especially in million-plus cities. Second, when we measure distribution of workers per thousand of population in different size-class of cities, data shows some evidence of dispersal of industrial and commercial activities in the post-liberalisation phase. However, the dispersal is largely confined to and around major industrial regions/clusters of India. In the post-reform period, some new clusters of industrial and commercial activities have emerged and prominent among them are the Hyderabad-Karimnagar-Karnool region and coastal Andhra Pradesh. In Andhra Pradesh, Tamil Nadu and Karnataka, the bases of industrial and commercial activities have been Tier 3 cities or small and medium towns, while in

Figure 5

Annual compound growth rate of workers in total and urban enterprises by districts, 1990–2005

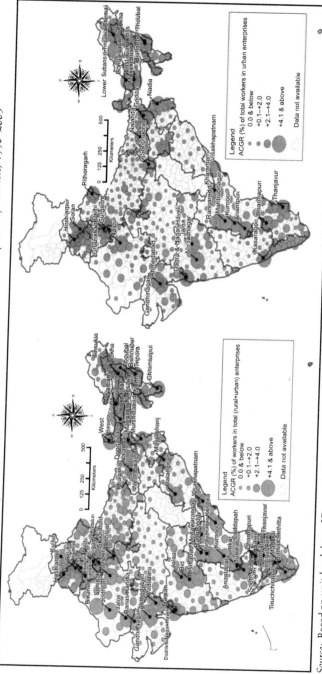

Source: Based on unit level data of Economic Census 1990 and 2005, obtained from Ministry of Statistics and Programme Implementation (MOSPI), New Delhi, on CD.

Figure 6

Annual compound growth rate (ACGR) of workers in urban formal and informal enterprises by districts, 1990–2005

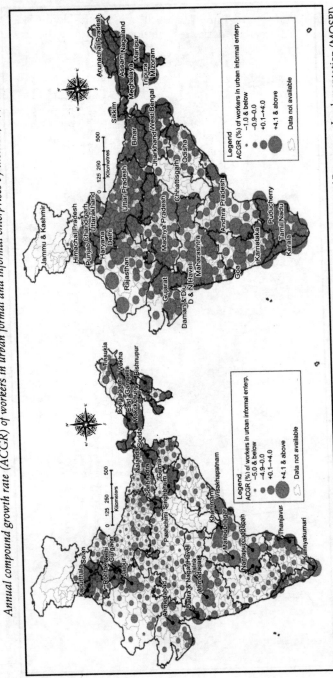

Source: Based on unit level data of Economic Census 1990 and 2005, obtained from Ministry of Statistics and Programme Implementation (MOSPI), New Delhi, on CD.

Mumbai-Pune-Surat-Ahmedabad belt, mega cities dominate the industrial and commercial activities. National Capital Region (NCR) and Chandigarh-Amritsar region are also growing and expanding very fast, and as such the industrial and commercial activities are moving to the small and medium towns of the region. Thus, the role of small and medium towns with regard to absorption and (geographic) expansion of industrial and commercial activities, and fuelling of further growth through expansion of market and provision of cheap factor of production is becoming very important in north-western, western and southern regions of the country. Overall, the location and distribution of towns show a strong association with industrial and commercial activities in southern, western and north-western India. However, the relationship between the size of urban centre and the size of industrial and commercial sector workers seems to be quite weak in Uttar Pradesh, Uttarakhand, Madhya Pradesh, Chhattisgarh, Bihar, Odisha and western Jharkhand.

Notes

1. An enterprise is an undertaking engaged in production and/or distribution of goods and/or services not for the sole purpose of own consumption. An agricultural enterprise for the purpose of Economic Census is defined as one engaged in livestock production, agricultural services, hunting trapping and game propagation, forestry and logging, fishing (corresponding to Groups 012, 013, 014, 015, 020 and 050 of NIC-2004). Enterprises engaged in activities pertaining to agricultural production and plantation (Group 011 of NIC-2004) are excluded from the coverage of Economic Census (MOSPI, n.d.).

2. In this paper, the unorganised sector and informal sector have been used synonymously. The enterprises employing less than 10 workers are defined as unorganised/informal sector, while the enterprises employing more than nine workers are defined as organised/formal sector.

References

Census of India (1991) *Primary Census Abstract 1991*. Office of The Registrar General and Census Commissioner. New Delhi: Ministry of Home Affairs, Government of India, Data on CD.

———. (2001) *Primary Census Abstract 2001*. Office of The Registrar General and Census Commissioner. New Delhi: Ministry of Home Affairs, Government of India, Data on CD.

Dutt, R.C. (1950) *The Economic History of India Under Early British Rule*. London: Routledge & Kegan Paul Ltd.

Dutt, R.P. (1940) *India Today*. London: Gollancz.

Gardiner, B., R. Martin and P. Tyler (2011) 'Does Spatial Agglomeration Increases National Growth? Some Evidence from Europe'. *Journal of Economic Geography*. 11: 979–1006.

Gore, C.D. (1984) *Regions in Question: Space, Development Theory, and Regional Policy*. London: Methuen & Co. Ltd.

Government of India (2006) *Report of the Expert Committee on Small Enterprises*, chaired by Prof. Abid Hussein, Government of India, 1996.

Helsley, R.W. and W.C. Strange (1990) 'Matching and Agglomeration Economies in a System of Cities'. *Regional Science and Urban Economics*. 20(2): 189–212.

Henderson, J.V. (1988) *Urban Development: Theory, Fact and Illusion*. Oxford: Oxford University Press.

High Powered Expert Committee for Estimating the Investment Requirements for Urban Infrastructure Services (2001) *Report on Estimating the Investment Requirements for Urban Infrastructure Services*. Ministry of Urban Development. New Delhi: Government of India.

Hirschman, A.O. (1958) *The Strategy of Economic Development*. New Haven: Yale University Press.

Karan, P.P. (1964) 'Changes in Indian Industrial Location'. *Annals of the Association of American Geographers*. 54 (3): 336–54. doi: 10.1111/j.1467–8306. 1964.tb00494.x

Krugman, P.R. (1980) 'Scale Economies, Product Differentiation and the Pattern of Trade'. *American Economic Review*. 70: 950–59.

——. (1991) 'Increasing Returns and Economic Geography'. *Journal of Political Economy*, 49: 137–50.

Lewis, Arthur (1978) *Evolution of the International Economic Order*. Princeton: Princeton University Press.

Marshall, A. (1890) *Principles of Economics*. London: Macmillan (8th edition, 1920).

Ministry of Commerce and Industry (2003) 'Foreign Direct Investment in India: Policy and Procedures'. New Delhi: Government of India. http://dipp.nic.in/manual/manual_0403.pdf (accessed on 19 November 2011).

Ministry of Industry (nd) 'Statement on Industrial Policy 1991'. New Delhi: Government of India. http://siadipp.nic.in/publicat/nip0791.htm (accessed on 18 November 2011).

Monsted, M. (1974) 'Francois Perroux's Theory of "Growth Pole" and "Development" Pole: A Critique'. *Antipode*. 6(2): 106–13.

MOSPI (2008) *Economic Census 1990*. Data on CD. New Delhi: Government of India.

——. (2009) *Economic Census 2005*. Data on CD. New Delhi: Government of India.

——. (nd) Instructions. http://164.100.34.61/dwh/data/economic_census/pdf/Instructions_ec5.pdf (accessed on 24 November 2011).

Myrdal, Gunnar (1957) *Economic Theory and Underdeveloped Region.* London: Duckworth.

Perroux, F. (1970) 'A Note on the Concept of Growth Poles'. In D.l. McKee, R.D. Dean and W.H. Leahy (eds). *Regional Economics: Theory and Practice.* New York: Free Press, pp. 93–103.

Planning Commission (1980) *Report on Industrial Dispersal.* National Committee on the Development of Backward Areas. New Delhi: Government of India.

———. (nd) *3rd Five Year Plan.* New Delhi: Government of India. http://planningcommission.nic.in/plans/planrel/fiveyr/3rd/3planch9. html (accessed on 18 November 2011).

Rangarajan, C. (1982) *Innovations in Banking: The Indian Experience.* New Delhi: Oxford and IBH.

Raza, Moonis and Y. Aggarwal (1986) *Transport Geography of India: Commodity Flows and the Regional Structure of the Economy.* New Delhi: Concept Publishing Company.

Rosenthal, S.S. and W.C. Strange (2004) 'Evidence on the Nature and Sources of Agglomeration Economies'. In V. Henderson and J. Thisse (eds). *Handbook of Urban and Regional Economics.* Vol. 4, Amsterdam: North Holland, pp. 2119–72.

Shaban, A. (2006) 'Regional Structure, Growth and Convergence of Income in Maharashtra'. *Economic and Political Weekly.* 41(18): 1803–15.

Venables, Anthony J. (2005) *New Economic Geography.* http://www.rrojasdatabank.info/newecongeogven05.pdf (accessed on 17 November 2011).

8

Financing and Access to Basic Amenities in Small and Medium Towns of India under Globalised Regime

DEBOLINA KUNDU

The Eleventh Five-Year Plan noted that the contribution of the urban sector to India's GDP is expected to increase to 70–75 per cent by 2030. It envisioned Indian cities to be the locus and engine of economic growth over the next two decades and suggested that the realisation of an ambitious goal of 9 to 10 per cent growth in GDP depends fundamentally on making Indian cities more liveable, inclusive, bankable, and competitive. In the coming decades, the urban sector is expected to play a critical role in bringing about growth of the entire economy and also sustaining it at high levels. Understandably, urban development has received major attention of the central government in recent years. The launch of the JNNURM, as a flagship programme of the government, with the twin objectives of ushering growth and dynamism in the urban sector as well as linking the programme to reforms to sustain the growth thus achieved, explains the importance accorded to this sector. JNNURM has been effective in catalysing significant investments into the physical infrastructure of cities as well as renewing focus on the urban sector across the country. Acknowledging the importance of urban centres in economic development of the country, the past decade witnessed a number of studies on urban projections and financial requirements for meeting the infrastructural backlog.

The McKinsey Global Institute (MGI) estimated that urban India would accommodate 40 per cent of the country's population by 2030, when an estimated 590 million people will be living in cities and towns.

The MGI report argues that India has a young and rapidly growing population, where an estimated 180 million new job-seekers would be entering India's workforce in the next two decades. Further, with an estimate of annual GDP growth of 7.4 per cent between 2008 and 2030, cities are expected to account for 70 per cent of the 170 million net new jobs created till 2030, account for more than 70 per cent of GDP, and register a fourfold increase in per capita income across the nation. The urban economy is expected to generate more productive agricultural jobs that are important for an eventual increase in agricultural productivity and income.

The report of the High Powered Expert Committee on Urban Infrastructure recently released estimates that India's urban population is expected to reach a figure close to 600 million by 2031. This would place cities and towns at the centre of India's development trajectory. In the coming decades, the urban sector will play a critical role in the structural transformation of Indian economy and in sustaining the high rates of economic growth. Ensuring high-quality public services for all in the cities and towns of India is an end in itself, but it will also facilitate the full realisation of India's economic potential, the report argues. The report comes to the conclusion that India's economic growth momentum cannot be sustained if urbanisation is not actively facilitated. Nor can poverty be addressed if the needs of the urban poor are isolated from the broader challenges of managing urbanisation. Cities will have to become the engines of national development.

The report further argues that the challenge of managing urbanisation will have to be addressed through a combination of increased investment, strengthening the framework for governance and financing, and a comprehensive capacity-building programme at all levels of government. The Committee has made projections for the period from the Twelfth Five-Year Plan to the Fifteenth Five-Year Plan, i.e., 2012–31. The investment for urban infrastructure (water supply, sewerage, solid waste management, storm water drains, urban roads, urban transport, traffic support infrastructure, and streetlighting[1]), over the 20-year period is estimated at ₹ 39.2 lakh crore at 2009–10 prices. The Committee is of the view that large expenditures on Indian cities and towns have to be combined with better governance structures, strong political and administrative will to collect taxes and user charges, and improved capacity to deliver. Cities must be empowered, financially strengthened, and efficiently governed to respond to the needs of their citizens and to contribute to the growth momentum.

Keeping the above concerns in view, the paper attempts to analyse the pattern of urbanisation in the country and its implications for providing infrastructure and other civic amenities in small towns in the second section. It also analyses the spatial pattern in the access to basic amenities in all the small and medium towns of India at the national and state levels vis-à-vis the big cities (Class I and above) based on the census data of 2001. The next section reviews the policies on urban development and their implication on the access to basic amenities in the small and medium towns, followed by an attempt to analyse the financing pattern of urban development across size-class of towns for the select states as well as at the national level based on the 13th Central Finance Commission data as well as allocations under the Central government programmes (JNNURM). The final section summarises the findings and delineates a policy perspective for balanced development.

Implications of Urban Growth on Provision of Infrastructure and Other Civic Amenities in Small Towns

The provisional figures of the population census suggest an increase in the level of urbanisation by 3.38 per cent[2] and an annual growth rate of 2.76 per cent during 2001–11, which is higher than that of the previous decade of 2.74 per cent only in the second decimal point. The growth rate had come down sharply from its peak of 3.83 per cent in the 1970s to 3.09 in the 1980s and further to 2.74 in the 1990s. This made policy makers at national and state levels concerned about deceleration in urban growth, particularly at a stage of rapid economic growth which had accentuated the rural-urban (RU) disparity in economic and social spheres.

The level of urbanisation in the country as a whole increased from 27.8 per cent in 2001 to 31.1 per cent in 2011 – an increase of 3.3 percentage points during 2001–2011 compared to an increase of 2.1 percentage points during 1991–2001. In the past decades, the total number of urban agglomerations and other cities and towns has increased sluggishly, at a rate much slower than urban population. The number had gone up only by 2,541 in the ten decades of the last century. The past decade makes a departure, as now it has gone up by 2,774 just in one decade. The phenomenal jump in the number of 'census towns' from 1,362 to 3,894 is unprecedented in the history of Indian Census. Of the new towns added, 2,532 are census towns and 242 are statutory towns. The 'impetus to urban dynamics' has understandably come at the lowest level. This is not reflected as much in an acceleration in the growth rate of small and medium towns but in a phenomenal increase in the number of census towns. The massive increase in the number of census towns, which are characterised by the absence of ULBs, would bring about a number of challenges in the field of urban development.

At the state level, the economically advanced states more or less show higher levels of urbanisation. The states of Punjab, Haryana, Gujarat, Maharashtra, West Bengal, and the southern states of Kerala, Karnataka, Tamil Nadu and Andhra Pradesh have higher urbanisation levels than the national average. States like Himachal Pradesh, Bihar,

Assam, Odisha, Uttar Pradesh, Rajasthan, Madhya Pradesh, Chhattisgarh and Jharkhand report lower levels of urbanisation than the national average. These are essentially the backward states. Also, most of the states reporting high levels of urbanisation report a large number of census towns being added in the 2011 Census.

It is difficult to assume that sectoral diversification in rural areas has already taken place to such an extent that there is a massive crop of new towns numbering 2,532 during 2001–11, in contrast to the decline in the number by 330 in the previous decade. It is nonetheless possible to hold that a few among these have been identified as 'census towns' due to the workforce here shifting from farm to non-farm employment. The share of primary workers in the rural male workforce has declined from 71 per cent to 63 per cent from 1999–2000 to 2009–10, which is higher than the corresponding shift from 74 to 71 per cent during 1993–99. In any case, the Central and state governments must recognise the possibility of urban impetus coming from the lower level by according 'statutory towns' status to the new census towns. They must also design a scheme similar to Jawaharlal Nehru National Urban Renewal Mission (JNNURM) to strengthen their infrastructure base and promote them as centres of distributed and inclusive growth.

Access to Basic Amenities in Urban India

It is possible to analyse the trend in the availability of drinking water and sanitation, using population census and NSS data. As per the census, the percentage of households having drinking water facility in urban areas had increased from 75.1 to 81.4 during 1981–91. The increase is not very impressive taking into consideration the fact that the eighties were declared as the Water and Sanitation Decade with specific programmes being launched to meet the target. The developments in the nineties are much more disturbing as one would infer from the NSS data. The percentage of urban households (HHs) having tap as the principal source of drinking water has gone down from 72.1 in 1988–89 to 70.4 in 1993 and further down to 70.1 in 1998. Also the percentage of urban households having water supply within their premises, which had gone up to 66.2 in 1993 from 58.3 in 1988–89, registered a marginal decline to 65.7 in 1998. The coverage, however, improved to 74.5 per cent in 2008–09.

Households having sole access to water source (not sharing with others), however, showed a significant increase from 34.8 per cent to 40.2 during 1988–93 but increased only by 1 per cent to 41.3 in 1998. The 65th round of the NSSO reported 47 per cent households having sole access to water source and 74.3 per cent of households with tap as a principal source of drinking water. It is important to note that within a span of two decades, the percentage of households having tap as a principal source of drinking water increased by only two percentage points, from 72.1 in 1988 to 74.3 in 2008–09.

The data available from the census of 2001, however, shows a distinct improvement in the coverage of HHs having access to safe drinking water, the percentage going up to 90.01, with the states of Andhra Pradesh, Punjab and Karnataka reporting the highest increase. Also, the percentage of HHs collecting water from outside the premises has gone down systematically during the Eighties and Nineties.

Population having access to toilet facilities in urban India was 58 per cent in 1981, which has gone up to 64 per cent in 1991 as per the Population Census. The coverage improved to 74 per cent in 2001, recording an increase of over 10 per cent. Going by NSSO, the percentage of households having access to toilet facility increased from 68 to 69 during 1988–93, the figure going up to 74.5 per cent during the next five years, which is impressive. In 2008–09, 88.7 per cent households reported having access to toilet facilities. Percentage of households having access to service latrine reported a decline from 11.7 to 1.6 during 1988–89 to 2008–09. Correspondingly, the percentage of households having access to septic tank and flush toilets has increased from 52.7 to 77.3 during the same period. Importantly, the developed states reported a higher coverage of households with septic tank and flush toilets.

Variation in the percentage of households covered by the amenities across size-classes shows regularity and a distinct pattern. The percentage of households covered by each of the amenities, viz, water supply, electricity and toilet increases systematically with the size-class of urban centres, except for Class VI towns. This is because many among these Class VI towns have been established or are managed by the government departments, public agencies, military establishments or private industries. These, therefore, enjoy a special status and higher level of amenities. It is indeed very disturbing that in Class V towns, having population between 5,000 and 10,000, the percentage of households not covered by toilet and drinking water facilities are 61 and 28, respectively, in 1991. The corresponding figures for the cities with more than 5 lakh population are 22 and 14 per cent only. Similarly, while 14 per cent of the people in Class V towns have none of these amenities, the corresponding figure for the 5 lakh plus cities is less than 3 per cent. On the other hand, the percentage of households having both the amenities in Class III, IV and V towns is about 30 per cent while that for Class I cities, it is twice as large. This can be attributed to small and medium towns having a weak base of manufacturing sector and a high percentage of workforce dependent on agriculture. As a consequence, many among these towns are not in a position to generate funds to provide civic services to all sections of population.

Most of the indicators of basic amenities show positive correlations with those of economic development across the states in the nineties. The percentage of households having flush toilets, for example, exhibits a very strong relationship with per capita income. For other amenities, like drinking water, toilets and electricity, too, the correlations are positive but not always statistically significant. One would argue that economically developed states are doing fairly well in providing their people access to basic amenities (Kundu et al., 1999). This trend is likely to continue in future years, implying that the improvements in the availability of these amenities would be higher in the relatively developed states.

The coverage of households through basic amenities across size-class of urban centres shows regularity and a distinct pattern. The percentage of households having all the three amenities goes down systematically as we move from higher to lower size-class of urban centres.[3] It is indeed very disturbing that in Class V towns (having population between 5,000 and 10,000), the percentage of households not covered by toilet, electricity and drinking water are as high as 61, 41 and 28, respectively, in 1991. The corresponding figures for the cities with more than half a million population are 22, 17 and 14 per cent only (Kundu et al., 1999). Going by the present trend, one would expect still higher inequality in the level of basic services across urban centres in different size-classes by the year 2020.

Access to Basic Amenities Across Size-Class of Towns (2001)

This section attempts to work out the access to basic services across size-class of towns based on the 2001 Town Directory data. The Class I towns have been further divided into three categories based on their population, viz., IA with population above one million, IB with population between 5 lakh and 1 million and 1C with population between 5 lakh and one lakh. Percentage of towns covered with protected water supply (through taps), and covered sewer facility have been worked out (Table 1).

Table 1

Access to basic amenities across size-class of towns in India – A state level analysis (2001)

State	Size-class		Percentage of towns with tap water supply	Percentage of towns with covered sewer facility
	IA	1 million +	80.6	83.9
	IB	5,00,001–1,00,000	90.0	52.5
	IC	1,00,001–5,00,000	83.5	27.3
	I	1,00,000+	83.9	33.6
All India	II	50,001–1,00,000	81.5	15.3
	III	20,001–50,000	75.3	10.3
	IV	10,001–20,000	73.8	7.7
	V	5,001–10,000	66.4	5.9
	VI	< 5,000	66.2	13.7
	All Urban		74.0	11.3

Source: Census of India, Town Directory, 2001.

Significantly, 83.9 per cent of the Class I towns report access to protected water through taps. The coverage declines systematically with lower order size-class. With regard to sewer facility, one finds low coverage in small towns and consequently high disparity in the coverage across size-class of towns. The million-plus cities report a fairly higher coverage of 84 per cent of the cities reporting closed sewer facility compared to the small and medium towns where the coverage falls to 6–7 per cent in Classes IV and V. This calls for immediate attention of policy makers as open drains directly affect the micro-environment of towns and cities.

The developed states of Punjab, Haryana, Gujarat, Maharashtra, Karnataka and Tamil Nadu show higher coverage with basic amenities. West Bengal is one state where the connectivity of tap water and covered sewer facility, water-borne toilets is much below the national level. The backward states of Rajasthan, Uttar Pradesh, Madhya Pradesh, Odisha, Bihar and Assam generally report coverages below the national average. However, Odisha and Madhya Pradesh report higher coverage of towns with tap water facility. Absence of covered sewered facility is a characteristic of all the backward states, and specially the small and medium towns.

People in small and medium towns in India, particularly those with less than 50,000 people, have low per capita income due to lack of employment opportunities in the organised sector, low incidence of secondary activities and poverty-induced growth of tertiary employment. The data from the NSS reveals that the incidence of poverty is very high in these towns compared to the metropolises or other cities. The percentage of people below the poverty line increases systematically as one goes down the population size categories (Dubey and Gangopadhyay, 1998). As per the 55th Round of NSSO (1999–2000), poverty level in small towns (< 50,000 population) was reported to be high (24.2%), in the middle size towns (50,000 to 1,00,000 population), poverty was lower (20.4%) and it was the lowest (14.2%) in the big cities. Understandably, many small and medium towns are not in a position to generate funds to provide civic services to all sections of the population and stabilise their economic base. The percentage of households not having access to basic amenities, viz., drinking water, toilets and electricity are very high here and the figure goes down with size-class of urban centres (Kundu et al., 1999).

It can be demonstrated that the larger cities are financially stronger and can take up public works and social infrastructure projects on their own, which is not so for smaller towns. With the decline in central or state assistance in recent years, it is not surprising that most of these smaller towns do not make any investment for improving infrastructure and basic services. This has compounded their problems of inadequacy of basic amenities.

Review of Urban Development Policies

Urban renewal, with a focus on inclusive development of urban centres, is one of the thrust areas in the National Common Minimum Programme of the government and accordingly, the Jawaharlal Nehru National Urban Renewal Mission (JNNURM) was launched on 3 December 2005 with an investment of ₹ 50,000.00 crores in the Mission period of seven years, beginning 2005–06. The Mission is the single largest initiative of the Government of India for planned urban development that integrates the two pressing needs of urban India: massive investments required for infrastructure development and at the same time, reforms that are required to sustain investments.

The Mission aims to encourage reforms and fast-track infrastructure development with a focus on efficiency in urban infrastructure and services delivery mechanism, community participation, and accountability of ULBs towards citizens. The primary objective of the JNNURM is to create economically productive, efficient, equitable and responsive cities. To achieve this objective, the Mission focuses on integrated development of infrastructure services; securing linkages between asset creation and maintenance for long-run project sustainability; accelerating the flow of investment into urban infrastructure services; planned urban development; renewal of inner-city areas and universalisation of urban services to ensure balanced urban development.

The Approach Paper to the Eleventh Plan reaffirms the concern regarding concentration of demographic and economic growth in a few large cities and deteriorating infrastructural situation in these that nonetheless 'provide large economies of agglomeration'. It, however, lays major emphasis on JNNURM launched in the Tenth Plan. Never before have the select large cities under any urban development programme received per capita allocation on such a large scale for infrastructural investment coming as project grants through additional central assistance. The Mission has also succeeded in getting the state and city governments to commit themselves to structural reforms, which the central government had failed to achieve despite adopting several measures and incentive schemes proposed since early nineties through other programmes and legislations (Kundu et al., 2007). In fact, a set of 23 mandatory reforms have to be introduced by the respective state governments and cities as per the commitments made by them in the Memorandum of Agreement (MoA) at the beginning of the Mission period.[4] 'It would be particularly necessary to ensure that there is no dilution in these reform requirements', the approach paper stipulates. Also, sanctioning of the funds under the Mission is contingent on the

City Development Projects (CDP), and detailed project reports being approved by the Central government. The JNNURM is thus a mission of macro-economic growth wherein ground conditions have been created through reform measures and infrastructural investment in 65 select cities[5] for attracting domestic and foreign investment.

The JNNURM has two sub-missions for the Mission cities, viz., (1) Urban Infrastructure and Governance (UIG), and (2) Basic Services to the Urban Poor (BSUP). Projects such as road, public transport, trunk network of water supply, sanitation, solid waste management and storm water drains, construction of multi-level parking lots and city beatification, etc., have been taken up under the UIG component. The main thrust is to ensure improvement in urban governance so that the ULBs become financially sound with enhanced credit rating and ability to access capital market for undertaking new projects. The JNNURM, besides attempting infrastructural development and reform in governance in the 65 select cities through its Infrastructural Development (ID) component accounting for over 60 per cent of the total stipulated funds, is expected to provide the poor in these cities access to basic services and land with tenurial security through its other component, called Basic Services for Urban Poor (BSUP). The latter accounts for about 40 per cent of the total funds directed to the Mission cities.[6]

The JNNURM is expected to cater to the non-Mission towns and cities under the two components, namely, the Urban Infrastructure and Governance (UIG) of UIDSSMT, and the Integrated Housing and Slum Development Programme (IHSDP). The programme is expected to cover all other Census towns under the Urban Infrastructure Development Scheme for Small and Medium Towns (UIDSSMT).[7] The existing programme of IDSMT (Infrastructure Development Scheme for Small and Medium Towns) and Accelerated Urban Water Supply Programme (AUWSP) has been subsumed under UIDSSMT. Likewise, the existing Valmiki Ambedkar Awas Yojana (VAMBAY) and the discontinued National Slum Development Programme (NSDP) have been subsumed in the IHSDP. Interestingly, the indicative allocation of JNNURM is biased against the non-Mission cities/towns as the share of UIDSSMT and IHSDP works out to be 12.8 and 8.9 per cent, respectively. The remaining share of about 80 per cent funds is directed towards the 65 Mission cities. The big city bias of JNNURM is also reflected in the per capita spending by the central government; the figure for the Mission cities works out to be ₹ 220 per capita per annum as compared to ₹ 119 for the non-Mission cities.

JNNURM is the first holistic programme aimed at urban renewal, taking the concerns of the urban poor as one of its agenda. The BSUP and

IHSDP are directed towards the urban poor in the Mission and non-Mission cities, respectively. Besides these, there are other reforms like internal earmarking of funds for the poor, provision of basic services to the urban poor and household level services where a comprehensive policy on providing basic services to all the urban poor has to be formulated, directed towards the poor. While the component of BSUP may be achievable, it is quite ambiguous how the component of security of tenure would be addressed. Also, the proposed scheme for affordable housing through partnership and the scheme for interest subsidy for urban housing which would be dovetailed into the Rajiv Awas Yojana would extend support under JNNURM to states that are willing to assign property rights to people living in slum areas. However, it is to be seen how property rights would be assigned to people occupying slums in prime locations in the metropolitan cities. Again, restricting the scope of the programme to only 250 Class I cities again brings out the big-city bias. Further, HUDCO funds, set up primarily to ensure balanced regional development, have gone in for retail financing, the rates of which are determined directly by the market. Refinancing of housing schemes, targeted towards the poor, seems to be a forgotten agenda in the era of liberalisation.

The Geographical Coverage of the JNNURM

As mentioned earlier, JNNURM focuses on 65 select cities in the Mission mode and the rest of the urban centres in non-Mission mode. In case of the Mission cities with urban agglomerations (UAs), all the ULBs within the UA have also been covered under mission mode. Thus, under JNNURM, 178 ULBs are to benefit from the 65 Mission UAs. The programme is also expected to cover all other towns under UIDSSMT, apart from the 65 Mission cities.

An analysis of the funds released till September 2009 shows that only 58 per cent of the urban population has been covered during the past four years (Table 2). And, if we assume the population of urban India to be static at the Census 2001 levels, the coverage percentage falls even further to 54 per cent. Of the 5,161 towns/cities as per 2001 Census, 4,207 towns/cities are yet to be covered under the flagship programme. Further, the coverage has been better in the developed states ranging from 50 to 80 per cent, except Haryana and Punjab where 68.45 per cent and 60.69 per cent population is yet to be covered. The less developed states like Bihar, Chhattisgarh, Madhya Pradesh, Odisha, Rajasthan and Uttar Pradesh have reported that about 60 to 65 percentage of their population is yet to be covered under the scheme.

Table 2

State-wise towns/cities yet to be covered by JNNURM & UIDSSMT
(population projected for 2009) *

States/UTs	% Population yet to be covered	States/UTs	% Population yet to be covered
Andaman & Nicobar	100	Lakshadweep	100
Andhra Pradesh	28.08	Madhya Pradesh	64.26
Arunachal Pradesh	23.08	Maharashtra	22.33
Assam	33.92	Manipur	36.99
Bihar	65.78	Meghalaya	28.02
Chandigarh	0	Mizoram	33.23
Chhattisgarh	79.22	Nagaland	0
Dadra & Nagar Haveli	0	Odisha	61.65
Daman & Diu	37.63	Punjab	60.69
Delhi	0	Puducherry	7.28
Goa	88.44	Rajasthan	66.48
Gujarat	22.32	Sikkim	33.03
Haryana	68.45	Tamil Nadu	51.75
Himachal Pradesh	65.44	Tripura	41.07
Jammu & Kashmir	22.08	Uttar Pradesh	59.45
Jharkhand	41.43	Uttarakhand	39.14
Karnataka	45.7	West Bengal	23.82
Kerala	59.71	All India	41.53

*as on 30 September 2009

Source: Data accessed from the MoUD website, http://urbanindia.nic.in and http://jnnurm.nic.in

The inability of the economically backward states to introduce reforms as per the MoA signed and to come up with technically correct and CPHEEO-verified DPRs are attributed to the sluggish flow of funds here.

Further, as per the stipulation of JNNURM, 35 per cent of the project costs are to be borne by the Central government in the case of million-plus cities under UIG. In case of BSUP, however, the central share is 50 per cent. Similarly, the central share of IHSDP and UIG UIDSSMT is 80 per cent. Inability to raise matching funds on the part of the state governments and the ULBs has resulted in discontinuity of flow of funds to some of these states.

Table 3

Class-wise distribution of the towns/cities yet to be covered by
*JNNURM & UIDSSMT, India 2001**

	Population yet to be covered	Percentage share of total pop. yet to be covered	% Pop. yet to be covered	Total no. of cities/ towns	No. of cities/ towns included	No. of cities/towns yet to be covered
Class I	42,917,767	32.53	24.08	441	126	315
Class II	27,292,423	20.69	79.22	496	100	396
Class III	34,632,187	26.25	82.22	1,387	289	1,098
Class IV	19,449,683	14.74	86.01	1,564	276	1,288
Class V	6,934,400	5.26	87.89	1,042	125	917
Class VI	693,396	0.53	84.50	231	38	193
Total	131,919,856	100.00	46.11	5,161	954	4,207

*as on 30 September 2009.

Source: Same as Table 2.

An attempt has been made to work out the coverage of JNNURM scheme at the size-class level. An analysis of Tables 3 and 4 shows that there is a systematic decline in the percentage of population covered with size-class. The Class I cities report 76 per cent of the population covered under JNNURM. The coverage falls to 21 per cent in Class II, 18 per cent in Class III, 14–15 per cent in Classes IV, V and VI, respectively. A state-level analysis shows higher coverage in Class I cities in the developed states (e.g., 95 per cent in West Bengal, 90 per cent in Tamil Nadu, 86 per cent in Maharashtra, 84 per cent in Gujarat and 75 per cent in Andhra Pradesh). The Class II cities, however, have a larger percentage of population uncovered, which ranges from 93 per cent in West Bengal to 59.39 per cent in Gujarat. West Bengal is one state where big city bias is very evident; where 95 per cent of Class I cities' population is covered against a figure of only 7–9 per cent in the small and medium towns. The coverage of towns declines systematically in the size-classes III to VI. The coverage of towns in the Class I cities of the less developed states varies from 57 per cent in Madhya Pradesh to 37 per cent in Bihar. The towns in the size-classes II to VI in the economically backward states show a much lower coverage as compared to their developed counterparts.

Table 4

Class-wise distribution of the towns/cities (state-wise) yet to be covered by JNNURM & UIDSSMT for 15 major states (Census 2001)*

States		% Popn. yet to be covered	Total no. of cities/towns	No. of cities/towns yet to be covered
Andhra Pradesh	Class I	25.39	47	30
	Class II	61.70	52	32
	Class III-VI	58.91	111	65
Assam	Class I	34.91	6	4
	Class II	77.40	7	6
	Class III-VI	75.25	112	82
Bihar	Class I	62.56	19	17
	Class II	86.69	19	17
	Class III-VI	87.90	92	80
Gujarat	Class I	16.56	27	17
	Class II	59.39	36	22
	Class III-VI	73.97	179	135
Haryana	Class I	65.41	20	16
	Class II	100.00	7	7
	Class III-VI	93.81	79	75
Karnataka	Class I	34.00	30	22
	Class II	78.16	28	22
	Class III-VI	80.77	212	173
Kerala	Class I	36.47	10	7
	Class II	80.72	24	19
	Class III-VI	81.66	125	102
Madhya Pradesh	Class I	43.11	25	19
	Class II	90.25	26	23
	Class III-VI	93.00	343	315
Maharashtra	Class I	14.50	40	23
	Class II	65.79	44	29
	Class III-VI	77.52	294	234
Odisha	Class I	46.33	9	6
	Class II	72.29	15	13
	Class III-VI	85.48	114	94

Cont'd...

...Cont'd

Punjab	Class I	43.08	14	10
	Class II	93.63	18	17
	Class III-VI	91.04	125	114
Rajasthan	Class I	62.00	19	17
	Class II	91.12	27	25
	Class III-VI	76.06	176	136
Tamil Nadu	Class I	9.60	26	18
	Class II	80.84	56	46
	Class III-VI	83.31	750	634
Uttar Pradesh	Class I	44.06	54	40
	Class II	84.27	55	47
	Class III-VI	89.80	595	531
West Bengal	Class I	5.67	58	7
	Class II	93.03	29	27
	Class III-VI	91.16	288	269
All India	Class I	24.08	441	315
	Class II	79.22	496	396
	Class III-VI	84.02	4224	3496

*as on 30 September 2009.

Source: Same as Table 2.

Table 5

Sector-wise distribution of funds released under UIG component of JNNURM & UIDSSMT* (in percentage)

Sector	UIG JNNURM	UIG UIDSSMT
Water supply	39.66	63.22
Sewerage, SWM & drainage/storm water drainage	38.30	28.17
Roads/flyovers, mass rapid transit and parking (roads only for UIDSSMT)	20.83	8.02
Urban renewal and preservation of water bodies	1.20	0.59
Total	100.00	100.00

*as on 30 September 2009.

Source: Same as Table 2.

Water supply and sewerage are the major areas of investment under JNNURM in both the Mission and the non-Mission cities (Table 5). An analysis of sector-wise distribution of funds released during 2005–09 shows that water supply and sewerage attracted 78 per cent of the funds released in Mission cities under UIG component, and roads and flyovers accounting for 21 per cent. The corresponding figures for the non-Mission cities are 81 per cent and 8 per cent, respectively. The share of urban renewal has been negligible in both the categories of cities.

An analysis of the information regarding the projects and schemes launched under the UIG component in different cities reveals that most of these have been designed to increase the total capacity of the basic urban services – water supply, sanitation and sewerage – at the city level. There is no explicit provision to improve the delivery of the facilities in the deficient areas within the cities or improve the access of the poor to these. Given the emphasis on reform, financial efficiency and cost recovery for each of the facilities and promotion of public-private partnership, it is understandable that those who have affordability will corner much of the benefits from this augmented system. This would further increase the spatial disparity within towns and cities.

The bias against pro-poor allocations is very clear if we examine Table 6. While the annual per capita fund released under BSUP is ₹ 66, the UIG component of JNNURM stands at ₹ 153. Likewise, the annual per capita fund released under IHSDP is ₹ 40, which is about half of that under the UIG UIDSSMT (₹ 78). The annual per capita funds released under urban development schemes work out to be ₹ 165. The pro-poor component accounts for ₹ 52 vis-à-vis ₹ 113 under the UIG component.

State of Municipal Finances in India across Various Size-Classes of Towns/Cities

This section attempts to analyse the percentage distribution of various sources of revenue and expenditure of ULBs across municipal corporations, municipalities and nagar panchayats for the major states of India based on the Thirteenth Finance Commission data. The percentage distribution of own tax and non-tax, own revenue and other sources of revenue and capital and revenue expenditure have been analysed for the years 2002–03, 2003–04, 2004–05, 2005–06, 2006–07 and 2007–08.

At the all-India level, own revenue formed about 63 per cent of the total revenue in 2002–03, which systematically declined to about 53 per cent in 2007–08. During this period, the share of own revenue declined the maximum for nagar panchayats (from 33% to 19%), followed by municipalities (from 46% to 32%) and municipal corporations (from 54% to 42%). Importantly, the share of own resources as a percentage of total revenue was maximum for the municipal corporations, followed by municipalities and nagar panchayats. The falling share of own revenues since 2005–06 shows the relative importance of central government transfers since the JNNURM was launched in that year and these grants form a sizeable share.

Table 6

State-wise annual per capita spending (₹) by the central government on different components of Urban Development Schemes (UDS) meant for mission and non-mission cities/towns since December 6, 2005*

Name	UIG JNNURM	UIG UIDSSMT	BSUP JNNURM	IHSDP UIDS-SMT	JNN-URM (UIG+BSUP)	UIDSS-MT (UIG+IHSDP)	UIG (NURM+UIDS-SMT)	Pro-poor Component (NURM+UIDSSMT)	UDS Total (NURM+UIDSSMT)
Andhra Pradesh	190.61	266.96	155.32	85.69	345.93	352.66	230.93	118.55	349.48
Arunachal Pradesh	2205.58	153.63	430.01	0.00	2635.59	153.63	548.95	82.84	631.79
Assam	161.25	77.28	82.35	21.92	243.60	99.20	98.79	37.40	136.19
A & N Islands	0.00	0.00	0.00	93.32	0.00	93.32	0.00	93.32	93.32
Bihar	96.55	35.91	76.57	20.85	173.13	56.75	51.41	35.10	86.51
Chandigarh	44.43	0.00	225.61	0.00	270.04	0.00	44.43	225.61	270.04
Chhattisgarh	324.74	38.57	208.68	48.88	533.42	87.45	89.05	77.07	166.12
Dadra & Nagar Haveli	0.00	4.74	0.00	4.20	0.00	8.94	2.94	22.98	25.92
Daman & Diu	0.00	11.07	0.00	10.36	0.00	21.43	4.74	4.20	8.94
Delhi	2.94	0.00	22.98	0.00	25.92	0.00	11.07	10.36	21.43
Goa	0.00	0.00	26.43	0.00	26.43	0.00	0.00	26.43	26.43
Gujarat	170.36	70.14	69.24	35.94	239.60	106.08	133.89	57.12	191.02
Haryana	172.28	26.55	34.18	41.45	206.46	68.00	57.58	39.91	97.49
Himachal Pradesh	265.73	39.19	61.65	87.01	327.38	126.20	97.66	80.47	178.13
Jammu & Kashmir	136.12	416.94	38.98	91.02	175.10	507.96	216.17	53.81	269.98

Cont'd...

...Cont'd

Jharkhand	76.59	32.02	27.23	32.89	103.83	64.91	56.87	29.74	86.61
Karnataka	150.63	57.57	29.72	21.95	180.36	79.52	95.12	25.09	120.21
Kerala	140.93	70.43	68.23	37.26	209.17	107.68	91.20	46.38	137.58
Madhya Pradesh	157.57	58.60	50.72	18.01	208.29	76.61	88.44	27.87	116.31
Maharashtra	181.54	148.83	74.10	77.31	255.64	226.14	169.39	75.29	244.68
Manipur	94.40	228.44	89.53	85.58	183.93	314.02	161.94	87.54	249.48
Meghalaya	389.22	77.52	127.23	134.73	516.45	212.25	265.25	130.21	395.46
Mizoram	29.29	91.11	155.04	193.87	184.33	284.98	52.34	169.51	221.85
Nagaland	128.18	0.00	1191.03	278.93	1319.22	278.93	37.48	545.65	583.13
Odisha	334.16	42.32	28.23	41.10	362.40	83.41	95.63	38.75	134.38
Punjab	110.35	57.10	7.07	5.84	117.43	62.93	73.81	6.23	80.03
Puducherry	194.15	0.00	79.79	31.52	273.94	31.52	145.60	67.72	213.33
Rajasthan	237.43	61.17	26.37	35.38	263.80	96.55	106.40	33.07	139.47
Sikkim	794.08	1,031.74	535.59	0.00	1329.67	1031.74	928.49	232.69	1161.18
Tamil Nadu	138.69	54.38	74.68	20.06	213.37	74.44	80.97	37.29	118.26
Tripura	195.54	207.85	77.51	69.45	273.05	277.31	203.63	72.22	275.85
Uttar Pradesh	130.04	41.26	60.75	23.12	190.79	64.38	68.98	34.87	103.86
Uttarakhand	136.38	37.59	16.78	2.21	153.17	39.79	75.95	7.87	83.82
West Bengal	61.09	63.49	70.66	124.22	131.75	187.71	61.88	88.24	150.12
All India	153.30	78.33	66.25	40.38	219.55	118.71	112.85	52.30	165.15

In Andhra Pradesh, the share of own revenue was stable at around 60 per cent in the municipal corporations during 2002–08. In Maharashtra, the percentage share came down from 87 to 69. The same pattern is observed in Haryana (96 to 69), Karnataka (72 to 47), Kerala (47 to 42), Maharashtra (90 to 82), Punjab (94 to 86), Tamil Nadu (48 to 47) except West Bengal, which registered an increase (55 to 60). Thus, the share of own resources constitutes a sizeable share of total revenues of Municipal Corporations (MCs) in the developed states, except Tamil Nadu. In the backward states, the share of grants and transfers are higher compared to own revenues. This is explained by the fact that the tax raising capacity, even of MCs, is much less in the backward states as compared to the developed states.

The share of own revenue of municipalities registered a decline in both the developed and the backward states during 2002–08, Gujarat (37 to 30), Haryana (73 to 17), Karnataka (46 to 19), Maharashtra (33 to 27) and Tamil Nadu (46 to 33), Assam (86 to 33), Bihar (73 to 18), Madhya Pradesh (16 to 8), Uttar Pradesh (22 to 11), Odisha (7 to 5) and West Bengal (10 to 5), except Rajasthan (38 to 42) and Kerala (35 to 38) where the shares increased.

In case of nagar panchayats, the share of own revenue registered a decline in both the developed and backward states during 2002–08, Karnataka (33 to 12), Assam (79 to 18), Bihar (71 to 7), Madhya Pradesh (13 to 7), Odisha (7 to 5), Uttar Pradesh (26 to 10), except Tamil Nadu (31 to 33) and Kerala (35 to 38) where the shares increased. In Punjab, the share was close to 93 per cent.

The share of own tax as a percentage of total own revenue remained at about 65 per cent for all ULBs during 2002–08 at the all-India level. In Andhra Pradesh, the share of own tax revenue increased from 55 to 58 per cent. The same trend is noticed in Assam (26 to 66), Odisha 72 to 78 and Punjab 79 to 81. The share was stable in the MCs of Haryana at around 35 per cent, in Maharashtra around 68 per cent and Uttar Pradesh around 71 per cent.

In Bihar, the percentage share declined from 92 to 57, in Gujarat from 86 to 78, Karnataka 67 to 60, Kerala (76 to 62), Rajasthan 23 to 4, Tamil Nadu 81 to 76 and WB 56 to 46. Rajasthan is the only state where the component of tax revenue even among MCs is very small and has declined over time. No pattern seems to be emerging in the case of nagar panchayats and municipalities in their shares of tax and non-tax earnings.

The share of capital expenditure registered an increase for all ULBs during 2002–08 at the all-India level. The increase has been noticeable since 2005–06 because of the JNNURM funds being available with the ULBs for capital expenditure. This trend is true for all classes of ULBs in the developed states of Andhra Pradesh, Gujarat, Haryana, Karnataka, Maharashtra, Tamil Nadu and West Bengal. The backward states of Odisha and Rajasthan also registered an increase. Uttar Pradesh and Punjab are the two states where the share of capital expenditure remained stable. Kerala is the only state where the share of revenue expenditure has gone up.

Conclusion and a Future Perspective

Within a span of two decades, the percentage of households having tap as a principal source of drinking water increased by only two percentage points, from 72.1 in 1988 to 74.3 in 2008–09. The coverage of households through basic amenities across size-class of urban centres shows regularity and a distinct pattern. The percentage of households having all the three amenities goes down systematically as we move from higher to lower size-class of urban centres.[8] The developed states report higher coverage of households with septic tank and flush toilets. The million-plus cities show a fairly higher coverage of 84 per cent compared to the small and medium towns where the coverage falls to 6–7 per cent in Classes IV and V. This calls for immediate attention of policy makers as open drains directly affect the micro-environment of towns and cities.

Only 58 per cent of the urban population has been covered under JNNURM, the coverage being high in the developed states and metropolitan cities. Of the 5,161 towns/cities, 4,207 are yet to be covered under the programme. An analysis of the JNNURM funding pattern, which is inbuilt in the component-wise indicative allocation, clearly brings out the big city bias. In fact, the developed states have had a larger share of the pie because of their ability to introduce the reforms as per their committed timeline. Moreover, a closer examination of the CDPs and DPRs, along with the mandatory reforms, makes it obvious that the Mission has a clear-cut mandate of producing 'global cities', disciplining them enough to adhere to the rigours of the credit rating agencies, which is a pre-condition to access capital market and other innovative sources of funding.

The concern for the small and medium towns and the urban poor is extensively present in the literature, especially since it has been made mandatory to include a chapter on the seven-point poverty linked charter in the CDPs. In practice, however, one finds greater bias on improving the efficiency in the functioning of the overall city economy and meeting the infrastructural deficiencies at the macro level rather than addressing the issues of distributional inadequacy and improving the access of the poor to these (Kundu et al., 2007). The design of the DPRs is such that even the subsidies built into the IHSDP or BSUP, meant for the urban poor, would substantially go to the non-poor. Unfortunately, this major shift in the thrust under BSUP and IHSDP has gone totally unchallenged and almost unnoticed in the corridors of policy making. Needless to mention that the number of slum-dwellers that would be rehabilitated through government programmes would go up to a couple of millions, far short of the figure of 24.7 million urban EWS housing shortage as estimated by the Ministry of Housing and Urban Poverty Alleviation at the beginning of the Eleventh Five-Year Plan.

It cannot be denied that the JNNURM has provided for substantial Central assistance to cities and towns for infrastructure development and housing the poor, and has indeed been effective in renewing the country's focus on the urban sector. However, the analysis exhibits a move towards polarised development and an inbuilt big-city bias, especially in the developed states. Also, only 45.5 per cent of the total allocations have actually been released under JNNURM till date. This phenomenon of large-scale under-utilisation of the JNNURM funds and inability of the smaller ULBs to prepare DPRs and generate matching resources can only be addressed by paying urgent attention to urban governance reforms, building capabilities at the ULB level and developing professional management capabilities of city governments in them, especially those in the economically backward states. Efforts should be taken to make special provisions for unconditional general grants addressed towards their infrastructure and housing needs till the time they develop the capacities to receive project funding. This will certainly help in making the growth process more inclusive, where the urban poor would be partners in the developmental process, and ensure equitable and sustainable urban growth.

There has been a declining trend in the percentage share of own revenue for all the ULBs during 2002–08, especially since 2005–06, which marks the launch of the JNNURM. The share of own revenues is high in the developed states, particularly in the MCs. Also, the percentage share of capital expenditure of ULBs started increasing since this year as JNNURM funds are basically for capital investments. The small and medium towns, which lack adequate access to basic amenities, also lack in technical know-how with regard to project formulation as well as reforms. Concerted action needs to be taken to build capabilities at the city and town level and developing professional management capabilities of city governments in them in order to bring about equitable economic development across states. The spurt in the number of census towns needs special policy focus. If indeed that has happened, the central and state governments must recognise their urban status 'statutorily' and design a scheme similar to JNNURM to strengthen their infrastructure base and promote them as centres of inclusive growth.

Notes

1. Given the volatility of land prices, the estimates do not include the cost of land acquisition.
2. The level of urbanisation increased from 27.81 per cent in 2001 Census to 31.16 per cent in 2011 Census.
3. The exception occurs in case of the lowest class of towns (Class VI) because many among these enjoy a special status, as mentioned above, and consequently have higher level of amenities.

4. In order to access funds, most states and cities were in a hurry to pass legislations and office orders to introduce the reforms without having much know-how as regards the reforms *per se* or their long-term consequences.

5. 63 cities were selected in 2005 as mission cities as per 2001 Census. In addition to the state capitals, seven cities with 4 million plus population, 28 cities with 1 million plus but less than 4 million population and seven cities of tourist importance comprised the Mission cities. Two cities, namely Porbandar and Tirupati, were added to the list in 2009 as religious/historic cities.

6. Notably, the Infrastructural Development (ID) component is being looked after by the Ministry of Urban Development while BSUP is being administered by the Ministry of Housing and Urban Poverty Alleviation.

7. According to the MoUD website, all cities and towns, as per 2001 Census, not covered under the Mission component of JNNURM are to be covered under UIDSSMT.

8. The exception occurs in case of the lowest class of towns (Class VI) because many among these enjoy a special status, as mentioned above, and consequently have higher level of amenities.

References

Dubey, Amaresh and Shubhashis Gangopadhyay (1998) *Counting the Poor: Where are the Poor in India?* Delhi: Central Statistical Organisation.

Economic Survey of India (2009–10) Ministry of Finance, Government of India.

Eleventh Five Year Plan (2007–12) Planning Commission of India.

http://jnnurm.nic.in

http://urbanindia.nic.in

Kundu, D. and D. Samanta (2011) 'Redefining the Inclusive Urban Agenda in India: A Critical Appraisal'. *Economic and Political Weekly*. Vol. XLVI, No. 5, 29 January.

Kundu, Debolina (2009) 'Elite Capture and Marginalization of the Poor in Participatory Urban Governance: A Case of Resident Welfare Associations in Metro Cities'. In *India Urban Poverty Report 2009*. MoHUPA and UNDP, New Delhi: Oxford University Press.

Kundu, A. et al. (1999) 'Regional Distribution of Infrastructure and Basic Amenities in Urban India: Issues Concerning Empowerment of Local Bodies' (with A. Kundu and S. Bagchi), *Economic and Political Weekly*. July, pp. 1893–906.

——. (2007) A Strategy Paper on Migration and Urbanisation in the Context of Development Dynamics, Governmental Programmes and Evolving Institutional Structure in India. A paper commissioned by United Nations Population Fund (UNFPA).

Mahadevia, Darshini (2006) 'NURM and the Poor in Globalising Mega Cities'. *Economic and Political Weekly*. Vol. XLI, No. 31, pp. 3399–403.

McKinsey Global Institute (MGI) (2010) *India's Urban Awakening: Building Inclusive Cities, Sustaining Economic Growth*. Washington, DC: McKinsey & Co., March.

Mukhopadhyay, Partha (2006) 'Whither Urban Renewal?'. *Economic and Political Weekly*. Vol. XLI, No. 10, 11 March.

NSSO (2004–05) Level and Pattern of Consumer Expenditure, 61st Round .

Patkar, Medha et al. (2007) 'Urban Renewal: At Whose Cost?'. *Economic and Political Weekly*. Vol. XLII, No. 11, pp. 17–23.

Raghu (2005) 'Urban Renewal Mission: Whose Agenda?'. *People's Democracy*. Vol. XXIX, No. 49, 4 December.

Report of the Thirteenth Finance Commission, 2010–2015 (March 2010) Delhi: Akalank Publications.

Sivaramakrishnan, K C. et al. (2005) *Handbook of Urbanization in India*. New Delhi: Oxford University Press.

Part Two
Case Studies

9

Urban Development and Small Towns in Punjab

R.S. SANDHU AND JASMEET SANDHU

India had only 10 per cent of urban population in 1901, which increased to 31.2 per cent in 2011. This shows an increase of only 21.2 per cent in eleven decades which appears less significant. But once this increase is seen in absolute numbers it becomes evident that the urban population of India increased more than 15 times, i.e., from 25 million to 377 million during this period. India's urbanisation is oriented towards metropolitan and Class I cities. This is evident from the massive increase in the percentage share of Class I cities, i.e., from 26 per cent in 1901 to 68.7 per cent in 2001. Metros accounted for 26.41 per cent of the total urban population in 1981, which increased to 37.81 per cent in 2001. The number of such cities has also increased from 12 to 23 and to 35 in 1981, 1991 and 2001, respectively. Although Class II, III and other classes of towns are growing in numbers, but their share in population has been declining steadily due to the rapid growth of metros and Class I cities (Census of India, 2001).

The colonial urban development in India was mainly in the form of the presidency and chief provincial cities which emerged along the main railway systems of hill stations. William Digby (1901) rightly pointed out, 'there are two countries: Anglostan, the land especially ruled by the English, in which English investments have been made, and Hindustan, practically all India fifty miles from each side of railway lines'. Post-colonial development also followed the British legacy and urban development took place along the major transportation routes (national/state highways and main railway lines). The National Commission on Urbanisation (Government of India, 1988) noted that the smaller urban centres remain impoverished and unable to provide even minimum level of infrastructure and services, whereas the larger ones suffer from acute inadequacy of services and distribution, creating zones of extreme deprivation. Kundu and Bhatia (2001) emphasised that the new development perspective and management solutions advocated for urban development in India do not take into cognisance the serious distortions in urban hierarchy and the spatial distribution of economic activities. Kundu (2011) again argued that although two plans (10th and 11th) considered low urban growth and weakening economic base of small towns as a serious problem, they placed the thrust of growth strategy onto 'increasing the efficiency and productivity of cities by deregulation and development of land.' High Powered Expert Committee (HPEC, 2011) on Urban Infrastructure and Services also recognised the fact that 'the small towns and medium towns have languished for want of an economic base'. The urban researchers have also focused their attention on metros only and small cities and towns have been ignored by them in India (Sandhu, 2011a). In 2011, a century-old observation of William Digby and the findings of the National Commission on Urbani-sation are still appropriate and relevant, in spite of a span of planning through 11 Five-Year Plan in the country.

Keeping the national scenario in mind, the present paper attempts to understand the nature and extent of urban development in Punjab in general and in small towns in particular. The Punjab state, with 33.95 per cent of urban population, was one of the most urbanised states of India (Census, 2001). Here, we shall try to understand the urban development in the state through some indicators such as level and pattern of urbani-sation in the state, process of planning and development, infrastructure and social characteristics. In the case of Punjab, there are 217 towns as per Census 2011. But detailed information about various classes of towns is not available yet, therefore, analysis in the present paper is based on the data from Census 2001. According to the Census 2001, there were 157 towns in Punjab, which included 14 Class I towns (including two metrop-olises) and 143 towns of Classes II to VI. The focus of this paper would be mainly on Class II to Class V towns. The paper is divided into four sections; the first section would deal with the trend of urbanisation in Punjab, the second will discuss the process of planning and development, the third part would explain the state of infrastructure and finally, the fourth would highlight the social characteristics of these towns.

Urban development includes the entire field of planning and execution of development works in towns/cities. Primarily, its basic function is to provide social and physical infrastructure to the people so that they could live in healthy surroundings and follow their social, cultural and productive activities with relative ease and efficiency. Planning and development is a 'state subject' under the Constitution of India. Therefore, the state government is responsible to enact legislations, establish authorities/agencies to carry out planning, development and maintenance in the state. Before moving to the first section, we would like to comment on the present data base available in Indian cities.

Data Base

We are more knowledgeable about stars and planets but are less aware of our own cities and towns. Ordinary cities and towns have been suffering from an information crisis, and it seriously undermines institutional capacity to develop and analyse and to have effective urban policy. The National Urban Observatory India (Town and Country Planning Organisation, 2002 & 2004) found, after studying 34 towns through various universities and research institutes in 2001–02 and 2002–03, that the 'urban data is scanty and scattered and it is generally aggregated at the district and the state level and the available information is neither reliable nor up-to-date'. Local bodies in Punjab do not have any systematic data base for the cities. Japan Bank of International Cooperation (2006) concluded, satirically, that 'it (data) is all in the heads of officials concerned rather than on the files'. When these officials retire or get transferred to other branches, all information goes with them. Further, data about same item varies within the Corporation from one branch to another. There is hardly any data from where income of a city can be calculated. Although there has been tremendous advancement in data base management system, yet a lot of information, particularly at the local level, remains unrecorded, unorganised and inaccessible; and officials consider it as confidential and personal property. The standardisation of data systems and their documentation is still at the rudimentary stage in the state. This situation is more precarious in the case of small and medium towns because they lack expertise and resources to create and maintain the data base. In the absence of reliable and upgraded data base, the present paper may fall short of available data; and it may be old and inadequate.

Urbanisation in Punjab

Before initiating any discussion on urbanisation in the state, it is pertinent to note that Punjab has been divided twice in the last 64 years and it lost its two capital cities. Firstly, Punjab lost its capital city of Lahore to West Pakistan in 1947, and later on at the time of its reorganisation in 1966, its capital city Chandigarh was declared as a union territory. Like India, Punjab is also considered predominantly an agrarian state though these days its non-agricultural sector contributes 75.08 per cent towards its GDP (Government of Punjab, 2011). According to 2011 Census, Punjab's total population stands at 27,704,236 persons, of whom 17,316,800 persons reside in rural areas and 10,387,436 persons in urban areas (Census of India, 2011). Accordingly, rural population accounts for 62.51 per cent of the state's population whereas the urban population constitutes 37.49 per cent of the total state population.

In 1951, the state's total population was 91.57 lakh. Rural population constituted 72.33 lakh, i.e., 79.0 per cent and the urban population 19.24 lakh, i.e., 21 per cent. During the last six decades, i.e., from 1951 to 2011, the total population of the state has increased to 277.04 lakh, an increase of 202.5 per cent. During the same period, the rural population increased by 139.4 per cent and the urban population by 440.6 per cent. In other words, the increase in rural population in the state during 1951–2011 was about 2.4 times, whereas the urban population increased more than five times, and the level of urbanisation went up from 21.0 per cent in 1951 to 37.49 per cent in 2011.

Table 1 shows that the growth rate of urban population during 1951–1961 was 29.06 per cent, which was higher than the growth rate (26.06%) of India's urban population. In the next three decades (i.e., 1971–2001), the growth rate of urban population in Punjab remained lower than the all-India growth rate. The lower growth rate of urban population in Punjab during 1961–91 can be attributed to two reasons. Firstly, the period between 1961–1971 and afterwards was the period of 'green revolution' in which the rural areas prospered and many small service towns developed, which usually supported agricultural and allied activities. D'Souza (1976) observed that there was a functional change of towns in Punjab during 1961–71 rather than higher growth rate of the urban population. These towns usually have lower growth rate as compared to the industrial towns because they mainly perform central place functions for their hinterland. Another reason for the lower growth rate of urban population in Punjab can be the government's policies favouring rural development. Moreover, agricultural development was also more or less uniformly spread in different regions of the state (Bhalla and Chadha, 1981).

Table 1

Urbanisation in Punjab and India during 1951–2001

Year	Total urban population (in lakhs) Punjab	Percentage of urban population		Growth rate of urban population		No. of towns
		Punjab	India	Punjab	India	
1951	19.24	21.0	17.29	20.02	41.42	98
1961	25.58	22.9	17.97	29.06	26.06	106
1971	32.16	23.7	19.41	25.27	38.23	108
1981	46.47	26.1	23.34	44.51	46.34	134
1991	60.01	29.7	25.72	28.45	39.19	120
2001	82.45	33.95	27.78	37.58	31.13	157
2011	103.87	37.49	31.2	25.72	31.81	217

Source: Census of India 2001 and 2011.

Table 1 and Figure 1 reveal a reversal in the trend that is, during 1991–2001, the urban population of Punjab grew at the rate of 37.58 per cent and this growth rate was higher than the growth rate for India (31.31%). During this decade, there was tremendous increase in the number of towns, i.e., from 120 in 1991 to 157 in 2001. According to the data, 41 new towns were declared for the first time and a few old towns were merged with the urban agglomerations. So, there was a net addition of 37 towns in Punjab state in this decade. The new towns added about one-fifth (or 4.4 lakh) of an additional urban population. In 2001, Amritsar city joined Ludhiana as another metropolitan city of the state. In all, Class I cities constituted about three-fifths (58.39%) of the total urban population, Class II and III towns together constituted 29.0 per cent of the total population. There was a slight decrease in the population in these towns although their number increased. Similarly, Class IV, V and VI towns also increased in number but their share of urban population relatively decreased.

Figure 1

Urbanisation in Punjab and India during 1951–2011

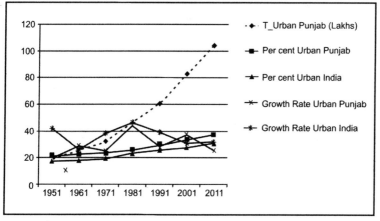

Therefore, in the last six decades (1951–2011), the level of urbanisation in Punjab has gone up from 21 per cent to 37.49 per cent, whereas the urban population has increased more than five times (19.24 lakh to 103.87 lakh), and the number of towns has increased by 102 per cent only (98 to 217).

Pattern of Urbanisation

With the above trend in the level of urbanisation and increase in total urban population in the state, distribution of increased population in different geographical regions and in different classes of towns in the state can now be analysed.

Geographical Distribution

The pattern of geographical distribution of urban population in the state depicts the uneven level of urbanisation and concentration of urban population in the districts of Punjab. It shows that there is a marked disparity among the districts of Punjab as far as the level of urbanisation is concerned. According to Census 2001, Ludhiana district, the most urbanised district, has more than one-half of its population (55.80%)

Map 1

Pattern of Geographical Distribution of Urban Population

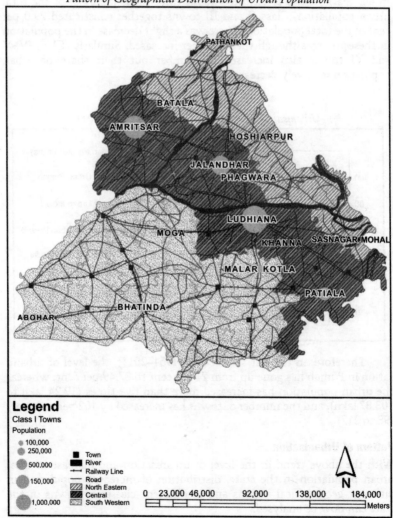

residing in urban areas. Nawanshahar is the least urbanised district of the state and it has just one-seventh of its population (13.80%) living in the urban areas. Besides Ludhiana, three other districts which have higher level of urbanisation than the state average are: Jalandhar (47.45%), Amritsar (40%) and Patiala (34.98%). These are the districts through which National Highway 1 (G.T. Road) passes. These four districts accommodate more than a half (54.46%) of the state's total urban population. There are two other districts, namely, Fatehgarh Sahib and Kapurthala, which are also located on the National Highway No. 1, but their level of urbanisation is lesser than the state average, and they accommodate only 5 per cent of the state's total urban population.

These six districts also form a contiguous belt that divides the state into three broad regions (as shown in Map 1), namely, North-eastern Punjab, Central Punjab and South-western Punjab, accommodating 15 per cent, 60 per cent and about 25 per cent of the urban population, respectively. Central Punjab is most urbanised of the three regions and all the major cities of the state, namely Ludhiana, Jalandhar, Amritsar and Patiala, are in this region.

As has been stated earlier, urbanisation and development share a positive relationship. Similarly, the most urbanised region, i.e., the central region is also the most developed region of Punjab. This is also more industrialised as compared to the other two regions of the state, and is the most important region for socio-cultural and economic activities. The districts falling in the other two regions of the state are lesser urbanised, lesser industrialised and lesser developed as compared to the central region.

Distribution of Urban Population in Different Classes of Towns

As stated earlier, there has been a substantial increase in the urban population in the state. Let us see how this growth is distributed in different classes of cities/towns. According to Census of India, there are six classes of towns. Table 2 presents the number of towns of different classes in the state and the percentage distribution of urban population in these towns (class-wise) for the six Census years, i.e., 1951, 1961, 1971, 1981, 1991 and 2001. It shows that in 1951, there were 98 towns in the state. There were three Class I cities, namely, Amritsar, Jalandhar and Ludhiana, accommodating one-third (33.11%) of the total urban population; another one-third (33.71%) of the population was accommodated in 19 Class II and III towns, and the remaining one-third (32.68%) of the total urban population of the state was accommodated in 76 Class IV, V and VI towns. This pattern of urbanisation showed an even distribution of population in towns of different classes, which is usually found in agricultural surplus states.

Table 2

Percentage of urban population in different classes of towns in Punjab: 1951–2001

Class of town	Census year					
	1951	*1961*	*1971*	*1981*	*1991*	*2001*
I	33.11 (3)	38.5 (4)	40.62 (4)	45.40 (7)	54.31 (10)	58.39 (14)
II	7.73 (2)	8.1 (4)	15.68 (8)	13.28 (9)	19.8 (18)	16.46 (19)
III	25.98 (17)	28.3 (23)	21.74 (22)	21.31 (28)	12.9 (25)	12.50 (35)
IV	14.14 (21)	11.2 (23)	13.78 (33)	11.07 (35)	10.5 (44)	9.82 (54)
V	13.18 (30)	10.0 (34)	7.00 (30)	6.72 (41)	2.0 (16)	2.52 (28)
VI	5.36 (25)	2.8 (17)	1.18 (11)	1.22 (14)	0.5 (7)	0.33 (7)
Total No. of Towns	98	106	108	134	120	157

Note: Number of towns in each category is given in parentheses.

Class I town = 1 lakh and above   Class II town= 50,000–99,999
Class III town = 20,000–49,999   Class IV town= 10,000–19,999
Class V town = 5,000–9,999   Class VI town= Below 5,000

Source: Census of India 2001.

The number of towns/urban agglomerations increased from 98 to 157 during 1951–2001. Table 2 also shows that in 2001, Class I cities increased in number from 3 to 14 and their share of urban population also increased from 33.11 per cent in 1951 to 58.39 per cent in 2001. The number of Class II towns also increased from 2 to 19 and these towns also gained in terms of their share of urban population. In 2001, 33 Class I and II cities and towns of the state together accounted for three-fourths (75.85%) of the total urban population. On the other hand, the remaining four classes of towns (Class III to VI), which contained 59.16 per cent of the total urban population in 1951, had only 24.15 per cent of the urban population in 2001. Thus, the gain of Class I and Class II towns has been the loss of remaining classes of towns. The growth rate for Class I towns was 48.31 per cent (as against the state average of 37.58%). It was merely 13.68 per cent for Class II towns, Class III towns recorded a growth rate of 33.08 per cent, Class IV returned 24.86 per cent and Class V towns emerged as the most promising towns and recorded the highest growth rate of 101.94 per cent. However, lowest category of towns (Class VI) returned a net negative growth rate of 4.53 per cent during the last decade. The higher growth rate of a particular class of towns is mainly due to the graduation of lower class of towns in them, as in the case of Class I towns, there was addition of four towns from Class II towns to Class I towns during 1991 to 2001. Same thing happened in the case of Class V towns by the addition of 12 towns from Class IV category.

Figure 2

Percentage of urban population in different categories of towns in Punjab, 1951–2001

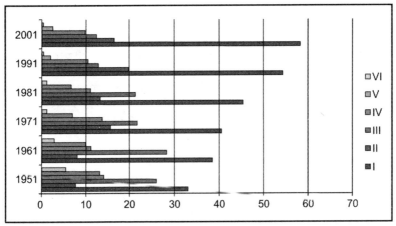

Source: Computed from Census 2001.

There was a tremendous increase in the number of towns in the state during 1991–2001. Their number went up from 120 in 1991 to 157 in 2001. This increase was observed in all the classes of towns except the Class VI towns. As many as 41 new towns were declared in the 2001 Census for the first time, a few old towns were merged with the urban agglomerations and there was a net addition of 37 towns in this decade.

Another feature of this decade (1991–2001) was the higher growth rate of urban population in the state as compared to the national average. In 2001, Amritsar city joined Ludhiana city as another metropolitan city of the state. Class I cities consisted of about three-fifth (58.39%) of the total urban population. Contrary to this, for India as a whole, it was 69 per cent, 83 per cent for West Bengal, 80 per cent for Maharashtra and 76 per cent each for Gujarat and Andhra Pradesh. Class II and III towns (54 in number) had 29 per cent of the total urban population of the state. There was a slight decrease in the proportion of urban population in these towns but their number increased from 43 in 1991 to 54 in 2001. Similarly, the number of Class IV, V and VI towns also increased but their share of urban population decreased.

Punjab's urbanisation presents a sharp contrast to that of mono-centric urbanisation in the states of Maharashtra or West Bengal, where a single metropolis dominates the scene (Dasgupta, 2000). Here, it is spatially dispersed and the biggest city of the state accounts for only one-sixth of the urban population of the state. However, in the last few decades, the trend is towards the concentration of population in Class I cities. This tendency could be attributed to increasing inequalities in the villages, resulting from the accumulation and transfer of capital by rich farmers to the cities. The major cities and the developed regions of the state are economically more vibrant and are attracting more migrants both from within the state and out of the state. For instance, Ludhiana city had 1,89,612 migrants in 1991 out of which about 50 per cent were from within the state and remaining were from other states and other countries (Singh, 2001). Industrialisation is also an important factor in the urbanising process. Further, natural increase and upgradation of Class II towns to Class I towns are also contributing towards the increase in proportion of population in Class I towns.

Process of Planning and Development in Punjab

The Punjab government has created a number of agencies at the state level such as the Town and Country Planning Department, Water Supply and Sewerage Board, Punjab State Electricity Board (now divided into two Corporations), Punjab State Industrial Development Corporation and, at local level, Municipal Corporations/Committees and Improvement Trusts to carry out the planning and development in the cities/towns of the state. Besides these, the Punjab Urban Planning and Development Authority (PUDA) was also established in 1995 to take care of overall urban development in the state. Under the umbrella of PUDA, six local-level development authorities have been created recently, which include Greater Mohali Area Development Authority (GMADA), Greater Area Ludhiana Urban Development Authority (GALDA), Amritsar Development Authority (ADA), Jalandhar Development Authority (JDA), Patiala Urban Development Authority (PatUDA) and Bathinda Development Authority (BDA).

Due to the multiplicity of authorities and lack of coordination among them, there is a lot of confusion and conflict among these agencies and ultimate victims are the people and urban development. The duplication of work among various developing agencies, cumbersome procedures, and organisational inadequacies lead to unauthorised and haphazard urban growth instead of planned development. These authorities have been functioning independently under their own Acts, and jurisdictions. The state Town and Country Planning Department (1974) found in its report that in Ludhiana, Amritsar and Jalandhar cities, the percentage of planned developed area was only 21.93 per cent, 26 per cent and 26.3 per cent, respectively. Around 30 to 40 per cent urban area was without water supply and 40 to 50 per cent was without sewerage system.

The state has thus remained backward in urban planning and development. In 1970s, Draft Master Plans were prepared for 35 cities/towns in the state but their non-statutory status made them ineffective. In spite of their non-statutory status, many residential urban estates, development schemes, town planning schemes and industrial nodal points were set up in conformity with the proposals of the master plans in the state. The department reviewed the earlier master plans and prepared new master plans for the period 1985–2001 for some cities, which were again revised in 1992 and 2000. New master plans for the period 2000–2021 were prepared, but these master plans lacked legal backing, which was considered as the main handicap in the implementation of these plans. With the enactment of the Punjab Regional and Town Planning and Development (Amendment) Act, 2006, simpler legal framework has been provided for the preparation of master plans for cities and towns of the state. Under this Act, now 35 master plans have been prepared by the Town and Country Planning Department and consultants mainly for Class I and II towns and for some small towns situated in their vicinity, but a majority of the small towns have been developing without any planning in the state.

Towns of the state have had inadequate infrastructure and massive increase in their populations could not be accommodated in a planned manner. This has resulted in uncontrolled and haphazard growth, non-conforming land use, and excessive strain on road network, utilities, services and facilities, housing shortage, proliferation of slums, traffic congestion, and overall degradation of urban environment. In other words, the skewed urban structure and spontaneous pattern of urbanisation has emerged in the state essentially because in the national planning process, 'explicit spatial policies ... have seldom been strong enough to alter existing spatial and hierarchical patterns and because spatial considerations have never received the attention they deserve' (Planning Commission, 1982). Till now there is no comprehensive urban policy at national or state level, and in the absence of any urban policy, such type of urban development is inevitable. Urban development is also a low-priority area for the state. Human Development Report (Government of Punjab, 2004) of the state was prepared and released through some consultants but urban development was conspicuous by its absence in the report, whereas urban sector has been contributing 75.08 per cent to the state GDP (Government of Punjab, 2010–2011).

The state has been boasting of preparing Master Plans for its towns and cities. But it is a widely accepted fact that the master planning method in India has not produced satisfactory physical environment and is not commonly used elsewhere (Rai, 2010; Planning Commission, 2008). Further, planners are of the view that 'it is not well suited to rapidly growing cities and multi-jurisdiction urban agglomerations. The master plan concept has also not been useful in addressing to India's large and widely spread slums. By locking in the supply of buildable land and space, the master plan, inter alia, inhibits the development of housing markets and contributes to proliferation of slums' (Planning Commission, 2008). Further, the existing Town and Country Planning Department of the state does not have adequate qualified planners and supporting staff to carry out any detailed exercise of planning. To illustrate the point, information was collected about the number of planners in the department since 1970s. In July 2010, there were 19 town planners against 53 sanctioned posts. Interestingly, the situation was much better in 1970s when a majority of the sanctioned posts (56) were occupied in the state Town and Country Planning Department. Since 1970s, the urban population has increased more than three times but the number of town planners has reduced to one-third. As per international standards, it is desired that there should be one planner for 5,000 urban residents (Ramanathan, 2008), but in Punjab, there is one planner for every 5,00,000 urban residents. It was found that master plans are prepared in the state in a very casual manner. For instance, during this study, it was noted that the master plan of one of the major cities of the state does not have existing land use plan of the city. Further probing revealed that the master plan was prepared hurriedly on the orders of the High Court without following the prescribed procedure in preparation of a master plan. It is bound to happen when there is scarcity of qualified planners and their supporting staff in the department. Even the planners working in the department feel that they are dictated by their bureaucrat bosses in formulation and planning of specific schemes, and compel them to plan by diluting the existing planning standards and norms. The planners feel that they have little say in the process, and they are there collecting only change of land use charges for the state by accommodating various promoters who violate the existing norms of planning, but have direct access to politicians and bureaucrats. Such a perception prevails because the urban space is considered a commodity which attracts investors, speculators and all those who have stakes in what has been termed 'urban fortunes' by Logan and Molotch (2007: 2–3). In this process, the planners who should be at the helm of affairs get marginalised, resulting in unplanned development.

Not surprisingly, Mr Jagmohan, the former Union Minister for Urban Development, made the following comments about Ludhiana city in 1998:

> Its present population exceeds 1.5 million. It is the biggest money-spinner in Punjab and a hosiery capital of the country. Its annual production in this area alone is about ₹ 10 billion. And yet, it is a city which has 50 per cent structures raised without any planning or regulation … . The level of air pollution is four times more than the toleration limit.

The Chief Administrator of the Punjab Urban Planning and Development Authority admitted that there were 3,075 cases of unauthorised colonies in Punjab in 2007. In the case of Bathinda, PUDA identified 26 unauthorised colonies (*Tribune*, 2010), and in Zirakpur (a small town located on the periphery of tri city of Chandigarh, Panchkula and S.A.S. Nagar) 71 unauthorised colonies have come up within the last few years. On 12 June 2011, the Deputy Commissioner of a district banned land registration in illegal colonies to check their mushrooming and illegal growth. But after two months, under political pressure, the DC of Sangrur lifted the ban on registration of land in illegal colonies within and outside the municipal limits (Majeed, 2011). The mushrooming of unauthorised colonies is a clear indication of unplanned urban growth in the state. It also reveals prevailing governmental planning (or non-planning), and attitude of development authorities towards planned development in the state.

Infrastructure

The quality of urban living is determined by the nature and type of infrastructure (social, economic, cultural and physical) provided to the people residing in the urban areas. It reflects the level of well-being of a particular community with emphasis on the quantity and quality of civic amenities and facilities like sewerage and disposal facilities, water supply, streetlights, sanitary services, roads, medical, educational, banking, recreational and other infrastructural facilities. In fact, the state of urbanisation and the quality of life tend to supplement each other. Access to basic amenities is the most important aspect of quality of urbanisation. The amenities like electricity, water, sanitation and clean fuel are the critical determinants of living conditions and health of the urban people (Clegg and Garlick, 1979; Ali and Rahman, 2004).

Punjab is more developed and urbanised than other states of India and it is also considered as the number one state in terms of the availability of infrastructure (Aiyer, 2010) in the country which includes social, economic and physical infrastructure. The present paper deals with social and physical infrastructure only. Under social infrastructure, health and educational facilities are examined; and under physical infrastructure, water supply, sewerage system, and roads are studied. There is a wide variation in the availability of infrastructure and services between various types of cities and towns. Usually, it is considered that larger cities have better institutional arrangement and quality of services. Small towns with limited resources always lack or are deficient of infrastructure. But recently, Bhagat (2011) observed that it is not always clear whether more urbanised states have better access to basic amenities or vice versa. Further, he feels that it is not clear whether the big cities are better off than small cities and towns. Keeping Bhagat's proposition in mind, let us examine the state of infrastructure in various classes of towns in Punjab.

Health Facilities

Punjab has taken bold steps in the improvement of health infrastructure services. As per the 2001 Census, the state has 2,852 Sub-Centres, 1,465 Subsidiary Health Centres (each having a medical officer and a pharmacist), 484 PHCs, 117 Community Health Centres, five medical and two dental colleges along with attached hospitals. There are 230 allopathic hospitals in the state. They range from 50-bed hospitals in smaller towns to larger hospitals attached to the five medical colleges, one each at Patiala, Faridkot and Amritsar, and two at Ludhiana, with facilities for dealing with complicated cases and acting as referral hospitals and teaching (CRRID, 2002a).

The availability of health institutions in the state increased 4.5 times (significantly 6.5 times in rural areas and two times in urban areas) between 1966 and 2001. In absolute terms, the total number of institutions rose from 496 in 1966 to 2,229 in 2001, the rural health institutions in the state rose from 275 to 1,777 during the same period, and the urban health institutions from 221 to 452 during 1966–2001. There has hardly been any increase in the number of health institutions after 1985. It has been observed that the percentage share of rural health institutions, which was 55.4 per cent among total health institutions in 1966, increased to 64.9 per cent in 1973, 79.1 per cent in 1980, and 81.6 per cent by the year 1990. During the 1990s, there was some additional emphasis on urban infrastructure. As a result, the share of urban health institutions increased slightly from 18.4 per cent to 20.3 per cent. The percentage share in the number of health institutions by ownership among the state government, local self-governments and voluntary organisations was 96.6 per cent, 1.1 per cent, and 2.3 per cent, respectively, in 2001.

Table 3
Health services by size and class of towns, 2001

Size-class of towns	No. of doctors (10,000 persons)	No. of nurses (10,000 persons)	No. of para-medical staff (10,000 persons)	Other personnel (10,000 persons)	Total no. of medical personnel per 10,000 persons	Total no. of beds	No. of beds per 10,000 persons
I	2.40	3.40	3.96	5.86	15.61	8,395	17.42
II	3.00	5.11	8.61	9.70	26.40	2,572	19.57
III	2.73	3.50	6.39	4.50	17.12	1,345	12.94
IV	2.85	3.71	6.37	5.50	18.42	1,253	16.30
V	4.43	7.00	13.34	8.15	32.91	346	22.20
VI	2.36	2.36	4.71	4.71	14.13	4	9.42
Total	2.62	3.78	5.43	6.32	18.15	13915	17.18

Source: Computed by Singh (2010) from:1. Municipal Statistics, Punjab, 2000–2001, pp. 94–104. Census of India, Punjab, 2001.

According to 2001 Census, the total number of medical personnel and beds in hospitals are registered as 14,706 and 13,915, respectively, in the state (Table 3). In other words, each medical personnel and each bed in the hospitals is for 551 and 582 urban residents, respectively. Whereas, according to the World Health Organisation norms, there should be one bed for 200 persons. Table 3 reveals that there are, on an average, 18.15 medical personnel and 17.18 beds in hospitals after every 10,000 persons living in Punjab. People residing in lower classes of towns have more medical personnel to serve than their counterparts residing in higher classes of towns. The position of Class I towns is still more depressing because they have to serve a large number of people residing in their service zone. The hospitals in bigger towns provide multi-specialty services that attract people from far-flung areas, which is not the case in lower class of towns, and the presence of better health facilities in bigger towns makes them better served areas in the state. These facilities are mainly concentrated in private medical institutions which are very costly for the common man, and governmental health institutions are in a bad shape due to their inefficient functioning because of many well-known reasons. (Peters et al., 2003) also noted, that the Indian public sector runs almost 200,000 primary health facilities and 150,000 secondary and tertiary facilities, but it is the private medical sector that accounts for 80 per cent of out-patient treatments and almost 60 per cent of the in-patient treatments.

Table 3 further indicates that, on an average, there are 2.62 doctors for 10,000 persons in the state but this ratio is lower in Class towns and is higher in case of other classes of towns. This is also true in the case of number of nurses, para-medical staff and other personnel for 10,000 persons in the state. Similarly, the number of beds is also more in case of Class II and Class V towns than Class I towns in the state. In short, it can be concluded that small towns are better-off than the bigger towns in terms of quantity of health infrastructure, but quality service is not provided by them, due to shortage of staff and medicines, low budget and lack of good governance. On the other hand, due to malfunctioning of health institutions in small towns, many unqualified practitioners are flourishing. A World Bank report (2004) found that, in Punjab, the absence rate for doctors and other health workers was 38.8 per cent and 43.8 per cent, respectively. The absence rate would be much higher in the case of rural areas and small towns which are away from the district headquarters. It has been observed that the availability of infrastructure does not ensure its delivery to the people. Even when government provision is extensive, this may not translate into substantial use unless there is good governance.

Educational Facilities

Literacy rate in the state was 58.51 per cent in 1991 and it increased to 76.68 per cent in 2011 (Census, 2011). The state has universal access to primary education. Except some remote areas/new habitations with small populations, there is a government primary school in almost every village. However, there are 61 per cent villages without middle cadre schools. In Punjab, the state government manages 90.8 per cent of the recognised educational institutions: 9 per cent are non-government, aided and/or recognised institutions and only a negligible number comes under the control of the Centre (CRRID, 2002b).

In terms of educational institutions per 10,000 persons, the state on the whole has 0.02 medical and engineering colleges, 0.03 polytechnic colleges and 0.26 arts/science/commerce/law colleges on the one hand, and 0.72 senior secondary schools, 1.19 secondary schools, 1.40 middle schools and 2.33 primary schools, on the other hand. Three main features relating to the distribution of educational institutions in urban Punjab can be observed from Table 4.

Table 4

Educational facilities by size and class of towns in 2001

Size and class of towns	No. of Medical and Engineering colleges per 10,000 persons	No. of Polytechnics (per 10,000 persons)	No. of Arts Sciences, Commerce, Law colleges per 10,000 persons	No. of Senior Secondary Schools per 10,000 persons	No. of Secondary Schools per 10,000 persons	No. of Middle Schools per 10,000 persons	No. of Primary Schools per 10,000 persons
I	0.02	0.03	0.19	0.56	0.96	1.11	1.91
II	0.04	0.03	0.27	0.62	1.14	1.44	2.31
III	0.02	0.04	0.40	0.96	1.46	1.71	3.10
IV	0.01	0.01	0.46	1.28	2.03	2.42	3.42
V	0.00	0.00	0.32	1.92	2.63	3.14	4.75
VI	0.00	0.00	0.00	4.71	4.71	4.71	9.42
Total	0.02	0.03	0.26	0.72	1.19	1.40	2.33

Sources: Computed by Singh (2010) from Census of India, Punjab, 2001.

First, all types of professional colleges, i.e., medical, engineering or polytechnic are mainly concentrated in bigger urban centres of Class I, II and III. It is particularly associated with relatively more demand for professional education and more educational awareness in highly developed and diversified economies of bigger urban centres, and existence of related facilities essential for the efficient functioning of these higher order institutions. An analysis of the spatial distribution of educational facilities within the towns reveals that usually slums are deprived of schools in them. In the case of Ludhiana city, about 50 per cent slums of the city do not have even a primary school. Further, the table indicates that the number of schools of various levels per 10,000 of persons goes on increasing as we move from the higher class of the urban centres to the lower ones. It reveals that the population pressure on school-level educational services in bigger urban centres is relatively more. As far as quality of education is concerned, it is a known fact that reputed colleges and schools are located in bigger cities and hence contribute towards better quality of education. A qualitative analysis of infrastructural facilities available in primary schools of the state reveals that more than 1,000 schools do not have buildings of their own. Even basic necessities such as drinking water and toilets are conspicuous by their absence in a large number of schools. An overwhelming majority of these schools are located in villages and small towns. Lack of good governance and inadequate staff (at present more than a half of the government colleges and schools are without regular principals) further makes these schools less attractive for the students. Consequently, there has been a mushrooming growth of private schools everywhere in the state. Their performance is better than the government-run schools because of their efficient management. Rather, they are growing because of the inefficiency of government-owned schools. Recently, it has been observed that there is an unexpected increase of professional colleges (engineering, dental, educational, nursing and management) in the state, especially in the rural areas near small towns because of the availability of cheap land. This makes small towns better served areas by the educational institutions, provided these professional institutions attract the local youths for higher learning, which is very doubtful.

It has been observed that the availability of infrastructure does not ensure its delivery to the people, especially in the government-run institutions. A World Bank report (2004) found that in Punjab, the absence rate for teachers was 35.7 per cent. The absence rate would be much higher in the case of rural areas and small towns which are away from the district headquarters.

Water Supply

At the national level, 20 per cent of country's urban households do not have access to safe drinking water, 58 per cent do not have safe sanitation, and more than 40 per cent of garbage generated is left uncollected for want of proper waste management (Sridhar and Mathur, 2009).

In urban Punjab, all have access to potable water but only two-third households have access to tap water and remaining one-third of them depend on hand pumps and other sources (Table 5). Three-fourth of them have this service within their houses but still one-fourth of the households have to go out to fetch water for themselves (refer Table 6). The availability of tap water indicates the higher degree of development and this situation varies from town to town and within the town also. Table 7 shows that in the case of Class I towns, 71.40 per cent households have the access to water tap facility; in case of Class II towns, it is 66.07 per cent, and further in Class V towns, it is minimum, i.e., 38.74 per cent only. From this, it can be concluded that the situation of water supply deteriorates as one moves from the higher class to the lower class of towns. Usually availability and sources of water depend on the size of population of a town. In the case of Class I towns, the situation is better than the smaller towns. Even in bigger cities, there are certain areas which lack piped water supply. In Ludhiana city, 85 per cent population gets piped water supply and 2.5 lakh population (about 15%) remains outside the water supply of the Municipal Corporation.

Table 5

Percentage distribution of households by source of drinking water

Source of Water	Percentage
Tap	66.81
Handpump	29.44
Others	3.74

Source: Census 2001.

Figure 3

Percentage distribution of households by source of drinking water

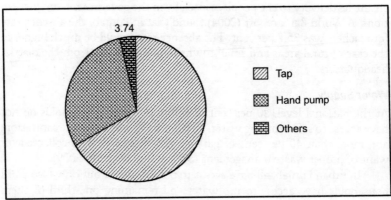

Table 6

Percentage distribution of households according to location of drinking water source

Location of water source	Tap	Hand pump	Others
Within premises	94.94	87.53	75.68
Near premises	4.16	10.61	15.73
Far away from premises	0.88	0.54	8.57

Source: Census 2001.

Table 7

Distribution of households in towns (class-wise) of Punjab according to availability of source of water

Town/ No.	HH_T	Tap	% of Tap	Hand Pump	% of Hand Pumps	Tubewell and Others	% of Tubewells and Others
Class I							
14	8,76,193	6,25,571	71.40	2,27,687	25.99	29,871	3.41
Class II							
19	2,31,333	52,845	66.07	67,742	29.28	10,746	4.65
Class III							
39	2,01,290	1,28,161	63.67	61,450	30.53	11,679	5.80
Class IV							
54	1,46,657	76,683	52.29	62,214	42.42	7,760	5.29
Class V							
29	38,481	14,909	38.74	20,625	53.60	2,947	7.66
Class VI							
8	3,09,905	2,24,254	72.36	77,796	25.10	7,855	2.53

Source: Computed from Census 2001.

Figure 4

Percentage distribution of households with water taps and class of towns

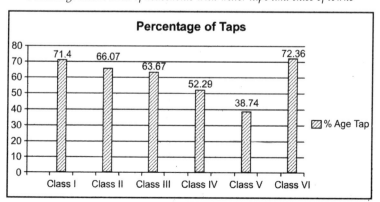

196 ◆ R.S. Sandhu and Jasmeet Sandhu

Sewerage System

The sewerage system is in operation in the state but its coverage varies from town to town. In Punjab, only 47 per cent of the households are connected with the sewerage system, while two-fifth of them are using pit latrine or other type of latrine, and 13 per cent households are without any latrine. In towns, municipal corporations/municipal committees operate and maintain the public underground piped sewerage system. Table 8 reveals that larger population is served with the sewerage system in Class I towns and this proportion declines in lower classes of towns. In case of Class I towns, 52.01 per cent of the households have water closet connected with the sewerage system. In the remaining classes of towns, it declines regularly. In case of Class V towns, less than one-fourth of the households are connected with the sewerage system. Further, the table reveals that a substantial percentage of households are without any latrine and this is negatively associated with the class of towns. In case of Class V towns, more than one-third of them are without latrine. Similarly, the situation of closed drainage system is better in Class I towns than the other classes of towns, as indicated in Table 8. It has been observed that even in Class I towns, water closet facility varies from 35.06 per cent to 84.44 per cent. S.A.S. Nagar (Mohali) is the only exception in the state where 84.44 per cent of the households have access to the sewerage system.

Table 8

Percentage distribution of households by availability of bathroom and type of latrines

Number of Towns	No. of total HH	Per cent bathroom	Type of latrine				% CD	% OD	% ND
			% pit latrine_HH	% WC_HH	% other latrine_HH	% no latrine_HH			
Class I 14	8,76,193	84.77	19.26	52.01	19.91	8.82	54.42	35.43	10.15
Class II 19	2,43,939	82.08	17.23	51.28	18.86	12.64	46.17	43.82	10.01
Class III 39	2,13,563	81.13	24.21	33.83	22.95	19.01	25.83	63.35	10.8
Class IV 54	1,36,572	83.07	26.00	34.74	16.33	30.32	25.98	69.88	10.51
Class V 29	38,481	74.95	32.83	22.11	10.13	34.93	13.7	75.14	14.89
Class VI 8	3,09,905	84.86	15.53	51.87	22.77	10.38	61.39	31.18	8.42

Source: Computed from Census 2001.

Figure 5

Percentage distribution of households in towns (class-wise) of Punjab according to availability of water closet and without latrine

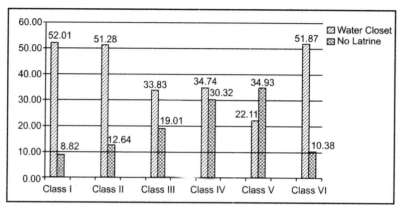

Source: Computed from Census 2001.

Roads

The average road length per sq km of areas in the state is 3.29 km in urban Punjab and it is relatively high in Class I towns. It decreases with the size and class of the towns. For instance, it is 4.91 kms in Class I towns and is lesser than the state average in the remaining classes of towns (Table 9). In other words, higher the size and class of the towns,

Table 9

Status of roads by size and class of towns-2001

Size and class of urban centres	No. of urban centres	Total population	Total area (in sq. kms)	Total Road length (in kms)	Road length per 10,000 population (in kms)
I	14	48,19,089	763.12	4.91	7.77
II	18	13,14,224	390.84	2.73	8.12
III	34	10,39,150	378.35	2.50	9.11
IV	51	7,68,586	354.90	1.73	8.01
V	21	1,55,875	89.13	1.54	8.80
VI	01	4,245	5.71	3.15	42.40
Total	139	81,01,169	1,982.05	3.29	8.06

Sources: Computed by Singh (2010) from Census of India, Punjab, 2001.

better is the status of the roads. It is mainly due to more developed industrial base, trade and commercial activities, good expansion of social institutions, residential areas, public utilities and services in large urban centres which are basically dependent upon good network of road infrastructure. Further, road length per 10,000 of population is found to be inversely related with the size and class of towns, i.e., it increases with the decrease in the size of urban centres. High concentrations of population and social and economic activities in the cities are main accountable factors behind it.

Social Characteristics

Levels of urban development reveal the quality of life and the social characteristics of the residents. Social characteristics have a significant relationship with the quality of life of urban dewellers, because these determine their affordability and accessibility of various urban utilities and services in the town. Further, the size of town indicates the level and availability of various services and utilities there. Social characteristics include occupation, education, caste, residential environment, religion, race, etc. In the urban society, role of traditional factors (caste, occupation, residential environment, religion, race) declines and 'modern' factors such as new occupations, modern education and man-made environment dominates in measuring the level of urbanisation and development. Usually, in cities, the ascribed statuses are replaced by the achieved statuses. More people in big cities are engaged in new occupations rather than traditional occupations. The larger cities are characterised by secondary occupations (non-agricultural), higher literacy, but also higher proportion of slum dwellers. In this background, we will try to analyse the situation in various types of towns in Punjab. In this section, only four indicators are being taken to know the level of urban development in the state. These characteristics include: level of literacy, level of agricultural workers, percentage of Scheduled Castes and proportion of slum population in different classes of towns.

Level of Literacy

Level of literacy is positively related with the size of town and degree of urbanisation. High literacy indicates higher socio-economic status of the residents of the town. In Punjab also, this is true as shown in Table 10. The Class I towns have higher literacy rate (80.50) whereas all the remaining classes of towns have lower literacy rate than the Class I towns. Class V towns have the minimum literacy rate.

Table 10
Size and class-wise concentration of urban literates, 2001

Size and class of towns	No. of towns	% of illiterates to total population
I	14	80.50
II	18	77.50
III	34	78.20
IV	51	74.60
V	21	71.90
VI	1	78.40
Total	139	79.00

Sources: Computed from Census of India 2001, Series 1, primary census abstract, total population.

Agricultural Workers

All activities in rural communities are locally-centred consumption, while in urban areas these are oriented towards the market-oriented products. The market is one of the basic features of non-agricultural activities because without organised exchange of goods and services, the urban dwellers would not survive. In other words, the town is basically a market place and non-agricultural activities are a predominant function of a town. All the bigger cities have lowest percentage of agricultural workers in their workforce. The higher level of agricultural workers indicates low income as well as lower socio-economic development of an area/settlement. It is also presumed that higher the concentration of agricultural workforce, the poor is the quality of urban living and degree of urbanisation. Agriculture workers constituted 5.89 per cent of total urban workforce of Punjab as against the national average of 7.52 per cent, in 2001. Table 11 shows that there is an inverse relationship between the percentage of agricultural workers and the size of town. In other words, smaller towns have higher concentration of agricultural workers than the bigger towns. The range of concentration varies from 3.12 per cent (in Class I towns) to 35.14 per cent in Class VI towns.

Table 11
Agricultural workers by size and class of towns, 2001

Size and class of towns	No. of towns	% of urban agricultural works to total workers	Average index
I	14	3.12	0.69
II	18	5.87	0.98

Cont'd...

...*Cont'd*

III	34	7.97	1.42
IV	51	16.21	2.69
V	21	26.60	4.39
VI	1	35.14	5.95
Total	139	5.89	2.24

Sources: Singh (2010), computed from Census of India 2001, Series 1, primary census abstract, total population.

Percentage of Scheduled Castes

Scheduled Castes accounted for 28.85 per cent of the total population of the state in 2001, much higher than the all-India average of 16.2 per cent. It could be accounted for due to good proportion of outside migrants entering the state for their meagre survival. In urban Punjab, they constituted 20.70 per cent. But their concentration varies from town to town and usually bigger cities have lower percentage of Scheduled Castes than the smaller ones. The size of town indicates the level of socio-economic development and concentration of Scheduled Castes. In earlier decades, D'Souza noted that fewer people among the Scheduled Castes go to the cities than among the rest of population and the greater is the occupational complexity of the city, the lower is representation of Scheduled Castes (D'Souza, 1975). However, in recent years, there are no town-wise (in terms of their size) studies available to analyse trends of mobility of depressed castes (migrants from outside or from within the state) to cities/towns. Table 12 shows that there is a negative relationship between the size of town and concentration of Scheduled Castes. Class I towns have lowest proportion (18.74%) of the Scheduled Castes and Class VI towns have the highest proportion (59.29%) of Scheduled Castes.

Table 12
Schedule caste population by size and class of towns, 2001

Size and class of towns	No. of towns	Total scheduled caste population	% of scheduled caste population to total urban population
I	14	8,78,898	18.24
II	18	2,79,488	21.27
III	34	2,59,293	24.95
IV	51	2,01,472	26.21
V	21	50,927	32.67
VI	1	2,517	59.29
Total	139	16,72,595	20.70

Sources: Singh (2010), compiled from Census of India 2001, Punjab, Series 4, final population totals.

Slums

The slum population in a society is a clear indication of the failure of the society and government to provide adequate habitat for human development (Aldrich and Sandhu, 1995) especially when the main objective of the national housing policy is 'shelter for all', and inclusive growth being the main thrust of the planning and development (11th Five-Year Plan).

Slums are an integral part of Indian cities and their proportion has been directly related to the size of cities. These are areas which lack or have inadequate basic services and are usually inhabited by the poor people, who cannot afford to live in better parts of the city. Due to rapid urbanisation, their number has been increasing regularly and their rate of growth is rather higher than the city population. In1981, there were 27.9 million slum-dwellers in India and by 2001, that number had increased to 42.57 million spread in 640 towns across 26 states and union territories (Census, 2001). They constitute 23.1 per cent of the total population of 640 towns. Punjab has 16.90 lakh slum-dwellers in its towns. They constitute one-fifth of the total urban population of the state, i.e., lower than the national average.

Table 13

Slum population by size and class of towns, 2001

Size class of towns	No. of towns	% of total urban population	Slum population	% of slum population to total urban population	% of slum population to total slum population
I	14	59.49	10,40,487	21.59	61.55
II	18	16.22	2,38,876	18.18	14.13
III	34	12.83	2,35,002	22.61	13.90
IV	51	9.49	1,57,283	20.46	9.30
V	21	1.92	18,871	12.11	1.12
VI	1	0.05	0	0.00	0.00
Total	139	10.00	16,90,519	20.87	100.00

Sources: Computed from:
(I) Census of India, 2001, slum population (640 cities and 7 towns reporting slums), Series 1, Vol. 1.
(II) Districts and regional local bodies, Punjab.

Table 13 reveals that in the state there is no direct relationship between the size of town and percentage of slum population. It shows that the proportion of slum population varies from zero per cent to 22.61 per cent in Class I to Class VI towns. The analysis of slum population within the same class of towns reveals big variation. For example, the percentage of slum population varies from 5.6 per cent to 35.27 per cent in Class I towns. But all the bigger cities like Ludhiana, Amritsar, Jalandhar and Patiala have about 20 per cent as the slum population. In Class II towns, their percentage varies from 0.63 per cent to 35.61 per cent (Sandhu, 2011b). This does not mean that some towns do not have slums. In fact, all classes of towns of the state have a substantial proportion of population living in slum-like conditions, but they have not been identified and notified as slums by the urban local bodies (ULBs). It has been noted that the inadequacy of infrastructure (water supply, sewerage system and drainage) in lower classes of town is very high and if the definition of a slum is objectively applied to them, a major part of Class II to Class V towns would qualify with having such slums. Although the poor in small towns which usually lack or have inadequate access to basic amenities have been living in slum-like conditions, yet they have not been identified as slum residents. In cities they are identified and are visible but in small towns their presence has been ignored officially. In this context, it can be concluded that small towns are ignored by planning and development process at the state level and the poor living in slum-like conditions in small towns are further marginalised by the local government by not recognising them as slum residents. The low level of literacy, high level of agriculture workers in the workforce, high percentage of Scheduled Caste population, inadequate basic amenities of life and weaker economic base are the predominant features of small towns in Punjab. Legally they are urban but due to their neglect by the state and local bodies, they can be called as semi-urban settlements which are on the periphery of the whole process of urban development.

Conclusion

In the last six decades (1951–2011), Punjab's level of urbanisation has gone up from 21 per cent to 37.49 per cent, whereas the urban population has increased more than five times (19.24 to 103.05 lakh), and the number of towns has increased by 60 per cent (98 to 157) during the same period.

The urban development in the state has more or less followed the colonial pattern of development. Accordingly, Punjab could be divided into three broad regions, namely, Central Punjab which accommodates 60 per cent of the urban population, and this is situated along the main railway lines and National Highway 1. It is the most urbanised of the three regions and all the major cities of the state, namely, Ludhiana, Jalandhar, Amritsar and Patiala, are in this region. Remaining two regions are the north-eastern Punjab, and south-western Punjab, situated on the either sides of Central Punjab, accommodating 15 and 25 per cent of the urban population, respectively.

The Class I cities and Class II towns have increased in number (from 5 to 33) and their share from 40.84 to 74.85 per cent of the urban population. On the other hand, remaining four classes of towns (Class III to VI), which contained 59.16 per cent of the total urban population in 1951, had only 24.15 per cent of the urban population in 2001. The gain of Class I and Class II towns was the loss of remaining classes of towns. The growth rate for Class-I towns has been higher than the lower classes of towns.

The trend of urbanisation in India is metropolitan and oriented toward Class I cities. Similarly, Punjab has also followed the same trend and its two metros and 12 Class I cities have three-fifth (58.39%) of the total urban population. Although in Punjab, the concentration of urban population was towards Class I cities, it was lesser skewed as compared to the national average and for some other states like West Bengal and Maharashtra. Unlike West Bengal and Maharashtra, Punjab's urban pattern is not that mono-centric and its population is more dispersed.

Although Punjab is more developed and urbanised than other states of India, its urban development has not remained a priority area for the state government. Master plans were prepared in the 1970s for some major cities and were revised regularly, but got their statutory status in 2006 only. In all the cities of the state, more than 50 per cent area is unplanned. Small towns developed organically without any systematic planning. The urban development in the state can be characterised as uncontrolled and haphazard growth, non-conforming land use, and excessive strain on road network, utilities, services and facilities, housing shortage, proliferation of slums, traffic congestion and overall degradation of urban environment. In other words, the skewed urban structure with spontaneous pattern of urbanisation has emerged in the state essentially because till now there is no comprehensive urban policy at the state level.

Punjab is the number one state in terms of the availability of infra-structure in the country. Small towns are better equipped with health and educational facilities than bigger towns particularly in terms of their quantity. But quality services are not available in them. Due to lack of good governance, the service delivery is also poor. In urban Punjab, all have access to potable water but only two-thirds of the households have access to tap water and remaining one-third of them depend on hand pumps and other sources. Three-fourths of them have water supply within their houses, but still one-third of the households have to go out to fetch water for their use. The availability of water taps is directly related to the size of towns, i.e., the situation deteriorates as one moves from higher class of towns to the lower ones.

In the state, less than a half (47%) of the households are connected with the sewerage system (water closet toilet), two-fifth of them use pit latrines or other type of latrines and 13 per cent households are without any latrine. Percentage of households without any latrine is negatively associated with the class of towns. In the case of Class V towns, more than one-third of them are without a latrine. Similarly, the situation of close drainage system is better in Class I towns than the other classes of towns. Similarly, higher the size and class of the towns, better is the status of the roads.

The Class I towns have higher literacy rate (80.50) whereas all the remaining classes of towns have lower literacy rate than the Class I towns. There is inverse relationship between the percentage of agricultural workers and the size of town. In other words, smaller towns have high concentration of agricultural workers than the bigger ones. The range of concentration varies from 3.12 per cent (in Class I towns) to 35.14 per cent in Class VI towns. There is also a negative relationship between the size of town and concentration of Scheduled Castes. Class I towns have lowest proportion (18.74%) of Scheduled Castes and Class VI towns have highest proportion (59.29%) of Scheduled Castes. There is a need of further analysis of mobility of depressed castes to different categories of towns and the reasons thereof.

In Punjab, there is no direct relationship between the size of town and percentage of slum population. It shows that the proportion of slum population varies from negligible to 22.61 per cent in various classes of towns. This does not mean that some cities do not have slums. Slums are there but have not been identified and notified by the local body. It has been noted that inadequacy of infrastructure (water supply, sewerage system and drainage) in lower classes of towns is very high and if the definition of slum is objectively applied to their settlements, a sizeable part of these towns (Class II to Class V) would qualify as slums. Although the poor in small towns which usually lack or have inadequate basic amenities are living in slum-like conditions, yet these areas have not been identified as slums. In bigger cities, partly they are identified and very visible, but in small towns their presence is ignored. This usually happens because the urban local bodies do not have systematic data base for housing conditions in towns in Punjab. In the absence of data, even non-slum areas are declared as slums whereas areas having all characteristics of slums are not identified as slums. This situation is worse in case of lower classes of towns.

In this context, it can be concluded that small towns in the state of Punjab are ignored by planning and development process at the state level, and the poor living in slum-like conditions in small towns are further marginalised by the Urban Local Bodies by not recognising their living areas as slums. Small towns are future cities of the state and the development of these towns needs to be guarded and nurtured through proper planning so that they do not graduate or annex to urban Punjab as unplanned and haphazard settlements or slums.

References

Aiyer, Shankar (2010) 'India's Best and Worst States'. *India Today*. 17 September.

Aldrich, B.C. and R.S. Sandhu (1995) *Housing the Urban Poor: Policy and Practice in Developing Countries*. London: Zed Books.

Ali, Osman Z.M. and M.R.A. Rahman (2004) 'The Effect of Urbanization on the Health of Urban Residents'. *Akademika*. Vol. 65, pp. 111–24.

Bhagat, R.B. (2011) 'Urbanisation and Access to Basic Amenities in India'. *Urban India*. Vol. 31, No. 10.

Bhalla, G.S. and G.K. Chadha (1981) *Structural Change in Income Distribution: A Study of the Impact of Green Revolution in the Punjab*. New Delhi: Centre for the Study of Regional Development, J.N.U.

Census of India (2001) *Punjab Provisional Population Total, Paper-2 of 2001: Rural-Urban Distribution of Population, Punjab Series 4*. Chandigarh: Directorate of Census Operation, Punjab.

———. (2011) *Punjab Provisional Population Totals, Paper-1 of 2011, Punjab Series 4*. Chandigarh: Directorate of Census Operations, Punjab.

Clegg, E.J. and J.P. Garlic (1979) 'The Ecology of Disease in Urban Societies'. *Current Anthropology*. Vol. 20, pp. 798–99.

CRRID (2002a) 'Health', *Punjab State Development Report 2002*. New Delhi: Planning Commission.

———. (2002b) 'Education', *Punjab State Development Report 2002*. New Delhi: Planning Commission.

D'Souza, Victor S. (1976) 'Green Revolution and Urbanization in Punjab during 1961–71'. In S. Manzor Alam and V.V. Pokshishvsky (eds). *Urbanization in Developing Countries*. Hyderabad: Osmania University.

Dasgupta, Biplab (2000) 'Contrasting Urban Patterns: West Bengal, Punjab and Kerala'. In Amitabh Kundu (ed.). *Inequality, Mobility and Urbanization: China and India*. New Delhi: Manak.

Digby, William (1901) *'Prosperous' British India*. London. pp. 291–92. Cited from A. Bose (1973) *Studies in India's Urbanization, 1901–1971*. New Delhi: Tata McGraw-Hill Publishing Co. Ltd.

Government of India (1988) *Report of the National Commission on Urbanization*. New Delhi: Ministry of Urban Development.

Government of Punjab (1974) *Integrated City Development Programmes Ludhiana (1974–79), Amritsar (1976–77 – 1980–81) and Jalandhar (1976–77 – 1980–81)*. Chandigarh: Town and Country Planning Department.

———. (2000) *Statistical Abstracts of Punjab – 1999*. Chandigarh: Government Press

———. (2004) *Human Development Report – 2004, Punjab*. Chandigarh: Government Press.

——. (2007) *Statistical Abstract of Punjab – 2007*. Chandigarh: Government Press.

——. (2011) *Economic Survey 2010–2011*. Economic and Statistical Organization, S.A.S. Nagar: Punjab Government Press.

HPEC (2011) 'Report on Indian Urban Infrastructure and Services', www.niua.org

Jagmohan (1993) 'Plan to Resuscitate Ludhiana'. *The Tribune*. 3 September 1997.

Japan Bank for International Cooperation (2006) *Special Assistance for Project Formation (SAPROF)*.

Kundu, Amitabh and S. Bhatia (2001) 'Industrial Growth in Small and Medium Town and Their Vertical Integration: The Case Study of Gobindgarh'. Discussion Paper No. 57, www.unesco.org/shs/most.

Kundu, Amitabh (2011) 'Politics and Economics of Urban Growth'. *Economic and Political Weekly*. Vol. XLVI, No. 20, pp. 10–12.

Logan, Johan R. and Harvey L. Molotch (2007) *Urban Fortune: The Political Economy of Places*. 20th Anniversary Edition, Berkeley: University of California Press.

Majeed, Shariq (2011) 'Illegal Colonies Let Off the Hook'. *Tribune*. 28 July 2011.

Peters, David H., Abdo S. Yazbeck, Adam Wagstaff, G.N.V. Ramana, Lant Pritchett and Rashmi R. Sharma (2003) 'Better Health Systems for India's Poor: Findings, Analysis and Options'. *Economic and Political Weekly*. Vol. 39, No. 9, pp. 907–19.

Planning Commission (2008) *11th Five Year Plan*. New Delhi: Oxford University Press.

Punjab Urban Development Authority (2010) *Master Plan of Amritsar (2010–30)*. Prepared by SAI Consulting Engineers Pvt. Ltd., Ahmedabad, Mohali, Punjab.

Rai, Anil (2010) 'Urban India-Issues and Challenges'. *Urban India*. Vol. 30, Issue 1, January–June.

Ramanathan, Swati (2008) 'India's Urban Phenomenon'. *Town and Country Planning*, February 2008.

Sandhu, Ranvinder Singh (2011a) *Urban Studies: A Trend Report*. Submitted to ICSSR, New Delhi.

Sandhu, Ranvinder Singh (2011b) *Urban Development in Punjab*. A report submitted to Punjab Governance Reforms Commission, Government of Punjab, Chandigarh.

Sandhu, R.S. and Jasmeet Sandhu (1998) 'Punjab Vich Sehrikaran Ate Sehri Vikas: Vartman Ate Bhivikh'. *Smajak Vigyan Pattar*. Nos 44–46, June–December 1998.

———. (2003) 'Urbanization in Punjab: Pattern and Development'. In M.S. Gill (ed.). *Punjab Society: Perspectives and Challenges.* New Delhi: Concept Publications.

Singh, Jaspal (2010) *Urbanization in Punjab: Geographical Analysis.* PhD thesis submitted to Punjabi University, Patiala.

Singh, Surjit (2001) 'Regional Migration in India: Some Issues of Urbanization'. In R.S. Sandhu, Sarup Singh and Jasmeet Sandhu (eds). *Sustainable Human Settlements: The Asian Experience.* Jaipur: Rawat Publications.

Sridhar, Kala S. and O.P. Mathur (2009) *Costs and Challenge of Local Urban Services: Evidence from India's Cities.* New Delhi: Oxford University Press.

The Tribune (2007) 'Unauthorised Colonies in Punjab', 31 May.

———. (2010) 'Illegal Colonies in Bhatinda', 12 June.

Town and Country Planning Organization (2002) *National Urban Observatory Pilot Studies, for Hyderabad, Guntur, Amritsar, Patiala, Mysore, Mangalore, Faridabad, Sonepat, Villupuram, Tiruvannamalai, Dehradun and Jaipur,* (Ministry of Urban Development and Poverty Alleviation). New Delhi: Government of India.

———. (2004) *National Urban Observatory: Pilot Studies.* Town Country Planning Organization, Ministry of Urban Development. New Delhi: Government of India.

World Development Report (2004) 'Making Services Work for Poor People'. *Economic and Political Weekly.* Vol. 39, No. 9, pp. 907–19.

10

The Changing Face of Urban India
Allahabad City in Context

K.N. BHATT AND LALIT JOSHI

The urban process under capitalism, according to David Harvey, implies among other things, the creation of material physical infrastructure for production, circulation, exchange and consumption. Furthermore, the existence of surpluses of capital and labour as well as mechanisms for pooling the two together create conditions that are conducive for the flow of investment into the built environment (Harvey, 1985: 13–14, 22). 'The use values necessary to the reproduction of social life under capitalism are basically produced as commodities within a circulation process of capital that has the augmentation of exchange values as its primary goal' (Harvey, 1985: 185). In fact, modern development strategies ensure that more and more urban space is utilised for exchange. This has been due to a perceptible shift from the managerial to the entrepreneurial approach to urban land by 1970s and 1980s (Harvey, 1989: 4).

Earlier, in a stimulating study, the French theorist Lefebvre declared that the industrial revolution of the 19th century was a precursor to the urban revolution of the 20th in which the urban problematic became decisive.[1] This trend continued throughout the 20th century until the present era of globalisation. Indeed, marked by massive migrations and wide-ranging displacement of people, contemporary urbanisation has generated fresh debates about the problems of planning and governance.[2] The idea of urban space, its meaning for different classes and communities as well as its diverse uses and forms of consumption is being re-examined. Urban planners and policy makers are being questioned for exclusion of marginal communities and neighbourhoods when preparing grandiose blueprints for urban development.

Central to this debate has been the concern towards the transformation of urban space into a commodity that attracts those who have stakes in what has been termed as 'urban fortunes' by Logan and Molotch. Deploying Marxist terminology, Logan and Molotch differentiate between 'use value' and 'exchange value' of urban land and clearly point out that maximisation of profit by promoters marginalises those who struggle for the 'use value' of land: that is for utilising land, buildings and communities as constituents of everyday life. Such marginalisation is possible because 'people make it happen – as individuals, as private companies, as voluntary organisations, as government units'. And finally, 'the flux of the city cannot be deduced from the laws of market or from some other ineluctable logic' (Logan and Molotch, 2007: ix, 2–3).

Gordon MacLeod views such entrepreneurial approach to economic development as an attempt to 'recapitalise the economic landscape of the cities'. Citing examples from the urban experiences of North America and Europe, he proposes that the withdrawal from the 'politics of redistribution' has sharpened 'socio-economic inequalities' among the urban population (MacLeod, 2002: 602–604). Powerful groups use institutional frameworks and other means to manipulate urban space in their own interests. Like MacLeod, Harvey Molotch also refers to the powerful nexus of builders, financiers and politicians as the 'growth machine' (Molotch, 1993: 31–32).

In South Asia, like many other geographical regions of the world, accelerated pace of urbanisation and growing incidence of urban poverty have become complementary processes. For example, the number of people living in slums and squatter settlements globally has increased to one billion; more than half of them living in Asia alone. In developing countries like India, the urban poor form 30 to 40 per cent of the urban population (NIUA, 2005: 1). Host to more than 31 per cent of India's population (as per the Census 2011 data), most Indian cities and towns are severely under strain in terms of the infrastructure and services available for their development.

Significantly, samples collected by the National Sample Survey (NSS) related to differential rates of decline in poverty levels in rural and urban India clearly reveal that in the recent years, poverty has declined faster in rural India than in the former. 'Compared to 1983, when rural poverty was 5–6 per cent higher than urban poverty ratios, by 2004–05 ... rural poverty ratio is only marginally higher by 0.9 per cent compared to urban poverty. That is, in the twentyone-and-a-half years since 1983, while rural poverty declined by 19.4 per cent, urban poverty declined by only 15.5 per cent ... . Quite clearly, increasing urbanisation has also been accompanied by urbanisation of poverty in India. And, importantly, the pace of urbanisation of poverty seems to have increased in the 1990s compared to the 1980s' (Himanshu, 2006: 4). Further, it has also been observed that poverty 'is no more confined only to the slums of large cities but in fact it is also spreading to medium cities along with growth of medium cities. As a result, increasing inequality is a concern not only for the large cities but also for some of the medium and small towns' (Himanshu, 2006: 23).

Seen in the context of rapid climate changes, urban India is more vulnerable to disasters, particularly in cities with high population density. 'Climate change risk to India should be seen in the perspective of an ongoing three-part transition: a demographic transition that will see India's population stabilising at about 1.6 billion in the 2060s; a simultaneous *rurban* transition, which will see an addition of almost 500 million people in an estimated 7,000 to 12,000 urban settlements over this period; and simultaneously ... environmental transitions. This complex-phase space provides for multiple sub-regionally nuanced strategies to respond to the climate crisis, drawing on considerable local experience of coping with uncertainty and far-from equilibrium systems (Revi, 2007: 2).' Menacing urban growth, alarm signals emanating from rapid climate change, ever increasing number of slum-dwellers and growing pressure on basic urban services call for a reworking of existing models and strategies of: (a) urban infrastructure development and service delivery, (b) environmental impact assessment, (c) urban governance, and (d) accountability of local bodies and active community participation.

With these introductory remarks on urbanisation and its political economy, the focus of this essay is the city of Allahabad. We explore the complex and varied nature of the urban experience in Allahabad keeping in mind some of the theoretical concerns raised by the scholars we have mentioned. We have also tried to examine the factors responsible for transforming Allahabad into a city which has become emblematic of overstretched civic amenities, poor infrastructure, environmental destruction and burgeoning ghettos. Finally, we also suggest a deeper critical engagement with complex and imbricated questions of planning and governance so that appropriate strategies can be worked out by planners and stakeholders alike.

Pre-colonial Allahabad

In the sacred literature of the Hindus, including ancient such as the *Vedas,* the *Puranas,* the *Mahabharata* and the *Ramayana* as well as many Buddhist texts, the city of Allahabad is alluded to as the sacred city of Prayag. In popular lore too, Prayag is sanctified as it is the meeting point (*sangam*) for the rivers Ganga, Yamuna and the mythical Saraswati. Around 600 B.C., Kaushambi (a separate district since 1997) of Allahabad became the capital of the *Vatsa* kingdom. Throughout the early period of

India's pre-colonial past, Allahabad continued to retain its status as an administrative outpost for the Maurya, the Sunga, Kushana and Gupta rulers. Hieuen Tsang, the Chinese traveller, has left behind a rich record of King Harshavardhan's 'religious assemblies' in the first half of the seventh century at the banks of the river Ganga (Nevill, 1911). The city is believed to have been washed away before the Muslim invasion in India (Tahseen, 1985: 4). However, the strategic importance of Prayag inspired the Mughal Emperor Akbar to rebuild a city ravaged by invasions and disasters. The result was the creation of a new administrative province or *subah* in 1580 (Sinha, 1974). Akbar also built a magnificent fort at the confluence of the rivers Yamuna and Ganga and named the city as *Illahabas* and which subsequently became known as Allahabad. Due to absence of major industries or artisanal activity, Allahabad did not experience large-scale urbanisation during the Mughal period.

Allahabad had barely any urban settlement or commercial activity of much significance, except for the Akbar's fort, Khusrobagh, a handful of *Sufi dairas* and *sarais* and traditional religious festivities. Bishop Heber, who reached Allahabad in 1824, observed that 'Allahabad ... occasionally the residence of royalty ... never happens to been a great or magnificent city, and is even more desolate and ruinous than Dacca, having obtained, among the natives, the name *Fakeerabad*, *beggar* abode' ... The only considerable buildings or ruins in Allahabad are the fort, the Jumna Musjeed, and the *serai* and garden of Sultan Khosroo (Heber, 1828: 283). The city attracts millions of pilgrims from across the world every sixth year ('Ardh-Kumbha') and once in every 12 years ('Kumbha'). However, despite all claims of it being rooted in antiquity, Maclean has recently demonstrated that the Kumbh Mela of Allahabad is actually a colonial creation (Maclean, 2003).

Colonial Allahabad

Colonial Allahabad evolved around the new urban space ceded by the *Nawab* of Avadh Saadat Ali Khan in 1801 to the East India Company. About three decades later, it was declared as the capital of the North Western Provinces, a status that it enjoyed until 1920. The city remained tranquil with a British garrison stationed in the old city until 1857, in which year rebels took over the administration. The British responded quickly and ruthlessly. The northern part of the city consisting of eight villages was forcibly appropriated and renamed Canning Town. It was around these villages that the new Civil Station or Civil Lines was rebuilt. For the British, Allahabad as the capital of the North Western Provinces of Agra and Avadh, was an ideal choice because of its rail links with Calcutta and 'easily defensible position' (Bayly, 1975: 19). Some of the finest buildings of the city such as the All Saints Cathedral, the University of

Allahabad, the Public Library and the Old High Court were built in the 19th century. Urban space around the Civil Station was also reworked to create the classic colonial bungalow-compound complex for its civil and military officials. The bungalow–compound complex situated along tree-lined wide-laned streets constituted the core of the colonial urban settlement (King, 1976).

Thus, Allahabad's engagement with colonial modernity began only with the creation of the Civil Station under the British. The German traveller Captain Von Elrich's (1845) impressions of the Civil Station bear further testimony to this fact: '... the houses of the civilian and military officials enhance the charm of this place, as they are surrounded with beautiful gardens. There are few places in India which have such beautiful and shapely buildings. The streets are long and wide with rows of trees between them. Some of these lead to the fort, some to the city and some to another famous place.'[3] Much of the building activity inside the Civil Station was facilitated by the creation of the Municipal Committee (a nominated body under the District Collector) in 1863 and later with the passage of the United Provinces Municipalities Act II of 1916. By the Act of 1916, real powers were conferred to the Municipal Board, many of whose members were now elected.

The urban landscape in Allahabad began to change perceptibly when the Allahabad Improvement Trust was constituted in 1919. New neigh-bourhoods were laid out or expanded, including Mumfordganj, George Town and Tagore Town. The Municipal Board was directed to transfer all properties held by it to the Trust. The scope of the Improvement Trust was also extended considerably to include Jhunsi, Naini and the Phaphamau regions of the district. Thus, between 1920 and 1947, around 30 housing schemes were initiated by the Improvement Trust in different parts of Allahabad (Pande, 1955: 339–40). Official reports expressed alarm at the state of housing on the eve of India's independence. The first of these was published as early as 1918.

The author of the report (Preliminary Report for the Improvement of the Town of Allahabad, 1918), Stanley Jevons, a Professor of Economics at Allahabad University, observed: 'There are striking examples in various market areas of the town, particularly in *Chowk* and Muthiganj, where the land on the roadside most suitable for shop purposes has not been protected from residential buildings. On the other hand there are instances of the invasions of the residential districts by some undesirable occupations or allied industries or business such as dyeing, washing or grain business.' Jevons suggested proper urban planning and dividing the city into business, residential, government, military, educational, industrial, railway, aviation, forest and other zones in order to stabilise all real estate values in all sections of the city.[4] Two decades later, in another report, based on a survey conducted in 1941–42 by Dr P.D. Gupta, Medical Officer at the Allahabad Municipal Board, it was observed: 'Much, as has been achieved by the Improvement Trust, Allahabad in improving them, still they have yet to proceed a pretty long way before the trust can claim to have provided better houses for inhabitants of all classes, creeds and vocations ... very successful schemes ... have simply afforded opportunities for the well-to-do class men to expand themselves in these areas.'[5]

By 1946–47, insanitary conditions prevailed in large parts of Civil Lines on account of the absence of adequate drainage (Pande, 1955: 358). Dr B.L. Sharma, the Medical Officer at the Municipal Board, also complained that the problem was compounded by demographic overcrowding and the 'condition of Civil Lines is worse than the slums'.[6] According to Gooptu, the problem began in the interwar years when many cities of Uttar Pradesh, including Allahabad, were inundated with labouring classes generating 'grave concern among urban propertied classes and local administrators alike.'[7] The constant reference to the new settlers as 'poor class people' or 'inferior classes' in middle class discourse perhaps stems from a feeling of disquiet and anxiety at the inability to deal with critical issues of town planning.[8]

The City after Independence

The crisis of Allahabad, as in the case of many other post-colonial cities, appears to be that of poor planning and governance, the roots of which go back to the skewed character of colonial urbanisation itself. Under colonial rule, the Civil Station was allowed to develop in a relatively planned manner while the old city was left to follow its own course. The morbid symptoms of colonial governance were manifest even after two decades of India's independence. 'The appalling congestion in the old city and the misuse of excess land in Civil Lines and the Cantonments, the acute shortage of houses in all parts, heavy traffic on the narrow and winding roads and lanes, unsatisfactory health and medical services, old human means of transport, illiteracy and the lack of modern industrial development are some of the unfortunate deficiencies of the diseased city' (Singh, 1966: 22). By the eighties, not only had the disconnect between the old town and Civil Lines become more apparent but also Civil Lines was being quickly turned into a site of unregulated development (Misra, 1984: 134). There is also evidence that mounting political corruption and a spate of land-related litigations pushed the city into the brink of stasis. Further, growing instances of financial corruption within the Allahabad Municipal Board made a mockery of the representative character of urban governance (Tahseen, 1999: 287–88).

The City Development Plan Allahabad, 2006 divides Allahabad city into three distinct geographical regions: (i) Trans-Ganga or *Gangapar*

214 ◆ K.N. Bhatt and Lalit Joshi

Plain, (ii) the Ganga Yamuna *Doab* (confluence), and (iii) Trans Yamuna or the *Yamunapar* tract. Urban Allahabad is spread over an area of approximately 82 square kilometres and described as an important centre of education and business, but also identified as one of the least industrialised and least polluted city in Eastern Uttar Pradesh (ANN, Part I, 2006: 7, 10). The Census of 2001, however, classifies Allahabad into three regions: (i) Allahabad Nagar Nigam (ANN) – (Municipal Corporation of Allahabad), (ii) the City Outer Growth and (iii) the Allahabad Cantonment.[9] The population of Allahabad city in 2001, including the cantonment area, was 10,18, 092 and divided into 87 administrative wards. In terms of population density, Allahabad is populated with 41 wards having less than 200 persons per hectare, 27 wards ranging between 200 to 400 persons per hectare, followed by only 6 wards which have more than 600 persons per hectare. The projected population of the city is estimated to be 16,37,296 for the year 2011 and 20,43,735 for 2021 as per the current Allahabad Master Plan 2001–2021 (ANN, Part-I, 2006: 10–12) ...[10]

The Master Plan includes an area of 21,689.13 hectares of land put under different uses in the city. As shown in Table 1, 35.14 per cent of the total area is delimited for residential purposes and is expected to go up to 36.11 per cent in 2021. The industrial area in the city was confined to only 5.61 per cent in 2001 and is projected to go down to 5.57 per cent in 2021. The highest decline is expected in the realm of public utilities, which as per projections will go down to 2.23 per cent in 2021 from 7.66 per cent in 2001 (ANN Part I, 2006: 30–31). This clearly reveals that there is a strategic move on the part of the planners to shift emphasis of the urban space from use value to exchange value.

Table 1

Land use pattern in Allahabad city

Particulars	Area covered ha. (2021)	Area covered ha. (2001)
Residential	11,164.48 (36.11)*	7,622.24 (35.14)
Commercial	746.2 (2.41)	545.43
Industrial	1,722.89 (5.57)	1,217.81 (5.61)
Administrative	2,624.5 (8.49)	1,871.09 (8.63)
Recreational	4,953.45 (16.02)	2,531.48 (11.67)
Public/semi-public	1,179.78 (3.82)	571.24 (2.63)
Public Utilities	690.05 (2.23)	1,660.53 (7.66)
Transportation	3,736.3 (12.09)	2,434.8 (11.23)
Other land uses	4,099.73 (13.26)	3,234.51 (14.91)
Total	30,917.38 (100.00)	21,689.13 (100.00)

* Figures in parentheses denote column percentages.

Source: Allahabad Master Plan, 2021 cited in ANN Part I, 2006: 31

The built space within the city according to the City Development Plan, 2006, is spread out into three main regions: (i) the Old city including Chauk, Ghantaghar, Bans Mandi, Katghar, Kotwali, Gaughat, adding other areas with similar characteristics like Daraganj, Bairhana and Katra; (ii) the New City originally founded by the British consists of Civil Lines, Ashok Nagar, Cantonment, Mumfordganj, Allenganj, Georgetown, Allahabad University; and (iii) the Outer Growth areas containing Jhusi, Naini, Phaphamau, Bamhrauli, Manauri, etc., (ANN Part I, 2006: 28). However, despite being the main business district of Allahabad, the old city languishes in neglect. Seven decades of planning and governance has not brought any relief from congestion, high-density population, traffic jams, encroachments and illegal constructions and the mushrooming of ghettos. The colonial city, in contrast, remained insular until the 1990s.

Allahabad Location Map

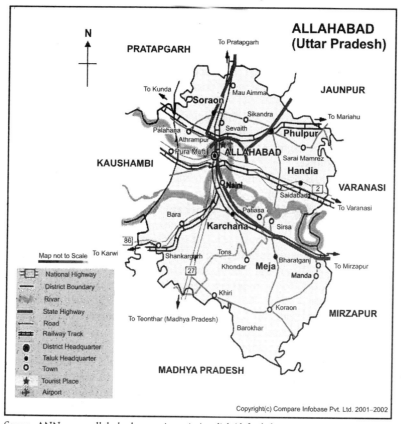

Source: ANN www.allahabadnagarnigam.in/english/default.htm

But a series of legislations destroyed its edifice as builders and planners colluded to reduce it into architectural disarray.

Allahabad today is home to thousands of transitory communities consisting of educated and unemployed youth. In some areas such as Allapur and Salori, migrant groups even outnumber the permanent residents. This has been facilitated by the mushrooming of private lodges, hostels and eateries for an ever-growing demographic profile. The creation of large-scale unorganised boarding has in turn stimulated a whole range of commercial activities, including the setting up of tea stalls, roadside eateries, books and stationery shops, vegetable and fruit vending, laundry and tailoring enterprises. One of the major attractions for the youth has been the dozens of coaching institutes dotting the crowded streets and lanes of the city. Some chase the dreams of successful careers in medicine and engineering, while others are lured by the glamour of the civil services.

Allahabad gets its steady stream of knowledge and informa-tion-seekers from neighbouring states like Bihar, Madhya Pradesh, Chhattisgarh and Jharkhand, in addition to other districts of Uttar Pradesh. Indeed, only a few cities in Uttar Pradesh can boast of the presence of such vast and diverse clusters of student populations. Although no empirical study to document the recent urbanisation of Allahabad has been conducted so far, it can be safely conjectured that due to an unprecedented demographic explosion, the infrastructure in the city is under tremendous pressure. Because the Civil Lines area has been the preferred site of builders and speculators, most indicators point at its imminent collapse.

The gradual dismantling of the 19th century bungalow-compound, which had remained until the 1980s, a ubiquitous marker of colonial architecture, can be plotted as a significant moment of departure in the history of Allahabad. Indeed, winds of change started blowing in the 1990s when the government of Uttar Pradesh passed several orders related to the management and disposal of *nazul* land (government land situated within the area of a municipality). Under the new dispensation, a new procedure for converting leased land into freehold land was adopted. Section 7 (1) of the Government Order of 1998 even permitted land illegally held (prior to January 1992), to be converted to freehold at 120 per cent of the existing circle rate.[11]

Huge bungalows belonging to former Kashmiri, Bengali and Khatri families were quickly bought, dismantled and sold to enthusiastic bidders. Builders also connived with local politicians and officials to appropriate prime land. In some instances, even state land was bought and sold in clear violation of existing laws. Thus, a clear transition from its earlier use value to the present exchange value in land can easily be mapped. Many of the buildings which came up in this period contravened building laws that had been in force since 1960. Builders have shown scant regard for the mandatory provisions of the 1960 regulatory framework. Moreover, most high-rise buildings in the city ignore obligatory fire and safety measures.[12]

Taking advantage of the relatively easy availability of office space in Civil Lines, a number of private banks and other financial institutions moved into the city. Around the turn of the century, major automobile companies opened showrooms in Sardar Patel Marg and Nawab Yusuf Road. The first mall of Allahabad (Atlantis) came up on Mahatma Gandhi Marg in 2006 followed by the Vinayak Mall in 2010 on Sardar Patel Marg. The American fast food chain McDonald's with its promise of 'total experience', cashed in on this opportunity by opening its franchise outlet in February 2006.[13] Close in its heels came Domino's in 2009. As the news of beverage chains like Café Coffee Day opening their outlets in Civil Lines trickles in, the further dismantling of the colonial bungalow promises to the youth of Allahabad, the belated yet the long-awaited transition to the era of capitalist globalisation.

The dismantling of the bungalow-compound has brought about extraordinary destruction of vegetation and illegal reclamation of ponds for building purposes. It has also triggered ruthless exploitation of groundwater resources. Besides, choked drains and the absence of any systematic policy of disposing urban waste have transformed many neighbourhoods into sprawling ghettos. A survey carried out by Oxfam in 2005, reveals that there are currently 283 slums in Allahabad that house 3, 62, 550 people, roughly equal to 30 per cent population of the city. Out of these, 27 slums are located in Civil Lines alone.[14] However, the Census of 2001 shows that only about 13 per cent population of Allahabad city lives in slums (Table 2).

Table 2

Slum Population in JNNURM City Allahabad

Particulars	Households	Population
Slum	18,558	1,26,646
Urban	1,50,157	9,75,393
% Slum	12.36	12.98

Source: Census of India, 2001, Primary Census Abstract, Series I, India, Slum Population, Cited in NIUA (2005): Urban Poverty, Urban Finance, Quarterly Newsletter, INDO-USAIDGFIRE(D)PROJECT, Vol.8, No. 4, October–December, p. 8

Thus, the Oxfam findings besides contesting the official figure of 183 slums in Allahabad also highlight the fact that slums have been in existence in the city for more than half a century and that their numbers are steadily growing.

ADA and 74th CAA

The mushrooming of slums in Allahabad places a serious question mark over the role of the Allahabad Development Authority (ADA), the nodal agency created by the state government in 1973 to implement its developmental agenda in the district. At the same time, the 74th Constitutional Amendment Act (74th CAA) which came into force on 1 June 1993, clearly empowers Municipal Corporations to formulate plans for economic development of the districts and implement schemes that are entrusted to them from time to time, including the 18 schemes enlisted in the Twelfth Schedule (Article 243W). Thus, the 74th CAA virtually disempowered and reduces the ADA into a vestigial organ of the state government.

Significantly, many of the schemes proposed in the ADA's Master Plan of 2001 have not yet taken off. These include the expansion of arterial roads both in the Civil Station and the old city, the construction of under-passes, flyovers, new bridges over the Ganga, a new bus terminus, river transport terminus, a new airport, conservation of heritage buildings, parks, etc. Meanwhile, the ADA has already submitted another Master Plan (2021) to the government. The handiwork of ADA's team, the plan aims to project Allahabad as a frontline city of India by 2021. Much in line with the tradition set in 2001, the ADA invited comments from the public only after the draft was ready. It is difficult to say whether there was any popular response to the draft at all or even if there was, did the final draft incorporate suggestions from the people?

The ADA has been in operation for more than 38 years. During this period, residential colonies, sans infrastructure, have been allowed to mushroom in several city localities, evoking charges of graft and corruption from the public. Of particular concern is the encroachment of parks, ponds and government land as well as the construction of nursing homes and commercial complexes in densely-populated neighbourhoods. The ADA has also been responsible for erecting two multi-storied structures in Civil Lines, namely, Indira Bhavan and Sangam Place. Both buildings are inferior in design, besides being poorly maintained.

All this suggests that despite the inadequacies of India's electoral politics, empowering the Municipal Corporation might be in the long run a better alternative than governance from 'above'. In addition to ensuring a greater democratisation of the planning and implementation processes, it may enable people to fix responsibility on elected representatives and urban local bodies (ULBs).

Conclusion

The city of Allahabad imagined in popular writings is limited to a small section of people inhabiting the Civil Station that came into existence after 1857.[15] There exists another Allahabad outside the Civil Station whose history still awaits exploration. For some, the disappearance of the bungalow signifies the passing away of the 'real' Allahabad (Mehrotra, 2007). In this paper, we have consistently distanced ourselves from such nostalgic lamentation. However, we are still tempted to ask a critical question. Can the fate of a city be left entirely in the hands of an indifferent government and a corrupt bureaucracy? Even after several years of independence, urban India has largely failed to evolve a community of committed citizens for conservation of its heritage and better civic life. Allahabad with all its claims of an enlightened and politically influential citizenry is no exception. The future of the city is rarely debated within the public sphere.[16] Voices challenging the monopolistic hold of the bureaucracy over the city's physical and cultural resources can be barely heard. Finally, vested interests ensure that all engagements with the present are deferred indefinitely so that the city can take refuge in exhilarated recalls of the past.

The systematic liquidation of the colonial town and the gradual demise of its cultural elite may not itself constitute sufficient ground for loss and mourning, but the situation does provide us with a vantage point to examine the claims made by the post-colonial state about the planned development of urban India. Furthermore, it also gives us an opportunity to understand the ways in which contemporary capitalism, driven by ruthless greed and competition, has forced to the brink of extinction forms of built space emblematic of colonial modernity. Nor has the project of planned development benefited the marginals. In fact, by privileging 'exchange value' over 'use value', urban development is increasingly becoming a major cause not only for the dislocation and displacement of the marginalia but also for its ghettos.

Thus, as pointed out by Harvey, urban planners, in order to save every city, need 'to acquire an understanding of how the built environment works in relationship to social reproduction and how the various facets of competitive, monopolistic, and state production of the built environment relate to one another in the context of often conflicting class and factional requirements ... appreciate how everything relates to everything else in an urban system, to think in terms of costs and benefits ... and to have some sympathetic understanding of the problems that face the private producers of the built environment, the landlord interest, the urban poor, the managers of financial institutions, the downtown business interests, and so on ... incremental understanding of what would be the 'best' configuration of investment ... to facilitate social reproduction' (Harvey, 1985: 176).

220 ❖ K.N. Bhatt and Lalit Joshi

In this synoptic survey of the city of Allahabad, we have tried to argue that neither the government nor its development agencies have the imagination or the resources to carry the urban project any further. As an alternative to bureaucratic governance, we suggest that an effective, responsive and transparent structure of governance by the Urban Local Bodies needs to be put in place. We hope that not only will this help fix the onus of development on the elected representatives, but will also help democratise a process in which the citizenry will become stakeholders in their futures.

Notes

1. Cited in Brian Harvey, 1985, p. 63. Further, Lefebvre states this in unambiguous terms, 'To present and give any account of the 'urban problematic', the point of departure must be the process of industrialisation.' Henri Lefebvre (1996): *Writing on Cities*, Selected translated and introduced by Eleonore Kofman and Elizabeth Lebas, Blackwell Publishing, Oxford, p. 64.

2. For example, see Baleshwar Thakur, George Pomeroy, Chris Cusack and Sudhir K. Thakur (eds), *City Society and Planning*, Concept Publishing Company, New Delhi, 2007; Saskia Sassen, *The Global City*, New York, London, Tokyo, Princeton University Press, 1992.

3. Cited in Srivastava, 1937, p. 55.

4. Cited in B.N. Pande, 1955, p. 42.

5. Cited in B.N. Pande, 1955, pp. 347.

6. Cited in B.N. Pande, 1955, pp. 358.

7. For details, see Nandini Gooptu, 2001, pp. 66–110.

8. Ibid.

9. Cited in ANN, 2006, CDPA Part I, Draft Report, p. 10.

10. All this and more can be examined in ANN, 2006, Allahabad Revised Master Plan 2001, Allahabad Development Authority, 2001, Allahabad.

11. For greater details, see The U.P. Regulations of Building Operations Act, 1958, Hind Publishing House, Allahabad, 2006, pp. 25–37.

12. Ibid.

13. One study demonstrates that the McDonald's chains have been advertising that a visit to its restaurant could mean an end to the 'drudgery' of everyday life. For more details, see Golden Arches East: McDonald's in East Asia cited in Vinaya Lal and Ziauddin Sardar (ed.), *The Future of Knowledge and Culture*, Penguin/Viking Delhi, 2002, p. 180.

14. This data on slums has been extracted from the Oxfam (India) Trust Rapid Survey of Slums of Allahabad (2005). The study does not indicate place of publication and is available on the Net.

15. For the narratives of nostalgia, see Dharamvir Bharti's *Gunahon Ka Devta*, Gyanpith, Delhi, 1998. Also see series of essays about Allahabad commissioned by the *Times of India* (Lucknow) between May and June 2006; Another nostalgic recall is Rameshwar Shukla's Allahabad: Ek Smriti-Samwad, in Satya Prakash Mishra (ed) Amrit Mahotsava Patrika, Sammelan Press, Allahabad, 1985; historian G.C. Pande's Introduction in Satya Prakash Mishra's Dastavez, Allahabad Museum, 2005, are replete with nostalgic remembering.

16. The situation, though, is different in certain metropolitan centres such as in Mumbai (www.maharashtra.gov.in/english/reports/citizens_action. htm) and Chennai (www.cag.org.in/membership.php) where citizens have begun to engage with urban problems.

References

Allahabad Nagar Nigam (ANN) (2006) *City Development Plan for Allahabad*, Feedback Ventures. Draft Report, Part I. www.allahabadnagarnigam. in/JNNURM/Part1.pdf

Bayly, Christopher (1975) *The Local Roots of Indian Politics, Allahabad 1880–1920*. Oxford: Clarendon Press.

Gooptu, Nandini (2001) *The Politics of Urban Poor in Early Twentieth Century India*. Cambridge: Cambridge University Press.

Harvey, David (1985) *The Urbanization of Capital*. Oxford: Basil Blackwell Ltd.

———. (1989) 'From Managerialism to Entrepreneurialism: The Transformation in Urban Governance in Late Capitalism'. Geografiska Annaler. Series B. *Human Geography*. Vol. 71, No. 1.

Heber, Reginald (1828) *Narrative of a Journey Through the Upper Provinces of India: From Calcutta to Bombay, 1824–1825*. Philadelphia: Carrey, Lea and Carey.

Himanshu, H. (2006) Urban Poverty in India by Size-Class of Towns: Level, Trends and Characteristics. pp. 1–26. www.csh-delhi.com/team/downloads/publiperso/urban_IGIDR_paper.pdf

King, A.D. (1976) *Colonial Urban Development*. London and Boston: Routledge and Kegan Paul.

Logan, John R. and Harvey L. Molotch (2007) *Urban Fortunes: The Political Economy of Places*. 20th Anniversary Edition. Berkeley: University of California Press.

Maclean, Kama (2003) 'Making the Colonial State Work for You: The Modern Beginnings of the Ancient Kumbh Mela in Allahabad'. *The Journal of Asian Studies*. Vol. 62, No. 3, pp. 873–905.

MacLeod, Gordon (2002) 'From Urban Entrepreneurialism to a "Revanchist City?" On the Spatial Injustices of Glasgow's Renaissance'. *Antipode*. Oxford: Blackwell Publishers. www.akira.ruc.dk/.../12-MacLeod-Urban-Entrepreneurialism-Spatial-Injustices-of-Glasgow.pdf

222 ◆ K.N. Bhatt and Lalit Joshi

Mehrotra, A.K. (ed.) (2007) *The Last Bungalow: Writings on Allahabad*. New Delhi: Penguin Books.

Misra, H.N. (1984) *Urban Systems of a Developing Economy: A Study of Allahabad City-Region*. Allahabad: International Institute for Development Research.

Molotch, Harvey (1993) 'The Political Economy of Growth Machines'. *Journal of Urban Affairs*. Vol. 15, No. I, pp. 31–32.

Nevill, H.R. (1911) *District Gazetteers of the United Provinces of Agra and Oudh*. Vol. xxiii, Allahabad: Government Press.

NIUA (2005) 'Urban Poverty'. *Urban Finance Quarterly Newsletter*. INDO-USAID(FIRE-D)Project, Vol. 8, No. 4, October–December.

Pande, B.N. (1955) *Allahabad: Retrospect and Prospect*. Allahabad: The Municipal Press.

Revi, Aromar (2007) Climate Change Risk: An Adaptation and Mitigation Agenda for Indian Cities, TARU, A Background Paper, Presented for the Global Urban Summit, Bellagio, Italy, 8–13 July, pp. 1–30. csud.ei.columbia.edu/.../Final%20Papers/.../Week2_Climate_India_Revi.pd

Singh, Ujagir (1966) *Allahabad: A Study in Urban Geography*. Varanasi: Banaras Hindu University Press.

Sinha, S.N. (1974): *Subah of Allahabad under the Great Mughals*. New Delhi: Gitanjali Publishing House.

Srivastava, Saligram (1937) *Prayag-Pradip*. Allahabad: Hindustani Academy.

Tahseen, Rana (1985) *Urban Administration in Allahabad, 1947–1972*. Ph.D thesis, abstract, Department of Political Science, New Delhi: Jamia Millia Islamia University. dspace.vidyanidhi.org.in:8080/dspace/handle/2009/905.

Tahseen, Rana (1999) *Urban Politics and Administration: A Case Study of Allahabad*. New Delhi: Deep and Deep Publishers.

11

The City of Terror

Deprivation, Segregation and Communal Conflicts in Malegaon

ABDUL SHABAN

Malegaon, a small city in the state of Maharashtra, for over one-and-a-half centuries, has been known for its handloom and powerloom-based textile industry. The city has also often been claimed as Manchester of the East. However, notwithstanding its glorious history, enterprising people and hardworking labourers, this city of about 4.5 lakh of population still remains underdeveloped and torn due to many social problems, including the communal strife between Hindus and Muslims even leading to bomb blasts. Although institutions and networks of mutual help and support among these ethnic communities do exist and are often portrayed as evidence of cooperation and symbiosis, at times they get ruptured and breached to allow inter-religious fights, brutal killings, looting and mayhem. The city is symbolised by extreme poverty, stark religious segregation, harsh working conditions of ordinary workers (often spanning to 12 to 16 hours), lack of housing, sanitation, educational and health facilities, and deafening sound pollution emanating from the powerlooms. In sum, the city has not only been faced with the terror acts and communal riots, but also extreme forms of underdevelopment and stigmatisation. The present paper attempts to look into these aspects of the city life of Malegaon with the following major objectives: (a) to examine the growth of population in the city, (b) to understand the levels and extent of socio-economic and infrastructural deprivation, (c) to study the lives of workers and entrepreneurs in the powerloom industry, and (d) to highlight the interdependence (especially economic) but also spatial segregation of religious communities, and the way these impact the residents and are also impacted by communal riots. The organisation of rest of the paper is as follows. We first discuss the growth of population and migration in the city, followed by income and infrastructural deprivation. The lives of workers and entrepreneurs in the powerloom industry are examined next, and are followed by the discussion on communal issues in the city and residential segregation of population. Notwithstanding the grinding poverty and penury in the town, the city dwellers show a strong taste of arts and culture. This aspect of the city life we discuss next and the final section concludes the chapter.

Population Growth and Migration

Migrants have played an important role in the emergence of Malegaon as a textile town.[1] The history of the town reveals that a sizeable number of people from Uttar Pradesh, Bihar Madhya Pradesh, and other North Indian states migrated to the town to escape the repression by the British colonisers during and after India's First War of Independence, in 1857. These migrants were largely the Muslims, as the repressive action of the Britishers was largely oriented towards Muslims who were blamed for the revolt in 1857. Such a repressive action of the Britishers against the Muslims continued for quite some time even after 1857. Muslims were denied government favours and postings in many sensitive/strategic positions in the government. The weakening of upper class Muslims, who acted as *jajman* for the poor Muslims, and also several famines during the period led to the mass migration of weaker sections (particularly Muslim weavers) from northern states southwards. These migrants got settled down at places favourable for their occupation and thus shaped the emergence of Burhanpur (in Madhya Pradesh), and Jalgaon, Malegaon and Bhiwandi (in Maharashtra) as the centres of textile industry. These centres played an important role during the freedom movement and provided needed clothes to Indians during Gandhiji's boycott of the British textiles.

The population of Malegaon town has slowly but steadily increased over the last hundred years. From a mere 19,054 in 1901, the total population of the town had reached 4,09,403 in 2001. As shown in Table 1, the town witnessed highest addition in number of persons during 1981–1991, but highest annual growth of the population in the town was during the decade of 1951–61. During 1991–2001, the growth rate of population in comparison to other decades has slowed down indicating that perhaps the town is now becoming economically moribund/stagnant and as such not able to attract higher number of migrants. However, it is projected that the population of the city will increase to 5,47,769 by 2021, and 7,61,154 by 2051.

Table 1

Recorded and projected population of Malegaon town

Year	Population	Decennial Variation	Decadal Variation (%)	Annual Growth Rate (%)	Projected Population (Linear Trend Based on 1951–2001 Recorded Population)
1901	19,054	—	—	—	—
1911	19,060	6	0.03	0.31	—
1921	23,505	4,445	23.32	2.33	—
1931	29,442	5,937	25.26	2.53	—
1941	36,780	7,338	24.92	2.49	—
1951	55,022	18,242	49.60	4.96	—
1961	1,21,408	66,386	120.65	12.07	—
1971	1,91,847	70,439	58.02	5.80	—
1981	2,45,883	54,036	28.17	2.02	—
1991	3,42,595	96,712	39.33	3.93	—
2001	4,09,403	66,808	19.50	1.95	—
2011	—	—	—	—	4,76,641
2021	—	—	—	—	5,47,769
2031	—	—	—	—	6,18,897
2041	—	—	—	—	6,90,025
2051	—	—	—	—	7,61,154

Source: Census of India, various years.

The city had 65 wards in 2001 but later it was reorganised into 72 wards. As per the Census of India 2001 data, 50.9 per cent of the total population in the city was living in slums, so much so that some eight wards in the town have more than 90 per cent of their respective population living in slums (Figure 1), while in 11 wards, 75.1 to 90 per cent, and in 13 wards, 50.1 to 75 per cent population lives in slum.

As per the Census of India 2001 data, Muslims comprised 75 per cent of the total population of Malegaon town. Most of these Muslims belong to the Ansari (*Julaha*) community, locally called Momins. The population shares of Scheduled Castes (SCs) and Scheduled Tribes (STs) to the total population of the town are 11 and 12 per cent, respectively (Census of India, 2001). Thus, about 98 per cent of the city's population comprises Muslims, SCs and STs.

Infrastructural Conditions

Infrastructural development of a town has bearing on lives of its residents. Among others, the provision of housing, schools, hospitals and dispensaries, sanitation and sewerage systems, roads and transport has

Figure 1
Ward-wise percentage of slum population in Malegaon, 2001

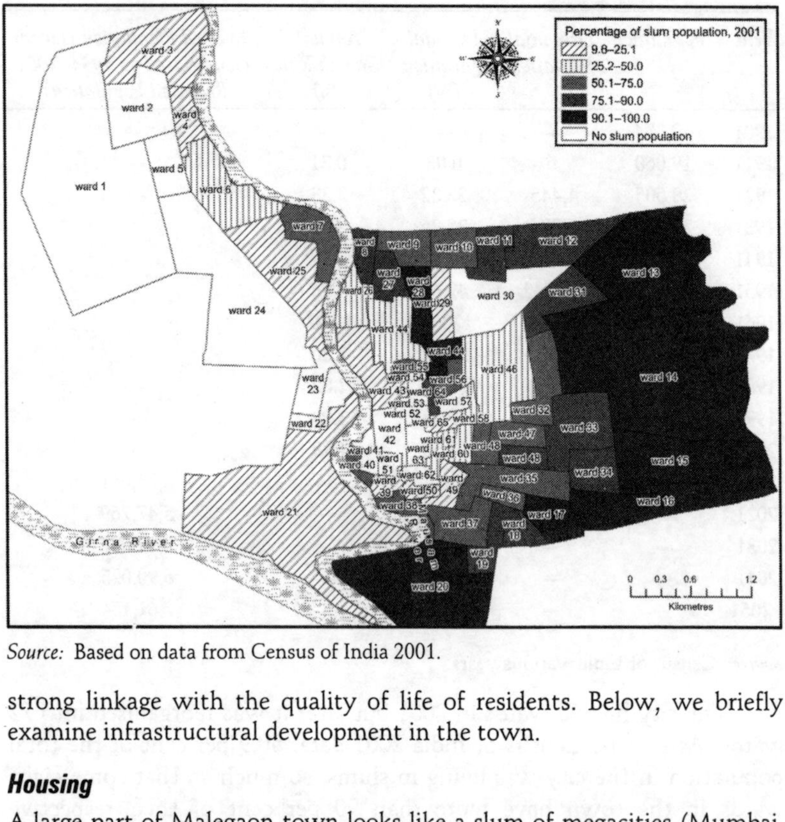

Source: Based on data from Census of India 2001.

strong linkage with the quality of life of residents. Below, we briefly examine infrastructural development in the town.

Housing

A large part of Malegaon town looks like a slum of megacities (Mumbai, Delhi, Kolkata) in terms of its make-up, congestion and, in fact, in areas even worse than that. Not only in slums, but across Malegaon, houses are typically made of tin sheets or wood, known as *patra* houses. Figure 2 shows dominant building materials and typical house types in Malegaon. The author had taken up a random sample (socio-economic) survey of 2,354 families/households from the town. The samples were taken from each ward in proportion to its share in total population of the town. The survey was conducted during March–October 2010 (henceforth called TISS Sample Survey, 2010). The survey shows that more than 48 per cent of the families live in 'huts with concrete wall and tin/plastic roofs', about 28 per cent in 'huts with iron/wooden pillar and tin/plastic roofs' and only 16.31 per cent of the families in the town have 'concrete houses or flats'. Religion-wise, more than 52 per cent of the Muslim families live in 'huts with concrete wall and tin/plastic roofs', while other 28.41 per cent live in 'huts with iron/wooden pillar and tin/plastic roofs' and only about 11 per cent have all concrete/flat houses. In contrast to the Muslims, over one-third of the non-Muslim families live in concrete houses/flats.

In the town, localities like Jooni Bhilati (Ward No. 1), Panchsheel Nagar and Bhilati (Ward No. 2), Kranti Nagar and Ganesh Wadi (Ward No. 7), Rahul Nagar and Khuddar Nagar (Ward No. 21), Yaseen Miyan Ka Takiya (Ward No. 45), Rehmanpura-Zaitunpura (Ward No. 46), Mahevi Nagar (Ward No. 48), Paath Kinara (Ward No. 50), Qila Khandak and Ghalib Nagar Jhoparpatti (Ward No. 56), Bohra Bagh Jhoparpatti and Byculla Jhoparpatti (Ward No. 60), Jamhoor Nagar (Ward No. 64), Ghayas Nagar (Ward No. 70) and almost the whole of Ward Nos. 9, 16, 20, 33, 34, 38, 47, 51, 52, 53, 57, 59, 63, 66, 67 and 72 have *patra* and plastic roof houses.

Public and Household Latrines

The sanitation (including the household) in the town requires considerable improvement. The public toilets in considerable parts of the town, specifically towards the east of the Mausam River, where most of the Muslim population is concentrated, are either not available or are in unusable condition. As per the information available from the Medical Officer, Malegaon Municipal Corporation, only about 34 per cent of the households have toilet facility in the town, while as per the City Sanitation Plan, 2010 (Malegaon Municipal Corporation), there are about 3,279 toilets (seats) in the town. However, these are official records and, on the ground, many of the toilets are missing or are in unusable conditions. At many places, they have even become a threat to public health

Figure 2

Major building material and condition of houses in Malegaon

Source: Photographed by the author in October 2010.

because of their un-cleanliness. There are about 81 open defecation spots in the town. As per the TISS Sample Survey, only 33.2 per cent of households in the town have latrines. It is important to note that in Malegaon town, there are wards where none of the households has toilet facility. These Wards are 2, 15 and 59. In Wards like 1, 10, 12, 21, 29, 35, 36, 56, 63, 66 and 69, even less than 10 per cent of the families have toilet facilities within house premises.

Source of Drinking Water and Supply

The supply of water in Malegaon is very erratic and unreliable. The tap water is supplied on alternate days and, in summer, the gap can be even of three days to a week. This necessitates that residents store water. Given the fact that most of the houses are too small to accommodate water storage tanks, cement water tanks are often put in front of the houses. The use of stored water not only results in water-borne diseases but also spoils the little space families have in front of their houses.

Presently, the water sources on which the town depends are insufficient to cater to the needs of families in the city, at the rate of 135 litres per capita per day (for per capita requirement of water, see Sharma and Shaban, 2007). The City Sanitation Plan (2010) of the town does identify the gap and proposes to develop the sources in future. As per the Plan, presently the total available sources contribute to only 31.5 million litres per day (MLD), while the requirement presently is of 55.27 MLD. The requirement is expected to rise to 96.56 MLD by 2026.

Electricity Supply and Streetlights

The city also faces shortage of electric supply. Particularly in the summer, due to long hours of power cuts, the situation becomes quite unbearable. Further, the powerloom industry and workers suffer immensely due to

Table 2

Streetlight infrastructure in Malegaon

Type of streetlight	Total number
High mast (90 poles)	391
Sodium fittings	5,623
T-5 fittings	999
40 Watt tubes	3070
Solar streetlight	100
Total	10,183

Source: Malegaon Municipal Corporation (2010): Malegaon Environmental Status Report 2009–10.

the power cuts. Many areas of the city are also unserved by streetlighting, and these areas mainly are the lanes in peripheral and slum areas of the city. The roads/lanes in these areas are also in a bad condition, often kutcha and full of ditches/potholes. The roads and streets remain waterlogged during rainy seasons and create additional inconvenience in the absence of proper lighting. The present available streetlight infrastructure in the city is presented in Table 2. However, one must keep in mind that these are the records on paper and many of the lights/poles are in a dysfunctional state, on the ground.

Sewerage System

A large part of the city is not having any underground sewerage system. The older part of the city where this exists is also in a poor condition and inadequately maintained. Even a moderate spell of water can flood the city. The roads, grounds, and even bus-depot of the town look like pools in rainy season. The water accumulation leads to breeding of mosquitoes and other health hazards, besides creating inconvenience to the residents. The city requires a thorough upgradation of its sewerage system and extension of the same to uncovered areas, particularly the slums located in the eastern part of the city.

Roads and Means of Transport within the City

The internal system of communication in congested *gaothan* area consists of narrow zig-zag roads and lanes. Even outside the congested part of the city, roads have uneven width and considerable meanderings. Many of the roads have been encroached by houses, shops and hawkers. This creates extreme congestion during the peak hours. On the top of it are the auto-rickshaws, cycle-rickshaws, cycles and motorbikes plying in all possible directions, following the traffic rules for namesake. The total road length in the city is about 384 kilometres. Out of this, 113.13 kilometres is the cement-concrete, 163.89 km is asphalt, and 106.99 km is the WBM (Water Bound Macadam; made of layers of compacted broken stone). Waterlogging on roads during the rainy season (due to lack of proper sewerage system) and immense dust during dry season are common features in the city.

Income and Poverty

A sizeable proportion of population in Malegaon town lives in poverty and penury. The TISS Sample Survey data shows that about one-third of the population in the town survives on per capita income less than ₹ 500. The share of population living below the poverty line income[2] is 56.5 per cent. The poverty among Muslims is more acute, a total of 60.7 per cent of the total Muslim population lives in poverty, while among the non-Muslims the share of population living below poverty line is 35.1 per cent. Figure 3 shows that about 82 per cent of the total population lives below the per capita income of ₹ 1,000, and thus can be considered highly vulnerable. The vulnerability among Muslims is significantly higher than the non-Muslim population in the city.

There are some wards in the town where the incidence of poverty is very high. In Wards 15, 18, 19, 25, 26, 51, 62, 65, 69 and 72, the share of BPL (below poverty line) population is between 75–95 per cent (Figure 3). Among the Muslims, the BPL population is specifically higher (above 75% of population) in Wards 1, 2, 15, 18, 19, 25, 26, 51, 62, 65, 67, 69 and 71, while among the non-Muslims, poverty is above 75 per cent in Wards 21, 29 and 36. A large share of population struggles in the city to keep body and soul together. Box 1 presents some cases of struggle by the women in the city.

Figure 3

Distribution of BPL population in Malegaon by wards, 2010

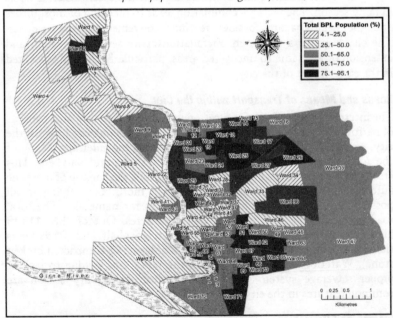

Source: TISS Sample Survey, March–October 2010.

Powerlooms in the Town

As per the informal sources (powerloom owners and workers), there are approximately 1,25,000 plain and outdated powerlooms installed in 6,500 units (a unit generally consists of 1 to 24 powerlooms) in the town. However, as per the Tax Department, Malegaon Municipal Corporation,

Box 1
Women and their struggle for economic survival

Zulekha Ansari, aged 65 years, is a resident of Nayapura (Ward No. 45). Despite her old age, she has to work on the *charkha*: spinning and putting colour into threads for saris. After labouring for a day, she manages to earn ₹ 20 only. Monthly, however, she just ekes out an income of not more than ₹ 450.

Manisha (age 30 years) lives in House No. 64, Ahire Gali, Sangameshwar (Ward No. 41). Her husband died due to a septic infection in 2009 and now she has to look after her family of seven, including mother-in-law and five children (all daughters and all below 14 years). Manisha works as a maid, earning just ₹ 1,000 every month. Only her one daughter (aged 14 years) is currently attending school – in 9th standard.

Shaqeela (age 39 years) lives in House No. 217, Tehzeeb Nagar (Ward No. 68). Being a widow, it's difficult for her to manage four children – all below 18 years. She works on a *charkha* and prepares the *nari* (thread) and manages to earn ₹ 350 every month. The family is dependent on community help for its survival.

Source: Based on personal interviews with the author.

there are only 56,194 powerlooms in the town. The lesser count of powerlooms by the Municipal Corporation is mainly due to the fact that those located in residential houses are not counted/or revealed by the owner. In fact, cloth weaving in Malegaon town has been a household industry and most of the (Muslim) families own a powerloom for their economic survival. The organised powerloom units in the town are also mainly located in residential areas. There are many advantages of the location of powerlooms in the residential houses as they can be operated by women and men, who can simultaneously do other household chores. However, they also cause many problems: from the sound pollution the hearing capacity of people gets affected, exposure to fibres causes asthma/TB, industrial garbage is dumped in residential areas, electricity supply scheduling and power cuts become difficult and chaotic.

Presently, the town processes about 85 lakh metres of cloth per day. People claim that the production was better in the past, with about 1 crore metres per day. It has come down in recent years mainly due to the power cuts for 6–8 hours daily at irregular intervals. Most of the powerlooms in the city run for 24 hours if power is available. Of the total cloth produced, 30 to 35 per cent is the cotton grey fabrics – Poplin and Cambric fabrics used for clothing and industrial purposes. These products are considered the best in the industry. The costing of these fabrics ranges from ₹ 6 to ₹ 15 per metre. Sixty per cent are man-made fibre grey fabrics – used for clothing and industrial purposes. These are considered as cheap products in the market. The costing of these man-made fibres grey fabrics ranges from ₹ 4 to ₹ 14 per metre. The rest 5 per cent is the yarn dyed fabric, used for direct clothing purposes. This yarn dyed fabric used as *saris* in rural areas once were the major and known products of the city. The cost of *saris* of 8.23 metres ranges from ₹ 85 to ₹ 350. A small proportion of this segment is the *lungi* of 2 metres; costs ranging from ₹ 36 to ₹ 110 per unit.

Given the lack of financial capital and government assistance to modernise the looms in the town, the weavers are mostly using outdated powerlooms, which are discarded by the textile mills. The weavers from Malegaon somehow manage with these old machines. Given the primitive type of powerlooms, the production per hour is lower and therefore, one needs to run the machine for longer hours. The electricity wiring and connection laid down at the beginning of electrification of the town, have never been upgraded/changed. Over time, the number of powerlooms has increased manifold, and sufficient electricity supply through the old networks/wires has also become an issue. Often there are electricity line faults and collapse of transformers.

Production and Supply Chains and Workers in Loom Industry

The cotton used for manufacturing cloth in the town is mainly grown in Vidarbha region of Maharashtra state. Given that most of the yarn-making industries are located in Gujarat (Malegaon has none, and attempts to open one in the past also failed), the cotton is sold to Gujarati traders by the farmers and is mostly routed through the districts of Nandurbar and Dhule to Gujarat. The cotton and polyester yarns are then imported by Gujarati merchants from mills of Ahmedabad, Surat, etc., and supplied to the powerloom owners of Malegaon. Marwari community monopolises the trade of yarn and cotton in the area. The Marwari community also has monopsony of grey fabrics and other products manufactured in the powerloom. It is often claimed that whatsoever is the profitability in the sector is mainly sucked by the fabric, yarn, and cotton merchants, while the cotton producers and fabric manufacturer are left with just only survival income/profits.

The local yarn merchants have made it a standard practice to fluctuate the yarn prices every hour, while mills fix up the rate for 15 days. This leads to the exploitation of the poor weavers, who can do nothing but buy the yarn. This often also leads to lower wages to the workers and sometimes non-payment of the wages to workers for days, as the owners of the looms try to meet the yarn price challenges which sucks most of their working capital. The multiple intermediaries in the yarn supply lead to undue increase in prices, which further erode the profitability of weavers. The buyers of grey cloth and other products generally delay the payment to the weavers/powerloom owners. The payment is generally made by cheque. Many a time, the merchants disappear without paying for the cloth they buy from powerloom owners. That leads to enormous losses to the weavers and keeps them indebted to the yarn suppliers.

The grey fabrics prepared at Malegaon are then sent to the many urban centres in Gujarat and Rajasthan and other cities like Kolkata and Mathura for further processing. It is often claimed by the loom owners that the merchant class has never allowed survival of yarn spinning mills, yarn banks, and additional processing of grey fabric in Malegaon town for the fear it may lose its highly-profitable business. Workers in the powerloom sector mostly get survival wages, along with health hazards like respiratory diseases. Again, for medical expenses, they remain indebted to the powerloom owners. Many of the workers, who often are migrants from other states, return to their homes and die there from respiratory diseases like TB. Social security of any kind does not exist for the workers and in case of some accidents (which are common given the old powerlooms used and almost nil protective gear available for the worker), workers are given a few thousand rupees and sent to their homes, and in case of death, ₹ 10–15,000 are provided to the dependents. The cases of accidents/deaths are often not reported to the police, or through bribing the police, the cases are concealed and shown as cases of natural death. Table 3 shows the wages, working conditions and common diseases associated with the work in the powerloom sector of Malegaon city.

Most of the workers in the powerloom sector are migrants from Uttar Pradesh and Bihar and mainly belong to Ansari (*julaha*) community. They are generally in the age category of 15–30 years, and are often uneducated or discontinuing their education at primary school level. They are generally pushed out of native homes due to poverty. Often, the new migrants are connected with someone (as relative or known) in the town. And as the opportunities of employment arise, the workers located in the town pass on the information to their relatives and known ones in villages or towns of Uttar Pradesh and Bihar. Learning operation of powerlooms is not very difficult. A worker can learn the same in 1–2 weeks. During the learning period, workers are paid ₹ 200–250 per week by owners of looms. The powerloom workers mostly live in dilapidated wood/tin houses in the eastern part of the town, which hardly has proper roads, streetlighting, sewerage system, schools, or tap water supply.

Table 3

Workers, working condition, diseases and wages in powerloom sector in Malegaon

Worker	General duration of work	specialisation and diseases	Weekly wage (₹)
Loom operator, also called 'majdur', or 'karigar'	12 hrs	• Looks after cloth-making on loom. • One *majdur* generally operates 8 looms • One *majdur* makes about 50 metres of cloth each day • Has to work in noisy and in the environment of cotton pieces flying in air for all 12 hours without any protective gear • Generally suffers from occupational diseases like leg pains, deafness, and asthma/TB	1,000–1,400 (mainly paid on piece rate basis)
Technician or 'mukadam'	12 hrs	• One technician manages 12 looms • They repair looms if some problem arises and also oil the looms	Fixed wages ₹ 1,000 to 1,500
Warper or beam-maker	12 hrs	• They run Kondi-Machines and also clean the shed • One warper runs 12 looms	₹ 800 to 1,400 (mainly paid on piece basis)
Metha or folders, who also measures how many metres' cloth is manufactured by each *majdur*	12 hrs	• Folds the manufactured cloth • Keeps records of which *majdur* manufactured how many metres of cloth	₹ 800 to 1,400 (fixed wage)
Tarasanwali	12 hrs	• Connects threads if broken in loom, generally females • One *trasanwali* is employed per 24 looms	₹ 700–1,000 per week (fixed wages)
Hammal/headloaders	12 hrs	• They carry beam, manufactured cloth from one place to another as needed • One *hammal* is employed per 24 looms or one shed	₹ 600–700 (fixed wages)

Note: One shed houses 24–50 looms; payment is made to workers every Friday (weekly basis).

Source: Based on interviews with powerloom workers and entrepreneurs.

Health: Mortality and Morbidity

The situation is also grave in the town with regard to health of the people. The death rate in the city is quite high and during the period 2003–2010, it ranged between 6.2 and 7.2 (Table 4). In fact, available data shows that the death rate has increased in recent years. The birth rate has also shown increasing trends in the town. It was 37.3 in 2003, and has increased to 43.7 in 2010. However, the town has experienced decline in the infant mortality rate from 40.5 in 2003 to 31.2 in 2010. Maternal mortality is also prevalent while 'still birth' is one of the major concerns. Surprisingly, the death and birth rate figures provided to us by the Malegaon Municipal Corporation are almost the same as for Maharashtra state as a whole.

Table 4

Birth and death, and infant and maternal mortality rates in Malegaon and Maharashtra

Year	Birth rate	Death rate	Infant mortality rate	Maternal mortality rate	Still birth
2003	37.3	6.5	40.5	1.2	14.0
2004	36.9	6.2	37.6	1.4	15.0
2005	37.9	6.3	36.6	0.9	13.3
2006	37.2	7.2	38.5	1.3	16.9
2007	37.9	6.3	31.7	1.2	14.6
2008	41.2	6.2	33.3	0.6	20.8
2009	42.4	6.9	32.8	0.7	14.3
2010	43.7	7.2	31.2	1.3	12.4
2011 (till May)	17.6	2.9	28.0	0.0	13.1
Maharashtra (2009–10)*	17.6	6.7	31.0	—	—

*Data for Maharashtra has been taken from Economic Survey of Maharashtra 2010, Directorate of Economics and Statistics, Government of Maharashtra, Mumbai.

Source: Medical Officer, Malegaon Municipal Corporation, Malegaon.

Causes of Death Among Muslims

As the data from other sources on causes of deaths could not be available, the data from death records of 'Bada Kabrastan' is used to find out the causes of death among Muslims in Malegaon. The data used for the purpose is from 27/12/2008 to 02/12/2010. The 'Bada Kabrastan' is the biggest cemetery in the town and almost 40 per cent of the burial of Muslims in the town takes place in this cemetery. The data throws a very disturbing picture on causes of death in the town. It shows that almost about 90 per cent of deaths of infants below one month is due to under-weight (may be resulting from lack of nutritious foods to mothers) and 4.8 per cent due to pneumonia (Table 5). Again, in the age group 2–12 months, 50 per cent of children die due to underweight and about 30 per cent due to pneumonia. Pneumonia and diarrhoea take most of the lives in the age group of 1–5 years. In the age-group of 6–14 years, underweight (malnutrition) remains a major cause of death, while in 15–35 years of age, TB and heart attack appear as the major killers. Heart attacks and TB also remain major causes of death in the age-group of 36–55 years while in the age group of 56–75 years, most of the people die due to old-age problems (perhaps due to weaknesses/insufficient nutrition and living conditions) and heart attack.

The higher death rate among the lower age-groups is mainly due to malnutrition, while TB is associated with poverty and working conditions in the powerloom industry. Heart attacks may be caused by consumption of beef (often of unhealthy buffaloes). Given the poverty, beef remains a major cheap source protein for the Muslim population. There also may be a link between drugs used on buffalos for milking and consumption of their meat, leading to heart attack. This needs to be researched.

Age-wise Deaths among Muslims

The data available from 'Bada Kabrastan' shows that 45.4 per cent of the total recorded deaths among Muslims are in the age-group of below 5 years (see Figure 4). The survival rate among population increases after they attain 5 years of age. Sex-wise data shows that as against total of 27.9 per cent of deaths in the age-group below one year, the same for the female and male groups in the age category is 29.8 and 26.3 per cent, respectively. Overall, 50.3 per cent deaths among females and 41.3 per cent deaths among males take place in the age-group of below five years.

Music, Literature and Cinema: Soothing the Strained Life

Penury and poverty of the majority of population in the town have not been able to stop the creativity of the residents of Malegaon. After toiling in powerloom and plastic industries or selling food on stalls and working in hotels, many of them gather at tea shops to discuss Urdu literature, recite their new poems and discuss about the new books they have read or published (see Box 2 for some case studies). *Sham-e-Mushaira* and *Ghazal* events are also regularly organised. Among these artists, there are also many talented actors who often gather together to make Malegaon's version of Bollywood's popular movies. Many of these actors copy the dialogue delivery style and actings of popular Bollywood actors. The films which are produced by spending tens of crores of rupees in Bollywood are

Table 5

Causes of deaths among Muslims in Malegaon town from 27/12/2008 to 02/12/2010

	Age								Total
	1 month and below	2–12 months	1–5 years	6–14 years	15–35 years	36–55 years	56–75 years	76 years and above	
Accident	0.1	0.3	5.5	5.8	7.1	3.0	0.3	0.0	1.6
AIDS	0.0	0.0	0.0	0.0	1.0	0.0	0.0	0.0	0.1
Anaemia	0.0	0.3	0.6	0.0	1.9	0.4	0.3	0.0	0.4
Asthma	0.0	0.0	0.0	1.4	1.3	8.5	13.6	2.6	5.3
Backbone problem	0.0	0.0	0.0	0.0	0.3	1.2	0.2	0.0	0.3
Blood cancer	0.0	0.0	0.0	0.0	0.6	0.2	0.0	0.0	0.1
Boils	0.0	0.0	0.0	0.0	0.3	0.0	0.0	0.0	0.0
Brain fever	0.0	0.0	1.2	2.9	3.2	0.8	0.6	0.0	0.7
Brain haemorrhage	0.0	0.0	0.0	0.0	0.6	1.6	0.6	0.0	0.4
Brain tumour	0.0	0.3	0.6	1.4	1.6	1.2	0.2	0.0	0.5
Burns	0.1	0.0	0.0	1.4	6.1	0.2	0.0	0.0	0.6
Cancer	0.0	0.0	1.2	2.9	4.8	8.7	5.1	1.1	3.3
Delivery	0.0	0.0	0.0	0.0	7.7	1.0	0.0	0.0	0.8
Dengue	0.1	0.0	1.8	1.4	0.0	0.2	0.0	0.0	0.2

Cont'd....

...Cont'd

Depression	0.0	0.0	0.0	0.0	0.3	0.0	0.0	0.0	0.0
Diabetes	0.0	0.0	0.0	0.0	1.0	6.1	4.9	0.4	2.3
Diarrhoea	1.6	7.0	14.7	8.7	2.6	1.6	0.3	0.0	2.3
Diphtheria	0.0	0.0	0.6	4.3	0.0	0.0	0.0	0.0	0.1
Drowned	0.0	0.0	0.0	4.3	1.6	0.0	0.0	0.0	0.2
Drowned in well	0.0	0.0	0.0	0.0	0.3	0.2	0.0	0.0	0.1
Electrocution	0.0	0.0	0.6	0.0	1.0	0.6	0.0	0.0	0.2
Epilepsy	0.1	1.4	1.2	7.2	1.0	0.2	0.1	0.0	0.5
Fever	0.6	3.1	1.2	4.3	0.6	0.2	0.0	0.0	0.6
Gangrene	0.0	0.0	0.0	0.0	0.0	0.2	0.0	0.0	0.0
Heart attack	0.6	1.0	3.7	2.9	10.9	33.9	24.8	0.0	13.4
Heat stroke	0.0	0.0	0.0	1.4	0.0	0.0	0.0	0.0	0.0
Hernia	0.0	0.0	0.0	0.0	0.3	0.0	0.0	0.0	0.0
Hysteria (Jhatka)	0.0	0.7	1.2	0.0	0.3	0.2	0.0	0.0	0.2
Intestinal problem	0.0	0.0	0.0	0.0	0.0	0.2	0.1	0.0	0.1
Jaundice	0.1	0.7	1.8	2.9	2.2	1.2	0.6	0.0	0.8
Joint pain	0.0	0.0	0.6	0.0	0.0	0.0	0.0	0.0	0.0
Kidney problem	0.1	0.3	0.6	4.3	4.5	6.9	1.5	0.9	2.1
Liver problem	0.0	0.0	0.6	0.0	1.3	2.6	0.1	0.0	0.5

Cont'd...

...Cont'd

Locomotion problem	0.0	0.0	0.6	0.0	0.3	0.0	0.0	0.0	0.1
Low BP	0.0	0.0	0.0	0.0	0.6	0.4	0.6	0.0	0.3
Malaria	0.0	0.0	0.6	1.4	0.3	0.2	0.0	0.0	0.1
Marasmus (Sukhandi)	0.9	1.4	8.6	0.0	0.3	0.4	0.0	0.0	0.8
Mental illness	0.3	0.3	3.1	1.4	3.2	0.6	0.2	0.0	0.7
Murder	0.0	0.0	0.0	0.0	1.9	0.4	0.0	0.0	0.2
Not known	0.0	1.0	0.6	4.3	1.6	0.6	0.1	0.0	0.5
Old age	0.0	0.0	0.0	0.0	0.0	0.0	40.7	91.3	24.6
Others (G.B.S.)	0.0	0.0	0.0	1.4	0.0	0.0	0.0	0.0	0.0
Others (Ghaweez)	0.0	0.3	0.0	0.0	0.0	0.0	0.0	0.0	0.0
Pneumonia	4.8	29.3	36.2	8.7	2.6	0.6	0.4	0.0	5.7
Poisoning	0.0	0.0	0.0	0.0	0.3	0.0	0.0	0.0	0.0
Polio	0.0	0.0	0.0	2.9	0.0	0.0	0.0	0.0	0.1
Rabies	0.0	0.0	0.0	1.4	0.0	0.0	0.0	0.0	0.0
Small pox (samowa)	0.3	0.0	4.3	0.0	0.0	0.0	0.0	0.0	0.3
Stomach disease	0.1	1.0	2.5	0.0	0.6	1.2	0.3	0.0	0.5
Stomach tumour	0.0	0.0	0.0	0.0	0.3	0.6	0.1	0.0	0.1
Stone	0.0	0.0	0.0	0.0	0.0	0.0	0.1	0.0	0.0
Suicide	0.0	0.0	0.0	0.0	1.0	0.2	0.0	0.0	0.1

Cont'd...

...Cont'd

Swine flu	0.0	0.0	0.0	0.0	0.3	0.2	0.0	0.0	0.1
TB	0.1	0.7	3.1	7.2	19.9	11.6	3.0	0.0	4.6
Throat cancer	0.0	0.0	0.0	0.0	0.0	0.0	0.1	0.0	0.0
Tonsil	0.0	0.0	0.0	0.0	0.3	0.0	0.0	0.0	0.0
Toothache	0.0	0.0	0.0	0.0	0.0	0.0	0.1	0.0	0.0
Typhoid	0.0	0.0	1.8	1.4	0.3	0.4	0.0	0.0	0.2
Ulcer	0.0	0.0	0.0	2.9	1.3	1.2	0.7	0.0	0.5
Underweight (weak)	89.9	50.9	0.6	10.1	0.0	0.0	0.0	0.0	22.4
Weakness	0.0	0.0	0.0	0.0	0.3	0.4	0.2	0.2	0.2
Weakness (swelling)	0.0	0.0	0.0	0.0	0.0	0.4	0.0	0.0	0.1
Total	100.0	100.0	100.0	100.0	100.0	100.0	100.0	100.0	100.0
Total number of deaths	693	287	163	69	312	508	904	530	3466

Source: Data compiled from official Register of 'Baba Kabrastan', Malegaon (REGD. NO. B-33).

Figure 4

Percentage distribution of total recorded deaths by age at 'Bada Kabrastan',
Malegaon from 27/12/2008 to 02/12/2010

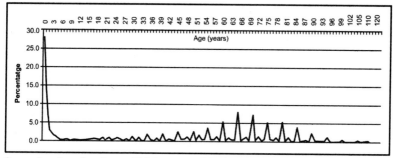

Source: Based on data from official register of 'Bada Kabrastan', Malegaon (REGD. NO. B-33).

remade as *copy* in Malegaon in a few thousand rupees. They often use normal *video* camera and hardly have any money to afford even for costumes, make-ups, etc. Some of the popular films made by the locals from Malegaon are: *Malegaon Ka Shole, Khandesh Ke Dil Wale Dulhania Le Jayen Ge, Gazni, Malegaon Ka Superman,* and *Koi Hil Gaya.* The local popularity of these films is huge, and the intensity and passion with which the actors perform their respective roles are appreciable. Some of the commercial TV serials, like *Malegaon Ka Chintoo,* have also been made with the help of local actors.

Film-making at low budget and improving conditions in the powerloom industry can play a transformative role for development of the town. They can lead to a generation of sizeable and better paid employments. There exists a huge potential in the town with respect to the cultural industry. The government must pay due attention and encourage investment in the industry and marketing of the products.

Communal Segregation and Riots

Since the beginning of 20th century, Malegaon town has experienced 11 major riots and two bomb blasts (Table 6). The frequency of riots has increased in the town after 1960. The recorded data shows that approximately 36 persons had died in these riots while 351 were injured. In contrast, in the two bomb blasts that took place in 2006 and 2008, a total of 37 persons died and 398 got injured. Thus, overall, the two bomb blasts have taken more lives in the city than 11 riots together since 1932.

The reason for the first recorded riot in the city is not known, but for other riots the major causes have been recorded. These reasons are based on *Times of India* reports (or other news papers). Some of the causes of riots in the town are identified/caused due to religious processions, more so in 1963 and 1983. In 1963, a Ganesha procession was reported to be disturbed by Muslims, while in 1983, the Muharram/Tazia procession was obstructed by the Hindu community. In 1982 and 2001, riots took place due to strained relationship between Muslims and the police. A distrust towards the police force runs very deep among majority of the Muslims in the town. They feel that the police itself is communalised and often acts in a partisan way against the Muslims. During the 1980s and 1990s, cricket matches between India and Pakistan were major causes of riots. A right-wing Hindu organisation much wanted to express its staunch nationalism by celebrating the defeat of Pakistan by India in cricket matches, while there were Muslims who, more to tease the Hindus or to express their love for cricket as a game, would celebrate the win of Pakistan. This often created acrimony between the two religious groups. Two riots (one each in 1982 and 1983) took places due to cricket matches and their celebrations. Other riots have taken place in the city due to cow slaughter allegedly by Muslims; the demolition of Babri Masjid by the Hindu right-wing, and fight due to personal reasons. The bomb blasts in the town have allegedly been the handiwork of a right-wing Hindu organisation.

Box 2

Some associated with Malegaon's film industry

 Rafique "Johnny" (aged 37 years): name "Johnny" was given after he played the role of Johnny Lever in "Malegaon Ke Karan Arjun". Studied till 7th and now works as a casual wage labourer in powerloom and earns about ₹ 2,500 per month; works in the night shift from 9 pm to 7 am. Also works part-time in film industry, with which he has been associated since 1996. He has played the role of Johnny Lever in "Malegaon Ke Karan Arjun" (2003); acted and produced "Khandesh Mein Dhoom" (2007); acted and written story in "Mamu Main Hoon Na" (2006);, and "Johnny Pareshan" (2003). His other films like "Khandesh Ka Veerappan", "Naak Mein Dum", etc., are also ready, but there are no distributors.

 Zia (aged 33 years) is a painter by profession and has been associated with the film industry since 1994. Has completed his BA; wanted to do BFA, but had no monetary support. In 1994, he worked as an Assistant Director in Khursheed Siddiqui's film 'Desh Ki Pukar'. In 1998, he wrote and directed 'Mere Hamsafar'. In 2000, his film 'Maut-The Haunting Shadow' was released.

Table 6

Chronology of riots in Malegaon, and their possible causes

Year	Reported killed	Reported injured	Duration (days)	Causes
1932	—	4	1	—
1963	7	80	1	Trouble broke out when a Ganesh Puja procession was passing by a place of worship, soda water bottles and bricks were hurled at processionists.
1967	4	9	1	Trouble broke out when the news spread about stealing and slaughtering of a cow.
1975	4	11	2	Trouble started between Hindus and Muslims over an altercation at a pan shop.
1982	—	19	1	The violence started when the police had lobbed tear-gas shells and imposed curfew in the town following the violent turn of an agitation by a group of Muslims protesting against certain 'objectionable' references in an eighth standard history book.
1983	4	178	4	Trouble broke out over the bursting of crackers near a place of worship after Indian victory in the Prudential World Cup cricket.
1983	—	—	—	same as above
1983	—	—	1	Trouble broke out at midnight of October 24th after some persons of a Muharram procession induiged in stone-throwing.
1987	7	1		Trouble broke out after a clash between two groups of people at Sangameshwar.
1992	4	43	4	Trouble broke out due to the Ayodhya controversy between Hindus and Muslims.
2001	13	several	—	Trouble broke out when a Muslim youth was distributing pamphlets outside a mosque which called for boycott of waiting police van.
Total (approx)	36	351	16	

Source: Based on data from Varshney (2002) and Centre for the Study of Society and Secularism, Mumbai.

Theoretical Understanding of Causes of Riots

Although many scholars have attempted to explain the causes of riots in India in their own ways (see for instance: Brass, 2003; Wilkinson, 2005; Jafferlot, 1995; Engineer, 1989, 199; and Puniyani, 2005), I, here, specifically focus on the explanations provided by Asutosh Varshney (2002). Varshney stresses on the existence or absence of civic ties between members of the two communities as the major factor that either leads to violence or to peace (Varshney, 2002). He recognises two types of civic networks:

1. *Associational forms of engagement:* business associations, professional organisations, film clubs, sports clubs, trade unions, etc.; and
2. *Everyday forms of engagement:* consisting of simple, routine interactions of life; that is, whether families in the neighbourhood from different communities visit each other, eat together, jointly participate in festivals, and allow kids to play together in the neighbourhood.

Varshney argues that the strength of associational forms to withstand national-level exogenous shocks is substantially higher than everyday form. Further, he also adds that an increase in number of parties competing for Muslim votes increases the incentives for state governments to prevent anti-minority violence. In the following section, we attempt to examine and map out the two forms of engagements in the town among Hindu and Muslim residents. These engagements have mainly been examined in terms of economic interdependence of the communities.

Interdependence of Communities: Everyday Forms and Formal Associations

In the town, there exists considerable interdependence of Hindus and Muslims on each other. There has emerged specialisation of some caste and religious groups on certain occupations/activities and they dominate those occupations, while others depend on the services/products. Table 7 provides details of major services/products offered by Muslims to non-Muslims and vice versa. Muslims are mainly the powerloom owners and largely depend on a few hundred Marwari Hindu/Jain business families for getting their yarn supply. Cinema house/theatre owners are largely Hindus; while the milk suppliers to almost half of the Muslim families in the town are the *Gowlis* (tribal group). The fodder grass (called *bilayati ghas*) used for feeding goats (often kept by Muslims) and other animals in the town is largely supplied by Hindus/Gowlis from nearby villages. Most of the barbers and *methas* (folders of cloth in powerloom factories) in the town are Hindus. In Muslim-concentrated areas, ration shops are also mostly owned by Marwaris or other Hindus.

Muslims buy yarn from local Marwaris (mainly Hindus) and sell the manufactured cloth back to them. Further, a majority of garage owners, air-conditioner/fridge mechanics, nurses, carpenters and watchmen in the city are from the Muslim community. They offer their services to the Muslims and also the Hindus alike. A large section of Hindus in the town depends on Muslims for these services.

Whether much of this association can be termed as *everyday form of association* remains a question. In fact, many forms of interdependence among the Hindu and Muslim residents, as outlined above (Table 7), are economic in nature and also very momentary. Some of them even lead to distrust and suspicion due to the exploitation of one community by the other. For example, many Muslim powerloom owners view that the yarn prices are manipulated by the Marwaris, and that is why Muslim handloom owners are not getting good prices for their products. The mistrust and disliking of one community over the other has made inroads, which get manifested while choosing an area for living or venturing by members of one community to other's areas during some festive occasions. It may flare up into physical violence. Extreme residential segregation of Hindus and Muslims in the town, which we discuss further, is the result of this distrust.

The town also has many formal Hindu-Muslim organisations. Some of them are Aman Committee (to enhance the interaction between the communities), Auto-Rickshaw Union, Majdur Kamgar Union, Kapda Union (makers of readymade clothes), Engineering Committee of Malegaon (this is the think tank for new development/innovation), Builders' Union, etc. Hindu-Muslims also jointly bid for the octroi contract for the town. These organisations create associational forms of engagement between the community members. However, it does not mean they prevent the communal riots to take place. In fact, there is a need to study the role of these associational forms and everyday forms of engagement during the 1980s, when most of the riots took place in the city.

Residential Segregation on Religious Lines

There exists very sharp residential segregation of Hindus and Muslims in different locations of the town. To the east of Mausam river is the Muslim-concentrated area, while to the west mostly the Hindus live. In the everyday life, this division is mentioned as *nadia ke is paar aur nadia ke us par* (this side of the river and that side of the river), without taking name of the communities residing there. Others are supposed to understand the symbolic description of the situation and be careful in dealing with those located on the other side of the river. Many claim the river as the border between India and Pakistan. Muslims do not call the part of the city dominated by them as Pakistan but others label so. Some Muslims claim that *Hindu Nashik ko apna shahar bolte hein, Malegaon ko*

Table 7

Inter-community dependence

Activities	Caste/religious groups involved	Dependence
		Dependence of Muslims on Non-Muslims
Yarn supply for handloom	*Marwaris*	Almost all Muslim handloom owners depend on the yarn supplied by Hindus
Cinema	Hindu owners	85 per cent of Muslim families/boys go to watch cinema in the cinema halls owned by Hindus
Milk supply	*Gowlis* from nearby villages supply milk between 6–8 a.m. to Muslim families	Almost 50 per cent of the Muslim families depend on this milk supply
Grass supply for goats	The contractors selling *bilayati* grass are Hindus and they bring grass from villages	Almost 40 per cent of Muslim families who own goats are dependent on these Hindu contractors
Hair cutting	*Nai* (barber) community from nearby villages	Almost 90 per cent of the barbers in the city are Hindu barbers and they offer their services in the Muslim-dominated areas and pockets in the city
Methas (folders of cloth)	They are from disparate Hindu caste groups	The folders of cloth in handloom industries belong to Hindu communities
Ration shops	*Marwaris* and also other Hindu castes	Almost 40 per cent of the ration shops in Malegaon in Muslim-concentrated areas are owned by the Hindus. Also, the petty Muslim shopkeepers get their stock from these Hindu businessmen
		Dependence of Hindus on Muslims
Activities	Caste groups involved	Dependence
Cloth manufacturing by powerloom	Mostly *Ansaris/Momins,* but also other Muslim castes	Hindu traders depend on these handloom owners for selling their yarn to the latter and then buying manufactured cloth

Cont'd....

...Cont'd

Drivers	Disparate caste groups from Muslims	Almost 70 per cent of the drivers of Hindu family-owned cars/vehicle are Muslims
Garage owners/car mechanics	Disparate caste groups from Muslims	Muslims dominate the occupation even in Hindu-concentrated areas
Fridge/AC mechanics	Disparate castes from Muslims	Muslims dominate almost 95% of the business
Supervisors and watchmen	Disparate caste groups from Muslims	Muslim dominate these occupations and serve in Hindu-concentrated areas
Nurse (boys and girls)	Disparate caste groups from Muslims	Muslim dominate this occupations in the city
Cushion/*gaddi* makers	Mansoories/Dhunias from Muslims	Almost Muslims have monopoly in this business in the city
Carpenters	Disparate castes from Muslims	Muslims dominate this business/occupation in the city and most of the Hindus buy furniture from their shops

Source: Based on field surveys and interviews.

nahin (for the Hindus, Nashik is their city and not Malegaon), because Malegaon is dominated by the Muslims.

On occasions, Muslims are scolded: *chal ... nikal Pakistan ja* (you ... go to Pakistan). However, this was more common in 1980s and 1990s when the communal flare-ups in India were at the peak. As mentioned earlier, the cricket matches were the cause of communal flare-ups many times in the town. Many Muslims from the city narrate that whenever India got defeated by Pakistan, they used to get abuses and stones as if India got defeated because of the Muslims. In fact, in day-to-day parlance, Muslims are blamed for many unfortunate happenings and situations, from defeat of Indian team by Pakistan or even Sri Lanka in cricket, or over-population to underdevelopment of the country (India). Malegaon was also referred to as 'chhota Pakistan' by a few Hindus during the field survey, mainly because of the higher concentration of Muslims in the town.

After 1992, the residential segregation between Hindus and Muslims has become even sharper. During the 1992 riots, a large proportion of Hindus and Muslims moved out from areas where the concentration of the other community was higher. Presently Hindus dominate in 17 wards in the city, and their concentration is very high in the Camp and the Sanghmeshwar areas. In Sanghmeshwar, neo-Buddhists are also very much concentrated.

Families belonging to both the communities make their strategic decision to locate themselves in safer areas. Hindus have left Datta Nagar and Zaitunpurar colony, where they were in majority but the area was surrounded by Muslim-concentrated areas. In Datta Nagar, there were 312 Hindu families in 1992, but presently, as told by locals, only 2 are remaining while others have moved out to other places. Hindus have also moved out from Bajrang Wadi. From all these places, they have mostly got settled in Soyegaon Naka. In the past, many Muslim families have also moved out from Camp Area, where Hindus are in a majority. As mentioned earlier, Muslims are mainly concentrated to the east of the river Mausam. There are some families of Muslims on the west bank of the river Mausam and they feel that they are on the border and can quickly escape to the other side of the river in case of some communal trouble.

Seeing all these spatial separations, a dejected Muslim stated: *Fasad se ab shahar mein kutch bhi nahien ho sakta kyun ki shahar but chukka hai, aur ab is se zyada kya bate ga (riots can do no more damage to the city, the city is already divided, what else is remaining to be divided?).*

Notwithstanding the riots and bomb blasts the city has gone through, there are also many examples of mutual existence, symbiosis, and respect for each other. The fate of both the religious communities largely remains tied to poverty and penury, and in these conditions many help each other to live the lives they have got. Some of the examples of mutual cooperation and respect for one religious community by the other in the town are: in Bajrang Wadi, Bhikku Chowk, a small Hanuman *Mandir* stands without any disturbance, and Muslims very much respect that, even after about 20 years of Hindus moving out from that area; the Mata Math Hindu temple and Ahle-hadith mosque in Motipura of the city share the same wall and both the communities enjoy this union. The priest proudly tells that the *mandir* gets water from the mosque and *muezzin* (the person responsible for saying 'azans' in a mosque) happily provides the water.

Conclusion

Although Malegaon falls under the category of Class I towns, it is more characterised by several developmental issues typical of small and medium towns in the country. Given that the city has been an important base of textile industry (mainly based on *kargha, charkha*, and handloom in the past, and the powerloom at present) for more than 150 years, the lack of development in the town shows continued apathy and lack of vision of planners and policy makers to harness the economic potential of such industrial towns and create labour-intensive industrialisation and urbanisation. At present, the town is besieged with poverty. The town suffers from infrastructural underdevelopment and the lives of workers and working conditions in the textile industry in the city remain pathetic (low wages, rampant diseases, living in slums, non-availability of protective gear at place of work, and lack of social security). Although this underdevelopment adversely affects the upward socio-economic mobility of a common resident of the town, yet it has become very 'facilitative' to political and culturo-nationalist organisations for dividing people in the town, through offers of token economic and/or non-economic favours. The town displays sharp residential segregation on the basis of religion, and has been plagued with frequent communal riots in the past, and bomb blasts in recent years. Malegaon represents one of the examples of subaltern urbanisation in the country – being socially, politically, and geographically outside of the hegemonic power structure and development – and exploitation of the poverty (by dividing the poor on religious, regional, and caste bases) by the political groups for their benefits.

Notes

1. The terms 'city' and 'town' are interchangeably used for Malegaon, as in population size it is more a city but in terms of living conditions, it's no more than a town.
2. The Expert Group on 'Methodology for Estimation of Poverty' chaired by Prof. Suresh D. Tendulkar, and constituted by the Planning Commission, Government of India, estimated poverty line income at ₹ 484.9 per capita

for rural areas and ₹ 631.8 per capita for urban areas in Maharashtra for the year 2004–05. See http://planningcommission.nic.in/reports/genrep/himanshu.pdf (accessed on 26 September 2009). Based on this estimate and taking inflation into account, the current study has taken ₹ 700 per capita as poverty line income. Persons having per capita income ₹ 700 or below are categorised as poor. We have used income approach to estimate the poverty as it is expected that the income of individual will be first used to satisfy the basic needs like hunger.

References

Brass, P.R. (2003) *The Production of Hindu Muslim Violence in Contemporary India*. Seattle: University of Washington Press.

Census of India (2001) Final Population Total (data on CD). New Delhi: Office of the Registrar General and Census Commissioner.

Engineer, Asghar Ali (1989) *Communalism and Communal Violence in India: An Analytical Approach to Hindu-Muslim Conflict*. New Delhi: Ajanta Publications.

———. (1991) *Communal Riots in Post-Independence India*. Hyderabad: Orient Blackswan.

Government of Maharashtra (2011) *Economic Survey of Maharashtra 2010*. Mumbai: Directorate of Economics and Statistics.

Jafferlot, Christophe (1995) *The Hindu Nationalist Movement and Indian Politics*. New York: Columbia University Press.

Malegaon Municipal Corporation (2010) *Malegaon Environmental Status Report 2009–10*. Malegaon, Maharashtra.

———. (2010) *City Sanitation Plan, 2010*. Malegaon, Maharashtra.

Puniyani, Ram (2005) *Religion, Power and Violence: Expression of Politics in Contemporary Times*. New Delhi: Sage Publications.

Sharma, R.N. and A. Shaban (2007) 'Water Consumption Patterns in Domestic Households in Major Cities'. *Economic and Political Weekly*. Vol. 42, No. 23, pp. 2190–97.

Varshney, Asutosh (2002) *Ethnic Conflict and Civic Life*. New Haven: Yale University Press.

Wilkinson, S.I. (2005) *Vote and Violence: Electoral Competition and Communal Riots in India*. New Delhi: Cambridge University Press.

12

Ethnic Conflicts in a Small City

The Case of Shillong

NIKHLESH KUMAR

The present paper is an attempt to understand the inter-ethnic relation-ships, more based on tensions and conflicts, in a small multi-ethnic and multi-religious city in the north-eastern region of India. To my mind, such an exercise should be made with a historical perspective as such relationships of conflict have their bases in historical experiences of the communities and their perception of each other. My focus presently is on the city of Shillong, which is the capital of Meghalaya. Fortunately, documents are available on the history of this city since the time of its creation.

My approach, in this long essay, would be to locate Shillong city in its geo-political context and to follow along the way how members of various communities happened to come there to live with the people who have claimed an indigenous status. Further, I have tried to point out the differences in the cultures of these communities and the implications thereof. In the process, it is examined as to how a relationship of suspicion and mistrust emerged between the tribal and the various non-tribal communities right from the very formative years of the city.

Emergence or growth of cities is not necessarily linked with the process of urbanisation or industrialisation. There is historical evidence about it from different parts of the world. However, Rao (1992: 93) makes a distinction between traditional and modern urbanisation in Indian historical context by 'taking the introduction of *Pax Britannica* as the cut-off point'. Descriptions are available in historical literature about the different classes of traditional towns in India according to their main functions, e.g., trade and commerce, manufacturing, administration, military, and education.

Various historical accounts also tell us that not all cities grew out of villages and the process of urbanisation went along different paths: administrative, political, commercial, religious and educational. Brush (in Rao, 1992: 217–27) argued that protection, prestige, and proximity could explain the distribution of population in pre-British Indian cities. These three factors could also explain the distribution of population in the cities even during the British period. But this was not always the case. Cities had emerged on their own without necessarily growing out of the villages in whatever form. However, it is also true that these cities might have absorbed populations migrating from villages, providing employment of various kinds.

Military and trading activities of several European nations along the Indian coasts resulted in the establishment and growth of cities. Shillong is such a case in point. Shillong, which during the British period was the seat of the Chief Commissioner of the Gauhati Province, subsequently became the capital of the then composite state of Assam after the independence of India, and is today the capital of the state of Meghalaya in the north-eastern region of India. It thus has over a century-old inter-esting history of existence and growth. There are not many cities perhaps whose history since inception is available in a documented form and this makes the study of Shillong more interesting. The history of Shillong is the history of British rule in the north-east; and the history of Shillong, till it became the capital of Meghalaya, is also the history of political and economic changes in the north-east which came about after the independence of India. During the process, Shillong has witnessed many agreements and accords of national importance, and even international events leading to the birth of Bangladesh in its neighbourhood.

Unlike many cities, Shillong did not grow out of any rural or urban base nor was its birth a result of industrialisation. Shillong is a city which was created by the British East India Company in the last quarters of the 19th century for setting up a military and civil station on the Khasi Hills due to its strategic location. It is, of course, true that subsequently some of the existing rural areas around it were included in its ambit. It is this historical fact that makes the case of Shillong inter-esting and different from that of many cities. The physical site at which this city was established by the British colonisers did not have any human habitation. The British officers and the 'native' (not the tribals of the Khasi Hills) subordinate staff were brought from outside to settle there. But all these 'natives' could not be accommodated there, so their population spilled over to the neighbouring villages inhabited by the Khasi population. This could be termed as the initial stage of contact between the Khasis and the 'outsiders'.

In order to understand the characteristic features of Shillong city, from the point of its ethnic composition and inter-ethnic tensions and conflicts, one has to go through, in some details, the historical circumstances of its creation and subsequent growth.

The East India Company was interested in extending its trade as far as China and in the pursuit of this interest it adopted the policy of diplomacy and reconciliation with the use of its superior military power. Control over the north-eastern region was considered vital by the Company in the pursuit of its long-term economic interests. It did not miss the opportunity to set its feet in the north-eastern region when the British India Company was invited to enter Assam, during the Ahom period, to drive away the Burmese invaders from there. The British after finally subduing the Burmese in 1826 entered into a treaty with them, which came to be known as the Treaty of Yandaboo.

Road communication by a shorter route was considered necessary by the Company to consolidate its grip over the Brahmaputra and the Surma valleys. This was possible by constructing the road through the Khasi Hills. Khasi Hills, a sparsely populated area those days as compared to plains in the mainland British India, had a unique political system totally unknown to the bureaucrats of the Company. They were only familiar with the political system in the princely states which appeared easy to understand and deal with.

Overtures were made to some of the Khasi tribal chiefs to allow the Company to construct roads through their territories for faster communication. The Company met with initial successes but in a short time a misunderstanding resulted in a protracted war. The Company eventually won with its superior fire-power.

There was another reason besides the road communication as the attraction for the Khasi Hills. This was for the yet unexploited mineral resources hidden under the surface of these hills. The Khasi and the Jaintia Hills were contiguous to the plains of the then East Bengal. The Company first set up its civil and military headquarters at Cherrapunji, which was termed Cherra Station. For this, a treaty was made with the Chief of Cherra who gave them unhindered passage from the plains of Sylhet to other parts of the Khasi Hills.

The Government of India, during the British period, had decided to create an Eastern Frontier district which had to be located either at Cherrapunji or Shillong. On the recommendations of a committee, the choice was made in favour of Shillong with portions carved out of upper Shillong and the Iewduh plateau. Soon thereafter, the process of acquiring the lands through direct purchase from the Chief of Hima Mylliem and other owners (clans as well as lineages) started for the construction of roads and the civil station.

But it was the Jaintia rebellion over the issue of imposition of house tax that prompted the British to shift their headquarters to a more central place from where the British forces could move more swiftly in all the directions. The choice fell in favour of a place which grew later into the present-day Shillong. The setting up of Shillong as a station by the British had more than one consideration. Some important ones were: (i) setting up a military station; (ii) setting up a civil station; (iii) setting up a sanitarium for the British population; and (iv) providing a place for retired British personnel to settle. The last point needs a little explanation. A proposal was submitted to the Government of India in 1858 (the year after the mutiny) that the European soldiers, veterans, and pensioners living in various parts of the plains be transferred to hill stations instead of giving them the option to settle wherever they were. The proposal was more particular about the pensioners. Such a proposal provoked the government to think seriously in terms of identifying hill stations and hill tracts for the purpose. In the North-East Frontier region, various locations on the Khasi Hills merited consideration. At last the location known now as Shillong seemed to be the most suitable (Hussain in Sinha, 1993: 65–66).

The Company had no control over the land identified by them for setting up the station. It purchased some land from the private owners and for more land it persuaded the Chiefs of Mylliem and Khyriem to cede some in their favour. Steps towards setting up Shillong as a military station started in early 1864 with the process of transferring 44th (Sylhet) Light Infantry (together with an Eurasian Artillery) to Shillong after the termination of Anglo-Bhutan War. It was finally in 1866 that civil departments of the government were removed to Shillong which then became the new civil station. Rules were also framed for the allotment of lands acquired from various sources. A four-fold classification of the lands was done for the settlement of the population: (i) lands purchased by government and reserved for public purposes; (ii) lands purchased by government and available for private persons for building purposes; (iii) lands purchased by government and deemed unsuitable for building purposes but available to private persons for purposes other than buildings; and (iv) the lands which were the private properties.

It is, however, an intriguing fact as to why did the tribal chiefs allow the British colonisers to interfere with their customary practices and political institution. The local chiefs had no rights of ownership or suzerainty over the land on the hills, yet they allowed these lands to alienate and pass over under the control of colonisers. Following the chiefs, the other local inhabitants also sold parts of their lands to the non-tribal settlers.

Lands purchased for public purposes were used for setting up of various government offices, police station, the jail, and residences of the European officers. Lands coming under class (i) were sold by auction to public for building purposes, and this opportunity was used by the European officers (whether in service or retired) and also those engaged in business, industry or plantations. Lands were also acquired by Missionary Churches gradually in subsequent years. Lands under class (ii) were taken by some Europeans to grow fruit orchards. Owners of lands under class (iii) sold some of their lands over a period of time not to the Europeans but Indian traders and merchants as well.

So far, I have narrated the circumstances resulting in the creation of the city of Shillong and how the British brought people (plantation workers, traders, lower service staff) with different ethnic backgrounds to settle here. In the following paragraphs, I shall try to explain how various measures taken by the Britishers over a long period of time influenced the tribal population.

Shillong, established in 1867 as the district headquarters, became capital of the Chief Commissioner's Province of Assam in 1874. Consequently, the Chief Commissioner's secretariat was transferred from Gauhati to Shillong, resulting in migration of more people to this city. Not all the migrant-employees could be settled in British-Shillong as a large part of it was either used for building government establishments and market or set aside exclusively for the European population and made out of bounds for the 'native' population. Such 'native' population had to spread in the adjoining villages. The Company also took steps to include some such villages within the jurisdiction of Shillong for providing some civic amenities to its employees settled there.

This was the first major step taken by the British colonisers to put the plainsmen in proximity of the hills people on the uplands. As stated by Datta Ray (in Goswami, 1979: 50): 'The first settlement was that of the administrative personnel round which accrued, in course of time, a trading community and civic services which catered to the need of the core population. This core comprised people inducted from outside for ministerial services from Bengal and for what it is now known Grade IV service staff from Bihar and Nepal, etc. The top level comprised European Officers.' The Khasi had been interacting with the plains people on the borders of the hills with the plains of Sylhet from earlier times in the course of their trading activities. But this was not the case with the Khasis from the uplands.

After the establishment of Shillong, work on a cart road connecting Shillong with Guwahati did not take long to complete. *Tongas*, pulled by ponies, were used as a means of transport by the people. Shillong then became more accessible to people from other parts of India, resulting in the increase in non-tribal population.

Some of the British officers were keen to allow missionary activities in the hills though the government was initially reluctant in this matter. Missionaries were permitted to come in as school teachers to spread modern education among the tribals, but the colonial government did not object to their spreading Christianity among them. The tribals needed a script in which the Bible could be translated. After experimenting with the Bengali script, the Missionaries settled for the Roman script. Schools were opened to teach the script and to inculcate western morality and values. Conversion to Christianity did not take place at the level of the collectivity (household, clan, or the village as a whole) but at the individual level and in the same kin group one could find a member following the Christian faith and other members continuing with their indigenous Khasi faith.

The Missionaries did not appreciate the matrilineal system of the Khasis and considered it as a 'primitive' practice which went against the Christian concept of family dominated by the male. It, however, took them time to realise the futility of changing the matrilineal practices by the Khasis. Learning through experience, they not only ignored this practice but even adopted some of the Khasi symbols in their own preachings. Use of cock, held sacred, as a symbol by the Khasis is a case in point.

While the British government did not lend a direct and overt support to the activities of Church institution, it did give support to the Mission-aries in the name of the cause of modern secular education. More and more Khasi youths started getting education and the brighter among them were given financial support to go to Kolkata for higher education. These educated Khasis were given employment in the bureaucracy, after their return, and they settled down in Shillong. This endeavour of the Missionaries had an unintended consequence of creating political awareness among the Khasi towards their future and identity.

Before the advent of Christianity, the Khasis maintained a religious affinity with their Bengali Hindu neighbours. The newly-converted Christian Khasi broke this affinity which later on was replaced with suspicion and contempt as a result of their training in the values of their new religion. In spite of this affinity, the non-tribal neighbours found the Khasi marriage system peculiar and considered the females of loose morality. This misconception also increased the social distance between the Khasi and the non-tribal populations.

Brahmo Samaj made its presence in Shillong in 1870. Ramakrishna Mission opened a centre near Cherrapunji in 1921, and later it started a centre at Shillong (Chaube, 1973: 37). However, this Hindu Mission remained confined to the Bengali Hindu population in religious matters, though its educational and health care activities spread to the Khasi population as well.

The efforts of the Missionaries in spreading secular education along with their religious activities took time in showing its impact. Many Khasi youth (both women and men) from the villages gradually started showing their skills and abilities, and some of the meritorious among them were sent to Kolkata for further education after they qualified in the entrance examinations. On the other hand, Ramakrishna Mission also contributed to the cause of secular education in the Khasi Hills and many of its tribal alumni played a significant role in the politics of the hills.

Gradually, Shillong acquired the reputation of an educational centre and also became the centre of administrative control over the region, where the indigenous Khasi population had little role to play. The Khasis were left to live their life the way they had been living and govern their own affairs the way they preferred till the interests of the British were not hampered. The British had no idea of the political system of the matrilineal Khasi tribe, yet they did intervene in it as they had done in other parts of the British India. This intervention had far-reaching consequences for the political stability of the region, which was perhaps never imagined by the Britishers then. However, the British rulers were cautious not to interfere too much in the local affairs.

Removing the district headquarters from Cherrapunji to Shillong could have been a matter of bureaucratic expediency from the administrative point of view but, from a sociological perspective, setting up Shillong as a civil and a military station had its long-term consequences for Shillong as well as its surrounding Khasi villages. The civil station at Cherrapunji had employed a large Bengali population from Sylhet in the then East Bengal (which is the present-day Bangladesh). They were given land on periodic lease near the jail and the police lines. Similarly, land on periodic lease was granted to the traders and shopkeepers in the adjoining area which later on was known as the Police Bazaar. Besides these, some other Bengali government employees and traders procured land on lease from the Khasi Chief of Hima Mylliem and the individual owners in the adjoining Khasi village of Laban. The Bengali settlements were either at the fringe of the civil station or outside it in the adjoining villages. What is important to note is that these were outside and away from the European settlements. Further, it is worth noting here that shifting of the district headquarters from Cherrapunji to Shillong civil station brought, besides the Bengali employees and traders, many Khasi employees and traders as well from Cherrapunji to Shillong.

The tribal lifestyle and consumption pattern were different from those of the non-tribals and Europeans. Consequently, there was a need to set up new markets to supply commodities for daily consumption to those who had settled there from outside. Area was earmarked for the market place. Bengali and Marwari traders were allowed to occupy the stalls for business activities. Over a period of time, the British also brought carpenters for constructing buildings and scavengers for sanitation works from as far as Punjab. Slowly, people belonging to various castes, e.g., washerman and cobbler also migrated from Bihar to provide services to the settled population.

With the gradual rise in population, the concerns of sanitation and other civic amenities were addressed by setting up a Town Committee. Shillong was declared a Station in 1878 after the Bengal Municipal Act of 1876 was extended to Assam. The Station Committee replaced the existing Town Committee. While making Shillong a station in 1878, the British wanted to include the areas of Mawkhar and Laban, to which the Chief of Hima Mylliem resented. The British persuaded him by offering the commissionership of the Station Committee. These two villages were not included as the British portions, yet the sanitary services were extended there as a large number of non-tribal employees had settled in these villages. 'Jurisdiction of the Shillong municipality, founded in 1910, went beyond the 'British territory' by virtue of Government's 'foreign jurisdiction' (ibid.: 19).

The importance of the above facts lies in the fallout of otherwise a simple-looking exercise of shifting the civil and military station from Cherrapunji to Shillong for purely administrative and military expediency by the Company in pursuit of its economic interests. The Company as well as the British government at those times might not have realised the long-term effects of their decisions. Implications could be seen, besides the influence on the various institutions of the tribal society, in terms of changes in the demographic composition.

The largest population of migrants belonged to the Bengali community hailing mainly from the plains of Sylhet. They belonged to a distinctly different culture and were educationally and economically more advanced as compared to the tribals inhabiting the Khasi Hills. Though they were put in the vicinity of the local Khasi inhabitants, their spheres of interaction were restricted and different. They were outside the political and social control of the Khasi. Conflicts or disputes between the Khasi and the others (which could be termed as between tribals and non-tribals) were taken care of by the British police and courts outside the tribal system of justice. The non-tribals looked down upon the tribals as inferior because of cultural differences. On the other hand, the tribals looked upon the non-tribals with suspicion considering them as the representatives of the British. But both the non-tribals and the tribals were treated as 'natives' by the British and accorded an inferior status, which was evident from the fact that the European Ward in Shillong was out of bounds for members of both the communities. However, the British followed a policy of keeping the tribals and the non-tribals segregated, which was clearly reflected by various regulations of exclusion passed by them.

A government notification of 1929 declared '... the British portions of the Khasi Hills District other than the Shillong Municipality and

Cantonment, ... to be backward tracts.' (Syiemlieh, 1989: 176–177). Consequently, no law passed by the Indian legislature of Assam could apply to these areas without the express notification by the Governor of Assam-in-Council. The areas under the Shillong Municipality and the Cantonment, being urban in nature and inhabited by educationally more advanced sections of the society, were kept out of purview of this notification.

In the meantime, through the efforts of an educated Khasi pastor, belonging to the Church of God, the Khasi chiefs organised themselves into a political body under the name of Khasi National Durbar in 1923, which in the following two years codified some of the Khasi customary land-laws (ibid.: 62). Hectic political activities that followed in the first five years of the formation of this Durbar, in the wake of the visit of Simon Commission, show amply clearly the political maturity of the Khasi elders in dealing with the intricacies of modern politics. Heated debates, which ensued after the submission of a representation by the Secretary of the Khasi National Durbar to the Simon Commission, show the emergence of differences in opinion among the Khasi leaders. These were the symptoms, to my mind, of the emergence of a modern political identity in the Khasi society which was asserted later after the British left India.

The Indian Statutory Commission, 1930, also known as the Simon Commission, recommended that the term 'backward tracts' be replaced by the term 'excluded areas'. The members of the Commission were of the opinion that the inhabitants of these areas required modern education so that they could look after their own interests. The term 'backward tracts' was replaced in the Government of India Act, 1935 by the terms 'partially excluded areas' or 'excluded areas'. The Government of India (Excluded and Partially Excluded Areas) Order, 1936 defined the British portions of the Khasi Hills District, other than the Shillong Municipality and Cantonment as the Partially Excluded Areas.

By this time, a number of educated, politically aware, and confident tribals had come up in the Khasi society who could articulate the aspirations of their society effectively. They started a debate in the society over the customary rights of the chiefs and questioned on the one hand the right of the chiefs to sell land to the British, and on the other, the British practice of issuing *sanads* to the chiefs, thus making the chiefs subordinate.

I think it took almost three-quarters of a century after the British government took over from the East India Company for a 'unified' Khasi identity to emerge. I have deliberately used the expression 'unified' as the Khasi were divided into a number of chiefships and a number of villages under each chiefship. Practice of *jhum* cultivation made them very mobile and they could easily migrate from one *Hima* to another. Their perception of affinity or allegiance at the lowest level was the lineage or the village while at the highest level it was the *Hima*, represented by the chief. Allegiance at the levels of lineage or the village, I would like to argue, could be termed as their primary identities. The idea of pan-Khasi identity, which I would like to term as the secondary, could be seen in its infancy with the formation of the Khasi National Durbar in the second decade of the 20th century. Formation of the federation of the Khasi chiefs was perhaps the first concrete step in this direction.

As per the political design of the British colonisers, these areas were kept, along with the other hill areas of the North-East, insulated from the Indian Independence Movement. In the third decade of the last century, the tribals inhabiting the partially excluded areas were permitted to politically interact with the Assamese living in the plains of Assam. I think it was around this time that the process of evolving a Khasi identity, cutting across kinship and village identities, set into motion. If it was the idea of Indian nationalism which was playing a crucial role during this period in British India, then it was the idea of Khasi nationalism which was guiding the Khasi-British and Khasi-Indian (non-tribal) relationships. After the departure of the British from India, the Khasi intellectuals and the political leaders thought it imperative to assert their Khasi identity more forcefully. This was clearly evident in the debates in the Constituent Assembly as shown in the following paragraphs.

This process was hastened, it appears, after the Government of India Act, 1935 was implemented which gave a Provincial Legislature to Assam. A coalition government was installed in Assam after the elections of 1937. This government did not prove to be stable as manoeuvres started to dislodge it. The tensions generated in the process resulted in the Khasi-Bengali clashes, which were though soon contained (ibid.: 67). This could be seen as the first case of inter-ethnic clashes in Shillong.

After the independence of India, Shillong became the capital of the then composite state of Assam. By this time, the population of highly-qualified Khasis of both sexes had increased considerably. It included medical practitioners, engineers, bureaucrats, politicians, teachers, traders, etc. Since facilities for higher education were available at Kolkata, exposure to the world outside the hills created wider awareness among the Khasi youths who had gone there for studies. These educated Khasis started taking interest in the politics of the state to safeguard interests of their tribe.

Khasis were not the only tribal community in the then composite state of Assam. They initiated and participated in the efforts to put up a united tribal front against the non-tribal Assamese, who were demographically larger and politically stronger in the parliamentary form of government. The tribals always suspected the Assamese and feared about the future of their communities under the dominance of the former. They had the examples of the tribals in other parts of India who had come under the influence of their Hindu non-tribal neighbours and in the process lost their individuality.

The mutual mistrust and contempt between the Khasis and the Assamese becomes evident as one reads through the debate on the Sixth Schedule in the Constituent Assembly soon after the independence of India (Hansaria, 1983: A-65). The arguments advanced, in the Constituent Assembly, by the non-tribal members from Assam against the draft of the Sixth Schedule to the Constitution of independent India throw light on the nature of such a relationship between the hill tribes and the plainsmen from Assam – their immediate neighbours. If the British had thought that the hill tribes were different from the people in the rest of India, the plainsmen from Assam ('the Indians!') had also found them to be different. If the British had wanted to keep them separate and preserve their culture, these 'Indians', on the contrary, had wanted unbridled interaction with the tribals so that they could be 'assimilated' into the culture of the plains (i.e., Assam). Rohini Kumar Chaudhury declared during the debate: 'We want to assimilate the tribal people. We were not given that opportunity so far. The tribal people, however much they had liked, had not the opportunity of assimilation' (ibid.).

The fears, in the tribal minds, came true soon when Assam moved the Official Language Bill making Assamese as the state language in 1960. The fear was that introduction of Assamese language would lead to the assimilation of all tribal communities into the Assamese community and loss of their tribal identity. The violent events that followed in the wake of this Bill hardened the discord between the tribals and the Assamese in general and the Khasis, in particular. Shillong, as the capital, became the seen of action and the ripples created by it spread across the Khasi Hills, thus threatening the harmony between the Khasi and the non-tribals (not necessarily the Assamese) living in the villages far and wide. I think that the process of the Khasi identity formation showed its culmination when almost three decades later serious concerns were voiced about the threat to their identity as a result of the passage of the Official Language Bill.

Tribal leaders started hectic political manoeuverings at both the regional and national levels, which required the greater participation and support of the masses as well as hardening of the anti-Assamese in particular and anti non-tribal attitude in general. City of Shillong, though small, remained the centre-stage of action. But, over a period of time, the demand for a Hill State started getting weak as many tribal communities thought that this would be dominated by the more advanced Khasi community. A common cause against the non-tribal communities could not crystallise into all-tribal solidarity and they remained fragmented and suspicious of each other. At last, Meghalaya was carved out of Assam as a separate state consisting of the two districts: United Khasi and Jaintia Hills District and Garo Hills District.

The Sixth Schedule as applicable to the state of Meghalaya provides for, among other things, protection of the customary practices of the tribes of Meghalaya. The Schedule provides for the creation of autonomous districts and autonomous District Councils in each of such autonomous districts in the state. These Councils are elective bodies consisting of members drawn from the tribal communities. The District Councils are empowered to make laws with respect to, among other subjects, control of markets and trading by non-tribals, inheritance of property, marriage, divorce, and social customs. However, certain provisions of this Schedule do not apply to the areas under the Municipality of Shillong.

Two very important legislations need special mention here as they have a significant bearing on the inter-ethnic relationships in Shillong: (i) regulation passed by the District Council to control trading by the non-tribals; and (ii) the Meghalaya Transfer of Land Regulation Act, 1971 (MTLRA) of the Meghalaya Legislative Assembly, controlling the transfer of land from tribals to non-tribals.

The regulation concerning control of trading by the non-tribals intends to safeguard the trading activities of the Khasi population. There is always a pressure on the District Council to discourage the issue of such licences to the non-tribals. Volunteers of the Khasi Students Union (KSU), the only association of the Khasi students in the state, very often go around various markets checking the licences of the non-tribal traders. The brunt of their anger has to be borne by the roadside hawkers or pavement vendors who do not possess any licence to carry out their trade activities. Their goods are destroyed and they are harassed and roughed up.

Some of the well-off and more enterprising non-tribal businessmen have found a convenient way to escape the provision of licence by entering into business partnerships with the Khasi or other tribal people, including the women, and running the business in their names, as if on their behalf. The tribals in such business pacts more act as the sleeping partners as they neither have any experience in different types of trade nor any capital to invest or any knowledge of the bigger markets outside Shillong. These tribal partners, however, get their share of profits from the business. Of course, this does not mean that such non-tribal businessmen remain comfortable as compared to the petty businessmen, and do not face any hostilities from the tribals.

The other point is about the Land Transfer Act of the Meghalaya Assembly, according to which land cannot be ordinarily transferred from a tribal to a non-tribal or from a non-tribal to another non-tribal. It means that in the case of a land transfer, the first claim lies with a tribal. Land could be transferred to a non-tribal only in the event of non-availability of a tribal buyer. This raises two important issues: (i) inheritance of land by the children of a non-tribal land owner; and (ii) buying of land by organisations, e.g., business houses, charitable organisations and religious organisations, since these organisations are considered as non-juridical persons who are treated as the non-tribals. This Act created difficulties for the Christian Missions who found it difficult to expand their activities. In due course of time, a way was found by the Churches to wriggle out of this situation. If the land could not be bought in the name of the Church as an organisation, it could definitely be bought in the name of any one of the Khasi priests of a particular Church or denomination. Similarly, any Khasi priest belonging to a Church could receive land as a gift donated to it. Individual non-tribal land owners then resorted to the legal provision of the power of attorney in order to transfer their lands without attracting the restrictions imposed by this Act.

It has been stated above that ever since its creation, Shillong city has enjoyed the distinction of being either the district headquarters or a capital city. Not only the state secretariat, offices of the East Khasi Hills district and the Autonomous District Council of the Khasi Hills but regional offices of various Central government organisations and banks are also located here. Besides these, the city has the distinction of being an educational centre in the country, with many well-known schools, colleges, North-Eastern Hill University and the North-Eastern Indira Gandhi Regional Institute of Health and Medical Sciences located in the city.

Many of these organisations required highly qualified or specially trained personnel which the local tribal community could not provide. This means that these personnel had to be recruited from other communities living outside the state. The local population could take up only unskilled work. They were generally denied the opportunity of joining white-collar jobs on the grounds of inefficiency, without sensitivity to the fact that the work environment in a bureaucratic organisation was unknown to the tribal-cultivators. Such a bureaucratic attitude was resented by the tribals and very often resulted in conflicts with the tribal youth leaders. Of course, some of the non-tribal businessmen have been employing Khasi women as sales girls to work in their establishments after the creation of Meghalaya, as women were considered more dependable and less hostile.

The special provisions under the Constitution bestow control to the tribals over political decision-making by reserving seats in the State Legislature as well as in the autonomous District Councils. Through these legislative bodies, the tribals are in a position to maintain control over their economy and regulate competition from outsiders in the market. The electoral politics centres around the contest between the candidates of the Indian National Congress, an all-India party, and the smaller state-level parties, popularly known as the regional parties – though they do not have a regional character. Tension is witnessed over the inclusion (or exclusion) of the names of non-tribals in the voters' list. The eligibility to vote in the elections for the seats in the State Assembly or Parliament is the same as anywhere else in the country but eligibility to participate in the elections of the Autonomous District Council as a voter is different. A non-tribal is eligible to vote only after completing 12 years of residency period.

The non-tribal voters prefer generally the candidates from the national party, much to the chagrin of the candidates of the local parties. This proves disadvantageous for the local parties who fail to form a government. Due to differences among them, the local parties do not succeed to form stable governments. Till about a decade ago, much tension was generated between the tribal and non-tribal communities over the names in the voters' lists. Similarly, tension surfaces over the alleged indiscriminate issue of trading licences to the non-tribal traders. Since 1979 till the early part of the last decade of the last century, such tensions frequently assumed violent forms causing fear in the minds of the non-tribal populations.

Raising the concern about preserving their ethnic identity, the Khasis have always opposed an increase in the number of Central government offices as they feared it would increase the non-tribal population in the state. They have been opposing even the extension of the railway line to their state on the same grounds. Thus, the formation of 'Khasi' identity has shaped for over 25 years now. It could be further stated that the events of the last two decades of the 20th century show an assertion of this identity.

Frequency of cases of overt conflicts though have reduced drastically at the turn of the last century. Conflicts erupted mainly over economic issues, often for employment in the government bureaucracy and retail trading in the market. Control over urban land is another factor which remains latent in such confrontations. Religion *per se* has not played much significant or direct role in such confrontations. Moreover, most of the conflicts have taken place in Shillong, and not in the interior rural areas for the simple reason that the non-tribal population is concentrated in Shillong, and no such competition or threat is perceived in the villages.

The present paper thus makes a modest attempt to explain the emergence and consolidation of the Khasi identity. Discussing various events since the creation of the city of Shillong, it is argued that the relationship of conflict between the Khasis and the non-tribals could be interpreted in terms of the process of emergence of the primary and the secondary identities in the Khasi society. At the end, it could be stated that there is also emergence of another identity, at the tertiary level, which is the identity as a Scheduled Tribe as per the provisions of the Constitution of India. This is manifested in their seeking advantages (reservations in education, jobs, etc.) in the spheres of both higher education and employment in the public sector as per provisions of the Indian Constitution.

References

Brush, John E. (1992) 'The Morphology of Indian Cities'. In M.S.A. Rao (ed.). *Urban Sociology in India: Reader and Source Book*. New Delhi: Orient Longman.

Chaube, S.K. (1973) *Hill Politics in North-East India*. New Delhi: Orient Longman.

Datta Ray, B. (1979) 'Shillong as an Administrative Centre'. In B.B. Goswami (ed.). *Cultural Profile of Shillong*. Calcutta: Anthropological Survey of India

Hansaria, B.L. (1983) *Sixth Schedule to the Constitution of India: A Study*. Guwahati: Gita Hansaria.

Hussain, Imdad (1993) 'Shillong: British Enclave to Tribal City'. In A.C. Sinha et al. (ed.). *Hill Cities of Eastern Himalayas: Ethnicity, Land Relations and Urbanisation*. New Delhi: Indus Publishing Company.

Rao, M.S.A. (ed.) (1992) *Urban Sociology in India: Reader and Source Book*. New Delhi: Orient Longman.

Syiemlieh, D.R. (1989) *British Administration in Meghalaya: Policy and Pattern*. New Delhi: Heritage Publishers.

13

Morphological and Demographic Changes in Port Blair Town and their Impact

UMESH KUMAR AND D.N. PANDEY

Port Blair town came into existence in 1951 with a population of 7,789 and an area of 7.87 sq km when nine villages, viz., Chatham, Haddo, Phoenix Bay, Aberdeen Basti, Aberdeen Bazar, Buniyadabad, South Point, Junglighat and Shadipur were clubbed together to form a town. However, the genesis of Port Blair can be traced back to 1857–58 when the British decided to open the second penal settlement in the Andaman Islands (Majumdar, 1975). It is situated in the South Andaman Island. The topography of the region is characterised by low range of hills enclosing narrow valleys and narrow coastal stretches.

Over decades, Port Blair town has grown in terms of both population and area. The population of the town increased very rapidly from 7,789 in 1951 to 1,00,186 in 2001. The rapid growth of population in each Census year was mainly due to emigration from mainland to this place. The availability of economic opportunity acted as a pull factor for people in mainland India. Similarly, the urbanisation of the surrounding villages led to the inclusion of a few more villages in Port Blair municipal town in 1979 and 1995. The area of Port Blair town increased from 7.87 sq km in 1951 to 16 sq km in 1995. The emergence of Port Blair as a place of tourist attraction since the latter half of 1990s has accelerated the pace of urbanisation of the surrounding area. However, Port Blair suffers from resource paucity. Unlike many other towns and cities of India, there are not enough resources in hinterland of Port Blair to sustain the rapidly increasing population of the town. Most acute of them is water. Potable water available in the surrounding areas of the town can sustain the population only for six months. The zone of influence of the town from the viewpoint of tourism has spread far beyond the formal boundary of the town and includes in its sphere of influence the Jarawa Reserve, the abode of one of the two most primitive population groups of the world. Consequently, it is adversely affecting them also.

The present paper endeavours to study the growth of Port Blair town against this backdrop of resource scarcity, in addition to its impact on the primitive tribal group.

The Andaman Islands are a group of over 200 scenic archipelagic islands, isles and rock outcrops which lie in the Bay of Bengal in the Indian Ocean, with India to the west and Myanmar to the east. The islands stretch over 464 kms in the Bay of Bengal, running almost parallel to the eastern coastline of the Indian mainland at a distance of about 1,000 kms from it (Tamta, 1990). The Nicobar group of islands, which lies to the south, is separated by the Ten Degrees channel from the Andaman groups. Together with the Nicobar Islands, they form the Union Territory of 'Andaman and Nicobar Islands'. They were included as one of the seven Union Territories of India in 1956. They are governed by the Central Administration of the Indian government through the Lt. Governor, who is appointed as the head of administration.

Port Blair, the only town in the Andaman and Nicobar Islands, is situated along the east coast of South Andaman Island, lying at a distance of 1,225 km from Kolkata, 1,190 km from Chennai and 1,200 km from Vishakhapatnam. The climate of the town is humid tropical but the breeze blowing from the surrounding sea makes it pleasant. Though Port Blair was declared as an urban area in 1951, its history dates back to September 1789, when Lt. Archibald Blair occupied the Chatham Island, which at present forms part of Port Blair municipal area. The settlement on Chatham Island was closed down for bad climate condition and other reasons in August 1791, but was again occupied in March 1858. The harbour and its surrounding area was named after Lt. Blair to honour him. In the growth of Port Blair town, the historical context is as significant as the present situation.

Andaman Islands during the Pre-Colonial Period

The islands remained shrouded in mystery for centuries. However, the Andaman Islands had found place in the accounts of sailors, travellers and traders since long, much before the colonial control over these Islands. For example, the Island of Buzacat, as described by Claudius Ptolemy in the 2nd century A.D., was probably the Andaman Islands. While the Chinese mentioned about it in their accounts of the 7th century, the Arabs in the ninth century and the Europeans in the 13th century (Mathur, 1968: 7). The central theme in almost all these references was the cruel nature and the demonic appearance of the cannibal inhabitants of the Islands (Portman, 1899: 51).

In the pre-colonial period, the South, Middle and North Andaman Islands were occupied by the Great Andamanese people and the Jarawa, two of the four Negrito tribes of the islands. In fact, the Great Andamanese originally had ten subgroups, namely the Aka-Chari, Aka-Jeru, Aka-Bea-da, the Aka-Kora, Aka-Bo, Aka-Kede, Aka-Kol, Okka-Juwai, Aka-Puikwar and the Aka-Bele and they were distributed from south to north in the Andaman Islands. In pre-colonial period, the area known as Port Blair was occupied by different groups of foraging people at different times (Radcliffe-Brown, 1948: 25).

The Colonial Period (1789 to 1947)

Detailed records of the Islands came out once the colonial empire in India realised the significance of the inaccessible islands as a natural prison for the convicts, and initiated the British colonisation of the islands. Colonial period can be divided into two distinct phases, i.e., the first penal settlement and the second penal settlement. During the colonial period, a number of events took place that shaped the history of the Islands and brought a great variety of changes in the human population, cultural fabric and environment of the Andaman and Nicobar Islands.

The First Penal Settlement was established by the British in September 1789 in Andaman Islands. In fact, a detailed documented account of contact with Negrito populations of Andaman and Nicobar Islands is available only through the first penal settlement (Majumdar, 1975: 52). When the British set their foot on the Andaman Islands in 1789, the behaviour of the Andaman Islanders was baffling for them, during the brief phase of colonisation. While the tribesmen on the northern side of Port Cornwallis (Port Blair of present day) were very hostile, those inhabiting the southern side were quite friendly. To the Britishers, both the groups were the same while, in reality, they were confronting two different tribes, the hostile Aka-Bea, a group of the Great Andamanese in the north, and the friendly Jarawa in the south. Lt. Colebrook and Archibald Blair were the first to encounter the Jarawa and described them to be indifferent (Portman, 1889: 76). There was practically no major confrontation even with the different groups of the Great Andamanese. Nevertheless, it was the first major contact of the Negrito tribes with the alien people or non-Islanders. However, the British vacated the Islands in May 1796 on many counts, and tropical diseases, particularly malaria, were one of the most important among the reasons.

The Second Penal Settlement in Andaman Islands was established in March 1858 after the acceptance of 'the Report of a Committee' formed to give its suggestion, regarding reoccupying the Andaman and Nicobar Islands and establish penal settlement at the 'Old Harbour' (renamed Port Blair) by the British Government (Records, Government of India, 1859: 31–33). This time, the outsiders were not welcomed by the aboriginals. As punitive measures, several expeditions were sent to teach a lesson to the autochthones. The government communication admitted that the settlement officials preferred to ignore the path of conciliation and selected to play the role of assailants (Portman, 1899: 271–73). The cruel and vindictive policy of the British officials posted in the area generated among the aborigines a definite spirit of hostility against the Britishers and a grim determination to drive them out from their habitat. It found expression in a series of attacks by them in quick succession during the months of April and May 1859. Important among them was the conflict of 17 May 1859, also known as the 'Battle of Aberdeen'. But the bow and arrows were no answer to the fire arms of the British. In this skirmish, many Great Andamanese were killed (Majumdar, 1975: 82–83). It was a revelation to the whole spectrum of contacts of the aborigines with the British, and the latter's relation with and attitude towards the aborigines. This argument is further strengthened by one of the attacks in which the Great Andamanese vented their wrath on the gangmen but were quite friendly with convicts who had iron rings round the ankles as distinctive marks. According to Portman (1899: 279), the Great Andamanese told him that they objected to the clearing of the forests. Portman (1899: 288) observed that far from being a ludicrous skirmish, these attacks were the desperate and determined attempts by the aborigines to drive the outsiders away from their area.

Table 1

Decadal population of Negrito Groups in Andaman Islands (up to 1951)

Sl. No.	Tribe	Estimated population					
		1858	1901	1911	1921	1931	1951
1.	Aka-Chari	100	39	36	17	9	
2.	Aka-Kora	500	96	71	48	24	
3.	Aka-Jeru	200	48	62	18	6	23*
4.	Aka-Bo	700	218	180	101	46	
5.	Aka-Kede	500	59	34	6	2	
6.	Okka-Juwai	300	48	9	5	—	
7.	Aka-Kol	100	11	2	—	—	
8.	Aka-Puikwar	300	50	36	9	1	
9.	Aka-Bea-da	500	37	10	1	—	
10.	Aka-Bele	300	19	15	4	2	
11.	Onges	700	672	631	346	250	150
12.	Jarawa	600	585	231	231	120	50

*It is the combined population of Great Andamanese groups from S. No. 1 to 10.

Source: MMathM (Mathur, 1968: 128–29).

Table 2

Decadal population of Negrito Groups in Andaman Islands (after 1960)

Tribe	Population					
	1961	1971	1981	1991	2001	2002
Great Andamanese	19	24	27	45	43	43
Onges	129	112	93	95	96	97
Jarawa*	500	275	200	280	240	265
Sentinelese**	50	82	100	100	39	39

*Population of the Jarawa is estimated till 2001. First time in 2002, a head count of the Jarawa population was done.

**Population of the Sentinelese is estimated.

Sources Census of India, 1961; 81; 91; 2001; AAJVS, 2002 and Directorate of Economics and Statistics, 2007.

By the end of 1860s, almost all the subgroups of the Great Andamanese had been slowly and gradually tamed following the policy of carrot and stick. The Aka-Bea-da was the first to be completely befriended, followed by other groups of the Great Andamanese.

By 1947, most of the tribal groups of the Great Andamanese had vanished except the three. Of the ten groups of Great Andamanese, only three were surviving and had a total population of 19 only in 1961 (Table 1 and Table 2). They were namely the Aka-Chari, Aka-Jeru and the Aka-Bea-da. Having been reduced in a number and without any territory of their own, they were living in a miserable condition in and around Port Blair. Finally, they were settled at Strait Island in 1970 (Sarkar, 1994: 7).

In the post-independence period, they were living in dilapidated conditions in and around Port Blair. Finally, the Andaman and Nicobar Administration settled them at Strait Island in 1974 (Chakraborty, 1990). Presently, their population is 41 (AAJVS, 2007). Now they are no longer full-time hunter-gatherers. Presently, a few of them are working in different departments of Andaman and Nicobar Administration also.

Like the Great Andamanese, the Onge also resented any intrusion in their territory which lasted for several years. In 1886, M.V. Portman succeeded in establishing friendly contacts with the Onges. Within a span of 20 years since their friendly contact with outsiders in 1886, the Onges had completely been befriended (Sarkar, 1994: 171). In the post-independence period, Little Andaman was opened for the rehabilitation of the refugees in 1967 (Pandit and Chattopadhyay, 1993: 171). It dealt a major blow to the Onges as it not only reduced the size of their territory but also curtailed their resource base. To compensate the loss of space (niche) and resources, they were settled in 1974 at two places in the

Little Andaman, namely, South Bay and Dugong Creek. Today, they are no longer solely dependent on hunting, fishing and gathering. Like the Great Andamanese group, the Onge population has also declined from 700 in 1858 to 150 in 1951 and 97 in 2002 (Table 2). In 2005, the total population of the Onges was only 97 (Kumar and Haider, 2007: 128).

The Negrito hunter-gatherers of the North Sentinel Island are known as the Sentinelese. They have been described as the world's most isolated population and hence the least known. The British in the absence of any urgent need for land and forest resources of this small island (area 50 sq km) off the west coast of the South Andaman did not make any effort to befriend them. In the post-independence period from 1967 onwards, occasional expeditions were sent to the North Sentinel Island, but the Sentinelese did not like it. Presently, the Andaman and Nicobar Administration is following the policy of non-interference with respect to the Sentinelese.

While all ten groups of the Great Andamanese and the Onge tribe had come under the influence of the British colonisers within the few years of the establishment of the Second Penal Settlement at Port Blair in 1858, the Jarawa, however, did not accept the friendly overture of the British. The Jarawa suffered violence because of the punitive expeditions sent by the British against them. The Jarawa continued with their defensive posture until the latter half of 1997, and then they became friendly with the non-Jarawa visitors.

Genesis of Community in Port Blair: Colonial Period

A little before Second World War, the settler population of the penal settlement consisted of the convicts, their guards, the government officials and their families, and the special community called 'local born' (Das, 1937: 73). The convicts came to the Andamans from different parts of India and some adjacent countries. According to one official version, the persons who were transported to Port Blair were 'either murderers' who for some reasons had escaped the death penalty, perpetrators of the more heinous offences against the persons and property'. There were both men and women among them. The convicts were always encouraged to settle down in the settlement after a certain period of imprisonment or after their terms of sentence were over. It is the descendents of such settled convicts who came to be known as the 'local born'.

During 1920s, the Moplah or Mopillah convicts, who were imprisoned in the jails of Madras, were shifted to the Andamans. They were, from the very beginning, given the status of self-supporters or were allowed as plantation workers. They were allowed to have their families with them and were resettled in villages adjacent to the Port Blair town. Later, another group of convicts, 'Bhantu', whom the British authority considered a criminal tribe, were transported to the settlements. These people were also settled as the 'self-supporters in the villages near Port Blair' (Mathur, 1968: 148). Around 1925, some Karen people were brought to Andaman Islands from Myanmar as free settlers and settled in the Middle and North Andaman Islands. The government also brought in some people from Chotanagpur plateau and adjacent areas to meet the demand of labour work in different government departments like forest and police.

Last census during the colonial period was conducted in 1931, when population of the Andamans was 19,223. Out of them, 18,845 persons (98.03%) were Indians. The non-Indians were from different countries like Ceylone, China, Nepal, Hong Kong and Japan. Among the Indians, 4,704 persons (24.47%) were born in the Andaman and Nicobar Islands. Others (69.93%) had migrated to the Andamans from different provinces or states of India, giving the settlement a cosmopolitan character (Mukhopadhyay, 2002: 5–26).

There were two kinds of settlers, the free and the convicts. The convicts could also earn the status of free settlers if they decided to settle down in the islands after the completion of the term of their sentences. Actually most of the free settlers were descendents of the convicts. As a part of the scheme of reforming the convicts, they were allowed to lead the households' life after the completion of a certain part of their sentences. In the later phase, the descendants of both kinds of settlers were known as 'local born'. In post-independence phase, the local born community was called pre-1942 population. The caste consciousness among the local born community is almost non-existent. The 'local born' community is still divided into Hindu, Muslim, and Christians. Earlier there were quite a few Buddhists among them.

Port Blair Town

Independence on 15 August 1947 was not only a boon to mainland India but also to the islands of Andaman. Till 1950, there was no urban area in this territory. Port Blair town came into being for the first time in 1951 with the urban population of 7,789 and an area of 7.87 sq km, when nine villages, viz., Chatham, Haddo, Phoenix Bay, Aberdeen Basti, Aberdeen Bazar, Buniyadabad, South Point, Junglighat and Shadipur were clubbed together to form a town (Kumar, 2002: 57–69).

The topography of the region is characterised by a low hill range enclosing narrow valleys and narrow coastal stretches. The hills go down the water edges which indicate that the hills form part of the submerged mountain range. Ridges and valleys cover most of the area of town except that of Mohanpura, Junglighat, Lambaline and some of the areas of Austinabad and Dollygunj, where some flat land is available. Because of the undulating nature of the terrain, drainage is not a problem in the town. However, in some of the areas reclaimed from the sea like Mohanpura, waterlogging is a problem during high tide and rainy season.

Figure 1
Port Blair Town

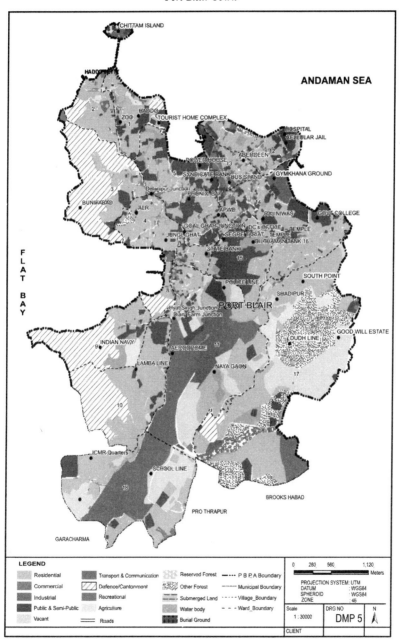

All the more, the environment of the region is almost free from pollution primarily due to diurnal change in wind direction and green umbrella of vegetation (see Figure 1).

Peopling of Port Blair: The Post-Independence Phase

On the eve of Japanese occupation of the Andaman and Nicobar Islands in 1942, a lot of people, mostly the government officials and free settlers, moved out of the Andamans. There were phases of emigration immediately after India became independent. This time s section of people who were settled in the Andamans by the penal settlement authorities also decided to move out of the islands. While the population of the Andamans was 19,223 in 1931, it grew to 21,316 in 1941, then dropped to 18,962 in 1951, even lower than that of 1931 (Census, 1951).

In the post-independence period, the Government of India accepted a proposal of further colonisation of the Andaman Islands on economic considerations. It was decided that the displaced families from East Pakistan would be settled in the islands with the view of attaining self-sufficiency in the matter of food. Those families were settled in the rural areas. Between 1949 and 1959, altogether 68 villages of refugees consisting of 2,328 families having a total population of 10,018 persons were established in the South and Middle Andaman Islands (Table 3). It was an open case of invasion of the Jarawa territory. During a span of seven years from 1949 to 1955, altogether 931 families were rehabilitated in various villages of South Andaman like Homfregunj, Herbertabad, Guptapara, Wimberlygunj and Shoal Bay.

Table 3

Year-wise achievement of the rehabilitation programme in South Andaman

Years	Number of villages established	Number of families rehabilitated	Population settled (in persons)	Area allotted for paddy cultivation (in acres)
1949	6	202	830	1,530
1950	10	265	1,165	1,765
1951	4	114	554	625
1952	8	123	595	789
1953	NA	NA	NA	NA
1954	3	97	400	575
1955	5	130	620	735
Total	36	931	4,164	6,019

NA= Data not available.

Source: Chakraborty and Dinda, 2002: 46.

The unfortunate part of the rehabilitation plan was that the refugees were settled near sources of fresh water, which effectively barred access of the Jarawa to this vital resource. The intrusion in their habitat and resultant loss of territory and life-sustaining resources because of establishment of refugee settlements must have made the Jarawa more and more hostile towards the non-Jarawa. Therefore, the Jarawa resisted rehabilitation, as there were 76 encounters with them between 1946 and 1961 in which 15 settlers and a number of Jarawa were killed (Census of India, 1961).

During the same period, many people migrated to Port Blair in search of jobs. Table 4 gives some information about the pattern of immigration to Port Blair town.

Table 4

Pattern of migration to Port Blair in 1961

State/Union Territories	Persons per 1,000 urban population
Andhra Pradesh	124
Assam	2
Bihar	22
Gujarat	2
Jammu and Kashmir	1
Kerala	102
Madhya Pradesh	3
Madras	143
Maharashtra	3
Mysore	4
Odisha	5
Punjab	10
Rajasthan	N
Uttar Pradesh	37
West Bengal	22
Delhi	3
Total	483

Source: Mukhopadhyay, 2002: 27–46.

In 1961, nearly a half of the population of Port Blair were migrants (485 migrants per 1,000 persons). It may be noted from Table 4 that a majority of the immigrants were from three states, Andhra Pradesh, Kerala and Madras. Within a span of two decades, the population of Port Blair town grew to 49,634. Out of this number, 27,503 persons were born outside the Andaman and Nicobar Islands, constituting 55.41 per cent of the population.

Of this population, about 1,360 persons (4.94%) were non-Indians, while the rest of 95.06 per cent were from different Indian states and union territories. Table 5 depicts the regional dimension of immigration from mainland India to the town of Port Blair.

Table 5

Migrant population in Port Blair Town (1981)

States/Union Territories	Migrant population
Andhra Pradesh	6,599 (25.24%)
Assam & Other North-East States	135 (0.52%)
Bihar	2,018 (7.72%)
Gujarat	90 (0.34%)
Haryana	122 (0.47%)
Himachal Pradesh	37 (0.14%)
Jammu and Kashmir	17 (0.06%)
Karnataka	226 (0.86%)
Kerala	3,878 (14.83%)
Madhya Pradesh	469 (1.79%)
Maharashtra	268 (1.79%)
Odisha	130 (0.50%)
Punjab	309 (1.18%)
Rajasthan	94 (0.36%)
Tamil Nadu	8,338 (31.89%)
Utter Pradesh	1,500 (5.73%)
West Bengal	1,690 (6.46%)
All Other Union Territories	226 (0.86%)
Total	26,146

Source: Census 1981.

Table 5 shows that there has been a preponderance of people from Tamil Nadu among the immigrants' population, followed by the persons from Andhra Pradesh and then Kerala. In fact the numerical dominance of people from three states was reported in 1961 Census as well. In 1981, the combined share of people from these three states was 72.96 per cent of the total immigrant population. The immigrants from Bihar (7.72%), West Bengal (6.46%) and Uttar Pradesh (5.73%) were other sizeable groups among the immigrants.

It must be noted that linguistic division of the population of Port Blair town does not reflect the linguistic situation prevailing in the entire Andaman and Nicobar Islands in the same year (1981). The most spoken language in households was Bengali (24.68%), followed by Hindi (18.14%), Tamil (14.81%), Nicobarese (11.98%), Malayalam (10.43%) and Telugu (9.86%) (Table 6).

Table 6

Number of persons with languages spoken

Language Spoken	Andaman & Nicobar Islands	Andaman Islands	Nicobar Islands	Andaman & Nicobar Islands
	1981	1991	1991	1991
Assamese	18	34	3	37
Bengali	44,147	64,108	598	64,706
Gujarati	110	1,930	0	1,930
Hindi	32,446	44,900	4,569	49,469
Kananada	234	292	31	323
Kashmiri	5	8	0	8
Malayalam	18,662	24,922	1,153	26,075
Marathi	332	337	202	539
Oriya	91	706	135	841
Punjabi	1,775	1,159	593	1,752
Sindhi	14	24	0	24
Tamil	26,485	49,543	3,993	53,536
Telugu	17,632	31,436	1,543	32,979
Urdu	1,797	1,439	53	1,492
Coori/Kadagti	19	10	0	10
Dogri	6	20	4	24
English	91	70	2	72
Nepali	254	324	19	343
Kheria	1,971	2,363	2	2,365
Konkani	24	62	2	64
Kurankh Oraon	5,761	8,595	658	9,253
Munda	1,866	2,678	267	2,945
Mundari	476	213	15	228
Nicobari	21,424	1,680	24,526	26,206
Santhal	6	339	57	396
Tulu	2	8	0	8
Gondi (Muria)	5	4	3	7
Lusai/Mizo	6	0	1	1
Other languages	3,226	NA	NA	NA
Total	1,78,885	2,37,204	38,429	2,75,633

Source: Basic Statistics, 1996.

The major ethnic groups found in Port Blair are the locals, the Moplahs, the Tamil, the Telugu, the Malayalis, the Bengalis, the Ranchis (people from Chhotanagpur region) and Valmikis. Depending on the time of immigration, the communities are divided in three groups; 'pre-42', the settlers and the later migrants. The first two terms have been accepted as official categories also. The 'pre-42' category consists of those people who came to the Islands before 1942 and the locals (local born); the Bhantus and the Moplahs belong to this category. Interestingly, the Karen and a section of the Ranchi people were not included in it though they had come before 1942. The second category, i.e., settlers, include the refugee population from East Pakistan who were brought by the government in post-independence period and settled at different places in the islands away from Port Blair. The third category, i.e., later migrants consists of people who immigrated to these islands on their own in search of livelihood.

Spatial Growth of Port Blair

The high growth rate of population in each census year was not a natural increase but mainly due to migration of people from mainland India to this place (Table 7). Besides, the sudden jump in population in 1981 was a function of both a huge number of immigrants from mainland and merger of seven new villages, viz., Lambaline, Nayagaon, Dudhline, Corbyn's Cove, Goodwill Estate, Minnie Bay and School Line (Figure 1). As a result of the merger of these villages, the area of Port Blair town also increased from 7.87 sq km in 1951 to 14.14 sq km in 1981. Similarly, in 2001 again, the above-mentioned two factors, i.e., immigration and extension of the municipal corporation limit of the town, accounted for phenomenal increase in the population. The area of Port Blair town was again extended in 1995 from 14.14 sq km to 16 sq km by incorporating two more villages, viz., Dollygunj and Austinabad. The most densely-populated areas of the town are Dairy Farm, Haddo, Delanipur, Phoenix Bay, Abardeen Bazar, Aberdeen Basti, and Junglighat.

Table 7
Decadal growth of population in Port Blair town

Year	1951	1961	1971	1981	1991	2001	2011
Population	7,789	14,075	26,281	44,634	74,955	1,00,186	1,31,000*

* Approximate population.

The sex ratio in the town in 1951 was very low, i.e., 315 females per 1,000 males, which later increased to 720 in 1981, 768 in 1991 and 806 in 2001.

The decadal census figures (Table 8) show how the economy of the town and occupations pursued by its inhabitants changed over a period of

50 years, i.e., from 1951 to 2001. Table 8 shows the rate of growth of Port Blair population and the corresponding change in the strength of working force in the population. The table shows that, male workers dominated the working force throughout the period. The presence of females in it was always very small. The table also shows the percentage of earners in the total population going down steadily, meaning a rise of dependent population in the town.

Table 8
Decadal variation in working population

Working Population	1951	1961	1971	1981	1991	2001
Population	8,014 (100%)	14,075 (100%)	26,218 (100%)	49,634 (100%)	74,955 (100%)	1,00,186 (100%)
Male Workers	3,766 (46.99%)	5,920 (42.06%)	11,156 (42.55%)	16,367 (32.98%)	22,677 (30.25%)	30,183 (30.13%)
Female Workers	272 (3.40%)	260 (1.85%)	589 (2.25%)	1,431 (2.88%)	3,013 (4.02%)	5,202 (5.19%)
Total Workers	4,038 (50.39%)	6,180 (43.91%)	11,745 (44.80%)	17,798 (35.86%)	25,690 (34.27%)	35,385 (35.32%)

Source: Census of India, from 1951 to 2001.

Table 9 depicts the division of working population into different occupational groups and presents the pattern of change in each of the occupational group across time. The above table shows that only a few people practised agriculture in 1950s. Though fishing and hunting have been clubbed together, Port Blair did not have a population of hunters. Secondly, the absolute number of people in this category has gone up, though the proportion of such people in working population has decreased. The occupations that have recorded real growth are construction, trade and commerce, transport, storage and communication. Another group of workers bracketed together under the category of 'other services,' which include the employees of different government offices, have always remained a considerably large part of the working population of the town.

Thus, the major occupational groups found in Port Blair are salaried jobs, trade, fishing, servicing and manufacturing. However, the overall impression that emerges from the trend is that Port Blair is primarily an administrative centre, followed by trade, commerce and related sectors like transport and construction.

The study by Mukhopadhyay (2002: 43) on the economic profile of Port Blair town discusses the community affiliation of traders at

Table 9

Decadal variation in occupation

Occupations	1951	1961	1971	1981	1991
Cultivation	196 (4.86%)	57 (0.92%)	69 (0.59%)	42 (0.24%)	70 (0.27%)
Agricultural labourer	4 (0.1%)	—	42 (0.36%)	34 (0.19%)	82 (0.32%)
Hunting, fishing, forestry, plantation, livestock, etc.	724 (17.93%)	1,216 (19.68%)	622 (5.30)	1,002 (5.53%)	1,758 (6.84%)
Manufacturing and servicing (household industries)	100 (2.47%)	79 (1.28%)	120 (1.02%)	118 (0.66%)	117 (0.45%)
Manufacturing and servicing (other than household industries)	589 (14.59%)	732 (11.84%)	1,880 (10.11%)	1,931 (10.85%)	1,533 (5.97%)
Construction	163 (4.04%)	1,407 (22.77%)	2,200 (18.73%)	2,895 (16.27%)	3,819 (14.87%)
Trade and commerce	448 (11.09%)	505 (8.17%)	1,440 (12.26%)	2,426 (13.63%)	4,140 (16.12%)
Transport, storage and communication	250 (6.19%)	254 (4.11%)	1,582 (13.47%)	2,148 (12.07%)	2,949 (11.48%)
In other services	1,564 (38.73%)	1,930 (31.23%)	4,482 (38.16%)	7,202 (40.46%)	11,222 (43.68%)
Total workers	4,038 (100%)	6,180 (100%)	11,745 (100%)	17,798 (100%)	25,690 (100%)

Source: Census of India, from 1951 to 1991.

Junglighat market area. It shows that there is a preponderance of Tamil traders followed by the Telugu, the Bengali and the Malayali. It also tells that the economy of Port Blair town is basically oriented to trading market and not manufacturing activities.

Urbanisation on Nearby Villages

Port Blair is directly influencing the daily life of the villages in its neighbourhood. The sign of urbanisation can be observed in all the villages at the periphery of the town. It is however, more pronounced in those villages which are near to or along the Andaman Trunk Road. Some of the villages are Partherapur (part), Birchgunj (part), Garacharma, Beadanabad, Mithakhari, Dundas Point, Wimberlygunj, Stewartgunj, Kanayapuram and School Line (part). Most of the offices and commercial establishments are located in Port Blair town only. These establishments provide a good scope for employment and marketing. Thus, one can very well observe that the persons from the above stated villages more or less come daily to attend their duties in various offices at Port Blair town and for marketing. The buses and boats coming from these areas to Port Blair may be seen as fully loaded with office-goers and vegetables. Milk and vegetables, which are produced in Bambooflat, Dundas Point, Ferrargung, Kanyapuram, Stewartgunj, Mithakhari, etc., are brought by both ferry services and road transport. The economic development of these villages has resulted in their semi-urban character.

Characteristics of Fringe Area

The term 'urban fringe' describes the built-up area just outside the corporate limit of a city. Smith's term was mainly concerned with the demographic characteristics of the area. Andrews (1942) and Carter (1972) have contributed some new thoughts on the fringe studies by attempting to differentiate the urban fringe from the rural fringe. The urban fringe, as described by them, is the active expanding sector of the compact economic city, while the rural-urban fringe lies adjacent to the periphery of the urban fringe. Thus, rural-urban fringe is an area with distinctive characteristics which is only partly assimilated into the growing urban complex and is still partly rural. Based on the above definition, the distinctive characteristics of rural-urban fringe of Port Blair town can be divided as (1) physical, (2) functional or organisational, and (3) cultural and normative. The physical aspects signify spatial characteristics that include small and fragmented farms, high-priced green belts, haphazardly distributed houses, many of which are in different stages of construction and finally, friction amongst various spatial uses. Study of the land use patterns of Garacharma, Bambooflat and areas on the north of Shippighat reveal that sub-divisions of the farms and fields are the most common features in these areas. Buyers with their speculative choice of site and building plan construct and finish at least with fencing or trace pillars. These sporadic, unplanned and uncontrolled constructions are a rule rather than an exception. Away from the main road (Andaman Trunk Road – ATR), this has often led to the creation of narrow and one-way lanes, sometimes ending in cul-de-sac. All those public institutions which require sufficient cheap spaces are located at the distal margin along major routes like Centre for Agricultural Research Institute, Centre for Soil Conservation, etc. Though there are institutions that are within the town like Regional Medical Research Institute, Institute of Polytechnique, godowns of Food Corporation of India, etc., when they were set up, they were outside the boundary of the town. Expansion of the town in the years 1974 and 1995 brought them within the corporate limits of the town. These public institutions are usually the chief channels of urban expansions. In big cities, the slum of commerce is also one of the attributes found in rural-urban fringe but in case of Port Blair town, it is absent till now, primarily because it is still a small town and has only very few manufacturing industries. Besides, growing intensities of the arteries of communication and the increasing transformational facilities are also important spatial aspects of the fringe of the Port Blair town. The 'kutcha' roads are being replaced by metalled roads. Besides, how a small change in the direction of main road can bring about a concomitant change in land use pattern is best explained by the short-distance directional change in the ATR. Earlier, the ATR passed through Austinabad village. But due to extension of runway, the road was straightened. Now, it has bypassed Austinabad village and directly connects Garacharma. Consequently, in Austinabad village, the conversion of agricultural land to non-agricultural uses slowed down while it has conspicuously picked up in Dollygunj area owing to its proximity to the ATR. The traffic and street density of the fringe is of an intermediate nature, i.e., more than that of the rural area and less than that of the urban area. Away from Shippighat, Buniyadabad, Brichgunj and Bambooflat, one notices that where the fringe is invading the countryside, it is marked by a basic change in the road pattern, i.e., road density has suddenly become less.

Functionally, fringe is almost synonymous with rapid change and transformation. Its most noticeable peculiarities lie in its ever-changing land use. The study of the villages of Garacharma, Bambooflat, and Bhatu Basti, which fall in the rural-urban fringe of Port Blair town, reveals that the various land uses, old houses, newer residential extensions, commerce, underlying farms, etc., are nearly sorted out into homogeneous areas but are intermingled in a random fashion, and it gives distinctive character to the land use pattern of the rural-urban fringe (Kumar, 2002: 57–69). In these villages, all agricultural and horticultural lands have been converted into non-agricultural lands. Generally, when one draws a functional cross-section of a fringe along the green belt to a nodal point, it begins with the cultivation of mostly marketable products grown with the meticulous care of the intensive cultivators and ends with relatively higher population density and functional facility. In case of the fringe area of Port Blair town, it begins from Shippighat in the south-east where green belts are prominent and ends at Garacharma, which has a relatively higher population. Similarly, in the north, it begins from Mannarghat and ends at

Figure 2

Port Blair and adjacent areas

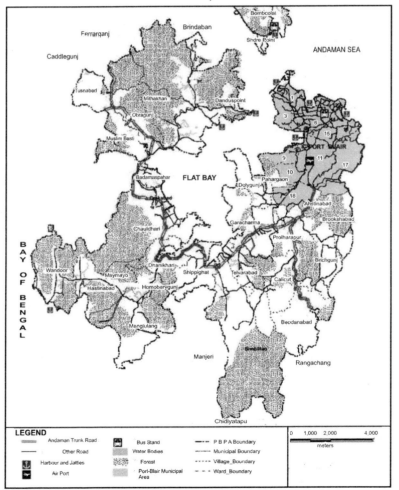

Bambooflat. But, there is no cultivation of marketable products most probably because of topographical constraints. So is the case with Bambooflat also. The intermediate section is found replete with a mix-up of well built as well as half-built houses; shops (commercial establishments) intermingled with greenery and farms (see Figure 2).

The above-mentioned physical and functional aspects combined together result in comparatively higher land value of the fringe. It may be taken as a common but temporarily dynamic denominator of the thickening of economic activities, which shadows with the process of urbanisation. The economic functioning is imprinted on the pattern of land use and land values are mutually determining. If the patterns of the marginal areas were truly assessed, it will to a great extent conform to the mosaic of the process of urbanisation taking place in the fringe zone. The sole function of the fringe is to provide constructional space whose value is summed up in the sole factor of proximity to Port Blair town.

The physical and functional aspects, as detailed above, contribute to the cultural composition of the fringe dwellers. The exiting population density is low and varies between 8–19 persons per sq km, with a tendency towards concentration along the ATR. Urbanisation of the fringe area appears to be a process of population concentration, which gains momentum with the growing provision of public services/facilities, which are still incomplete. Most of the fringe dwellers usually travel daily back and forth between the place of employment and their residences. Their inclination and drift to the town is oriented by their status, nature, kith and kin already serving in the town, nature of employment already available and their related association. Unlike other cities and towns, there is very little migration from fringe to Port Blair town for the distance travelled is very less and never exceeds more than 10 km. However, the changing social and behavioural pattern of the fringe dwellers is one of its remarkable aspects. The growing enrichment of their behaviour over time and with a cross-section of associations, changing taste and temperament regarding food, clothing and shelter, polished and tactful talk, dextrously developed mental faculty, etc., are some of the aspects of their personality which are thickening and bringing them closer to urbanity.

Thus, it is clear from the above observations that the fringe is a significant development of Port Blair town. The incoherent land use pattern, which is occurring due to outward growth process of the town, may be taken as a representative of the fringe. In other words, it is this space into which the town is extending due to the process of dispersion and creating the rural-urban fringe. Considering all these characteristics, this haphazardly developed zone of twilight may be viewed as a zone of constantly changing pattern of land occupancy, small farm size, mobile population of low density, incomplete provision of public utilities and services, speculative sub-division and building plots – all resulting in a continual movement or dynamism.

Area of Further Extension of Town

Based upon the land use map and personal investigations into the field, the possibility of further growth of the town towards different directions outside the present municipal limit has been assumed, which would be a tentative limit of the urban fringe. There is no possibility of the physical extension of the town in the adjoining north, east, and west directions because of the natural barrier, i.e., the sea. Similarly, the town is bounded by sea on the north also, which restrains the extension of built-up area in the Bambooflat area. Thus, we find that the sea acts as a strong natural barrier for the physical expansion of the town in this direction. On the other hand, the town is growing very fast towards south and south-east mostly along the ATR. The present trend suggests that most of the future development will take place in this direction. A number of commercial establishments are developing fast in a ribbon-type manner along the Andaman Trunk Road and the link roads due to the availability of better infrastructure in the form of linkage, accessibility, suitability of land, etc.

The existing land use pattern of three villages, namely Garacharma, Bhatu Basti and Bambooflat, shows that the lands under categories of forest and agricultural uses have significantly decreased while the lands in the categories of non-agricultural land and wastelands have increased (Kumar, 2002: 57–69).

Under the impacts of these factors, the area having strong interaction with the town is slightly linear. Hence, the southern boundary of the rural-urban fringe extends up to 10 km, i.e., up to Shippighat from the centre of the town while the northern boundary extends up to Bambooflat. But beyond Bambooflat, the attributes of the fringe suddenly decline. It is because of the existence of the natural barrier, i.e., the sea.

Non-agricultural Workers in Fringe Villages

One of the important attributes on which the impact of the town may be markedly discernible is the occupational structure of the villages. The settlements in the vicinity of the town/city, particularly those which are close to ATR, seem to be changing their character more conspicuously than those situated away from it. These villages are Bhatu Basti, Garacharma, Bambooflat and Shippighat, followed by Brichgunj (part), Calicut, and Teylerabad, etc. In fact, a high percentage of non-agricultural workers (80% approx) in the working force of the rural areas of the first three villages is an approximate measure of the urban zone of influence.

This particular group is composed of the persons engaged in construction, trade and commerce, transport and other services. These people live in the fringe areas that are classified as rural, yet they are engaged in non-agricultural activities.

Change in Density in Fringe Villages

The change in density during 1981–91 and in some cases during 1991–2001 has been taken to be the other indice of measurement of influence of the town. In 1991, the density of Port Blair town was 5,300 persons per sq km which increased to 6,262 persons per sq km in 2001. During the corresponding year, the density of the Garacharma increased from 9 persons per sq km to 16 persons per sq km and of Bambooflat from 13 persons per sq km to 22 persons per sq km Though this criterion provides a haphazard picture, the rate of change is more in the area situated comparatively nearer to the ATR in the south. In the west also, the settlements that are close to the main road are undergoing faster changes than those away from it. There is a greater tendency of increase in density towards the south of the town.

Population Growth in Fringe Area

Like the density, population is also an important determinant for delimiting the urban fringe. The growth of 50 per cent or more of the population during the years 1991–2001 has resulted in delineating the fringe boundary of Port Blair town. In many villages, the population increase was almost 100 per cent. It increased from 4,993 to 9,431 in Garacharma, 472 to 729 in Shippighat, and 4,726 to 6,790 in Bambooflat, between 1991 and 2001. In the case of Pahargaon (part), Protherapur (part) and Calicut villages, their populations increased from 1,339 to 3,184, 996 to 2,184 and 679 to 1,169 between 1981 and 1991. This phenomenal increase in the population of these villages is due to immigration from mainland India as well as migration from other rural areas to these villages. In fact, the villages of Garacharma and Bambooflat have crossed the yardstick of 5,000 population in the year 2001 and have been accorded the status of census towns. Besides, 75 per cent of the male population of these two villages is also engaged in non-agricultural activities.

Sex Composition in Fringe Villages

Incessant migration of male population from mainland India in search of employment has resulted in higher proportion of male population in the nearby villages. Keeping this view in mind, 800 females per 1,000 of males population has been selected as an index of the extent of the urban fringe of Port Blair town (Census, 2001). In the villages adjacent to Port Blair town, a sex ratio of 800 females or less per 1,000 males has been recorded (Census, 2001).

Extent and Form of Urban Fringe

All these determinants when taken together and superimposed one over the other provide satisfactory results. There is a zone in which more of the variables co-exist in the space and at the same time, there is also a zone where a few are conspicuous by their absence. All those villages which have fulfilled at least any three of the above indices (physical landscape, occupational change and demographic change) and which are contiguous to the town have been included in the urban fringe of Port Blair town. Those villages are Garacharma, Bambooflat, and part of Shippighat. Towards the inner side, they merge into the town, and towards the outer side, they grade into the peripheral rural areas. The inner boundary of the fringe coincides with the municipal limits of the town that existed at the time of the previous Census.

Delimited on the basis of attributes discussed above, the fringe of Port Blair town does not form a concentric zone around the city but semi star-shaped, and it extends from 3–10 km of distance from the urban limit of the town. The extension of the fringe is, thus, approximately along the transport network, especially along the ATR and the link road.

Certain villages departing from the norms also exist in the urban fringe of Port Blair town. These villages are undergoing a transformation in terms of their physical, occupational and demographic structure at a somewhat rapid rate than other villages beyond. At the same time, they are not only facing a tremendous change in their economic structure, population growth, density and sex composition, but they have also confronted an unplanned growth of the built-up area.

Growth of Tourism in Port Blair

Andaman Islands have been one of the preferred locations for the Indian tourists. Tourist arrivals have been consistently increasing in Port Blair over the years from 9,596 in 1980 to 1,27,504 in 2006, except the drop in 2004–05 due to the tsunami of 26 December 2004 (Table 10). Domestic tourism in the post-tsunami period has increased significantly given the increased incentives offered to tourists using the leave tour concession (LTC) to visit the Andaman Islands in place of their using the hometown LTC. The rate of tourist arrivals as percentage increase in tourist arrivals is also seen to be growing over the years. It has led to the expansion of tourism industry in Port Blair town. It has resulted in the expansion of transport, trade and commerce and servicing sectors.

The tourism vision statement of the Andaman administration identifies tourism as the thrust sector for economic development, revenue and employment generation on the Islands.

Impact of Urbanisation

As discussed, the population of Port Blair town has increased rapidly over the years from 7,789 in 1951 to approximately 150,000 in 2001. This rapid

Table 10

Tourist arrivals at Port Blair (1980–2006)

Year	Domestic tourists	Foreign tourists	Total tourists
1980	7,500	2,096	9,596
1982	13,444	1,102	14,546
1984	16,000	3,152	19,152
1986	20,942	1,791	22,733
1988	34,589	3,663	38,252
1990	29,019	6,697	33,716
1992	35,817	2,435	38,252
1994	50,737	3,798	54,535
1996	57,958	5,796	73,754
1998	74,732	4,915	79,647
2000	81,432	4,684	86,116
2002	90,629	4,707	95,336
2004	1,05,004	4,578	1,09,582
2006	1,18,648	9,051	1,27,504

Source: ActionAid Report on Rethink Tourism in Andaman, 2008: 26.

increase in the population is telling on the limited resource capacity of the town, particularly water. In addition, the growth of tourism is adversely impacting the coral growth in and around Port Blair town and directly or indirectly impacting the primitive tribal groups.

Water Scarcity

The Andaman and Nicobar Islands receive abundant rainfall, with average annual precipitation of 3,100 mm. The South-West Monsoon (May to October) predominates, though the North-East Monsoon also brings some rain. Thus, it gets some eight months of rainfall. At present the total population of Port Blair is approximately 1,60,000. The water demands of this population translate into a requirement of 27.18 million litres per day. Against the demand of 27.18 million litres per day, there is a supply of about 17.79 million litres per day. Thus, there is a shortfall of 09.39 million litres of water per day (Table 11). The shortfall in Port Blair is 35 per cent according to the PWD. However, Zila Parishad paints an even grimmer picture of 45 per cent shortage. The above mentioned water requirement has not taken into account the additional demand for water created by the arrival of tourists.

Besides the surfacewater, the groundwater is also an important source of potable water. Water table is available at the depth of about 50 feet (Figure 3). In order to meet the water requirement, many borewells have been sunk. But sinking of more number of borewells is depleting the

Table 11

Water: Demand and supply (Port Blair Town)

Name of locality	Sources of water	Population (in Lakh)	Projection for 2007		
			Demand @ 135 LPCD (in MLD)	Water availability (MLD)	Excess/Shortfall (MLD)
Port Blair Municipal Area including Minibay, School Line, Part of Austinabad.	Dhanikhari	1.32	22.28		
Junglighat, Prem Nagar, Vijay Baugh, Part of Dairy Farm area.	Jawahar Sarovar, Lamba Line Diggi	0.12	2.02	17.79	−9.39
Raj Niwas area	Dilthaman	0.13	2.20		
Nayagaon	Nayagaon and	0.03	0.51		
Chakkargaon	Chakkargaon Diggi	0.01	0.17		
Total		1.61	27.18	17.79	

Source: Andaman Public Works Department, 2008.

groundwater. The biggest of the hurdles is the formation of aquiclude by the marine sediments, which are clayey in nature, at the subsurface. This prevents development of any groundwater aquifers. However, there are borewells in and around Port Blair which are yielding water, while borewells in North Andaman altogether have failed to yield water.

The GPS mapping of some of the borewells in different parts of the town and other parts of the South Andaman shows that more than 50 per cent of the borewells lie in a depth range of 40–50 feet and a bell curve phenomenon can be seen. Not much correlation could be found between the water table and the distance from the coastline.

In post-tsunami period, many borewells are reported to have dried-up due to changes in the position of the tectonic plates. It has further aggravated the problem of water shortage in Port Blair town and surrounding area. In order to meet the challenge, the administration will have to evolve a long-term measure of raw water storage (rainwater reservoir) to ensure the sufficient availability of water. In addition, the proposal to convert the tsunami-affected low-lying areas into sweet water lakes has to be implemented.

Threat to Environment

Port Blair is fast emerging as an upmarket destination for tourists and is characterised by high volume and low-value tourism. The tourism vision statement of the Andaman administration identifies tourism as the thrust sector. During their stay at Port Blair, tourists visit and enjoy snorkelling and underwater coral watching. The presence of too many

Figure 3

Number of wells (with their depths) in the Islands

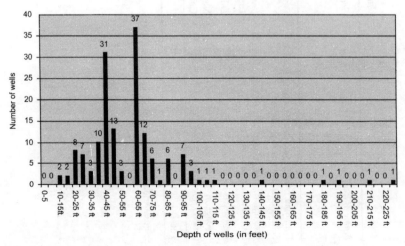

Source: Water and Island's Development, Regional Seminar, 12 March 2008.

people is adversely affecting the growth of coral. The areas most affected are the North Bay and Wandoor.

Impact on the Jarawa Tribe

The zone of influence of the town from the viewpoint of tourism has spread far beyond the formal boundary of the town and includes in its sphere of influence the Jarawa Reserve, the abode of one of the two most primitive population groups of the world. In the wake of the Jarawa becoming friendly, the tour and travel operators have used this new situation as an opportunity. The tourists, who visit Port Blair, are promised to be taken through the 'Jarawa Reserve' with all possibilities of seeing and meeting the homo sapiens who are still in Stone Age. Consequently, it has found expression in terms of a sudden spurt in the number of vehicles plying on the Andaman Trunk Road, which passes through the Jarawa Reserve. It is directly related with the sudden increase in the number of tourists visiting the Andaman and Nicobar Islands. In the year 1996, a total of 3,695 buses and 5,802 other vehicles crossed the Jirkatang check post either way. By applying the IRC norms for calculation of volume of traffic, one finds that the road was used by only 515 persons daily or a total of 1,87,895 persons in the entire year (Acharya, 2002:169). By 2004, there was 150 per cent increase in the traffic volume with more than 1,500 persons crossing the Jarawa Reserve every day. A large section of them are in fact the tourists desirous of seeing the Jarawa. The movement of so many vehicles across the Jarawa Reserve disturbs the tranquillity of their habitat, scares away their prey and poses danger of accidents to the Jarawa people. The unwanted contact with outsiders has exposed them to some health problems. Diseases that are very common among sedentary populations can be fatal for such hunting-gathering communities. The same pattern has been repeated time and again in different parts of the world. For example, in the Andaman Islands, the Great Andamanese suffered from an epidemic caused by such diseases like measles and pneumonia, which were largely responsible for rapid population decline of the Great Andamanese and to some extent of the Onges (Cipriani, 1966). The diseases, which have witnessed sudden increase among the Jarawa, are anaemia, skin diseases, and respiratory tract infection. Besides, it is also tempting them to barter their implements for certain goods offered by the tourists.

Conclusion

The genesis of Port Blair can be traced back to the establishment of 'second penal settlement' by the British colonisers at Andaman Islands in 1858. During the colonial period, the population of Port Blair comprised mainly two categories of people; one who were brought as prisoners and the other who worked for the colonial rulers. In between, some more people were brought to work as labourers to clear the forests and to assist in the establishment of settlements. It attained the status of an urban area almost after nine decades in 1951. In a span of five decades (1951–2001), Port Blair registered more than twelve-fold increase in its population. This increase in population is attributed to the in-migration in addition to natural increase of population. During the same period, the urbanisation of adjacent villages resulted in their merger with Port Blair, leading to spatial extension of the municipal limit of the town from 7.87 sq km to 16 sq km. The process of urbanisation is still strong and two adjoining villages of Garacharma and Bambooflat have been accorded the status of Census towns in 2001. The town is growing towards south and south-east, mostly along the ATR, and a number of commercial establishments are developing in a ribbon-type manner along it due to availability of better infrastructure in the form of linkage, accessibility, suitability of land, etc. The present trend suggests that most of the future development will take place in this direction. However, in present time, Port Blair town is facing an acute shortage of water and the gap between the demand and the supply is expected to increase in coming years in the absence of other sources of water except the rainfall. In addition, the emergence of Port Blair town as a tourist destination is threatening the coastal ecology of the Andaman Islands, particularly the corals.

References

Acharya, S. (2002) 'Andaman Trunk Road and the Jarawa Situation'. In K. Mukhopadhyay, R.K. Bhattacharya and B.N. Sarkar (eds). *Jarawa Contact: Ours with Them and Theirs with Us*. Kolkata: The Anthropological Survey of India, pp. 166–73.

ActionAid (2008) *Rethinking Tourism in Andaman: Towards Building a Base for Sustainable Tourism*. Research Report.

Andaman Adim Janjati Vikas Samiti (AAJVS) (2007) *Reports on Primitive Tribal Groups*. Port Blair.

Andaman Administration (2007) *Statistical Handbook on Andaman and Nicobar District 2005–2006*. Port Blair.

Andaman Public Work Department (2008) *Report on Demand and Availability of Drinking Water*. Unpublished Report. Port Blair.

Andrews, R.B. (1942) 'Elements in the Rural Urban Fringe Pattern'. *Journal of Land and Public Utility Economics*. Vol. 18, pp. 169–83.

Awaradi, S.A. (1990) *Master Plan (1991–2021) for Welfare of Primitive Tribes of Andaman Islands*. Andaman and Nicobar Administration, Port Blair.

Basic Statistics (1996) *Andaman and Nicobar Islands*. Directorate of Economics and Statistics, Andaman and Nicobar Administration, Port Blair.

Carter, M. (1972) *The Study of the Urban Geography*. London: Edward Arnold Ltd.

Census of India (1911) *The Andaman and Nicobar Islands*. Calcutta: Superintendent of Government Printing.

——. (1951) *The Andaman and Nicobar Islands.* Vol. XVII, Calcutta: The Government of India Press.

——. (1961) *The Andaman and Nicobar Islands.* Vol. XVII, New Delhi: Publication Division, Government of India.

——. (1971, 1991) *The Andaman and Nicobar Islands: Economic Tables.* New Delhi: Publication Division, Government of India.

——. (1981) *Special Survey Report on Port Blair, Series 24.* Andaman and Nicobar Islands. New Delhi: Publication Division, Government of India.

Chakraborty, D.K. (1990) *The Great Andamanese.* Calcutta: Seagull Books.

Chakraborty, S. and A. Dinda (2002) 'The Jarawa and their Neighbour: The Post-Independence Scenario'. In K. Mukhopadhyay, R.K. Bhattacharya and B.N. Sarkar (eds). *Jarawa Contact: Ours with Them and Theirs with Us.* Kolkata: The Anthropological Survey of India, pp. 43–57.

Cipriani, Lidio (1966) *Andaman Islanders.* London: Wiedenfeld and Nicolson.

Danda, A.K. (1993) 'Indigenous Small Populations of Andaman and Nicobar Islands'. In A. Basu, J. Sarkar, and A.K. Danda (eds). *Andaman and Nicobar Islanders: Studies on Small Populations,* 10 Anthropological Society Occasional Papers, Kolkata: Indian Anthropological Society, pp. 85–100.

Das, F.A.M. (1937) *The Andaman Islands.* New Delhi: Asian Education Services.

Golledge, R.A. (1960) 'Sydney Metropolitan Fringe: A Case Study in Rural-Urban Relation'. *Aust. Gwgr.* Vol. 7, pp. 243–55.

Imperial Gazetteer of India (1909) *Provincial Service Andaman and Nicobar Islands* (reprint). Jullender: Sterling Publications.

Kumar, U. (2002) 'Morphological and Demographic Changes in the Rural-Urban Fringe of Port Blair Town'. *Journal of Anthropological Survey of India (Special Issue).* December, Vol. 4, No. 4, pp. 57–69.

Kumar, U. and R. Haider (2007) 'Impact of Tsunami at the Onge Settlements at Dugong Creek, Little Andaman'. In Anthropological Survey of India, *Tsunami in South Asia: Studies on Impact of Tsunami on Communities of Andaman and Nicobar Islands.* Delhi: Allied Publishers Pvt. Ltd., pp. 103–19.

Majumdar, R.C. (1975) *Penal Settlement in Andamans.* Delhi: Gazetteers Unit, Department of Culture, Government of India.

Man, E.H. (1883) (reprint) (1975) *The Aboriginal Inhabitants of the Andaman Islands.* Delhi: Sanskaran Prakasan.

Mathur, L.P. (1968) *History of the Andaman and Nicobar Islands (1756–1966).* Delhi: Sterling Publishers Pvt. Ltd.

Mukhopadhyay, C. (2002) 'Economic Profile of Port Blair Town'. *Journal of Anthropological Survey of India (Special Issue),* December, Vol. 4, No. 4, pp. 27–46.

Pandit, T.N. (1974) 'Jarawa: Story of a Century of Mutual Hostility'. *Daily Telegrams,* 16 and 18 March, Port Blair.

——. (1976) 'The Ethnic Situation in the Bay Islands'. *Yojana.* Vol. 20.

——. (1989) 'Tribal Policy in the Andaman and Nicobar Islands: The Impact of Nehru's Philosophy'. In K.S. Singh (ed.). *Jawaharlal Nehru: Tribes and Tribal Policy*. Calcutta: Segal Books, pp. 83–92.

——. (1990) *The Sentinelese*. Kolkata: Seagull Books on behalf of the Anthropological Survey of India.

Pandit, T.N. and M. Chattopadhyay (1993) 'Meeting the Sentinelese: The Least Known of the Andaman Hunter-gatherers'. In A. Basu, J. Sarkar and A.K. Danda (eds). *Andaman and Nicobar Islanders: Studies on Small Populations*, 10 Anthropological Society Occasional Papers, Kolkata: Indian Anthropological Society, pp. 169–78.

Portman, M.V. (1899) *A History of Our Relations with the Andamanese: Compiled from Histories and Travel Records of the Government of India*. New Delhi: Asian Education Services.

Radcliffe-Brown, A.R. (1948) *The Andaman Islanders*. Illinois: The Free Press.

Records of the Government of India (1859) *The Andman Islands, with Note on Barren Islands*. No. XXV (Home Department), Calcutta, pp. 31–33.

Sarkar, J.K. (1994) *People of India: Andaman and Nicobar Islands*. Vol. XII by K.S. Singh (General Editor), Madras: Affiliated East-West Press Pvt. Ltd., pp. 96–105.

Singh, R.L. (1955) *A Study in Urban Geography*. Allahabad: Nand Kishore and Bros.

Smailes, A.E. (1962) *The Geography of Towns*. Hutchinson University Library, London: South Impression.

Srivastava, B. and R. Ramachandran (1974) 'The Rural-Urban Fringe'. *Indian Geography Journal*. Vol. XLIX, pp. 1–9.

Tamta, B.R. (1990) *India: The Land and People*. Andaman and Nicobar Islands. New Delhi: National Book Trust, India.

Water and Island's Development – Regional Seminar 12 March 2008, Port Blair http://www.unicef. org/rosa/media_2582.htm

Wehrwein, G.S. (1967) 'The Rural-Urban Fringe'. In H.M. Mayer and C.F. Kohn (eds). *Reading in Urban Geography*. Allahabad: Central Book Depot.

Young, M. (1962) 'Some Geographical Features of the Urban Fringe'. *The South Eastern Geography*. Vol. 2, pp. 1–6.

14

Complexities in Growth of Tura Town in Meghalaya

SUMIT MUKHERJEE AND AMLAN BISWAS

Tura as one of the oldest towns in Meghalaya state has been functional as the headquarters of the entire Garo Hills Division since 1866. As one of the earliest district headquarters in North-East India, Tura became the fastest growing town in Meghalaya following the formation of the state in 1971, with an abnormal growth of 127 per cent recorded during 1971–81. Then, it showed a reverse trend considering that it took almost a decade for Tura to become a Class II town in 2001, with a population of 58,978, as against 64 per cent growth for the state as a whole. This uneven growth has been explained mainly due to the formation of the state of Meghalaya and the consequent spurt in urban activities centring around the administrative functions in the town, and partly due to the readjustment of municipal boundary when 11 villages were brought under the jurisdiction of Tura Municipal Board. But its growth rate has fallen steadily (29% in 1991–2001) during last two decades, against 37.59 per cent for the sate as a whole, indicating perhaps the non-supportive trend of urbanisation in an isolated hill town established as an administrative headquarters by the colonial government, in absence of suitable factors of urbanisation. At present, the urban land use of Tura Municipal Board area depicts a very high share of residential area (72%) of the total area of 18.3 sq km, with insignificant land under commercial, industrial, recreational and transport activities. Tura is largely inhabited by the Garo tribes, although it slowly assumed a cosmopolitan nature due to various other tribes and non-tribal people entering the town. While examining the causes for steadily falling growth rate of the Tura Municipality, the present paper reveals several locational disadvantages as well as lack of industrialisation and urban planning for developing civic facilities as the causative factors. Even being a picturesque hill town, Tura failed heavily in drawing tourists for certain reasons otherwise common in North-East India.

Urban History of the Region

Processes related to the growth of urban population and urban areas in North-East India and its tribal states in particular differ in certain aspects from that of rest of India owing to various regional uniquenesses. Differences in terms of genesis, location, traditional pattern of land holding and land tenure system, economic traditions, migration, ethnic and demographic characteristics, etc., need to be understood carefully and contextually. Barring a few large cities like Guwahati, Dibrugarh, Jorhat and Bangaigaon, with specific historic, commercial and industrial background, almost all the towns in North-East India are overgrown villages administered to become a town. In fact, majority of those have originated as administrative headquarters of a state or a district. The British Indian towns grew out of suitability factors, viz., weather, strategy, business, and were decided by the colonial rulers imposed upon a predominantly rural tribal situations. Such imposed urbanisation has resulted in a socio-cultural dichotomy with purposively brought non-local and non-tribal communities as government servants and the non-participating tribal communities in subsistence form of economy. Shillong city, the then capital of undivided Assam state, has a history more of conflicts than co-existence amongst the local Khasi tribesmen and the early emigrants from Assam and eastern Bengal being the British servants or *babus* (Joshi, 2004: 77). Similarly, Tura was chosen, primarily owing to its milder weather of the hill top, as the headquarters of the Undivided Garo Hills to conquer over the Garo country as early as 1866. The town took a century to attain Class II town status in 1971 (Bahadur, 2009: 87).

The urban system of North-East India, in continuum with many other parts of the world, is characterised with an uneven growth where a few large cities accommodate largest portion of urban population and a large number of smaller cities share strikingly fewer urbanites. There were no Class I cities in 1951, and their number came to nine in 2001. During this period, population in smaller towns gradually declined whereas stable growth in larger ones indicated a continuous migration from those towns. Alike rural population, these small town dwellers migrate perhaps in search of better socio-economic options and civic amenities (Bahadur, 2009). At present, there are around 200 urban centres in North-East India with only one million-plus city, and with absolute majority of medium and small towns. Those small towns, having no or negligible surplus economy or a well-connected steady market to boost commercial or industrial development, grew when the administrative machinery expanded and migration of rural population occurred under certain social and economic compulsions. The Class I cities (including the only million-plus Guwahati UA, estimated 2.3M in 2011) are almost equal in size to the medium (Class II and III) and jointly hold 66 per cent of the urban population in North-east India, whereas the small towns account for 64 per cent of all towns sharing just 34 per cent population (Census of India, 2001, List of Towns: Assam, p. 2).

Though these states showed high population growth, it is only after independence that the tempo of urbanisation became distinct with rural urban migration. The lower level of income from *jhum* and settled cultivation was the main push factor as the land: man ratio declined, along with the land-carrying capacity. The lower level of income from agriculture, including that from once flourishing plantation economy after its fall particularly during the famine in Bengal (1942), was a compound impact during and after the Second World War. The growing timber market along with other trades in mineral, etc., had not been strong enough for an occupation shift (Chakraborty, 2004: 181). Even the growing timber market suddenly got the big blow due to the Supreme Court order against commercial movement of timber outside the state in 1996.

Further, the new constitutional administration, i.e., Autonomous District Councils, though apparently with good objectives, never became popularly accepted because it failed to mingle with all the variants of existing tribal customary laws in tribal societies. In fact, the traditional tribal societies had already experienced painful bruises from the parallel administrative organs like Laskars and Sirdars imposed by the British rulers.

The recent rapid rate of urbanisation in north-eastern states does not bespeak of a corresponding growth of industry but a shift of people from a low-productive agricultural employment to yet another sector marked by low-productivity employment, namely, handicraft production, retail trading, domestic service and transport in urban areas (Bahadur, 2009). The town of Tura was born as one of the oldest district headquarters in North-East India and now it is a Class II town, the second largest in Meghalaya, and the headquarters of West Garo Hills district. The town recorded an abnormally high growth rate just after formation of the Municipal Board in 1972 when several new villages were added to it. But the growth of population sharply declined to 27 per cent during 1991–2001.

With the skewed and complex backdrop of urbanisation prevailing in the region and particularly in case of Tura town, an attempt is made here to outline the major and important trends, causes and dynamics. Mostly secondary data and information have been utilised, complemented with direct observations and interviews with local community members during a field visit in 2010.

Geo-political and Socio-economic Scenario

Meghalaya is one of the tribal states in North-East India situated along the international boundary with Bangladesh on the south and shares the state boundary with Assam on the north, west and east. This is one of the smaller states in India in terms of area (22,429 sq km) and a population of 29,64,007 in 2011. It has 86 per cent Scheduled Tribe (ST) population dominated by three groups: the Khasis, Garos and the Jaintias. All these three communities are matrilineal in societal form. Density of population is also low (132 per sq km) in this predominantly rural (79.02%) state, where urban population is only 20.08 per cent. The decadal growth of population was 27.82 per cent during 2001–2011 (Census of India, 2011).

Geographically, Meghalaya (the abode of clouds) is coterminous with the plateau of the same name, a geological extension of the Chhotanagpur plateau, and receives highest rainfall in the world from south-west monsoon. The central axis of the plateau runs east-west with two highest points, viz., the Laitkor or Shillong Peak (1961m) on the east and Nokrek (1412 m) on the west in Garo Hills. Hence, the whole state has a typical plateau landscape with flat skyline bounded almost on all sides by the 150 m contour line. The central axis of the plateau landscape which runs in the east-west direction raises up to 1,900 m above mean sea level (Figure 1).

There are two distinct physiographical divisions, viz., (i) the Khasi Hills or the Eastern Meghalaya covering almost 60 per cent of the total area

Figure 1

Location and profile of the study area

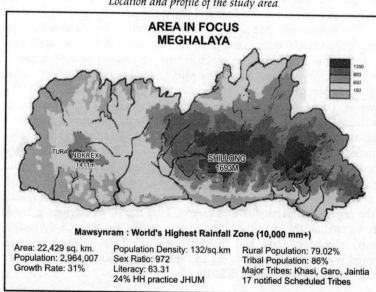

and four out of the seven districts of the state, namely, Jaintia Hills, East Khasi Hills, Ri Bhoi and West Khasi Hills; and (ii) the Western Meghalaya or the Garo Hills consisting of all three Garo Hill districts (Singh, 2004). The Garo Hills or Western Meghalaya has a lower average altitude with low-rounded hills and intermittent plains with an average altitude of 600 m. The Garo Plateau rises to a distinct east-west range known as Kailash or Tura range. The central plateau ridge culminates here, reaching the Nokrek peak (1,412 m) near Tura. Another relatively lower range runs north-south between Maheshkhola and Adokggre, separating the western and central parts of the Garo Plateau. Its western and northern parts along the left bank of Brahmaputra River are characterised by low hills and limited plain areas drained by the Dudhnoi, Krishnai and the Jinjiram rivers. The Simsang is the longest river in the region draining southwards to enter Bangladesh as Someswari. The Mahadeo and the Mahes Khola are the other two south-flowing rivers which flow through deeply-cut valleys in the South Garo Hills (Taher and Ahmed, 1998).

In general, Meghalaya enjoys a sub-tropical monsoon climate. Remarkable variation in temperature and rainfall is observed due to orographic prominence and the maritime air mass from the Bay of Bengal on the south.

The Garo Hills or the Western Meghalaya with relatively lower altitude enjoys a fairly higher air temperature for major part of the year (February to October). April is the hottest month with mean minimum and maximum temperatures of 33°C and 22°C, respectively. January is the coldest month and the mean temperature varies from 24°C to 12°C. The average annual rainfall is also lower (3,300 mm) in the Western Meghalaya and winter is particularly dry. The amount of rainfall decreases from south to north as the South-West Monsoon wind gets obstructed by the Tura Range and causes heavy orographic rainfall on the southern slopes.

Excessive rainfall and wet climate has endowed the region with a thick cover of sub-tropical rainforest, rich in species diversity. The natural vegetation of Meghalaya varies from sub-tropical pine forest over the higher altitude zone to the dense mixed tropical wet evergreen type in areas with moderate altitude but receiving high rainfall. On the other hand, tropical moist deciduous forest cover is widely found in the lower hills and valleys of the Garo Hills districts. The vegetal cover of Meghalaya was estimated at 69.70 per cent of its total geographical area based on imagery data (Forest Survey of India, 1999) but as per legally notified area under forest, the cover was only 37.80 per cent (NEC, 1995). It is important to notice that there has been a loss of 110 square kilometres of forest cover during a short span of two years in 1991–1993 only due mainly to shifting *(jhum)* cultivation and commercial exploitation in the dominantly private forests. In fact, around 90 per cent of the total forest area is under private individual or clan ownership in this tribal state under the provisions of the Sixth Schedule of the Indian Constitution.

Scott David's efforts in introducing foreign crops like potato, turnip, beat, millet, maize, etc., in 1830s started gaining popularity after rice and cotton began to dwindle during 1872 (Joshi, 2004: 309). People of Meghalaya are still largely dependent on agriculture, though plantation agriculture is continued along with patches of settled paddy cultivation but still about 23 per cent practice shifting cultivation. Only 9 per cent area is under settled cultivation and another 1.5 per cent in horticulture producing potato, ginger, turmeric, bay leaf, broom stick, orange, lemon, areca nut, etc. (NEC, 2001).

To interpret the paradox that Meghalaya is, being quite rich in mineral resources like limestone, coal, sillimanite, uranium, etc., and being the only state with a surplus power generation in NE India and yet devoid of any major industry, let's dig into the complexities of the existing administrative system, society and their economic traditions. Most of these resources are exploited and sent outside only in raw form. There are little value addition activities in the state. CMIE index for infrastructure development of Meghalaya was 65 in 1992–93. The contribution of the tertiary sector to the state remains pathetically low. It seems true that the pre-migration income of the immigrants was lower than that of the urban poor, which led to overurbanisation. The well-known tourism potential apart from the potential of agro-based products still remains very much an isolated affair and there is hardly any attempt to decentralise tourism outside Shillong city and its periphery.

Urbanisation in Meghalaya

In general, urbanisation in Meghalaya has maintained a low but steady growth. As per 2011 Census, the state has only 20.08 per cent urban population, which is much lower than the national average of 31.16 per cent. The lower urbanisation indicates a rather poor economic development of the state as a whole as urban centres are found to be the nerve-centres of growth and development. The level of urbanisation in all the districts except East Khasi Hills (44.42%), which includes capital Shillong, is well below the state average. Three out of four districts recorded a decline in urban share of population with a huge contrast with remarkable increases, e.g., in Ri Bhoi and South Garo Hills districts which are located on the border with Assam and Bangladesh, respectively. West Garo Hills district ranks third in urban population but houses only 11.68 per cent urban dwellers, and showed a slight increase over 2001. The decadal growth rate of urban population in Meghalaya has become almost at par with that of India during 2001–2011 (Table 1). It is again interesting to find that Ri Bhoi recorded highest rate of 90.85 per cent followed by South Garo Hills 50.92 per cent, whereas West Garo Hills ranked fourth showing 27.30 per cent growth during the last Census decade. Compared to the transport linkages vis-à-vis accessibility among the districts, connectivity is the single-most factor associated with higher urban growth in the bordering districts. But, the same fact indicates a higher rate of in-migration in those districts, even cross-border movement from Bangladesh is highly suspected in case of the abnormally high rate in the newly-formed Baghmara MB, the headquarters of the South Garo Hills (Table 1).

Table 1

Percentage share and growth rate of population by residence, 2011

	2001		2011		Growth Rate 2011		
	Rural	Urban	Rural	Urban	Total	Rural	Urban
India	72.19	27.81	68.84	31.16	17.6	12.18	31.8
17 Meghalaya	80.42	19.58	79.92	20.08	27.82	27.04	31.03
01 West Garo Hills	88.37	11.63	88.32	11.68	26.73	26.66	27.3
02 East Garo Hills	85.77	14.23	86.07	13.93	25.84	26.28	23.21
03 South Garo Hills	92.16	7.84	90.85	9.15	29.38	27.49	50.92
04 West Khasi Hills	88.31	11.69	88.85	11.15	30.25	31.04	24.25
05 Ri Bhoi	93.16	6.84	90.26	9.74	34.02	29.85	90.85
06 East Khasi Hills	57.98	42.02	55.58	44.42	24.68	19.53	31.79
07 Jaintia Hills	91.62	8.38	92.75	7.25	31.34	32.96	13.67

Source: Census of India, 2011: Provisional Population Totals.

Presently, the state has 16 urban centres, predominant being the Shillong UA comprising municipality, cantonment area, census towns, etc., under the Shillong Municipal Board and Cantonment Board and Town Durbars – a traditional urban body. Tura is also a Municipal Board and a district headquarters of West Garo Hills. As per 2011 Census, there are 22 towns of which 10 are statutory and in addition there are 12 Census towns in Meghalaya. In absence of further details, the following Table shows the growth trend of towns up to 1991–2001 (Figure 2).

Table 2

Size-Class wise distribution of population in towns of Meghalaya 2001

Size class	Number of towns	Total population	Per cent to total urban pop
I	1 (Shillong)	2,67,881	59.2
II	1 (Tura)	58,391	12.9
III	2	47,026	10.4
IV	5	70,761	15.6
V	1	8,643	1.9

Source: Urbanisation in North-East India (Bahadur, 2009).

Figure 2

Trend of decadal growth in the urban centres of Meghalaya

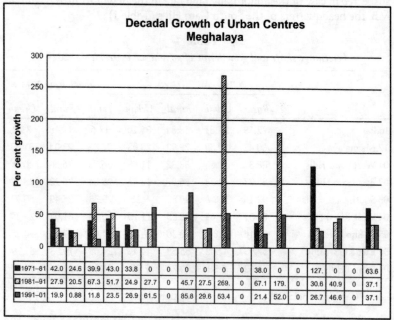

The clear imbalance in distribution of urban population is visible from the table above. Almost 60 per cent share of urban population is with the only Class I town Shillong, followed by Tura in the next category. In fact, the remaining eight smaller towns together share only 27.9 per cent, i.e., just one-fourth of the urban population (Table 2).

Tura Town

Just after the first general election, District Councils were constituted in most of the hill districts of North-East India. These councils were vested with powers to make laws with respect to the allotment, occupation, use of land management of unreserved state forest, use of canals and water for agriculture, regulation of *jhum*, and establishment of village and town committees.

A provisional Tura Town Committee was constituted by the Garo Hills Autonomous District Council on 30 July, 1953. As per demands made by the town dwellers of Tura, the Government of Meghalaya established a municipality constituting Tura Municipal Board consisting of 11 members, including a chairman, on 13 August 1979, replacing the TTC (www.tmbonline.in). The name Tura is said to be a corruption (by the British) of the local god's name 'Dura'.

The town is located approximately along 90°: 9':30" – 90°:19':00" east longitude and 25°:33':30" north latitude and has average altitude of 1,300 metres above the sea level. Tura town lies at the foot of Tura Peak, which has an altitude of 1,412 metres above sea level and forms the main landmark dominating the eastern boundary of the town. This urban body is environmentally sensitive owing to its location on the western boundary of the Core Area of the Nokrek Biosphere Reserve.

Tura town falls under the Central Main Plateau Region. The main physiographic features of the area are the WNW-ESE Tura range with steep southern as well as western faces. This range has an average height exceeding 1,300 m with a maximum height of 1,412 m at Nokrek Peak (Figure 1). The geographical isolation is evident from the available communication options. The nearest rail head is in Krshnai, Assam, some 110 kilometres north and the air linkage and nearest city is Guwahati, located more than 200 kilometres away, communicable through NH 51. The capital city of Shillong is 323 kilometres away and can be accessed via buses via Assam. On the southern side, the border of Bangladesh at Dalu, is situated at a proximity of only 50 kilometres.

Tura is largely inhabited by Garo tribes with a section of non-tribal populace mostly composed of Bengali, Assamese, Marwari and Hindi linguistic groups, although it is slowly assuming a cosmopolitan nature with various other tribes and non-tribal people pouring into the town as it grows. The growth of the town is being propelled by the expansion of service sector which brings with it in-migration from different communities. The town has an area of 18.3 sq km, housing a total population of 58,978 (in 2001) with a population density of 3,223 per sq km. A vast majority of people belong to Scheduled Tribe (72%) communities like Koch, Hajong, Rava, etc., other than the Garos. Scheduled Caste population shares only 3.5 per cent and the remaining 24.5 per cent are the non-tribal communities.

Urbanisation in Tura

Tura had its urbanisation conceived as early as in 1866 when it became functional as one of the oldest district headquarters of North-east India. But, in practice, the town did not experience any remarkable growth until the formation of the state of Meghalaya in 1971, being essentially an administrative centre and located in a far corner with very poor communication. The growth rate of population in Tura town has not been significantly upward. The most spectacular growth in the population of the town was observed during 1971–81 when Tura experienced a massive 127 per cent rise in its population. This abnormal growth has been explained mainly as due to the formation of the state of Meghalaya and the consequent spurt in urban activities centring around the administrative functions and partly due to the readjustment of municipal

304 ◆ Sumit Mukherjee and Amlan Biswas

boundary when as many as 11 villages were brought under the jurisdiction of Tura Municipal Board.

The population growth of the town (Figure 4) reveals that there has in fact been a marginal decline of 0.43 per cent in the growth rate of population in Tura town between the decades of 1981–1991 and 1991–2001. The annual average growth rate of population between 1991–2001 has been 0.03. In fact, it took almost a century for the town to attain Class II status (Figures 3 and 4).

It is interesting to find from Figure 5 that the density of population is high in Wards 2 to 5 which are traditionally the most congested residential areas and also house many offices and educational institutions. But it is evident from the graph that the lower density in Ward 1 is perhaps due to the main market area with more commercial establishments than residential. It is also notable that non-tribal population density is higher only near the core of the town, including the main residential areas, indicating that they are the early migrants in this old administrative town.

Figure 3

Absolute and Exponential Population Growth Graph of Tura

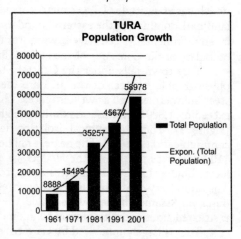

Figure 4

Temporal trend of decadal growth in Tura

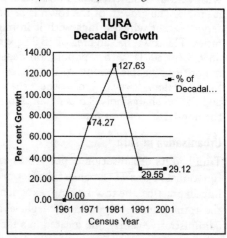

The unusually high share of residential area and very low percentage under industrial, commercial and transport sectors are the good indicators of a town with hampered growth and weak future (Table 3). An effective corrective measure is already adopted in the Tura Master Plan for a more balanced urban land use through its expansion.

Figure 5

Ward map of Tura town with location of markets (Tura Municipal Board Map)

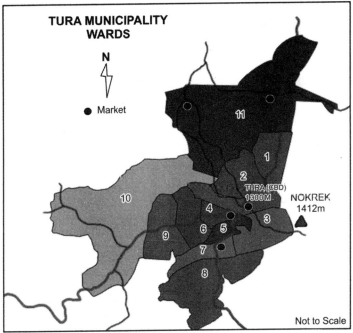

Figure 6

Ward-wise density of population of Scheduled Tribes and non-tribal people

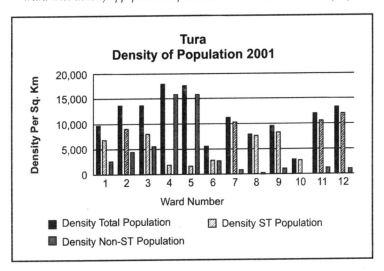

Table 3
Urban land use, Tura 2001

Land Use	Per cent to Total Area	Hectare/1,000 Persons
Residential	73.1	20.19
Commercial	1.22	0.31
Industrial	0.1	0.02
Public and semi-public	17.14	4.35
Security	3.78	0.22
Transportation	4.66	1.12

Source: Tura Municipal Board.

Tura: The Growth Process

Having the backdrop narrated, let us now focus on the major issues which are found to be directly or indirectly responsible for the trend and present state of growth of Tura town.

The new political institutions, created after independence, were in fact eroding the powers and functionality of traditional councils instead of improving upon them. Though these constitutional institutions are meant for and committed to economic, social and political changes towards modernisation (Joshi, 2004). District Councils were instituted in the tribal areas of Assam, Meghalaya, Tripura, and Mizoram under the Sixth Schedule of the Indian Constitution in order to protect the rights of the tribal communities. The District Councils are authorised to manage forests for the purposes of agriculture or grazing, for residential and non-agricultural purposes, and also for the regulation of *jhum* and the establishment of village or town committees or councils (National Commission to Review the Working of the Constitution, 2001).

The establishment and evolution of District Councils, contrary to the expected outcome of recognising and strengthening the traditional systems of governance, has generally resulted in more alienation of the communities from the state governments. The reasons cited by the communities include: (1) the District Councils were established and operated following a uniform set of rules that did not accommodate local variations, including differences among tribes and their traditional practices; (2) the District Councils were promoted as a democratic set-up, mostly alien to the tribal communities, and there have been cases of elite capture; (3) a district is a large entity, and could be home to a number of tribal communities. The traditional systems of inter-tribe dialogue and conflict resolution have not been integrated into the District Councils; and (4) district Councils were created as parallel institutions, and many of these councils have been managed through official bureaucracy. Yet, the District Councils lack full autonomy or power.

Traditionally, the Garo socio-political organisation is well structured in hierarchy of Nokma (village head), Mahari (family) or Machong (clan) and Chatchi (a group of clan). The different tiers show an acknowledgement of decentralisation as a political principle and secondly the principle of local self-government. Village Nokmas were powerful chiefs in the past; but the councils in which elders from the clans or groups of clans sat, presided over by Nokmas, decided all issues such as foreign policies, war and peace, inter-villages and land disputes and judicial cases. This council was called 'Mela-salbonga'. King Nokmas assumed positions because they held and managed land on behalf of their wife's Maharis' (Joshi, 2004).

Village Nokmas are the custodians of village rights, hence they are supposed to be resourceful. The power of Nokmas was broken down after the annexation when the Laskars were instituted by the government, entrusted with collection of house tax and revenue with a power to decide petty cases, while the Deputy Commissioners exercised overall jurisdiction on behalf of Government. The modern system of administration had the advantages in breaking down the old village isolation and integrating the groups of people inside the district. Nokmas still supervise temporal affairs and were the authoritative interpreters of the local customary laws and customs of the people. Nephews succeed to their maternal uncle's office in which through the system of their marriage, nephews attain that position. The Nokmas represents his wife's Mahari and is entrusted with the maintenance and management of land for which he consults the Mahari's representatives in vital issues as consistence worth the sanction of the customary laws (Bareh, 2001: 68–70).

Under the Sixth Schedule of the Constitution, all forests other than the government reserved forests are to be managed by the District Council, but the bulk of the forestland is in the hilly areas where customary laws are applicable. This hinders effective management of the forests for both the District Council and the communities. In the West Garo Hills (Meghalaya), the two parallel governing institutions – the tribal customary laws under the Nokmas and the statutory laws of the District Council – have overlapping authority over management of the forests. This prohibitive overlap is seen as one of the reasons for the mismanagement of forests in the Garo Hills.

The whole picture of administrative multiplicity can be narrated by quoting para 8.4 of Urban Development (Chapter VIII) in the Meghalaya State Development Report 2005, as follows: 'A complex legal framework vis-à-vis the constitutional status of the State dominates the urban governance and management in the State. Except for the Shillong Municipality, all the areas of the State are classified as 'Tribal Area' as per Article 244 of the Constitution of India whereby powers to make laws and rules on a number of subjects have been vested in the Autonomous District Councils.

The Meghalaya Town and Country Planning Act, 1973 (The Assam Town and Country Planning Act, 1959 as adopted by Meghalaya) as well as the Meghalaya Municipal Act, 1973 (The Assam Municipal Act, 1956 as adopted by Meghalaya) are in force over the whole state. While Municipal Boards have been constituted in some towns under the provision of the Municipal Act, managements of some towns are with the Town Committees constituted by the Autonomous District Councils. In some towns, like Sohra, there is no urban local body. However, because of various underlying problems, these bodies are yet to establish themselves firmly and are mostly dependent on the government for most of their obligatory functions. In this scenario, government departments and parallel agencies, besides traditional village bodies, have been involved in the civic management and service delivery in most of the towns.'

The pulse of the Garo people on this issue of administrative multiplicity can be well understood from a letter to the Editor published in widely circulated English daily written by a Garo leader (please see Annexure I), which even challenges the goodness of the development schemes under JNNURM in lieu of the traditional rights on land and forest. Such is the depth of feeling existing amongst the local people.

Garos in Garo Hills

The delimitation of Garo Hills district by the British administration during the late 19th century actually created a division between the considerable population of the Garos living in the plains of Bengal (now Bangladesh) and Assam. The Garos have a long history of migration from northern mountains across the Himalayas and subsequent phases of movement in North-East India and Bangladesh during times of war and conflicts with earlier habitants before the majority of them settled down in the western part of Meghalaya. They belong to Bodo family of Tibeto-Burman race and call themselves 'Achiks' (Sangma, 1981: 15)

The number of Garos living in the Garo Hills in 1901 was 1,03,538. The vast majority of the people living in the district at that time were the Garos themselves. The same census shows that the number of Garos living outside the Garo Hills at that time was considerable, including 34,180 in Mymensingh (now in Bangladesh), 10,842 in Goalpara district, 5,768 in the Khasi and Jaintia Hills and 5,144 in Kamrup district (Simon, 1996).

It would seem that the comparatively sparse population in the Garos' own habitat was due to the unhealthy climate prevailing there in former times, which kept the population down. It is on record that the cases of that dreaded disease, Kala-azar, were first detected in the occupied portion of the Garo Hills in 1869.

The figures of the Garos settled in areas outside their homeland are evident even from the Census Report for 1961, which showed that as many as 14,780 Garos were living in the neighbouring United Khasi and

Jaintia Hills district, 3,316 in the United Mikir and North Cachar Hills district (Table 4). While the number of those living in Assam dropped to 4,487, no figures could obviously be obtained for Mymensingh. The Garo population in the home district was 2,39,747, representing 78 per cent of the total. By this time, progress in medical science and health services had led to the opening up of the interior and the number of people living in the district had begun to take an upward trend. The Census of 1971 shows that there were then 4,06,615 people living in the Garo Hills, of whom 3,06,804 or 75.45 per cent were Garos. On the flip side, there were 53,485 Bengalis, 9,472 Assamese and 3617 Hindi and quite a large number (figure not available) of Gujarati speaking people, who were recorded living in entire Garo Hills when the state was formed in 1971. The feelings of identity crisis, a normal outcome of urbanisation, matched by the desire for political dominance, have led to political unrest, extortion, extremism and terrorist activities in the states of the North-eastern region. On the other hand, the mal-distribution of population in each growing city has jeopardised the whole urban planning endeavour (Bahadur, 2009: 127).

Table 4
Geographical distribution of Garo habitats in North-East India

Year	Garo Hills	Khasi and Jaintia Hills	Assam	Bangladesh
1901	1,03,538	5,768	10,842	34,180
1961	2,39,747	14,780	4,487	NA
1971	3,06,804	25,000	6,500	NA
2001/2005		6,89,639	10,500	1,20,000

Source: Meghalaya District Gazetteers: Garo Hills (1958) and Census data for respective years. T-5 Census of India. 2001. Data Highlights-Migration Tables.

Till today, most of the commercial establishments in Tura, like wholesale and retail market, are dominated by non-tribal people though in most cases the trade licence is taken in the name of a Garo. In fact, there are many instances of early migrant Bengali and Assamese men married to a Garo lady and possessing the property and business in a diluted form of matrilineal family. Such and other kind of dominance over the Garos in their homeland has caused a sense of economic and cultural insecurity among the Garos. The present generation of the Garos, particularly those 'hybrid' siblings, are showing some kind of dissent attitude to make the situation in such urban areas further complicated.

Migration
Rural-urban migration is a complex process and its effects are multidimensional. In case of heavy and continuous flow of selective migration of young males from rural to urban areas, stagnation of economic growth

may take place in rural and economically-depressed areas due to the loss of active labour force. But rapid growth occurs in urban destinations in terms of population and labour force, economic development, morphological structure and functional interactions. These are known as pull factors of migration. Migration occurs due to economic gains and social ties in any urban centre. The migration from rural to urban areas is mainly caused due to the availability of different types of employment. The villagers perform the job of coolies, rickshaw-pullers and as servants in shops of different types. Some of them are coming to the urban areas for higher education, as government servants and for other sort of recreation. As there are lack of jobs in rural areas, villagers are forced to settle in urban settlements. Table 5 and 6 present data on migration status. Table 6 highlights migration of people within Meghalaya state. Intra-district migration has been a dominant factor for mobility of people, though in all only a small proportion of population has migrated, as shown from the Census 2001.

Table 5

Top ten states in rural-urban and urban-rural migration by last residence, India, 2001

Rural to Urban		Urban to Rural	
State	Per cent	State	Per cent
Mizoram	39.1	Goa	26.7
Meghalaya	27.4	Kerala	13.3
Nagaland	26.8	Nagaland	13.2
Arunachal Pradesh	26.1	Sikkim	11.8
Gujarat	25.9	Tamil Nadu	11.5
Tamil Nadu	23.3	Meghalaya	11
Haryana	21.9	Mizoram	8.5
Maharashtra	21.2	Andhra Pradesh	8.4
Karnataka	21.2	Maharashtra	8.2
Jammu & Kashmir	21.1	Karnataka	7.4

Source: Census of India 2001. Data Highlights-Migration Tables.

Table 6

Migration by place of birth, Meghalaya, 2001

Migrants	Persons	Per cent to total Pop.	Males	Females	Sex ratio
Intra-district migrants	2,09,891	9.10	1,10,853	99,038	893.4174
Inter-district migrants	44,108	1.91	23,891	20,217	846.2182
Inter-state migrants	92,088	3.99	51,798	40,290	777.8293
International migrants	12,360	0.54	7,410	4,950	668.0162
Total	3,58,447	15.54	1,93,952	1,64,495	848

Source: Census of India 2001. Migration Tables.

Table 7

Actual and natural annual growth rates of population and their growth differentials in North-eastern States, 2001

States	Natural annual population growth rate			Actual annual population growth rate			Growth differential (Actual-Natural)		
	Urban	Rural	Total	Urban	Rural	Total	Urban	Rural	Total
A.P.	1.39	1.82	1.78	10.14	1.60	2.60	8.75	–0.22	0.82
Assam	1.51	2.02	1.97	3.62	1.67	19.00	2.11	–0.35	-0.07
Manipur	1.24	1.49	1.39	1.28	3.76	30.00	0.04	2.27	1.61
Meghalaya	1.22	2.33	2.15	3.71	2.96	30.00	2.49	0.63	0.85
Mizoram	0.96	1.27	1.14	3.87	2.10	2.92	2.91	0.83	1.78
Nagaland	1.18	0.00	0.00	6.79	6.27	6.44	5.61	0.00	0.00
Sikkim	1.34	1.58	1.56	6.22	3.00	3.30	4.88	1.42	1.74
Tripura	1.14	1.24	1.19	2.88	1.40	1.57	1.74	0.16	0.38

Source: SRS Bulletin, October 1999 and Census of India 2001.

The natural and actual growth differential of population can help examining the extent of rural-urban migration as well as international migration in this frontier state. As expected, Meghalaya showed a remarkably high positive growth differential in case of urban population (2.49) and in case of rural (0.63) as well (Table 7). Interestingly, the higher sex ratio in the slum population of Meghalaya also indicates a migration with family, which usually happens from far-flung rural areas (Bahadur, 2009: 79).

Urban Economy

The agro-climatic factors prevailing in Meghalaya as a whole are quite favourable for horticulture of vast range like fruits, vegetables, spices, etc., but the emphasis is given to foodgrains, chiefly paddy, both in terms of total cultivated area and allocation of state budget. On the contrary, only 22 per cent of the state area is good for settled cultivation of which only 14 per cent is irrigated and 12 per cent under multiple crops. The state is yet to become self-sufficient in foodgrains and the annual shortfall was 1,52,000 tonnes in 2006–07. On the other hand, the level of industrialisation is relatively low and so is the opportunity of employment outside the primary sector.

As per the Meghalaya State Development Report (Government of Meghalaya, 2009) on Agriculture, the rural-based occupation in primary and secondary sectors didn't develop significantly compared to the tertiary sector in the urban or semi-urban areas. Still, existing traditional low-return *jhum* cultivation has failed to provide the food security whereas once profitable plantation agriculture like cotton, orange, areca nut, cashew, tea, rubber, etc., have either failed or declined due to poor marketing facilities. The per capita worker income in rural areas increased marginally from ₹ 3,096 in 1980–81 to ₹ 4,358 in 1992–93, compared to a much higher increase in the urban income from ₹ 9,055 to ₹ 12,280. Therefore, the trend is creating severe inequalities between rural and urban workers, resulting in a renewed urban pull factor but in absence of sufficient growth of industries and entrepreneurship in those medium and small urban pockets. The anomaly calls for reshaping of the institutional set-up to gear up agriculture and rural production output. On the other hand, the tertiary sector occupational avenues in the urban areas, like that for Tura, are neither organised nor sufficient to absorb the rural unskilled migrants other than as petty vendors or wage labourers in the service sectors.

Still today, there is no manufacturing unit in West Garo Hills and South Garo Hills districts. Even the WGH district is contributing only 9 per cent to the state small-scale industry sector with a declining trend of per worker output. In the district, short-term demand-based factories are maximus in number; followed by the forest and mineral based. The only brighter side of the canvas is the Self-Help Groups (SHGs). Both in terms of absolute number (4,458) and per cent share (47.45%), WGH district tops the list. Animal husbandry-based activities dominate the scene (24%), followed by trade and petty business-based (19.73%), horticulture-based (14.68%), skill-based, viz., weaving, handicraft, etc., (10.81%) and service-based activities (9.31), in 2008 (ibid.).

The Census statistics also show a low rate of work participation in Tura town (27.86) in 2001. Though participation in work is high among the males of all ages, but only 15 per cent of the females had participated at least one day in the previous year (Table 8). The fact that 97 per cent main workers were engaged in works other than agricultural activities is also satisfying for Tura to be a statutory town, as per Census 2001.

Table 8
Work participation rate, Tura, 2001

Total Work Participation Rate	27.86
Male Work Participation Rate	40.27
Female Work Participation Rate	14.83
Total Main WPR	25.13
Total Main Other WPR	95.91
Male Main Other WPR	96.77
Female Main Other WPR	93.17

Source: Census of India. 2001. B Series Tables, Meghalaya.

Civic Amenities

There is no sewerage system in any of the urban centres in Meghalaya. In the state only 47.54 per cent urban households have sanitary latrines, whereas 52.46 per cent and others have pit latrines (Tura 45%) and 8.4 per cent have no latrine. A major problem is the absence of adequate drainage system in all the towns. Tura has only 9 per cent closed drains and 34 per cent open drains whereas 57 per cent have no drainage facility linked to their houses. Only Shillong has a centralised waste disposal and treatment facility. In other Municipal Boards like Tura, sweeping of roads and garbage collection are in vogue.

Along with dilapidated roads, besides shortage of residential houses, there is an utter lack of sanitation, water supply and repair of roads in most of the towns of the North-eastern region. Water and sewage disposal is an important area least managed by the local bodies in most of the urban centres of the North-eastern states. Lack of drainage facilities and lack of any policy relating to the recycling of solid wastes and garbage have created an urban chaos in the region.

The transport sector seems to be entirely neglected in most of the urban centres. Further, the difficult topography and concentric form of unplanned settlement growth have aggravated the transport system. In case of Tura, as in many other cases, the main highway runs through the town, resulting in regular conflict between the inter and intra-city vehicles. Traditional bazaars transformed into complex wholesale and retails market areas, jostled together in the CBD, are mostly located in the heart of the city. There are five such traditional weekly *Hat* or bazaars in Tura which are still in existence, and in a slow transformation into a daily and modern market place. The Tura super market, directly related to the genesis of Tura town, adjacent to the traditional bazaar is posing a growing problem in the already congested heart of the town.

Tura town, compared to Shillong, has never been given any perceptible importance and impetus to be a tourist destination. In spite of being treasured with the bio-diversity in the forests, hills, fruits, caves, tribal festivals like Wangala, etc., perhaps due to the hurdles of transport, disease prevalence, lack of planning and investment, Tura has yet to get a proper launching pad for tourism industry. It is unfortunate to observe that there is no tourism office at Tura and even the Forest Department has no visible promotional efforts.

In the Tura Master Plan, already accepted by the state government, the present municipal area of 18.32 sq km is proposed to be increased to 39.16 sq km by including ten villages, including Danakgre, Badagongre, Agilanggre, Doldegre, Bokmagre, Robagre, Dopgre, Walbagre. It is stated in the Plan that the emphasis is to be given to expand conservation areas of existing vegetation and open space, parks and gardens, transport, industry, public services and obviously a good portion for housing. But nothing is said clearly regarding expansion of income opportunities and boosting the entrepreneurship.

Concluding Remarks

The declining rural agricultural economy vis-à-vis per capita rural income, shortfall in foodgrains and growing rural population pushes people to the nearest urban areas in Meghalaya. This is because urban income levels are still higher than that of rural areas and still growing; but without industrial-isation, towns like Tura suffer badly from an unhealthy economy resulting in slum-like conditions. People are forced to choose between weak and declining subsistence agriculture and marketless plantation agriculture or the marginally higher income options in the mal-developed urban economy.

The urban development initiatives are not getting real shape due to the complex and conflicting parallel legal systems of traditional and modern origins. The urban development schemes like JNNURM, Urban Infra-structure Development Scheme for Small and Medium Towns (UIDSSMT), etc., are not being launched unless there is an elected municipal body in Tura. This situation focuses a vital administrative dilemma whether the same old Municipal Act should be in place contradicting the Autonomous District Council Acts or there can be a new amendment to the ADC Act to empower the existing urban local bodies in North-east India to accept and implement such development schemes on their own.

It will not be illogical to deduce that though Tura town had acquired the statutory status of a town some 40 years back, it has failed to emerge as a healthy growing urban area. With its Master Plan on the cards, it is expected that by the next Census there will be another steep growth period for Tura, leaving the dilemma as such. In fact, it is already agreed and explained that urbanisation in a town like Tura is actually a complex process. But from the above discussion, certain areas of highest concern can be stated here for further study and analysis, and for the urban planners and economists to pay some heed:

• Given the Garo Hill Region as a unique eco-cultural and economic zone of the state, a separate comprehensive Master Plan is the need of the day. The town of Tura cannot be treated as an isolated case for development. Unless both the rural and urban economies are taken as an integraced one, the existing crisis of urban development cannot be addressed meaningfully.

• A public consensus needs to be developed for effective adminis-trative reforms which can suitably address both the traditional values and modern development initiatives. The primary emphasis may be given on development of health, education, transport and communication, housing and civic amenities by involving the local people in the development process. This will be a step forward to mitigate the grievances of inequality and disparity and feeling of insecurity among the sons of the soil, who are more participating in separatist movement amounting to the insurgency.

• To reverse the disadvantages of location, tourism may be the main area of focus for Tura town which can play as the gateway to the

Garo Hills other than itself offering a better tourist facility. The nearby Nokrek Biosphere Reserve with unique biodiversity can be offered as a place for eco and ethno-tourism in a controlled situation.

• Through empowerment and orientation of rural artisans and other indigenous skills towards small entrepreneurships, the migrant population can be accommodated in the town as an contributing urbanite than a slum-dweller.

• The fact that border town Baghmara is growing at a faster rate than Tura, as per 2011 Census, further enquiry is to made to understand the relative advantage of the former towards a learning process of development directions.

References

Bahadur, T.K. (2009) *Urbanization in North-East India*. New Delhi: Mittal Publications.

Bareh, Hamlet (2001) *Encyclopaedia of North-East India: Meghalaya*. New Delhi: Mittal Publications.

Barling, Robbins (1963) *Rongsanggri: Family and Kinship in a Garo Village*. Philadelphia: University of Pennsylvania Press.

Census of India (2001) *List of Towns: Assam, Town Directory*. www.censusindia.gov.in/towns/asm_towns.pdf

———. (2011) *Provisional Population Totals*. www.censusindia.net

Chakraborty, M. (2004) *The Famine of 1896–1897 in Bengal*. New Delhi: Orient Blackswan.

Forest Survey of India (1999) *State of Forest Report 1999*. Dehradun: Forest Survey of India.

Government of Meghalaya (2009) *Meghalaya State Development Report*. www.megplanning.gov.in/report.htm

Joshi, Hargovind (2004) *Meghalaya: Past and Present*. New Delhi: Mittal Publications.

North-East Council (NEC) (2001) *North-East India: A Profile*. Shillong: North East Council.

Playfair, Alan (1909/1975) *The Garos*. Guwahati: United Publishers.

Sangma, Milton S. (1981) *History and Culture of the Garos*. New Delhi: Book Today.

Simon, I.M. (ed.) (1996): *Meghalaya District Gazetteer: Garo Hill District*. Shillong: Government of Meghalaya.

Singh, R.L. (2004) *India: A Regional Geography*. Varanasi: National Geographical Society of India.

Taher, M. and P. Ahmed (1998) *Geography of North-East India*. Guwahati: Mani Manik Prakasan. www.tmbonline.in: Official Portal of Tura Municipal Board.

Annexure I

A clipping from the Editorial Page of *The Shillong Times,* dated 7 July 2011:

Municipal elections illegal!
Editor,

The decision of the Government to hold elections in the Municipal Areas declared by the Government is illegal and unconstitutional. The Municipal areas as notified by Meghalaya Government are not actually Municipal areas. The Government notified certain towns and district headquarters as Municipal areas only for the purpose of administration. For instance, the villages of Williamnagar like Kusimkolgre, Kolmesalgre, Ampangdamgre, Do'betkolgre, Denggagiri, Bangonggre and Nokil A'we which are under the A'king Nokmaship and the direct control and administration of the District Council have been illegally declared as Municipal areas by the Government. Villages like Rongreng Baija, Chidekgre and Rangmal Badim also have been declared by the government as Municipal areas but those are actually a State Forest Reserve under the control of the Autonomous District Council.

Likewise the Municipal areas of Baghmara, Resubelpara and Tura are actually the land of A'king Nokmas and under the control of Autonomous District Council. The so-called Municipality Boards are not boards in real sense but can be explained away as town planning committees. And all these are in the Sixth Scheduled areas. Article 243 Z(C) of the Indian Constitution clearly states that Municipality cannot be extended to Scheduled and Tribal Areas. Holding Municipal elections in the above mentioned areas is tantamount to illegal implementation of Part IX-A of the Indian Constitution which deals with Municipality.

Imagine what would happen if we establish an Autonomous District Council for the Delhiites right in the middle of Delhi city. Can there be two systems for a single area?

Article 243 Z(C) also says that state government unilaterally cannot amend any law in regard to the extension of municipalities to the Scheduled and Tribal Areas except the Parliament, by law. The MUA Government is trying to pass Community Participation Bill and hurriedly conduct elections in Garo Hills just to fulfil the terms and conditions of JNNURM scheme. Only after much hue and cry by ordinary people of Garo Hills and various NGOs and traditional institutions of Meghalaya, has the NCP decided to set up a committee to study the controversial Meghalaya Community Participation Bill, which is too little, too late. Just because a Municipal Election is allowed, will Baghmara turn into a miniature version of Shillong (even after 50 years)? The people of Tura,

Williamnagar, Baghmara and Resubelpara strongly protested against the Municipal elections last year and should launch a stronger protest this time too. Accepting Municipality means the surrender of our rights and ownership which is guaranteed under Constitution of India to protect tribals. It is an excuse for Meghalaya Government to say that it had to act on the direction of the High Court based on the petition filed by municipal candidates. If the Government could not conduct elections for Shillong Municipal Board, then why do they want to have the elections only in Garo Hills, that too for Town Planning committees? Does the Government think that the people of Garo Hills can be taken for granted?

Yours, etc.
Wilberth Marak

15

Urban Governance and Planning in Karnataka*

V. ANIL KUMAR

Towns, cities, are turning-points, watersheds of human history. When they first appeared, bringing with them the written word, they opened their door to what we now call *history*.

—Fernand Braudel (1992: 479)

This work is a product of research in progress on district-level urban governance in Karnataka. This is being done with special reference to one town namely Dharwad in northern Karnataka. The research idea came up and the first clues of the research problem were taken from the prior study done on district planning with reference to Tumkur district in Karnataka. In Tumkur, we basically focused upon the rural planning but the problem of urban planning came to our notice in the study and we touched upon the subject in that study (Vaddiraju and Sangita, 2011).

The state of urban governance and planning vis-à-vis district and 'taluk' towns in India is in a deplorable state. The subject is in need of urgent and fresh consideration and thinking. District towns and 'taluk' towns play a crucial role in development. They form the nodal points of the sinews of development process. They are the nerve centres of all development in India so far as majority of ordinary, non-elite people in this country are concerned. Cities and towns are also of civilisational importance. The term *civitas* in Roman refers to city. The term is also historically inextricably linked to citizenship and governance. It was

---

* The revised version of this paper was published by the author in *Economic and Political Weekly*, Vol. XLVIII, No. 2. The original paper is included here with due permission of the journal.

always the cities from which political power flowed and cities have been the centres of political power.

Research Questions

The central question for this study is how the district and small cities are governed. Is the governance process at this level conforming to what is postulated in the Constitution?

How is the planning function taking place? According to the Constitution, the district is the place where all planning – rural and urban – has to be centred and particularly the function of decentralised planning is the responsibility of the urban bodies. Is that happening at all?

The Challenge of Urban Governance

Karnataka is one of the six most urbanised states in the country with 33.98 per cent of urban population (Sivaramakrishnan, Kundu and Singh, 2010). Most district towns in Karnataka are neglected. The bulk of the concentration on urban development and planning goes to Bangalore and Mysore, which are sought to be made into global cities. The other district towns and municipalities are grossly underemphasised in urban planning and development. The many small towns in Karnataka, as our earlier field work in Kolar, Bellary, Davanagere, Chamarajanagar, Bidar and other places shows, are in a state of urban slums. This is not in consonance with constitutional amendments on urban governance. The media and civil society attention too is limited largely to the cities of Bangalore and Mysore. We find attention to small cities only in the local newspapers or local editions of major newspapers. What is happening in Karnataka is clearly a reflection of what Amitabh Kundu called exclusionary urban development (2003; 2011). We will discuss more about this below. Suffice is to say it here that this urbanisation process is not a friendly one to the poor in the larger cities as well as a majority of the poor in the small and medium cities.

What is more glaring in Karnataka is the neglect of North Karnataka in comparison to other parts of Karnataka and therewith the neglect of towns and their populations in Northern Karnataka. This came out so evidently in our field work and interviews with many scholars in Dharwad. Particularly the scholars at the Centre for Multi-Disciplinary Research, Dharwad, informed that at least part of the explanation for the backwardness of Dharwad and other towns in Northern Karnataka stems from the neglect of overall development and conditions in that region. Earlier, many committees were appointed to address the question of regional inequalities in Karnataka, but the recommendations of these committees have not made a significant impact on the region of North Karnataka and its towns and cities.

Exclusionary Urbanisation

Earlier we have mentioned that the nature of urban development in India in general and Karnataka in particular is exclusionary urbanisation as

Amitabh Kundu has noted. The concept of exclusionary urbanisation points to specific features of urbanisation. These are as below:

Cities Becoming Unwelcoming to the Poor Migrants from Rural Areas

One of the main features of exclusionary urbanisation is the phenomenon of the extreme levels of cost of living and lack of employment opportunities for the poor migrants from still smaller towns and rural areas. This is a marked phenomenon of urbanisation in Karnataka. While both the above said aspects of exclusionary urbanisation are true, the most important one is the lack of employment opportunities for the poor in a highly capital intensive development, which is not conducive to the healthy accommodation of newcomers into the city. The prohibitively high cost of living in cities too is a major factor that excludes a vast section of aspirants into the city.

Cities Being Captured by Local Elite

According to Amitabh Kundu, another major feature of exclusionary urbanisation is the elite capture of the cities. The elite of major cities form a highly-influential interest group that favours benefits to its own self from the state. These happen to be the articulate middle class, the business class and the industrial houses that consistently demand better services and conditions at the expense of the poor and newcomers to the city. The frequent demolitions of slums in the name of beautification of the cities, the attempts to privatise basic services in the name of the efficiency gains are some of the features of exclusionary urbanisation that favour the elite at the expense of the local poor or the new entrants. Often privatisation and outsourcing of basic services and the consequent user charges imposed on them happen to be some features that can work against the poor. Another feature of the elite capture is the 'voice'. In urbanisation in India, the voice of the articulate upper class elite is often more prominently heard than that of the poor. The poor are generally not only property or assetless, they are also voiceless.

Urbanisation Being Spatially Skewed Towards Big Cities

Another major feature of exclusionary urbanisation process in our country is the spatially skewed nature of this process. Big cities as I have already mentioned above are favoured. Bangalore is highly favoured over Bidar. Mysore is highly favoured over Chamaraja Nagar; and this is not limited to Karnataka alone. The small cities and towns are losers in this phenomenon unless and until they are saved through deliberate interventions. This point is of special importance to this paper as it deals with exclusion of small cities and towns in the globalisation-led development process. Globalisation favours big cities. That there is concentration of all attention by the state and capital on the big cities is innate to the logic of globalisation. Following the tendency for capital to spatially also to concentrate, the state provides and develops those cities where the capital and its managers are at ease. All amenities and services and facilities are provided in such places so that more and more capital can be attracted to these places. And in the process, an attempt is to create 'global cities' with global standards of living for a few in the country while majority areas, including towns and cities of the rest of the country, are neglected. The argument of economies of scale comes handy to legitimise this process of concentrated and distorted development process. The urbanisation process thus is not spatially distributed and decentralised to incorporate all the cities, including the small cities, but is limited to only a few mega cities.

Methodology

In the context of the above framework, the attempt here is to conduct a study with reference to a specific town, Dharwad in northern Karnataka. Dharwad is on the Bangalore-Pune Highway and is a link, in many ways than one, between Karnataka and Maharashtra states of India. Dharwad in many respects is a remarkable city. It is supposed to be the gateway to the hilly region of the state (*malnad*), connecting the hilly region to the plains region (*bayalu seeme*) in Karnataka.

We intend also to study one 'taluk' town along with the district town. We intend to study particularly Navalgund 'taluk' of Dharwad district with special reference to its rural linkages. The inspiration for these ideas comes from the importance to study the linkages between urban and rural areas in the development process. Precursors to this idea are found in development literature but Marxist historians have also argued with regard to specific importance of towns as radiators of capitalism. This debate has taken place between historians on the transition from feudalism to capitalism in Europe. The two poles of these debates were held by competing stand points of Maurice Dobb and Paul Sweezy. Many other historians joined the debate (Hilton, 1978).

The major methods used in this study are review of secondary data, interviews with officials at district level, interviews with key informants in the city and field observation. As part of the secondary documents, we have included writings by scholars and documents on urban governance. As part of the interviews with officials, we have interviewed officials in the urban government cell in the Deputy Commissioner's office, the Chief Planning Officer and other officials. We have also interviewed officials pertaining to planning in the Zilla Panchayat office. As part of the interviews with key informants, we have interviewed scholars in the Centre for Multi-Disciplinary Research, and also scholars at the Institute for Social and Economic Change (ISEC) as part of the feedback made at the ISEC. Library sources at the ISEC and CMDR have been quite helpful. This study is based on primary research and the author has visited the city under study, Dharwad, a number of times. As mentioned above, this is an ongoing research and further visits to Dharwad and 'taluk' town of Navalgund are due. The author hopes to uncover further aspects of the governance, planning and development/marginalisation of small towns once the entire field work is complete.

Urban Governance and Small Cities

This paper deals with urban governance and planning, which is particularly that of small and medium towns/cities. Some of the major problems addressed here are: the implementation of the 74th amendment to the Constitution; the planning function within that and the question of the relationship between the rural areas and urban areas or the rur-urban continuum; also this raises the questions of addressing the needs of the existing population as well as planning for the future; the priority to be given for civic amenities and the question of preserving the distinct identity of the place. We deal with these questions vis-à-vis Dharwad city in particular and Karnataka in general. We attempt to understand the above from the point of view of small cities and towns.

Urban Governance at District Level

The Laws

In Karnataka, the urban governance process comes under two important laws. These are: (a) the Karnataka State Municipalities Act of 1964, and (b) the Karnataka State Municipal Corporation Act of 1976. The 74th Amendment Act comes as an add-on law and most of the urban and municipal governance is carried out under the former two laws. The structure of urban governance in Karnataka is as presented below.

Figure 1
The structure of urban governance in Karnataka

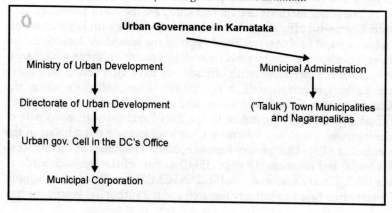

As the above figure shows, there are two streams according to which urban governance is carried out in Karnataka. One, the Ministry of Urban Development and the other, the Department of Municipal Administration. The Ministry of Urban Development governs through the Directorate of Urban Development to which all the urban government cells in the Deputy Commissioner's offices report. The municipal corporations of the state come under this. Whereas the second stream is that of Department of Municipal Administration under which all the town municipalities, which are not corporations, come under. Interesting point, however, is that both the streams only pay a token attention to the 74th Constitutional Amendment. The process happens largely in terms of bureaucracy and not much political representation of the citizens happens or matters in either case.

Urban Planning at District Level

District planning in Karnataka, and for that matter in any Indian state, is supposed to happen via the urban bodies. It is not the rural local bodies such as the Zila Parishad currently but the urban local bodies which are supposed to perform the planning function. The planning function for the district is situated in the 74th amendment and not in the 73rd amendment to the Constitution. The latter is specifically pertained only to the rural areas. In the light of this constitutional division of responsibilities, it would be interesting to see the reality on the ground.

It is a part of political mystery to understand as to why the District Planning Committee (DPC) and the planning function for the district are envisaged in the 74th Constitutional Amendment. The District Planning Committee is supposed to plan for the entire district and perform the major functions of integration of urban and rural plans and conduct all planning related to the governmental schemes not only in rural and urban areas, but also supposed to perform the function of planning for the entire district – rural and urban parts together – according to the resources, opportunities and vision that the conditions can allow to be developed. The DPC is supposed to be an elected body from both urban and rural areas and is also envisaged to meet regularly and coordinate the planning process. Though the DPC has no decision-making authority, it has the major function of advising and approving all the planning process at the district level. All this is important to say here because most of the small and medium cities and towns in the country are situated at the district or sub-district level. Therefore, urban planning at the district level is synonymous also with the planning for small and medium towns and cities. It is not only the planning function in India but the entire governance process of small and medium towns that is supposed to be carried out from the district offices. In this context, it would be interesting to examine as to how these processes are operating at the district level. The megapolises in the country are replete with their own organisations to govern and plan for them. It is the small and medium towns in the country whose condition is inextricably linked to the district planning.

Some Issues of Concern

Given the above scheme of things, it would be interesting to see as to what is taking place in reality in Karnataka. Often the process of district planning in general and urban planning in particular are not happening in an ideal manner. Some of the features of the existing urban planning process at the district level in Karnataka are as below:

The urban cell in the Deputy Commissioner's office conducts all urban planning for the district. In almost all the districts of Karnataka, there is no separate office for urban governance and urban planning. The urban governance process is looked after by the Deputy Commissioner's office. There is often a small section in Deputy Commissioner's office which looks after all the district's urban affairs. This section is led by an officer of the rank of 'tehsildar' and is responsible for urban governance as well as urban planning. This is despite the fact that there is often great need for urban planning in each district. This office reports directly to the Deputy Commissioner without any accountability to either the DPC or to the elected urban representatives. What in reality exists is often a small cell in the DC's office which cannot even be called an urban governance office. This is too ill-equipped in terms of expertise, staff and scope to meet the demands of urban governance and urban planning. Often urban governance and planning at district level not only involve the district town but also numerous small towns, which are 'taluk' towns or other municipal areas. Sometimes these towns are fast growing or most of the times badly in need of governance, civic amenities and planning. We can hardly expect the urban cell in any district of Karnataka to meet these needs.

To make matters worse, the bureaucracy stifles even the work of what there is. The urban governance cell in the collectorate as mentioned above is accountable only to the Deputy Commissioner and reports directly to him. The office is not answerable to any of the elected representatives. Consequently, this urban cell also does not see itself as a part of the district planning process. This leads to non-cooperation by the cell with the District Planning Committee. The Chief Planning Officers that we met in Karnataka often felt that the urban cells in the office of the Deputy Commissioner do not share information and data or urban plans in time. This is only aggravated with the situation that the plans are integrated and consolidated in the actual process in the Zilla Parishad whose function is to plan for rural areas. Consequently, often the rural plans, at least in Karnataka, are prepared ahead of the urban plans and when the CPO asks for the urban plans from the urban planning office, the same are not supplied. The urban planning cells at the district level often have some reluctance to participate in the planning process because the planning process is done by the DPC with elected members in it, whereas the urban cell is only accountable to higher levels of bureaucracy.

The net result of the above processes is that often the district plans are prepared either without the urban component, or the integration of rural with urban plans does not happen. And, this problem is aggravated with the fundamental fact that the Zilla Panchayat/Parishad basically remains as rural panchayat/parishad than something that reflects plans both for rural and urban areas of a district. In Karnataka, traditionally, rural decentralisation has received considerable attention and focus. Therewith the rural planning process as well as the offices concerning the rural governance are strengthened, but the same has not happened with urban local governance or planning. There is a need to recognise and emphasise on this dimension while continuing with the efforts on rural planning.

This is an important aspect to consider as to why in any district the Zilla Panchayat should only be the Zilla Rural Panchayat. There is a renewed need to consider the importance of urban local government and urban planning at the district level on par with the rural government and planning. The need for this is only going to increase rather than decrease in the future; the earlier policy makers realise the slum-like circumstances our urban areas will take. This is not only true for Karnataka but for the country and all the states.

Dharwad City

Dharwad is a city at least with 900 years of history. Recorded history of the city is existent from before the times of Vijaya Nagara Empire. There are many legends, to the name of Dharwad as well. Besides these legends, the most important aspect is that Dharwad is geographically situated in northern Karnataka with the hilly region of the state starting from Dharwad. Therefore, Dharwad is also called the gateway to Western Ghats. Also, it is an important point that the city is the mid-point between Bangalore and Pune and is situated on the Bangalore-Pune highway and as such reflects the influences of both.

Dharwad is a city with great cultural and literary prominence. Famous vocalists of Hindustani Classical music, Pandit Bhimsen Joshi, Gangubai Hangal, Kumar Gandharva, Mallikarjun Mansoor hail from this district. The city even today has a very lively tradition of hosting classical music concerts and festivals. Besides this, the district and the city have also produced many literary giants of Kannnada language. A number of them have been decorated with the Gnanapeeth Awards. When we visit the city we are also told that city's literary giants are not only awarded honours but they also are members on the committees that award honours such as Gnanapeeth Award. For a small district and district town, what is mentioned above is a great achievement and that is what makes this city remarkable in many ways.

Besides being a cultural centre, Dharwad is also a major educational centre of Northern Karnataka. Dharwad is home to Karnatak University, a university of agricultural sciences and a number of reputed colleges and institutions of higher education. Many students and youths from the rest of Northern Karnataka come to Dharwad in search of education and higher learning. Dharwad is governed by a municipal corporation and population of the twin cities of Hubli-Dharwad is 13 lakhs. Dharwad's population alone is around 7 lakhs.

Some Problems of the City

Drinking Water

The basic civic amenities of drinking water and sanitation are major problems in Dharwad. The supply of drinking water is not on 24x7 basis. Some wards receive water on 24x7 basis but only on experimental basis; this is as part of an ongoing World Bank project on drinking water in the city. Otherwise, the city faces severe shortage of drinking water. A majority of wards only receive water once in three to four days and if it is summer season, they get water once in seven days. There are plans for the city that if the World Bank Project succeeds, the entire city may be provided water on 24x7 basis. But this is still only a dream for most of the residents in the city.

Sanitation

Dharwad has an open drainage system. Majority areas of the city, including the newly-built expanding areas, have only to rely on an open drainage system. Actually there are two parts of the city. One part of the city built during the colonial time and with underground drainage system, and the second part of the city that developed later and has no underground drainage. Since the city built during the colonial time is now only a small part of the city, majority areas of the city do not have underground drainage. This leads to many problems. Often there is no regular cleaning of the overground drainage, consequently this results in very poorly maintained hygiene, with pigs, stray dogs and mosquitoes all around. This further leads to many other diseases and health problems. The most vulnerable areas in this regard are the ones where the poorer populations live. These are even worse than the rest of the city. Plans exist to build an underground system but it may take at least ten or more years. A picture shown here speaks volumes about the state of affairs of sanitation and drainage in Dharwad city.

Picture 1

STINK AND FILTH: Overflowing dustbins in Heggeri Maruti Nagar attract stray pigs and dogs

The above described conditions bring to light the question of governance of the small cities and towns in the country. These even include towns with exceptional literary and cultural prominence. Most of these small cities are in transition and are growing at varying pace and these lack any planning and attention. There are serious questions to be asked as to where do we go so far as the governance and planning of these towns is concerned. Serious issues emerge regarding the uncertain future of these small cities and towns that are facing neglect and apathy.

What Citizens of Dharwad Say?

In the above context, it would be interesting to know as to what the citizens of Dharwad have to say on their urban situation. A random sample of letters to the *Times of India* have the following contents:
• Drain overflowing
• Clean open sites
• Unbearable stink
• Garbage piles up
• Provide interior roads

These are some of the major problems that our small cities and towns are confronted with. The first aspect of the problem is the unplanned and haphazard nature of whatever growth that is taking place. The expansion of small cities is happening without any thought being given to it. This growth process has often little connection with the district planning process. The second most important problem is that the question of civic amenities to the growing urbanisation process is completely ignored in these small towns and cities. The third problem is that the specificities of these cities are being neglected. A city like Dharwad requires better transport, concert halls, reading places, libraries and so on, in addition to drinking water and sanitation. We could not find such amenities in any of the small towns where we have done field work in Karnataka. The fourth one of the important aspects is that the links of the small towns and cities with their hinterlands are lost sight of, in the process. Finally, and because of the factors mentioned above and their combinations often, there is little or no perceivable governance and planning.

Conclusion

Finally can we generalise the Dharwad condition? Though the city of Dharwad is exceptional in terms of its cultural and literary achievements, the poor state of most district towns in Karnataka is the same. We have earlier witnessed the same conditions in Bellary, Chamarajanagar, Bidar, Davanagere, Kolar, and Tumkur and recently in Haveri. All these are district towns. Why are these in the condition described above? In fact, in Karnataka, according to the State Institute of Urban Development (SIUD, Mysore), the cities of Dharwad and Udupi in Karnataka are better governed and better planned than most of other small cities and towns in the state. This shows amply what the situation in other small cities would be. The reasons for most of this state of affairs can be traced to what Kundu called 'exclusionary urbanisation' process in the country. The big cities and large urban agglomerations such as Bangalore and Mysore are favoured over small cities and towns. The governance and planning of the latter languishes without being noticed. Indeed Karnataka has a rich history of decentralisation and local government reforms. But most of these are related to Panchayati Raj institutions and rural areas. Now, the state has to concentrate on urban areas, governance and planning of small towns. The condition of Dharwad reflects the condition of small towns in other contiguous states too. Since we began this paper with a quotation from Braudel, we also end with what Braudel says about small cities and towns in historical process: '... urban history has to be extended to cover these small communities, for little towns as Spengler observed, eventually 'conquer' the surrounding countryside, penetrating it with 'urban consciousness', meanwhile being themselves devoured and subordinated by agglomerations more populous and more active. Such towns are thus caught up into urban systems orbiting regularly round some sun-city' (Braudel, 1992: 482).

References

Bhagat, B.R. (2011) 'Emerging Pattern of Urbanisation in India'. *Economic and Political Weekly*. Vol. XLVI, No. 34, 20 August, pp. 10–12.

Bhattacharya, Prabir B. (2002) 'Urbanisation in Developing Countries'. *Economic and Political Weekly*. Vol. XXXVII, No. 41, 12 October, pp. 4219–28.

Braudel, Fernand (1992) 'Towns and Cities'. In *Civilization and Capitalism, 15th–18th Century: The Structures of Everyday Life, The Limits of the Possible*. Berkeley: University of California Press, pp. 479–558.

Gupta, Naryani (2004) 'The Indian City'. In Veena Das (ed.). *Oxford Handbook of Indian Sociology*. New Delhi: Oxford University Press, pp. 142–55.

Hilton, Rodney (ed.) (1978) *Transition from Feudalism to Capitalism*. London: Verso.

Kundu, Amitabh (2003) 'Urbanisation and Urban Governance: Search for a Perspective beyond Neo-Liberalism'. *Economic and Political Weekly*. 19 July, pp. 3079–87.

———. (2011) 'Politics and Economics of Urban Growth'. *Economic and Political Weekly*. Vol. XLVI, No. 20, 14 May, pp. 10–12.

Nandy, Raj (1985) 'Introduction and Background to the Study'. *Developing Small and Medium Towns: An Evaluation of Administrative Machinery in a Medium-Sized Town*. New Delhi: Indian Institute of Public Administration, pp. 49–55.

Prasad, Lalta (1985) 'Introduction'. *The Growth of a Small Town: A Sociological Study of Ballia*. New Delhi: Concept Publishers.

Shaw, Annapurna (1999) 'Emerging Patterns of Urban Growth in India'. *Economic and Political Weekly*. Vol. XXXIV, Nos. 16&17, pp. 969–78.

Sivaramakrishnan, K.C., Amitabh Kundu and B.N. Singh (2010) *Oxford Handbook of Urbanization in India*. New Delhi: OUP.

The Times of India (Bangalore), Monday, 25 July 2011, Hubli/Dharwad/Belagaum section.

Vaddiraju, Anil Kumar and Satyanarayana Sangita (2011) *Decentralised Governance and Planning in Karnataka, India*. Newcastle upon Tyne: Cambridge Scholars Publishing.

16

Munger

A Bazaar Town in Decline

SHEEMA FATIMA

Why a Bazaar Town

Most of the literature available and research work carried out in the field of urban studies has been negligible in the state of Bihar. In the past, very little has been done to chronicle the many important British-period towns within the state, like Bhagalpur, Munger, Motihari and West Champaran, which held l importance. Most of the work has been done on Patna city, which is also the capital, and Gaya, which being a Buddhist religious destination has its own relevance.

This paper attempts to make insights into the town of Munger,[1] which has historically been a significant district town along River Ganga and became particularly relevant to the Britishers. The town in the past served as a strategic centre for political, economic and geographical activities in the region. And yet, a place which thrived for decades has no resemblance to its past. A scenario where it would have carried forward its legacy and material importance to the present time, but on the contrary what we have today is a stagnated, sleepy town and a reminiscence of its bygone days. In this interpretation of Munger as a bazaar town, what needs to be seen is whether it reaffirms the fact that most colonial centres were a part of the administrative and economic benefits for the Britishers without creating any strong urban dynamics.

The above proposition should hold true in the case of Munger in many respects which subsequently got exaggerated post-independence, because of poor governance as it did for many other small and medium towns. When we talk about the decline of Munger as a bazaar town, we do not talk about it being a small town, instead like any other small and medium towns, its population has grown exponentially and the town physically, resulting in congestion, crowding and poor living standards.

Rather, the focus is on the human and social aspect of urbanism; in terms of the quality of life it provides, particularly in comparison to what it possibly could because of the potential it carries. The same or similar kind of opportunities would show a different type of urban growth pattern. Therefore, in many aspects, Munger town also symbolises the urbanisation process in the state of Bihar. The paper makes an attempt to understand the possible causes of stagnation of Munger town and further use it as a metaphor to reflect on the urbanisation process in the state of Bihar.

Munger: Its Origin and History

The history of Monghyr is replete with stories of battles and wars. It starts with the Mahabharata that records the encounter of Bhim with the ruler of Modagiri, and concludes with the defeat of Mir Kasim in 1763 at the hands of East India Company. In between, it saw the rebellions, sieges and battles fought between Pala Kings, Turks, Mughals, Afghans, Marathas and English.

Pre-historic Time

The territory included within the district of Monghyr formed part of the Madhya-desa or 'Midland' of the first Aryan settlers. It has also been identified with Mod-Giri, a place mentioned in the Mahabharata, which was the capital of a kingdom in Eastern India near Vanga and Tamralipta (O'malley, 1926). Traditionally, it is stated that the foundation of the town was laid by Chandra Gupta, after whom it was called Guptagarh, a name which has been found inscribed on the stones of Kastarnighat near the fort.

However, the first historical account of the district appears in the travels of Hiuen Tsiang, who visited this area towards the close of the first half of the 7th century A.D. and observed: The country is regularly cultivated and rich in producing flowers and fruit being abundant, the climate is agreeable and manners of the people simple and honest. There are 10 Buddhist monasteries with about 4,000 priests and a few Brahminical temples occupied by various sectaries (Imperial Gazetteer of India, 1931).

Medieval Era

During the medieval era, it changed hands as did the rest of the country under different rulers and kings. In the 9th century A.D., Monghyr conceded under the Pala kings' rule. They ruled till the middle of the 11th century where Rampala, a frustrated and helpless Pala king, drowned himself in the Ganga at Monghyr in 1130 A.D. (Kapoor, 2002).

Then followed Bakhtiyar Khilji, who in 1195 invaded and conquered Bihar. He made Monghyr the second-most important town in south Bihar after Patna under his rule. Later, Babar invaded Bihar in about 1530 and Monghyr became the headquarters of the Bihar army. In 1533–34, Sher Shah Suri conquered Monghyr and it remained under his rule till Bihar was conquered by Akbar in about 1563, thus bringing it under Mughal Empire (O'malley, 1926). In fact, Sher Shah loved Monghyr because of his early success here which later paved his way to the throne of Delhi. Monghyr was a crucial territory and provided the rulers with a strategic geographical location along the Ganga river after Patna. It helped the subsequent rulers to have a military headquarters right before the territory of Bengal started up in the east. Throughout Muslim period, the fortune of Monghyr oscillated between the power of the Delhi kings and the prowess of the Bengal sultans and for a brief period it went to the Sharqis of Jaunpur (Kapoor, 2002).

Mughal Era

During the early Mughal period, we get a few references to the district in the famous book *Ain-i-Akbari*, according to which Sarkar Monghyr consisted of 31 Mahals or Parganas. After 1590, when Akbar established his supremacy over the Afghan chiefs of Bengal, Monghyr was for a long period the headquarters of his general, Todar Mall; and it also figures prominently during the rebellion of Sultan Shuja against his brother, Aurangzeb. The territory hence featured prominently for the Mughal rulers, and changed hands right from the time of Babar, who invaded in 1530, till we last saw the presence of Mughal rule under Aurangzeb. Soon after the disintegration of Mughal Empire, Monghyr had to witness new changes. Bihar came to be joined with the Suba of Bengal, which had become independent of Delhi. Later, we see its reference when the Maratha expeditionary Balaji Maratha entered Bihar and advancing through Tekari, Gaya, Manpur, reached Monghyr while travelling towards Bengal (O'malley, 1926).

The second significant phase for the history of Monghyr starts from 1762 onwards, when Mir Kasim, the Nawab of Bengal, chose Monghyr as his capital instead of Murshidabad in Bengal. Mir Kasim was attracted to this town due to the Ganga. It was like a hill station, on its three sides were mountains and the other side was Ganges; therefore strategically secure and important. He shifted base from Murshidábád to Monghyr, a strong position of the Ganges, and commanded the only means of communication with the west. There he proceeded to organise an army, drilled and equipped after European models. Mir Kasim took with him all his effects, his elephants, horses and treasures, comprising cash and jewelleries of the harem, and even the gold and silver decorations of the Imambara, amounting to several lakhs in value, and bade farewell to the country of Bengal. At Monghyr he remodelled his army on European lines (Imperial Gazetteer of India, 1931). From here he wanted to keep an eye on the increasing influence of East India Company, who were on an expedition to expand their base.

Mir Kasim, once settled in the town, established an arsenal for the manufacture of fire-arms and it is from this time that Monghyr can trace back its importance for the manufacture of guns. Its craft was well praised in Britain, though later it lost its importance when they started importing guns and pistols from Britain, thereby affecting the local manufacture. Two Dutch travellers De Graafe and Oasterhoff, who visited Monghyr in 1670, wrote: The town stands upon an ascent, the river bank by it being 8 or 10 yards high, the brick wall by the river side at the south end of Monghyr was about 5 yards high and 20 yards long with a little tower at each end and each wall is a fortification to place the gun on it (O'malley, 1926). The Dutch travellers give a vivid account of the town and how well placed was its fort along the mighty River Ganga, which kept on attracting rulers to its shoreline.

British Period

Monghyr was a place of considerable importance since the earliest days of the British occupation of Bengal although it did not become a civil station until 1812 and consequently, the old fort was occupied by the regiment of East India Company. It consisted of two distinct portions – the fort, within which were situated the public offices and residence of the Europeans; and the native town, stretching away from the former eastward and southward along the river. With the arrival of East India Company, the railways followed soon to the town, thereafter making it far more favourably situated for the purpose of trade now both by rail and river; formerly the trade was carried exclusively by river, but soon a greater part was diverted to the Railways. It was connected by a short branch with the loop line of the East Indian Railway and by a steam ferry with the railway system on the north of the Ganges. The Ganga's breeze and climate even brought

Picture 1
A vast view of Monghyr

Source: http://www.bl.uk/onlinegallery, retrieved on 5 December, 2011.

renowned poet and writer Rabindranath Tagore, who wrote portions of his famous book *Gitanjali* staying at his hill residence at Pir Pahari Mountain. Joseph Hooker speaks of Monghyr, 'By far the prettiest town, Munger was celebrated for its iron manufacture, especially of muskets, in which respect it is the Burmingham of Bengal.' Stone work, silver works were exemplary and were exempted from heavy duty transit levied on inland trade during those days. Particularly after the battle of Plassey, the European servants of the Company began to trade extensively on their own account and claimed a similar exemption for all goods passing under the Company's flag and covered by Dastak or certificate signed by the Governor or any agent of the factory. Mir Kasim resentfully complained that his source of revenue had been taken away and that his authority was completely disregarded (Imperial Gazetteer of India, 2030).

The earliest record of Monghyr in the collectorate appears to be the letter from the Commissioner of Bhagalpur to the Secretary of the Sadar Board of Revenue at Fort William, dated the 29 May 1850. He wrote: 'It appears from the record that the native town and bazaar of Monghyr have for a long period been considered government property. This though constituting one Mahal (fort), was divided into 13 Tarafs, viz., (1) Bara Bazar, (2) Deochi Bazar, (3) Goddard Bazar, (4) Wellesly Bazar, (5) Munger Bazar, (6) Gorhee Bazar, (7) Batemanganj, (8) Topekhana Bazar, (9) Fanok Bazar, (10) Dalhatta Bazar, (11) Belan Bazar, (12) Rasoolganj, and (13) Begampur' (O'malley, 1926).

Monghyrs' popularity did not translate into progress and development as it continued to be a mere station with a little garrison that had caused a mutiny in 1766. During the early part of 19th century, Monghyr became an invalid station for British soldiers. The subsequent history of the district is uneventful as with the extension of the British dominions in other parts of the country, the town of Monghyr ceased to be an important frontier post. There was no arsenal, no regular garrison was kept and no attempt was made to bring the fortification up-to-date. Monghyr, however, was still important for its fine situation and salubrious air and was used as a sanatorium for the British troops; so great a resort that it was the journey up the Ganga followed by a stay was regarded of as healthy as a sea voyage (O'malley, 1926).

Reading the Bazaar Town

When we look at Munger as a bazaar town, we do not limit ourselves just at the economy of the town but at the whole system of bazaar (Anand, 2006). The writer talks about the bazaar town not in isolation but as microcosms containing a representational array of the elements comprising a regional environment. Markets provide a compressed display of an area's economy, technology and society – in brief, of the local way of life. Studies of markets in India continue to draw their conceptual sustenance from the central place theory, which highlights markets as nodes in a complex pattern of economic and social exchanges organised hierarchically as well as by factors like economy, geography, transportation, political and administration. These factors for Monghyr to command a central place urban node were well in place during the British and the reason for their presence in town.

The bazaar town had very narrow lanes, widely known as *sakri gali*. Besides the wheels of public transport in the town were tom-toms, which were commonly used. While the upper class passengers liked to travel in *baghis*, automobiles were only owned by the White Sahibs and some big *zamindars, rajas* and *nawabs* who were rarely seen on the roads. But, the fate of Monghyr that definitely had a great change was after its reconstruction due to the devastating earthquake of 1934, which had virtually demolished the buildings and houses of the city and affected even the oldest fort known as Munger Qila. It was actually after the redesigning of the city by the English administrators that it acquired the proper shape of a town, having been divided into *chowks* and cross-roads with roads interlinking each part of it. All the administrative houses were mostly located within the fort area. 'The native town is irregular, and in many parts extremely picturesque, several of the bazaars stretching in long lines beneath the umbrageous shelter of magnificent groves. At the south and eastern gates of the fort there are streets, composed of brick houses, sufficiently wide for carriage to pass. But the remainder consists of scattered dwellings, chiefly built of mud' (Roberts, 1836). This passage from Emma's travelogue portrays a vivid picture of a vibrant bazaar town in Monghyr, where the Britishers had a strong presence living mostly within the fort area and the indigenous population lived in mud houses and in a not-so-planned manner.

The Ganges divided the district into two portions. The northern, intersected by the Bur-Gandak and Tiljugâ, two important tributaries of the Ganges, was liable to inundation during the rainy season, and was a rich flat, wheat and rice cultivating land, supporting a large population. A considerable area, immediately bordering the banks of the great rivers, is devoted to permanent pasture. Immense quantities of buffaloes are sent every hot season to graze on these marshy prairies; and the ghee, or clarified butter, made from their milk forms an important article of export to Calcutta. To the south of the Ganges the country is dry, much less fertile, and broken up by fragmentary ridges. The soil consists of quartz, mixed in varying proportions with mica. Ranges of hills intersect this part of the district, and in the extreme south form conical peaks, densely covered with jungle, but of no great height (Old Indian, 1866).

Monghyr Bazaar was the main centre for many adjacent villages and smaller *kasba* like Tarapur, Surajghara, Bariyarpur and Kharagpur. Its centrality was primarily because of the presence of major rail, road, and ferry-steamer connections. The Ganges intersected the district from west to east for 70 miles and was navigable at all seasons by river streamers and the largest country boats, and saw the presence of a considerable amount of river traffic. Villagers brought their agriculture produce from adjacent villages to Monghyr market and they were exported further on to big markets in Calcutta. The streamers of India general and river steam navigation companies conveyed goods and passengers between Calcutta and Patna. Even boat steamers were also equally common for transporting passenger and consumer goods. Out of 10,000 boatmen who pass every year by a certain tower of the castle of Monghyr (Imperial Gazetteer of India, 1931).

Market and Economy of the Bazaar Town

Monghyr had vast tracts of land under agricultural cultivation, but the most important manufacture, however, was that of indigo, conducted by means of European capital and under European supervision. The total area under indigo is estimated at about 10,000 acres with an average out-turn of 2,900 ewes of dye. The Governor General passed Monghyr the prosperity of which district of unrivalled fertility is greatly promoted by the indigo cultivation and its landscape being highly improved by the appearance of the commodious mansions of the planters which with they are studded. At Monghyr the Governor General and suite embarked on board the Hon. Company's steamer Hoogly which was there waiting for his lordship, and dropped down the Ganges coming through the Sunderbans to Calcutta in seven days (Asiatic Journal, 1830).

The market was very active particularly along the River Ganges, it has been mentioned repeatedly by the traveller writers who passed Monghyr town on their way to Bengal. In his *Narratives of a Journey through the Upper Province of India from Calcutta to Bombay, 1824–25*, the author speaks about the town in detail: 'The ghat offered a scene of bustle and vivacity which I by no means expected. There were so many budgerows and pulwars that we had considerable difficulty to find a mooring-place for our boat, and as we approached the shore we were beset by a crowd of beggars and artisans who brought for sale. Guns, knives, and other hardware as also many articles of upholstery and toys were for sale. They looked extremely neat but as I meant to buy none, I woult not raise expectation by examining them' (Heber, 1827). He further goes on to say, 'The district is very fertile and most articles of production cheap. The people are quiet and industrious, and the offence which come before the magistrate both in number and character for less, and lessatrocious, than case either in Bengal or Hindostan. The peasant are more prosperous than in either, which may of itself account for their decency of conduct. They get three crops in succession every year from the same lands, beginning with Indian corn then sowing rice, between which, when it is grown to a certain height, they dibble in pulse, which rises to maturity after the rice is reaped' (Heber, 1827). In an account, written by Emma Roberts in her travelogue *Scenes and Characteristic of Hindostan* to describe about the people and their livelihood, she says,

'Upon the arrival of a budgerow at Monghyr, the native vendors of almost innumerable commodities repair to the waterside in crowds, establishing a sort of fair upon the spot. And both the ghaut, when vessels are passing up and down, and the bazaars, present a very lively scene, from the variety of the commodities and the gay costumes of the people. Agriculture as well as manufactures flourishes in the neighborhood of Monghyr, grain of all kinds, sugar and indigo are in great abundance and the country is celebrated for opium' (Roberts, 1836).

'The town comprises of sixteen markets, scattered over a space a mile and a half long from north to south and a mile wide. The houses are generally small; they have sloping roofs of red tiles, and gables ornamented with earthen ware figures. It is a thriving place, having a great number of manufactories and shops for the fabrication and sale of hardware and fire arms' (Old Indian, 1866). Bekapur was famous for goldsmiths and excellent blacksmith craftsmanship and Gola bazaar had a big grain market. Suturkhana had a camel market and a thriving bird market crowded with main-shiqaris (bird catchers). The art of inlaying sword-hilts and other articles with gold and silver gave employment to many. Minor industries included weaving, dyeing, cabinet-making, boot-making, soap-boiling, and pottery. The principal exports, sent to Calcutta both by rail and river, were oil-seeds, wheat, rice, indigo, gram and pulse, hides, and tobacco; and the chief imports consist of European piece goods, salt, and sugar. When the Ganges is in flood, carriage by boat is preferred; but the native merchants are always ready to use the railway when immediate dispatch becomes of importance. Trade is chiefly in the hands of immigrants from lower Bengal and Musaalmans who monopolise the export hides.

Industries included the manufacture of firearms, swords and ebony work. During World War I, Monghyr gun manufacturing was prominent and production of cartridge was undertaken on a large scale. Cannons were made at Topkhana Bazar but subsequently they shifted to making guns like ML Guns and capped gun. Till the shifting of the factories to the jail campus, it was manufactured at Chuabag and Kassim Bazar. Britishers banned the use of guns by private persons by enforcing Act 18 in 1841, Act 30 in 1854. Its manufacture was then also banned by Act 28 of 1857, then up to 1860 by Act 31 of 1860. In 1879, New Arms Act came into existence on 6 March 1879 and provisions were made for the manufacture of guns under licences scheme. During the First World War, the Munger gun manufacturing again came into prominence and production of cartridge gun was also developed. Munger was perhaps the only city in India where gun manufacturing took the shape of a cottage industry and became a popular profession.

Later skills of the same craftsmanship led to the establishment of Jamalpur workshop, which started on 8 February 1862. It was the largest and oldest locomotive repair workshop. British chose this place due to availability of skilled workers who were descendents of acclaimed

Picture 2
Native workmen at Jamalpur

gun-makers and fabricators of weapons for Nawab of Bengal Mir Kasim. Jamalpur has the distinction of manufacturing locomotives well before the Chittaranjan Locomotive Works.

By 1890, the workshop had 3,122 men, which grew to 9,528 by 1906. Since there was virtually no industry in the country, the workshop grew to be totally self-sufficient. It set up the country's first rolling mill in 1879, as well as the railway's first captive powerhouse, which was set up in 1895. The iron foundry was amongst the best in the country and even produced cast iron sleepers; a total of 214 locomotives were built at Jamalpur between 1899 and 1932. With the phasing out of steam locomotive, which produced 600 standard units per month in 1962–63, it declined in late '60s and came to a halt in August 1992.

The other important industry in town was ITC, which started as Peninsular Tobacco Company on 6 November 1907, because of easy availability of tobacco and good connectivity due to River Ganga.

Explaining the Decline, the Colonial Narrative

The question then turns out to be: how did a town, with all its natural assets – one that had long prospered economically and socially – come to be the underdeveloped, stagnant, and unmotivated urban centre that it is today? This decline in the growth and prosperity of Munger needs to be enquired as mentioned in the beginning at two levels. At the very onset, we

Map 1
Municipal ward map of Munger showing the main bazaar (Year 2007–2008)

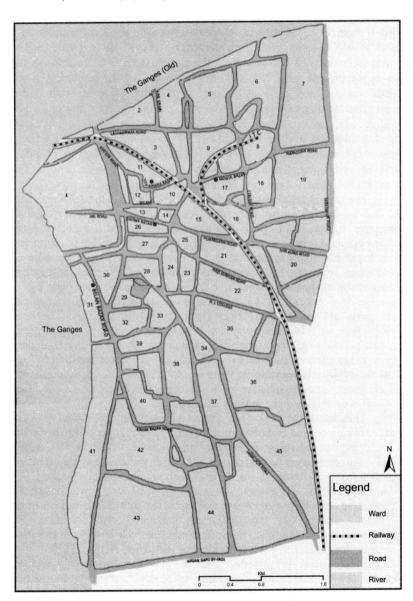

Source: Munger Municipal Nagar Nigam.

need to explore in the real sense how far did the colonial presence influence its growth? And, subsequently, on the role of the post-colonial state of Bihar, and its functioning, particularly in reference to urban development.

The British-controlled economy in India may have been prosperous, but the native economy – developed and run by the local population – was always a lesser one. Such a contrast proved disastrous once the colonial forces were removed from the picture with decolonisation in the mid-1900s (Abdullah, 2002). As referred earlier, by the beginning of the 19th century, Monghyr was no more an important frontier town and it ceased to be of much relevance to the British. The raw materials like indigo, rice, grains, spices were shipped to Calcutta from Monghyr port by big steamers and boats and later by trains. There was no activity towards its value addition. So, there has never been any factory or industrial unit for agriculture-based processing unit or production centres. The two main factories were the ITC and the railways.

The Jamalpur railways was built by the colonisers in such a way that it was far and away from the main town of Monghyr; it served their purpose of connectivity but at the same time kept it disconnected. Most of the employers were British and Europeans and the local population was employed for labour work. Employees' colonies and bungalows were far and away from the local population. There was a special railway line connecting the Jamalpur station with the Munger fort put in place by the East India Company. It was like the dual city with its indigenous city alongside but physically distinct from the British annexes. The same stood true for ITC factory and the town of Monghyr. The cigarette manufacturing factory is an island of its own, their raw material came from other parts of the country and only the labourers required to keep the factory machines running were employed from the local population. Both these factories till date have not been able to create any ancillary factories or employment in their vicinity.

Their economy was broken down because these large towns were also primarily processing and offloading centres, to supply goods further away. The symbiotic relationship between large number of handicrafts, service and commerce-based towns, on the one hand, and their small hinterlands of primary production on the other, which was historically evolved, was disrupted and the former were allowed to die or became centres of primary processing and off-loading of raw materials. The immediate impacts of the economic and political transformations associated with colonisation, by definition, constrained societies into dependent relationships so that they were no longer able to sustain themselves (Raza and Habib, 1991).

(The) distortions introduced in the spatial structure of the economy during the colonial period in response to the exploitative requirements of the imperialist rule, how did these distortions condition the process and pattern of urbanisation (Raza and Habib, 1991) but, in many ways these distortions in urbanisation during the colonial time period carried the effect of weak centripetal pulls even centuries later. The colonial set-up was such that it created no value addition in its immediate hinterland, Monghyr town was merely a treasure house of natural resources, which the East India Company harnessed to the best of its capacity. By the early 19th century, the Company became less influential and Crown had become more predominant. Once the centre of power changed and river was no longer the primary source of communication, the presence of the Company started decreasing.

The bazaar town with its diverse natural resources, its strong heritage, and central physical location had the making of an urban centre with multiple functions and of indispensable importance. It grew but did not develop; its growth reflected not the healthy processes of urbanisation but the diseased process of urban accretion (Raza and Habib, 1991). This leads us to reflect at the current situation of Munger town and what kind of urbanisation it is experiencing.

Explaining the Decline, the Post-colonial Narrative

The present town of Munger, whose geographical location was once considered to be of strategic importance, has now proven to be a major impediment in its expansion. Earlier the undivided district of Munger was well connected by road through Khagaria and Begusarai, connecting right up to Guwahati. In 1972 and 1981, the districts of Begusarai and Khagaria respectively were carved out, thus cutting of its main transportation arteries, leaving it handicapped. On the other hand, the plan to connect the town of Munger with a bridge on River Ganga which would further connect it to NH-30 has been on paper since 2000, but the work remains largely incomplete.

The Munger Municipal Council has 42 wards. Of the total population, 39.23 per cent lives in slums and 25 per cent of these slums are on unauthorised lands. The municipality has been able to connect only 57 per cent of its city population with piped water supply. Households largely depend on hand pumps, borewells and dug-up wells. The city has been sanctioned a separate fund of ₹ 47 crore in the 12th Five-Year Plan for water facilities and sanitation, which has not moved beyond the Detailed Project Report (DPR). The city has no sewerage system and septic tank/pit are the main form of sanitary waste disposal. The city still has manual scavengers who are gradually being employed by the municipality and efforts are being made to rehabilitate them (DPR, 2011).

As discussed earlier, the population size has been increasing but this growth does not get reflected in the city's economy. Ganga, which acted as a communication artery carrying immense business for the British, lost its glory with the advancement of railways and road system. Eventually the Ganga river also started shrinking, leading to closure of the big steamers in later part of 1990s. Neither the state governments nor the district administration could optimise on its past glory for economic or tourist purposes. Thus, these 'antiquated means of transportation' could never be replaced and rather left Munger town cut off from the growth process. By late 1990s, the law and order situation became unfriendly for the local business and eventually led to outmigration of people to Patna, Delhi and other parts of the country.

At the same time, the colonial rule left the city with many instances on the positive side too, reflected in its public amenities like Town Hall, hospital, and other infrastructure. These public amenities dot our small towns but today they are symbols of negligence. The state and local administration have not been able to maintain such infrastructure and in the last 10–15 years, even the local business class which looked after the upkeep of the town's bazaar and *chowks* has migrated out, leaving it in derelict condition.

Like many other Indian small and medium towns, Munger municipality lacks institutional set-up, with most of the posts being vacant and almost negligible capacity building at municipal and ward levels. The employees in the municipality are mostly untrained for the work they are expected to perform as implementing officers. As expressed in personal interviews with the municipal employees, in many cases they have implemented the government urban area related projects in the wrong way or are not able to understand the scope of the work itself. Munger was sanctioned the Integrated Development of Small and Medium Towns (IDSMT) project in 2008–09, but because of lack of permanent officials in the municipality, it remained incomplete and in the case of Swarna Jayanti Shahari Rozgar Yojana (SJSRY), they were not able to understand the scope of work, leading to its non-implementation. In most of the cases, under the above situation, by the time the programmes are somehow finally implemented, orders for new programmes stream in, leaving them with more confusion.

Thus, even the post-colonial state shares equal responsibility for the conditions in which our small towns are. They were no doubt exploited under the garb of colonialism but the state in post-colonial period has left these towns neglected, paying no attention to reviving their potentialities.

Munger as a Representation of the Urbanisation Process in Bihar

Historically, those who have been most subject to *zamindari* rule are economically the least developed today (Mathew and Moore, 2011). The classical political economy and Marxian political economy view that the erosion of feudal relations and attainment of capitalist conditions/relations in agricultural economy are preconditions for development of industries and urbanisation. This stands true in case of Bihar, which was a feudal setup and largely agriculture-based. Post-independence, it saw a poor land re-distribution process, agriculture practices saw no improvisation as was the case in several other states. So, the raw material was being mostly exported out with no value addition process being carried within the state.

Poor infrastructure and negligible supply of continuous electricity were the major reasons for the failure on this front.

The other impediment to this process of urbanisation of the state has been at the policy level. The realisation of these growth engines was not more than they being district headquarters. They were not treated as important centres of agglomeration, having prospects to prosper. Needless to explain, Bihar has always been looked at as a seemingly backward state and primarily agriculture-based. The focus has always been rural areas and agricultural growth. Urban centres could not garner much attention in terms of policy making or investment. The public service system was purposely kept weak and unattended. The reasons can be accumulated on many fronts, and look exaggerated in the years from 1990 to 2005, when the state was governed particularly badly (Mathew and Moore, 2011). The public servants who were needed to go through formal training, accounting and spending procedures were either not in place, or not given the discretion they needed to get things done in time. The conditions of the urban local bodies were severe because vacancies in state government offices, particularly at the middle and senior levels, were left unfilled; they lacked engineers, town planners and other technical staff required for implementation of urban programmes. Thus, the nature of the state and governance was such that it did little for the business to flourish, for cities and towns to grow and be able to develop a strong infrastructural system. The functions under 74th Amendment Act have not been fully devolved to urban local bodies. The fiscal autonomy and demarcation of roles in the urban local body are negligible in Patna and worse in other district headquarters of the state. By late 1990s, the law and order situation became unfriendly for the local business and eventually led to outmigration. For over a decade, students, families, doctors and many more have been migrating out from the state, ready to adjust and accommodate in the by-lanes of Delhi, Mumbai, Pune and other parts of the country for better living conditions.

To conclude, one can say that with such impediments for over a decade, many potentials and avenues of investment, improvements were lost in these small town bazaars and *kasbas*. They could never reach the take-off stage and encash on their potentials to become centres of higher functions and grow further. The lack of governance and policy implementation made matters worse. And thus, what we see today is a situation of haphazard urban growth, with poor infrastructure and complete absence of an economic base to support a natural progression towards urbanisation.

Note

1. When I use Monghyr, I refer to the pre-independence town, but Munger connotes the present town.

References

Abdullah, A. Nusrat (2002) Underdevelopment in Dependent Societies: Breaking the Colonial Bond. Unpublished thesis. Washington: Georgetown University.

Anand, Yang (2000) *Bazaar India: Markets, Society, and the Colonial State in Gangetic Bihar*. New Delhi: Munshiram Manoharlal.

Asiatic Journal and Monthly Register for British and Foreign India/China and Australia (1830). Vol. III, London.

Detailed Project Report (2010). Munger.

Heber, R. (1827) Narratives of a Journey Through the Upper Provinces of India from Calcutta to Bombay 1824–25. Asian Educational Service, retrieved on 10 December 2011. http://books.google.co.in/books?id=mOA2D1mQv 64C&source=gbs_navlinks_s

Imperial Gazetteer of India (1908–1931) *His Majesty's Secretary of State for India in Council*. Oxford: Clarendon Press, retrieved on 5 December 2011. http://dsal.uchicago.edu/ reference/gazetteer

Kapoor, Subodh (2002) *The Indian Encyclopedia: Meya National Congress*. UK: Genesis Publication, retrieved on 9 December 2011. http://books. google.co.in/books?id=ncL8Ve9FqNwC&dq=joseph+hooker,monghy& source=gbs_navlinks_s

Mathew, S. and M. Moore (2011) *State Incapacity by Design: Understanding the Bihar Story*. IDS Working Paper 366, Institute of Development Studies, University of Sussex. http://munger.nic.in/distdept.html

O'malley, L.S.S. (1926) *Bihar and Orissa District Gazetteers: Monghyr*. New Delhi: LOGOS Press.

Old Indian (1866) From Calcutta to the Snowy Range, retrieved on 5 December 2011. http:// books.google.com/books?id=JmYBAAAAQAAJ&oe=UTF-8.

Raza, M. and Habib Atiya (1991) 'Characteristics of Colonial Urbanisation: A Case Study of the Satellistic "Primacy" of Calcutta'. In M.S.A. Rao, Chandrashekhar Bhat and Laxmi Narayan Kadekar (eds). *A Reader in Urban Sociology*. New Delhi: Orient Longman.

Roberts, E. (1836) *Scenes and Characteristics of Hindostan: With Sketches of Anglo-Indian Societies*. Philadelphia : Carey, Lea & Blanchard, retrieved on 10 December 2011. http://books.google.co.in/books?id=KFwqAAAAYAAJ &printsec=frontcover&dq=Scenes+and+Characterstics+of+Hindosta n+by+Emma+Roberts&hl=en#v=onepage&q&f=false

University of Chicago Archive, retrieved on 5 December 2011. http://dsal.uchicago.edu/reference/gazetteer/pager.html?objectid=DS40 5.1.I34_V17_404.gif

Contributors

R.N. Sharma is a sociologist by training. He did his Ph.D. from IIT, Kanpur in 1978, and the same year, joined the Tata Institute of Social Sciences (TISS), Mumbai as a faculty in the Unit for Urban Studies. Since then, he has been associated with the TISS in various academic positions. He was appointed as Professor and Head of the Unit for Urban Studies from 1989 to 2005. In 2005, during the 'restructuring phase' of TISS, he became the first Dean of School of Social Sciences. He retired as Professor from the Centre for Development Studies at TISS, in 2012.

Prof. Sharma has conducted over 35 research projects funded by national and international organisations. He has to his credit two edited books and over 30 research papers published in national and international journals. His main areas of interest are: urban development, urban social planning, housing poverty, research on small cities and towns, and involuntary displacement both in rural and urban contexts.

Prof. Sharma has been associated with several governmental/academic organisations on matters of research, social interventions and policy matters (e-mail: rnstiss@ yahoo.com).

R.S. Sandhu retired as Professor of Sociology from Guru Nanak Dev University, Amritsar. He has been Dean, Faculty of Arts and Social Sciences, U.G.C. Visiting Fellow to the Netherlands (1998), Overseas Fellow of Human Science Research Council of South Africa (1995),

Visiting Professor in Winona State University, Winona, Minnesota, USA (1991–92), British Council Visiting Fellow (1990), and Head of the Department of Sociology (1989–1991). He has eleven books to his credit which include *Urbanization in India* (2003) and *Housing the Urban Poor: Policy and Practice in Developing Countries* (1995). He has also been Editor of *Guru Nanak Journal of Sociology* (1989–1991) and Guest Editor (1998) and member of Editorial Board of the *Habitat International*. He has organised and chaired many sessions in various international conferences/World Congresses held in Vancouver, (2007), Durban (2006), Singapore (2004), Milan (2003), Brisbane (2002), Montreal (1998), Bielefeld (1994), Montreal (1992), Madrid (1990), Amsterdam (1988) and New Delhi (1986). His main areas of interest are Urban Studies, Urban Planning and Sociology of Development (e-mail. ranvinder@yahoo.com).

Swapna Banerjee-Guha, presently Professor of Development Studies at the Tata Institute of Social Sciences, Mumbai, was formerly Professor of Human Geography at the University of Mumbai where she taught for 26 years and currently holds the position of an adjunct faculty in the Department of Economics. She received her initial training and Ph.D in Human Geography from Calcutta University way back in 1970s following which she started her teaching career in Burdwan University, West Bengal. A Postdoctoral Fulbright Fellow at the Johns Hopkins University, USA in 1984–85, Dr Banerjee-Guha has taught and researched in several universities and research institutes in North America, Europe and Asia and supervised research of students from various social science disciplines in India and abroad. She has been the external expert of Human Geography at Jawaharlal Nehru University, University of Calcutta and several others. A steering committee member of the International Critical Geography Group since its inception in 1997 and Honorary Director of Spaces for Democracy Network initiated by Newcastle University, UK in 2007, Dr Banerjee-Guha is an author of *Encyclopaedia Britannica* and a regular contributor to journals at home and abroad. She has more than 100 research articles and a number of books to her credit. Her current areas of interest are urban, social and development issues at national and international levels in the current globalisation era. She is a bilingual writer, writes both in English and Bengali (e-mail: sbanerjeeguha@hotmail.com).

Annapurna Shaw is a Professor at the Public Policy and Management Group, Indian Institute of Management, Kolkata. An urban geographer by training, she has a Master's degree from the Centre for Regional Development, Jawaharlal Nehru University, New Delhi and a Ph.D from the Department of Geography, University of Illinois at Urbana-Champaign, USA. Her research interests are in the areas of urban policy and planning, sustainable cities, the informal sector and economic development. Her publications include *The Making of Navi Mumbai* (2004) and *Indian Cities in Transition* (edited, 2007) (e-mail: ashaw@iiimcal.ac.in).

Rowena Robinson is presently Professor of Sociology at the Department of Humanities and Social Sciences, Indian Institute of Technology, Mumbai. She has taught earlier at Delhi University and Jawaharlal Nehru University. Among her publications include *Tremors of Violence: Muslim Survivors of Ethnic Strife in Western India* (Sage, 2005); *Christians of India* (Sage, 2003); edited (with Sathianathan Clarke) *Religious Conversion in India: Modes, Motivations and Meanings* (Oxford University Press, 2003); and edited (with Marianus Joseph Kujur) *Margins of Faith: Dalit and Tribal Christianity in India* (Sage, 2010) (e-mail: rowena@iitb.ac.in).

Rajesh Gill is Professor in Sociology, and Chairperson, Departments of Sociology and Women's Studies, Panjab University, Chandigarh. She has published four books and about 65 research articles in reputed journals and books. She contributes regularly to national newspapers on such themes as gender, education and corruption. Her areas of specialisation include Urban Sociology, Gender Studies, Poverty Studies and Governance. She is on the Editorial Boards of numerous reputed journals. She has completed four research projects on Urban Slums, City Planning, Women's Reservation in Urban Local Governance and Youth in Slums (e-mail: rajeshgill09@yahoo.com).

Biraj Swain works on issues of essential services, development policy and civil liberties in South Asia and Sub-Saharan Africa. She calls herself an academic vagabond, trained in Economics, Journalism, Sociology and Human Rights Law. She blends these disciplines for democratising governance of essential services and public sector reforms for greater citizens' engagement. An avid consumer of popular culture and soccer, she is a regular contributor to various journals, academic and mainstream, and believes in the imperative necessity for dissent and debating matters. She is an international faculty with

United Nations University, Tokyo and the UNESCO-MISARC (e-mail: biraj_swain@hotmail.com).

Abdul Shaban is presently Associate Professor at the Centre for Development Studies, Tata Institute of Social Sciences, Mumbai. He has authored a book *Mumbai: Political Economy of Crime and Space* (Orient Blackswan, 2010), and edited another book *Lives of Muslims in India: Politics, Exclusion and Violence* (Routledge, 2012). He has also published many papers in reputed national and international journal on issues related to urban and regional development in India. Dr Shaban has been Visiting Professor at the Department of Geography, University of Paris 7, and at the University of Masaryk (Brno) and Palacky University, Olomouc, Czech Republic. He has also been a Fellow at the Department of Geography and Environment (in 2008–09), and Cities Programme (in 2011–12), and London School of Economics and Political Sciences, London (e-mail: shaban@tiss.edu).

Sanjukta Sattar is Reader in Geography at the Department of Geography, Gokhale Memorial Girls' College, Kolkata. She has authored a book on *Tourism in Sikkim India: Impact on Economy, Society and Environment* (VDM Verlag, Germany, 2010). She has also published papers in international journals and contributed chapters in edited books on issues related to 'social exclusion' and 'environment' in India cities (e-mail: sanjukta.sattar@gmail.com).

Debolina Kundu is Associate Professor at the National Institute of Urban Affairs, New Delhi and has over 15 years of professional experience in the field of development studies. She has a Ph.D on urban governance from Jawaharlal Nehru University, New Delhi and has been a fellow at the Local Government Initiative, Hungary. She has been engaged as a consultant with several national and international organisations, e.g., National Institute of Urban Affairs, Indian Institute of Dalit Studies, UNDP, UN ESCAP, KfW Germany, GTZ India, and Urban Institute, Washington on issues of urban development, poverty, governance and exclusion. She is also a visiting faculty to Jawaharlal Nehru University, New Delhi, YASHADA, Pune, Indian Institute of Dalit Studies, and School of Planning and Architecture, New Delhi. She had also been the head of research team for Ministry of Commerce and Industry in the 'Doing Business with City Governments' project. She has a large number of publications in journals and books of international and national repute with the Sage, Oxford, EPW etc. (e-mail: dkundu@niua.org).

Jasmeet Sandhu is Professor of Sociology at Guru Nanak Dev University, Amritsar. She has been Head of Sociology Department (1995 to 1998) and Editor of *Guru Nanak Journal of Sociology* (1995 to 1998). She is the author of four books and several research papers published in academic journals in India and abroad. She has participated in many international and national conferences. Her areas of interest include Population Issues, Sociology of Family and Marriage and Sustainable Development (e-mail: jsmtsandhu@yahoo.com).

K.N. Bhatt is presently Associate Professor at G.B. Pant Social Science Institute, Allahabad University, Allahabad. Specialises in environmental economics and social development issues, Dr Bhatt teaches Environment and Natural Resource Management. He has directed and authored/co-authored 21 research projects in interdisciplinary social science issues relating to development education, child labour, human development, hill development, decentralisation, disaster management, innovative farming practices, etc. Most of these projects have been sponsored and funded by national or international organisations. Dr. Bhatt has published five books and three dozen research papers in journals and edited volumes (e-mail: knbhatt1@rediffmail.com).

Lalit Joshi teaches Modern and Contemporary History at the University of Allahabad. His areas of academic interest include Cultural Globalization, Environmental History of Colonial India, Urban History as well as the History of Cinema. He has presented papers in several national and international conferences and has published extensively in Hindi as well as in English. Prof. Joshi was a Teaching Assistant in Syracuse University (New York) from 1987 to 1991. His forthcoming book on Colonial Kumaun deals with the complex links between colonial policy, the Himalayan environment and the ordinary people of Kumaun and how these were seen in literary writings of the period. His major publications include *Houseful* (2004) and *Bollywood Texts* (2011).

Nikhlesh Kumar did his postgraduate studies at the Department of Sociology, Delhi School of Economics and doctoral studies in the area of sociology of occupations and professions at the North-Eastern Hill University, Shillong. He started his teaching career at the Department of Sociology, North-Eastern Hill University in 1978. He is at present Professor and Head of the Department of Sociology in the University. Besides working in the area of sociology of occupations and professions, he has also been working in the areas of sociology of organisations, traditional institutions in tribal societies, panchayati raj institutions and development issues in the tribal communities of the north-eastern region of India. He has conducted empirical studies in the areas of institutions of self-governance, disability, and development in Tripura (e-mail: archikans@yahoo.co.uk).

Umesh Kumar is a Human Ecologist with the Anthropological Survey of India (AnSI) and presently posted at Kolkata. He obtained his Master's degree in Geography from University of Delhi in 1990 and was awarded doctoral degree in 2009 from North-Eastern Hill University. After a brief stint as a lecturer in K.M. College, University of Delhi, he joined the AnSI in 1997. He has completed a number of projects and important among them are studies of tribes of Andaman and Nicobar Islands, particularly the Jarawa, the Onges, and the Nicobarese, and impact assessment of the tsunami on Little Andaman. He is presently engaged in biosphere reserves studies. He has published more than two dozen papers in different journals and books (e-mail: umeshkumarpb@gmail.com).

D.N. Pandey is a Senior Ecologist with the Anthropological Survey of India (AnSI). He obtained his Master's degree in Geography from Banaras Hindu University, Varanasi. He joined the AnSI in 1983. He has worked in different areas of Human Geography. During his posting at Andaman Nicobar Regional Centre, Port Blair, he completed research projects on the tribes of Andaman and Nicobar Islands, particularly the Jarawa, the Great Andamanese and the Shompen. He has also been associated with 'People of India' project particularly for the Bihar and Andaman and Nicobar volumes. In addition, he has carried out a number of other studies, important among them are: Narmada Salvage Project, Environment and Ecology of Coal Mining Areas, Regionalism and Development, Biosphere Reserve Studies and Social Impact Assessment Study in Pachamarhi and Achanakmar-Amarkantak Biosphere Reserves. Many of his research works have been published in different journals and books (e-mail: digpan@gmail.com).

Sumit Mukherjee did his Master's in Geography from University of Calcutta and doctoral degree in the field of geography of health from North-Eastern Hill University, Shillong. The twenty years of his association with Anthropological Survey of India as Research Associate in Human Ecology, and six years in the Census of India earned him extensive experiences in field-oriented research and digital cartography. He has authored three books on scheduled tribe and scheduled caste populations of India. He has published several research articles in international and national journals and edited volumes (e-mail: sumitmkj@gmail.com).

Amlan Biswas is presently with Anthropological Survey of India, Kolkata as Statistical Investigator. He has vast experience of socio-economic studies on various subjects under National Sample Survey and publications in other socio-cultural journals. His areas of interest are society, development and perception of development. He worked as a member of the team to study Nokrek Biosphere Reserve, Meghalaya (e-mail: biswas.aj@gmail.com).

V. Anil Kumar is Assistant Professor at the Centre for Political Institutions, Governance and Development, Institute for Social and Economic Change, Bangalore, where he teaches Political Theory, Indian Government and Politics and other courses. His research interests include civil society and its relation to governance and public policy, policies towards child labour, policies towards decentralisation, aspects of rural and urban governance, and social and political theory. He has earlier published four books on the following themes: agrarian change; drinking water as a basic right; developmental politics in south India; and decentralised planning in Karnataka. He has written numerous articles. He did his doctorate from the University of Delhi (e-mail: anilkumar@isec.ac.in).

Sheema Fatima has taught for two years at School of Social Science and Policy, Central University of Bihar, Patna. She has a Master's in Geography from Delhi School of Economics and M. Tech. in Public Policy & Planning from CEPT University, with further specialisation in GIS and Remote Sensing from ITC, Netherlands. She has worked with governmental and non-governmental organisations in Ahmedabad and Bihar. At present she is based at Mumbai working as an independent researcher and is a visiting faculty at Tata Institute of Social Sciences, Mumbai. Her areas of interests are urban studies and political economy of Environment (e-mail: fatimasheema@gmail.com).

Index